WILLIAM PETTY

WILLIAM PETTY

And the Ambitions of Political Arithmetic

TED McCORMICK

OXFORD
UNIVERSITY PRESS

ıⵚⵚ⁊⁊⁊⁊Ꝩ⁊

*This book has been printed digitally and produced in a standard specification
in order to ensure its continuing availability*

OXFORD
UNIVERSITY PRESS

Great Clarendon Street, Oxford OX2 6DP

Oxford University Press is a department of the University of Oxford.
It furthers the University's objective of excellence in research, scholarship,
and education by publishing worldwide in

Oxford New York

Auckland   Cape Town Dar es Salaam   Hong Kong   Karachi
Kuala Lumpur Madrid Melbourne Mexico City   Nairobi
New Delhi Shanghai   Taipei Toronto
With offices in
Argentina Austria Brazil Chile Czech Republic France Greece
Guatemala Hungary Italy Japan South Korea Poland Portugal
Singapore Switzerland Thailand Turkey Ukraine Vietnam

Oxford is a registered trade mark of Oxford University Press
in the UK and in certain other countries

Published in the United States
by Oxford University Press Inc., New York

© Ted McCormick 2009

ISBN 978-0-19-954789-0

To Theresa

Contents

Preface

By design, this is a somewhat unusual book. My aim has been to explore what the title refers to as the 'ambitions' of political arithmetic; exploring these has compelled me to delve deeply into the intellectual biography of William Petty, political arithmetic's inventor and for approximately two decades its sole practitioner. The result is neither a simple biography of Petty nor a straightforward study of political arithmetic, but an attempt to locate the origins, means, and ends of political arithmetic in the multiplicity of intellectual, political, and social contexts Petty inhabited. The few conventional biographies that narrate Petty's birth, ascent, apogee, decline, death, and historical significance are apt to ascribe his multifarious interests and innumerable projects—scientific, economic, political—to his 'genius'. This notion of genius is, in effect, a black box: less an explanation than a blank space where an explanation, if we only had one, would go. The many studies of Petty's political arithmetic, on the other hand—though increasingly alive to its multifaceted nature—invariably dwell on his 'contribution' to later developments in the social sciences, and in particular to recognizable components of economic theory. That the boundaries of current theory can be applied to his work without hampering historical understanding is never more than provisionally questioned.

I have avoided reference to Petty's 'genius' and reserved for the final chapter my consideration of his 'contribution' to later social science. My own approach, from the beginning, has been to pursue political arithmetic through Petty's manuscripts and printed works (very much in that order), and to build up from the evidence preserved in the archive a picture of what Petty intended his invention to do, how, and why. I could not have foreseen when I began just how far afield—or through how many fields—this pursuit would ultimately take me, but it became apparent early on that grasping political arithmetic would require paying closer attention to Petty's intellectual background and political concerns than to any retrospectively composed canon of economic literature. Two points have grown progressively clearer over the course of my work. First, political arithmetic was intended not to describe the economy but to assist the state; it was less about representation than intervention. Second, both the mechanisms of intervention Petty proposed and the framework within which these made sense were derived from natural philosophy.

This book traces the process by which Petty evolved something that could later be taken for social science from an engagement with certain strands of seventeenth-century natural philosophy and a series of political crises in Interregnum and Restoration England and Ireland. Central to this process were Petty's growing 'ambitions': scientific ambitions with political implications, and political ambitions that mobilized scientific resources. If political arithmetic's ambitions resonate more closely with early modern science than with modern economics, however, its established place in the historiography of social science raises intriguing questions about their fate. Petty's extension of corpuscularian matter theory, alchemical transmutation, and a mechanical worldview facilitated the 'Operations of Authority' by reducing land and population to elementary particles, homogeneous and politically vacuous units at the disposal of the crown. It reoriented policy—as Francis Bacon and his followers sought to reorient philosophy—from playing with words to manipulating things. It promised, finally, to end history: perhaps not, as Bacon had predicted, in an apocalyptic sense, but rather in the sense that it would confer on the crown the power both to undo the damage of past policy and to remake both land and people—again and again, if necessary—in its own image. If all this sounds foreign to modern social analysis and antithetical to liberal democracy, it is well to remember that our own age has seen social scientists proclaim 'the end of history' and politicians claim the power to 'create [their] own reality'. Only by setting aside the question of theoretical 'contributions' and treating 'genius' as an explanatory tool of last resort can we see that political arithmetic's most grand and terrible ambitions are also our own.

Acknowledgements

This book began at Columbia University in 2001, when David Armitage asked me what I knew about William Petty. During my ensuing doctoral research, and well beyond, David has been a perceptive reader and an extraordinarily supportive mentor. Without implicating him unduly in the shape it has finally taken, it is the simple truth that this book would never have existed without him. Nor would it exist in anything like its present form without Nicholas Canny, who acted as mentor during two years of unencumbered research and writing at the Moore Institute, National University of Ireland, Galway. Nicholas's attentive reading and active support were invaluable, as was the time and space for work and discussion that the Institute provided.

Carl Wennerlind, Matthew Jones, Martha Howell, and Karl Bottigheimer served on my dissertation committee; Carl in particular has been a continuing source of advice and support through the subsequent expansion of my investigation. Courses with Nadia Abu El-Haj and Peter Bearman at Columbia and Emma Rothschild and Katharine Park at Harvard helped me begin to navigate some of the fields I have found myself traversing. Julian Hoppit supervised my doctoral research in London; conversations with him, Negley Harte and David Ormrod helped me see political arithmetic as my real subject. Besides those already named, Toby Barnard and Mordechai Feingold shared their wisdom and read large portions of the manuscript at different stages; Toby's generosity, especially early in the research stage, and Moti's support at the beginning and end of the writing process deserve special thanks.

Conversing, corresponding, and comparing notes with Adam Beaver, Nessa Cronin, John Cunningham, Jane Grogan, Kristin Heitman, Vera Keller, Rebekah Klein-Pejšová, Jason McHugh, Lindsay Sharp, and Matthew Underwood helped shaped my approach to Petty and his various contexts. Special thanks to Hugh Goodacre for an engaging e-mail exchange and for the chance to test my ideas in the forbidding forum of the University College London (UCL) Department of Economics, and to Rhodri Lewis for permitting me to see and cite his valuable forthcoming edition of Petty's 'Scale of Creatures', as well as for his hospitality during a late visit to Oxford. Daniel Carey offered both good conversation and a wonderful month of house-sitting, allowing me to ponder Petty's misdeeds while looking out across Galway Bay. The occasional coffee or pint with many of the above and with Edward Collins, Barry Crosbie, Enrico Dal Lago, Tomás Finn, John Gibney, Ellen Gilmore, Rick Graff, Orla Power, Mark Stansbury, and the rest of the 'axis of medieval' at Galway reminded me of a world beyond Petty altogether.

Time in the archive was not only essential but also perhaps the most enjoyable part of working on the book. For that pleasure I owe a large debt of gratitude to the staffs of the British Library (and especially to Frances Harris, archivist of the Petty Papers), the Royal Society Library, and the National Archives in London; the Bodleian Library at the University of Oxford (and the staff of Duke Humfrey's Library in particular); the Trinity College Library in Dublin; the Huntington Library in Pasadena; the Folger Shakespeare Library in Washington; and the Osler Library for the History of Medicine at McGill University in Montreal. The libraries of Columbia, Harvard, UCL, the University of Maryland, College Park, and NUI Galway furnished both essential secondary works and, in many cases, agreeable workspaces.

A number of sources provided essential funding for my work at each stage. A 2003–04 Institute of Historical Research–Andrew Mellon Dissertation Research Fellowship allowed me to get started; a summer fellowship from the Department of History at Columbia and a 2004–05 Visiting Fellowship at Harvard allowed me to see the dissertation through. The bulk of the book as it now exists was written with the support of a 2006–08 Government of Ireland Fellowship, generously provided by the Irish Research Council for Humanities and Social Sciences.

I have road-tested versions of my arguments with variable but always informative results. Thanks to the members of the 2004 Mellon Summer Seminar on 'Intellectual History and Other Forms of History' at Caltech; the Early Modern History Workshop and the Early Science Working Group at Harvard; the Early Modern Europe Group at Columbia; participants in the 2006 conference '"Without Let or Hindrance": Inclusion and Exclusion from the Medieval to the Modern' at Lancaster University; Gearóid Ó Tuathaigh and audiences at the history seminar series and the 2007 'Crossing Cultures' conference at NUI Galway; the Research Seminar in Irish and British History at Trinity College Dublin; the Inter-Disciplinary Seminar in History and Philosophy of Economics at UCL; the

British History Seminar at Concordia and McGill; and audiences at the 2007 History of Science Society and 2008 North American Conference on British Studies annual meetings.

My thanks to Wiley–Blackwell for permission to use my article 'Transmutation, Inclusion, and Exclusion: Political Arithmetic from Charles II to William III', *Journal of Historical Sociology* 20:3 (September 2007), 259–278, parts of which appear in Chapter 8, and to Ashgate for permission to use my book chapter, '"A Proportionable Mixture": Sir William Petty, Political Arithmetic, and the Transmutation of the Irish', in Coleman A. Dennehy (ed.), *Restoration Ireland: Always Settling and Never Settled* (Aldershot: Ashgate, 2008), 123–139, parts of which appear in Chapters 3 and 5.

Christopher Wheeler and his staff at Oxford University Press have made the publication process a great deal smoother and much less mysterious than it might have been. In addition to owing the usual debts, I must also thank them for fixing the title of the book, wisely rejecting my awkward stabs at describing what, in retrospect, seems straightforward: the 'ambitions' of political arithmetic. I am grateful, too, to the anonymous readers, for their very helpful advice.

As this is my first book, there will be no better time to thank several people who helped shape me as a historian before William Petty entered my head. Wendy Shrock introduced me to both the early modern period and the history of science years before I had any inkling of what they would mean to me. Denys Judd put me on to the history of empire at a critical time (I was a philosophy student). The late Wim Smit shepherded me through my first year of graduate work and offered a model of broad and deep historical scholarship very few can hope to match. Caroline Bynum encouraged me to be bold.

Joel and Ginny McCormick were my first writing instructors and have remained careful readers and constructive editors—as well as immensely supportive parents—ever since. I hope the book is half as clear as they would like. It's probably twice as long.

Theresa Ventura has been my first and last reader, critic, enthusiast, sounding board, and best friend, from beginning to end. She has seen the project through from prospectus to book, while helping the author keep it in perspective. This book is dedicated to her, with love.

List of Illustrations

List of Abbreviations

The following abbreviations will be used throughout the notes.

Libraries and Archives:

Beinecke   Beinecke Library, Yale University, US
BL   British Library, London, UK
Bodl.   Bodleian Library, University of Oxford, UK
NA   National Archives, Kew, UK
Osler   Osler Library, McGill University, Canada
RSL   Royal Society Library, London, UK
TCD   Trinity College Dublin Library, Ireland

Works:

CHSCP Daniel Garber and Michael Ayers (eds), *The Cambridge History of Seventeenth-Century Philosophy*, 2 vols. (Cambridge: Cambridge University Press, 1998).

CSPI 1663–65 Robert Pentland Mahaffy (ed.), Calendar of State Papers relating to Ireland, Preserved in the Public Record Office. 1663–65 (London: Stationery Office, 1907).

CSP Thurloe Thomas Birch (ed.), A Collection of the State Papers of John Thurloe, Esq; Secretary, First, to the Council of State, And afterwards to The Two Protectors, Oliver and Richard Cromwell, 7 vols. (London: The Executor of the late Mt. Fletcher Gyles, Thomas Woodward and Charles Davis, 1742).

EW William Petty (ed. Charles Henry Hull), *The Economic Writings of Sir William Petty*, 2 vols. (Cambridge: Cambridge University Press, 1899).

HMC Fourteenth Report Fourteenth Report of the Historical Manuscripts Commission, Appendix, Part VII: *The Manuscripts of the marquis of Ormonde, preserved at the Castle, Kilkenny*, 2 vols. (London: Historical Manuscripts Commission, 1895).

HMC Ormonde Calendar of the Manuscripts of the Marquis of Ormonde, K.P. Preserved at Kilkenny Castle, New Series, vols 3–7 (London: Historical Manuscripts Commission, 1905–12).

HP The Hartlib Papers: A Complete Text and Image Database of the Papers of Samuel Hartlib (*c*.1600–62) (2nd edn. on CD-ROM, HROnline for the Humanities Research Institute: University of Sheffield, 2002).

JRS Allan P. Farrell, S. J. (trans.), *The Jesuit* Ratio Studiorum *of 1599* (Washington: Conference of Major Superiors of Jesuits, 1970).

Oxford DNB Oxford Dictionary of National Biography, (Oxford: Oxford University Press, 2004; online edn., 2007) [http://www.oxforddnb.com].

PP William Petty (ed. Marquis of Lansdowne [H.W.E. Petty-Fitzmaurice]), *The Petty Papers: Some Unpublished Writings of Sir William Petty*, 2 vols. (London: Constable & Co., 1927).

PSC Petty (ed. Lansdowne), *The Petty-Southwell Correspondence* (London: Constable & Co., 1928).

Note to the Reader

Original spelling has been maintained in all quotations from primary sources and interpolations are marked; however, early modern characters, abbreviations and ligatures no longer in use have been silently modernized, as has use of '£' and similar symbols. When quoting from modern editions of early modern works, I have maintained the editor's conventions. William Petty's handwriting was notorious even in his own time, and the exact transcription of his words is in some cases open to question. When in doubt I have put my guess in brackets with a query.

Introduction: William Petty and Political Arithmetic

Hic jacet author & magister rerum,
Hic jacet author politico-arithmeticae,
quam nemo a Pythagora ad Cartesium descripsit,
Hic jacet qui fecit quod erat faciendum,
qui demonstravit, quod erat demonstrandum.[1]

William Petty (1623–1687)

William Petty's name is not particularly well known today. Unlike that of his celebrated associates, Thomas Hobbes, Robert Boyle, and Samuel Pepys, Petty's fame, considerable in the seventeenth century, declined rapidly thereafter. In some respects this is not surprising: Petty did not, like Hobbes, produce a comprehensive and shocking political philosophy, nor did he, like Boyle, give his name to any scientific law, nor, like Pepys, leave behind an entertaining diary. In other respects, however, Petty's low historiographical profile is harder to understand. No less an authority than Karl Marx thought him 'the founder of political economy', and economists and historians of economics still locate in Petty's 'political arithmetic' the roots of the classical liberal economics of Adam Smith and David Ricardo.[2] Petty's interest in population data, meanwhile, has earned him

---

[1] 'Here lies the author and master of things,/Here lies the author of political arithmetic,/which no-one from Pythagoras to Descartes described,/Here lies he who did that which was to be done,/who demonstrated, that which was to be demonstrated.' This is how Sir Peter Pett imagined Petty's epitaph: 'Sir Peter Pett's Pindarick on the Politicall Arithmetick' (undated), BL MS Add. 72899, f.61.

[2] Karl Marx (trans. Emile Burns). *Theories of Surplus Value, Part I* ([1861]; Moscow: Progress Publishers, 1967), 1. See Wilson Lloyd Bevan, 'Sir William Petty: A Study in Economic Literature', *Publications of the American Economic Association* 9:4 (1894), 13–102; Charles Henry Hull, 'Petty's Place in the History of Economic Theory', *Quarterly Journal of Economics* 14:3 (1900), 307–340; E. A. J. Johnson, *Predecessors of Adam Smith: The Growth of British Economic Thought* (New York: Prentice Hall, 1937); William Letwin, *The Origins of Scientific Economics* (London: Methuen, 1963); Joyce Appleby, *Economic Thought and Ideology in Seventeenth-Century*

a place among the founders of statistical demography, alongside his friend John Graunt; Graunt's seminal 1662 *Natural and Political Observations ... upon the Bills of Mortality* is sometimes even attributed to Petty.[3] On any account, Petty played a major part in the 'pre-history' of social science.[4]

His role in the seventeenth-century revolution in natural philosophy and in the rise of experimental science is less well known but nevertheless significant.[5] Trained as a physician and skilled in mathematics, Petty became by turns an active member of Samuel Hartlib's circle of reform-minded inventors and philosophers, a Professor of Anatomy at the University of Oxford (where, besides participating in the 'Experimental Philosophy Club', he restored a hanged woman to life), and briefly of Music at Gresham College in London; after the Restoration, he was one of the founding Fellows of the Royal Society, and made substantial contributions to the Society's projected 'History of Trades', a wide-ranging study of manual crafts. An inveterate innovator—his most famous invention was a 'double-bottomed boat' designed to sail faster and with a smaller crew

England (Princeton: Princeton University Press, 1978); Tony Aspromourgos, 'Political Economy and the Social Division of Labour: The Economics of Sir William Petty', *Scottish Journal of Political Economy* 33:1 (1986), 28–45, 'The Life of William Petty in relation to His Economics: A Tercentenary Interpretation', *History of Political Economy* 20:3 (1988), 337–356, and 'New Light on the Economics of William Petty (1623–1687): Some Findings from Previously Undisclosed Manuscripts', *Contributions to Political Economy* 19 (2000), 53–70; Andrea W. Finkelstein, *Harmony and the Balance: An Intellectual History of Seventeenth-Century English Economic Thought* (Ann Arbor: University of Michigan Press, 2000). Explicitly Marxian appreciations of Petty include Alessandro Roncaglia, *Petty: The Origins of Political Economy* (Armonk: M. E. Sharpe, 1985) and Ellen Meiksins Wood, *The Origin of Capitalism: A Longer View* (London: Verso, 2000).

  [3] See Chapter 4.
  [4] Richard Olson, *The Emergence of the Social Sciences, 1642–1792* (New York: Twayne Publishers, 1993); Charles Emil Strangeland, *Pre-Malthusian Doctrines of Population: A Study in the History of Economic Theory* (1904; New York: Augustus M. Kelley, 1966); James Bonar, *Theories of Population from Raleigh to Arthur Young* (London: George Allen and Unwin, 1931); Karl Pearson and E. S. Pearson, *The History of Statistics in the 17th and 18th Centuries* (High Wycombe: Charles Griffin and Company, 1978); Alain Desrosières (trans. Camille Naish), *The Politics of Large Numbers: A History of Statistical Reasoning* (Cambridge, MA: Harvard University Press, 1998); Ian Hacking, *The Emergence of Probability: A Philosophical Study of Early Ideas About Probability, Induction and Statistical Inference* (2nd ed., Cambridge: Cambridge University Press, 2006). On the political implications of these developments, see Peter Buck, 'Seventeenth-Century Political Arithmetic: Civil Strife and Vital Statistics', *Isis* 68:1 (1977), 67–84; Edward Higgs, *The Information State in England: The Central Collection of Information on Citizens since 1500* (Basingstoke: Palgrave Macmillan, 2004); Paul Slack, *From Reformation to Improvement: Public Welfare in Early Modern England* (Oxford: Oxford University Press, 1999) and 'Government and Information in Seventeenth-Century England', *Past and Present* 184 (2004), 33–68.
  [5] See Chapter 2.

than conventional ships of the same tonnage—Petty later helped organize the Dublin Philosophical Society, sister to the Royal Society of London, and served as President. Petty and his associates brought the Scientific Revolution to Ireland.

It is in Ireland that Petty is best known.[6] There he went in 1652 as Physician-General to the Cromwellian army, which had recently re-conquered the country after ten years of war following the Ulster rebellion of 1641. Petty quickly found favour under Henry Cromwell (Oliver's younger son, effectively in charge of governing Ireland), and by 1654 he was charged with conducting a massive survey of lands confiscated from the 'rebel' Irish and slated for reallocation to English troops in Ireland and in-vestors in London. The resulting 'Down Survey' was lauded then and since as the first scientific mapping of much of Ireland. It was also, perhaps more importantly, the central instrument in a series of land settlements—under Cromwell, after the Restoration, and, finally, after the Glorious Revolu-tion—that shaped the politics of the Restoration in Ireland and ultimately anchored over a century of 'Protestant Ascendancy' in the country. It es-tablished Petty's reputation as both an expert on Irish land and population and a beneficiary of Irish suffering—a reputation that has endured.

Petty has not, then, been totally ignored. Far from it: whole books have been devoted to his contribution to economics and demography, and numerous articles to his scientific ideas and Irish adventures. Yet there have been few sustained attempts to connect these different parts of Petty with each other; the only book to do so on the strength of original archival research appeared in the late nineteenth century.[7] This neglect derives in part from the nature of the sources themselves: his sizeable manuscript archive was in private hands for much of the twentieth century. In its absence, scholars have largely depended on a small group of printed sources: an 1899 compilation of Petty's *Economic Writings*, a two-volume selection of miscellaneous manuscripts printed in 1927, and a 1928 edition of Petty's correspondence with his friend Robert Southwell.[8] These sources reflect

[6] See Chapter 3.

[7] Edmond Fitzmaurice, *The Life of Sir William Petty, 1623–1687* (London: John Murray, 1895); other biographies include Erich Strauss, *Sir William Petty: Portrait of a Genius* (Glencoe, IL: The Free Press, 1954) and Thomas E. Jordan, *A Copper Farthing: Sir William Petty and his Times, 1623–1687* (Sunderland: University of Sunderland Press, 2007). P. G. Dale's booklet, *Sir W.P. of Romsey* (Romsey: Lower Test Valley Archaeological Study Group, 1987), gives an interesting picture of seventeenth-century Romsey. An up-to-date summary is Toby Barnard, 'Petty, Sir William (1623–1687)', *Oxford DNB* <http://www.oxforddnb.com/view/article/22069>.

[8] *EW; PP; PSC.* See also Petty (ed. Thomas Aiskew Larcom), *The History of the Survey of Ireland, Commonly Called the 'Down Survey'* (Dublin: Irish Archaeological Society, 1851).

and reinforce another problem: the division of scholarly labour among a variety of fairly narrow historical subfields—the historiographies of Ireland and England, of science and politics, of natural and social science, even of economics, statistics, and demography. Economists can study Petty's economics, Irish historians his role in Ireland, and historians of science his contributions to the Royal Society; but connecting these things and assessing their relationships requires mastering literatures that have developed along separate lines, printed sources that come pre-packaged for subdisciplinary use, and manuscript sources that have, until recently, been hard to consult at all. Bringing in the still wider range of interests that Petty's manuscripts reveal is no easy task.

Yet even scholars working within well-defined disciplinary traditions have recently begun to pay more attention to Petty's wide range of interests and to the connections between them.[9] Precisely because of this range, a full-length study is worthwhile both for the light it can cast on an underexamined but important figure and for the unique window it can open onto the broader political and intellectual world in which he operated. At Petty's birth, in 1623, England was a small nation in the midst of economic depression and political crisis, sitting uneasily on the sidelines of an expanding Continental war it could hardly afford to enter. Its colonial career in the Atlantic was barely off the ground (even the Ulster plantation was just over a decade old). Francis Bacon had yet to publish his *New Atlantis*, with its scheme for 'Salomon's House'—a fictional scientific institution that, four decades later, the Royal Society would partially realize. By 1687, when Petty died, England's colonial empire had grown explosively, an expanding plantation system flooding the home market with new commodities, feeding a new consumer society and drawing ever more labour, free and enslaved, across the Atlantic. England itself, having been through rebellion, regicide, and Restoration, was on the verge of a revolution that would bring in its train the rise of Parliament and the growth of a

---

[9] Frances Harris, 'Ireland as a Laboratory: The Archive of Sir William Petty', in Michael Hunter (ed.), *Archives of the Scientific Revolution: The Formation and Exchange of Ideas in Seventeenth-Century Europe* (Woodbridge: Boydell Press, 1998), 73–90; Tony Aspromourgos, 'The Mind of the Oeconomist: An Overview of the "Petty Papers" Archive', *History of Economic Ideas* 9:1 (2001), 39–102. See also Sabine Reungoat, *William Petty: Observateur Des Îles Britanniques* (Paris: Institut National d'Études Démographiques, 2004). The most comprehensive prior attempt to study Petty's intellectual production is Lindsay G. Sharp's D.Phil. thesis, 'Sir William Petty and Some Aspects of Seventeenth-Century Natural Philosophy' (University of Oxford, 1976).

modern fiscal-military and bureaucratic state—not to mention renewed supremacy over Ireland, Union with Scotland and war with much of Europe. Newton's *Principia*—the foundation of physics for more than two centuries and as good a marker as any for the birth of modern science—appeared that same year. Once a political, economic, and intellectual backwater, England (after 1707, Britain) was a 'great power' in every sense.

Petty played a part in these transformations. His signal contribution to them, in the eyes of both contemporaries and successors, was something he called 'political arithmetic'. Differences arise, however, over just what political arithmetic was. For historians of economics, statistics, or demography, it was a 'pre-Smithian' economics, a proto-statistics or a first step towards demography; for historians of science it stood for the extension of empirical method to the social or political sphere; for political historians it signified the systematic gathering of quantitative demographic and economic data, or at least the aspiration to gather such data, in the service of the state.[10] There is broad agreement that political arithmetic was a seventeenth-century methodological innovation that brought the quantitative techniques and empirical spirit of the Scientific Revolution to practical questions of economy, society, and politics, paving the way for the recognizable social science of the Enlightenment. But little is known about how it did this, and still less about what political arithmetic meant at the time of its creation and how it came into being in the first place.

This book is about William Petty, but at its core is the problem of political arithmetic: how, when, and why did Petty create it? What did he understand by it? What did he want it to do? How did it work? How did he present it, and how did his audiences respond? And how, finally, did it come to be understood as a method somehow fundamental to later social science? Political arithmetic was the work of decades, both before and after Petty coined the phrase, and perhaps more than some other inventions, its fortunes were tied to those of its inventor, who remained, as long as he lived, its sole self-conscious practitioner. At the same time, it was by its very nature a social enterprise, provoked by Petty's engagement with his intellectual and political surroundings and dependent

---

[10] Phyllis Deane, *The State and the Economic System: An Introduction to the History of Political Economy* (Oxford: Oxford University Press, 1989), 23; Bonar, 84; Geoffrey Holmes, 'Gregory King and the Social Structure of Pre-Industrial England', in Holmes, *Politics, Religion and Society in England, 1679–1742* (London: Hambledon Press, 1986), 285.

for its effect on a network of contacts and potential exponents in England and Ireland. Answering these questions therefore requires delving deeply into Petty's life and the contexts in which he lived it. His education, his intellectual, personal, and political relationships, the places where he went, the groups he joined, the interests he served, the philosophers, courtiers and kings to whom he presented his ideas, and the problems these ideas were intended to solve are all part of the story. Conversely, grasping Petty's intellectual biography means understanding the ambitions of political arithmetic.

The Petty papers

This will become more evident if we turn from what political arithmetic meant to the material form that it took. Despite the neat appearance of Petty's edited *Economic Writings*, political arithmetic was neither summed up in a single work nor fully presented in print at all. It was, rather, strewn across scores of manuscripts—some of considerable length, some mere scraps of paper, a few destined for print, the vast majority not.[11] Of course, the authors of the most polished books leave masses of manuscript drafts and notes behind; one might still argue that the books should have the last word. But in the seventeenth century 'publication' was not yet synonymous with print. At a time when censorship and sedition laws were the norm and political power—at least, the power to frame policy—was concentrated in a relatively small elite, politically sensitive material could be more safely and often more effectively 'published' by being circulated in manuscript from hand to hand, copied and recopied, among select coteries of readers.[12] Petty printed comparatively little, but he circulated a very great deal. Doing so enabled him to address delicate questions frankly, to keep close track of his proposals, and to reach the people who mattered—and no one else. A full study of Petty both provides and necessitates, among other things, a close look at 'scribal publication' in action.

The manuscripts in Petty's archive take many forms. Some, like those that ultimately became his best-known printed works (in particular *Political Arithmetick* and *The Political Anatomy of Ireland*), are lengthy essays,

[11] Harris, 'Ireland as a Laboratory'; Aspromourgos, 'Mind'.
[12] Harold Love, *The Culture and Commerce of Texts: Scribal Publication in Seventeenth-Century England* (Amherst: University of Massachusetts Press, 1998).

organized as self-sufficient treatises on their chosen topics and divided into chapters covering different aspects of those topics; others discuss religious, political or economic questions more informally, through fictionalized dialogues; others are still rougher sketches of the pros and cons of a given proposal; many are mere lists (sets of 'heads') of Petty's current projects, ideas, or desiderata. Easily the largest group, however, are Petty's short tracts, or *tractiuncli*. These are usually between two and four folios in length, typically devoted to quite specific policy projects, and divided into separate sections, each containing a set of numbered or otherwise ordered points—laying out Petty's proposal, describing the problem it is designed to solve, how it is to work and what resources it requires, the probable costs of not adopting it, and the short- and long-term benefits of following it through. Their format reminds us that Petty was, to use a seventeenth-century term, a 'projector'. His papers, as he produced them, were designed not so much to reveal scientific or social-scientific truths to the wide world as to sell economic, political, or social projects to a carefully selected and assiduously pursued audience of powerful men. Political arithmetic, correspondingly, was not set forth wholesale in a treatise, but spun out little by little as a web of projects.

Taking these manuscripts into account does not simply mean supplementing the printed volumes with new material. It requires rereading many of the familiar printed texts *as* manuscripts themselves, since this was how they circulated, alongside other manuscripts, in Petty's time. This, in turn, means coming to grips with a new set of problems. Many of the papers were *ad hoc* responses to the challenges of the moment; while they often address specific problems—ranging from unemployment, to Irish land, to English sovereignty at sea, to church government, to theology and beyond—they rarely enunciate general principles. Because Petty addressed his tracts to a 'specialist' audience, they assume familiarity not only with the matter at hand but also, often, with Petty's own earlier proposals. Many of the papers make no sense by themselves, and seeing the bigger picture requires setting what can look like very different papers alongside each other. Beyond even this lies the problem of the archive's temporal structure. Petty's production palpably accelerates at certain periods of apparent crisis, and slackens at other times; even allowing for material that does not survive, the periodicity of the papers is yet another link between Petty's intellectual work and his political surroundings.

Understanding political arithmetic thus means reconstructing the complex relationships between papers of different genres and periods, as well as between these papers and the world around them. Individual tracts may employ ideas developed in earlier dialogues; sets of heads may tell us which *tractiuncli* belong together, juxtaposing proposals that seem at first completely unrelated; correspondence may tell us which papers went where, how they were received, and how they changed. And reconnecting these papers allows, indeed compels, us to re-establish ties between ideas whose links would otherwise remain invisible. All this has serious implications for our understanding of political arithmetic and of Petty. It is not difficult to see in the carefully selected *Economic Writings* the makings of a proto-scientific approach to economic analysis or to discern precocious anticipations of modern theories. It is much harder to look at hundreds of papers on everything from the shortage of coin to Native American marriage practices to the duties of the parish priest and see the same thing. The application of quantitative methods to economic questions may be part of political arithmetic's legacy; but its meaning in its time was plainly something more rooted and complex. Until we grasp this richer meaning, it will be hard to see the legacy in a clear light.

Political arithmetic in context

We can get some idea of what is in store by considering Petty's introduction of political arithmetic, in a 1672 letter, as part of 'the Politicall Medicine' of Ireland.[13] At the time, the Irish land settlement, which Petty had helped to shape, was under attack by an increasingly powerful Irish Catholic lobby at the English court; Petty's addressee was Arthur Annesley, earl of Anglesey, who as Treasurer of Ireland after the Restoration had also worked on the settlement. Petty was shortly to circulate the manuscripts of both *Political Arithmetick* and *The Political Anatomy of Ireland*, which he evidently regarded as part of the settlement's defence.[14] From its inception, then, political arithmetic was not a neutral mode of economic analysis but part of an explicit political program: here, the protection of the Irish land settlement, in which Petty had both a personal and a professional stake. Yet it is more complicated and more interesting than that. What made the Irish settlement's Catholic critics particularly

---

[13] Petty to Anglesey, 17 December 1672, BL MS Add. 72858, f.73.
[14] On Anglesey, see Michael Perceval-Maxwell, 'Annesley, Arthur, first earl of Anglesey (1614–1686)', *Oxford DNB* <http://www.oxforddnb.com/view/article/562>.

menacing in late 1672 was that a combination of other events—England's unpopular alliance with Catholic France against the Protestant United Provinces; King Charles's recent Declaration of Indulgence for religious dissenters (spurred by a secret clause in the 1670 Treaty of Dover between England and France); widespread and justified suspicion that the heir to the throne, James, Duke of York, was Catholic—all seemed to portend a slide towards 'Popery' which would spell the end of the English church, English liberties, and English supremacy in Ireland. It might even open the road, as some feared, to the Universal Monarchy of the Most Christian King, Louis XIV.[15]

Petty does not seem to have worried much about the fate of true religion or the danger of Universal Monarchy.[16] However, he worried a great deal about English authority in Ireland, upon which the land settlement depended and which was bound up with the politics of religion throughout the Three Kingdoms and with English strength still further afield. It is these larger questions, rather than the narrower one of the land settlement, that political arithmetic came to increasingly embrace over the course of the 1670s and 1680s. In addressing them, Petty shifted from stop-gap defensive tactics specific to Ireland to a much more aggressive and inventive strategy which would create conditions of lasting stability in Church and State throughout the Three Kingdoms and the English Empire. This strategy certainly included the pursuit of economic improvement and the interest in systematic data gathering by the state about its resources with which Petty has been credited. But it also projected new administrative structures for governing both the Three Kingdoms and the English colonies around the world, a more comprehensive church settlement and toleration for religious dissent, and, underpinning all the rest, the systematic state manipulation of demography. Political arithmetic, in other words, was chiefly concerned with political stability. Economic 'development', to use an anachronism Petty invites, was a means to that end.

Petty's analysis of the threats to the Stuart monarchy gave more weight to internal than to external factors; like some recent historians, he

---

[15] Tim Harris, *Restoration: Charles II and His Kingdoms, 1660–1685* (London: Penguin, 2006), especially 8–135; Harris, Paul Seaward and Mark Goldie (eds), *The Politics of Religion in Restoration England* (Oxford: Oxford University Press, 1990); John Miller, *Popery and Politics in England, 1660–1688* (Cambridge: Cambridge University Press, 1973).

[16] As he wrote to Robert Southwell: 'I find, by looking far back upon the paucity of people in the Assyrian, Persian, and other first Monarchyes, how easy a Thing twas for a few resolute fellowes to conquer the World as then it was; and that (whatever the King of France may think) the Universall or Great Monarchy doth and will grow every Century more and more difficult by the Course of nature.' Petty to Southwell, 20 August 1681, *PSC*, 93.

attributed the vulnerability of the Crown to stresses inherent in multiple monarchy. There were, inevitably, problems involved in attempting to govern different nations separated by culture, custom and institutions simultaneously, and further problems attended the partial and ongoing colonization of one of the Stuart kingdoms, Ireland, by the other two.[17] In 1641 this friction helped ignite a rebellion in Ulster, which rapidly spread south through Ireland, spurring on, in turn, the outbreak of the Civil War between King and Parliament in England and, ultimately, a decade of sporadic war throughout the Three Kingdoms.[18] Ireland was at once a member of the Stuart multiple monarchy, causally linked to its overall instability, and an imperfect microcosm of it, wherein each national, religious, and political division was reproduced (though with local complications and variations, and not to scale). In trying to stabilize Ireland Petty confronted the instability of the Three Kingdoms as a whole, which he interpreted as the product of multiple, nationally and confessionally distinct populations whose identities, through a series of unfortunate events, had become vested with dangerous political significance. Political arithmetic was designed to solve this problem either by removing the political sting of these differences—through religious toleration, for instance—or by removing the differences altogether.

The tools it used to do this included many of the features which have earned political arithmetic its place in the historiography of the social sciences: the quantitative analysis of human and natural resources, the advocacy of economic and social policies based on empirical criteria, and numerous practical schemes for improving infrastructure, agriculture, manufactures, and trade. But it also relied on a set of altogether less familiar instruments: the planned, and if necessary coerced, 'transplantation' and 'counter-transplantation' of different national and confessional subpopulations and their 'mixture' and 'union' through intermarriage and generation—a programme initially directed toward 'the transmutation of the Irish into English' but ultimately applicable to the politics of religion in England and the challenges of colonization across the Atlantic. Political arithmetic emerges not as an early economics but as an ambitious art of government by demographic manipulation.

---

[17] J. G. A. Pocock, *The Discovery of Islands: Essays in British History* (Cambridge: Cambridge University Press, 2005); Nicholas Canny, *Making Ireland British, 1580–1650* (Oxford: Oxford University Press, 2001).

[18] Allan I. Macinnes, *The British Revolution, 1629–1660* (Basingstoke: Palgrave Macmillan, 2005).

This complicated art drew on an astonishing range of sources, from contemporary economic writing to the political thought of Hobbes and Harrington to the literature of Irish plantation from Spenser and Davies on. Above all, it relied on developments in natural philosophy and allied fields—not least, as 'transmutation' suggests, alchemy. Like alchemical transmutation, the demographic transmutation political arithmetic promised would produce natural results by artificial means. Forcibly transplanted to Irish households, thousands of English women might, Petty suggested, function as the natural objects of their Irish husbands' passions and the natural teachers of language and manners to the resulting children—cementing a 'natural and lasting' union between the English and Irish populations. Deploying natural processes to govern diverse populations, manipulating their cultural characteristics and thus their political allegiance, Petty offered an instrument of government tailor-made for a composite monarchy and a colonial empire.

If the practical empiricism of Bacon and his followers, the mechanistic worldview of Descartes and Hobbes, and the corpuscularian matter theory of Gassendi and Boyle made political arithmetic possible, the peculiar mutability of Restoration politics—when no national or confessional group's loyalty went unchallenged, and when the religious identity of the Crown itself was in flux—made it necessary. In order to work, it relied on an equally localized set of assumptions about human nature, the natural world, and, most importantly, the susceptibility of natural processes to human knowledge and manipulation, particularly through the medium of policy. Circulating his ideas and promoting his new brand of expertise led Petty to mobilize a carefully cultivated network of friends, contacts, and potential patrons in political and scientific circles on both sides of the Irish Sea. Only after 1688, finally, did a second generation of self-conscious political arithmeticians rearticulate Petty's creation as a method of social and economic analysis subsequently seen as fundamental to modern social science. All this is the subject of this book.

Overview

In one sense, this book has two distinct halves. Chapters 1–4 focus on Petty's life and intellectual world from his birth in 1623 to his invention of political arithmetic at the beginning of the 1670s. Chapters 5–8, by contrast, focus on the political arithmetic that Petty drew on this

background to create, which he applied successively to political challenges in Ireland, the American colonies, and finally the Three Kingdoms
as a whole, and which was radically reinterpreted after his death as
something more like the social science we recognize today. Chapter 1
looks at his youth in England, his Jesuit education in France, and
his philosophical and medical training among Cartesian academics in
the Low Countries and exiled English royalists—including Thomas
Hobbes—and French physico-mathematicians in Paris. Chapter 2 follows Petty back to England and extensively examines his wide-ranging
experimental and philosophical work with the neo-Baconian Hartlib
Circle during the later 1640s—probably the most important phase of his
intellectual development from the perspective of his later work—and ends
with his brief academic career at Oxford and then Gresham College.
Chapter 3 traces his career in Cromwellian Ireland, from his appointment as Physician-General for the army to his scramble to secure the
extensive estates he had accrued after the collapse of the Protectorate, focusing on the Down Survey, considered both as a specimen of
Baconian science and as Petty's real introduction to practical politics.
Chapter 4 picks up at the Restoration and examines Petty's turn towards
economics in light of his encounter with James Harrington, the demographic work of John Graunt, and his own continuing commitment to
practical and experimental science, both within and beyond the Royal
Society.

   Although the focus of the last four chapters falls on Petty's political
arithmetic rather than Petty, the division is in fact somewhat artificial: as
will become clear, the man and his creation were always closely connected. Chapter 5 treats Petty's first major political-arithmetical manuscripts
(*Political Arithmetick* and *The Political Anatomy of Ireland*) as responses to
political, religious, and economic anxieties in Britain and Ireland that drew
on both his own natural-philosophical background and certain strands
of contemporary economic discourse, promoting peace and prosperity
through social engineering, initially through 'the transmutation of the
Irish into English'. Chapter 6 pursues Petty's 'instrument of government'
through the later 1670s and 1680s, as he applied it first to the management of colonial population in the Americas and finally, under James,
to balancing the demographic strength and political power of different confessions in the Three Kingdoms. Chapter 7 offers a synchronic
reconstruction of the network of contacts that made Petty's 'scribal publication' of his manuscripts possible and upon which the political reach
and force of his ideas depended. Chapter 8, finally, shows how Petty's

political arithmetic was reinvented by a second generation of political arithmeticians, who—drawing on his printed work, and in ignorance of his manuscripts—transformed his aggressive program of demographic manipulation into a putatively objective analytical tool, a 'computing faculty'. Even this final transformation, however, was in some ways more apparent than real.

CHAPTER I

From Romsey to Paris

It cannot be denied, but Outward Accidents conduce much to *Fortune*, Fauour, Opportunitie, Death of Others, Occasion fitting Vertue. But chiefly, the Mould of a Mans *Fortune*, is in his owne hands.[1]

Vastly more ink has been spilled regarding Petty's later work and its effects than on the sources, influences, and contexts that shaped his intellectual development. Yet the first three decades of his life, from his birth in 1623 to his appointment as Physician-General to Cromwell's army in Ireland in 1652, deserve careful consideration not only for what they tell us about the last three but also because they are interesting in themselves. These were the years, naturally enough, that shaped Petty's intellect and interests, in which he forged his first lasting relationships, and in which he produced his first work. They were also years that shaped early modern philosophy, when mechanistic and corpuscularian views of nature began seriously to challenge the dominance of Aristotelianism in the universities, when experimental and chemical approaches to medicine began to displace the traditional reliance on Galen, when mathematics began to assert its centrality to the investigation of nature, and when practical science began to compete for control of the philosophical agenda.

Petty was a product of this early stage of the Scientific Revolution. For most of these years he was only a student, to be sure, though by the end of the 1640s he had acquired a peculiar philosophical reputation of his own. But if he played at best a minor role in these intellectual surroundings at this stage, they would play a major role in his conception of his work then and later on. And although some of the influences Petty encountered at this time are familiar and even predictable—Thomas Hobbes in politics, for instance, or William Harvey in medicine—a great many are less obvious. For one of the most striking things about Petty's education is its

---

[1] Francis Bacon, 'Of Fortune', in *The Essayes or Covnsels, Civill and Morall, of Francis Lo. Verulam* (London: Printed by Iohn Haviland for Hanna Barret, 1625), 235.

very heterogeneity. From an artisanal family in a small English town, he moved through a Jesuit college in Normandy, two or three Dutch universities, overlapping Parisian intellectual circles, and finally between the academic world of Oxford and the philosophical hotbed of 1640s London. His interests were literary, artistic, philosophical, mathematical, medical, alchemical, and technological (to say no more); his intellectual world and work may better be seen as an eclectic synthesis of disciplines and approaches—mechanism, corpuscularianism, mixed mathematics, iatrochemistry, and craft knowledge—than the natural product of one or two decisive influences or traditions. By looking at Petty's wide-ranging practical and intellectual training, culminating in his work with the Hartlib Circle, we can see how this peculiarly mid-seventeenth-century synthesis, crucial to political arithmetic, began to take shape.

Young William Petty

> I who a Country Boy was put to School
> Where I was borne, to a pedantic foole
> And there formed verbs, did scan construe and parse
> Make verse and Themes but all to save my arse.[2]

William Petty was born on 26 May 1623, in the small town of Romsey, Hampshire, England, eight miles upriver from Southampton. He was the third child of six born to Anthony and Frances (or Francesca) Petty, who had married in 1618, but the first of only three to survive childhood; a sister, Dorothy, and a brother, Anthony, followed. Founded in the Middle Ages, Romsey was dominated then, as it is now, by a thirteenth-century abbey that survived the Reformation as the parish church. Through the early seventeenth century its population hovered around 2,700, and it supplied a steady trickle of emigrants both to London and—perhaps reflecting the local tendency to Protestant dissent—to the English colonies across the Atlantic.[3] Its principal trade was fulling and dyeing wool, and Aubrey records that the elder Anthony Petty 'was by profession a clothier, and

---

[2] From Petty's English version of his poem written to the Jesuits of the University of Caen, 1638, quoted in Dale, 7. The 'Palinodia Ad Patres Soc. Jesu. Cadomaeos' is printed in *PP*, 2:245–246.

[3] Strauss, 18. Petty later supplied John Graunt with ninety years' worth of data on christenings, marriages, and burials in the parish of Romsey; see Graunt, *Natural and Political Observations, Mentioned in a following Index, and Made upon the Bills of Mortality*, (5th ed., London: Printed by John Martyn, 1676), 86–95.

also did dye his own clothes'.[4] He reports, too, that Anthony, who died in 1644, 'left little or no estate to Sir William', though his own father, John Petty, had been one of the 'capital burgesses' of Romsey in 1607 and left the family a prominent house in the centre of town (which Petty later inherited, and which stood well into the nineteenth century). It seems that the trade depression of the 1620s, which hit the English textile industry particularly hard, hit Romsey and the Petty family too.[5] Anthony Petty was in and out of debt for the rest of his life.[6]

This background of work and worry marked Petty, and against it his subsequent rise to fame and fortune stands out all the more brightly. Aubrey describes a precocious child:

> Rumsey is a little haven port, but has most kinds of artificers in it: when [Petty] was a boy, his greatest delight was to be looking on the artificers, e.g. smiths, the watchmaker, carpenters, joiners, etc.: and at twelve years old could have worked at any of these trades. Here he went to school, and learned by 12 years a competent smattering of Latin, and was entered into the Greek.[7]

Petty himself later recalled, in a similar vein, that he 'could att the first hearing remember any 50 Nonsensicall Incoherent words; and not only repeat them readily forwards and backwards, but alsoe readily which was the 3rd, 19th, 37th &c.'—adding, with a self-depreciation characteristically leavened by contempt for others, that 'It was a thing of noe use but to get the admiration of foolish people.'[8] Most of his recollections, however, have a different hue.

His chief surviving forays into autobiography are in his last will and testament and in a few letters to Robert Southwell, and the central theme throughout is money. 'I have drawn out a paper,' Petty announced to Southwell in the summer of 1686,

> shewing what money I had at Xmas 1636—which was 1s. How it rise to 4s 6d, then to 24s, then to 4£. Then to 70. Next how it fell to 26, then rise

[4] John Aubrey (ed. Richard Barber), *Brief Lives* (Woodbridge: Boydell Press, 1982), 241.
[5] The same crisis provoked a seminal debate over the nature of trade; see Appleby, 24–51.
[6] Dale, 1–3; Strauss, 18–21; Barnard, 'Petty, Sir William', *Oxford DNB*. Little more than her name is known of Petty's mother, who died in October 1663. The younger Anthony outlived his father by only five years, dying in October 1649.
[7] Aubrey, 242.
[8] Petty to Southwell, 16 August 1687, *PSC*, 284. By the time Petty rendered this judgement he was quite familiar with Francis Bacon's *Advancement of Learning*, and may have had Bacon's words in mind: 'the art [of memory] ... may be raised to points of ostentation prodigious: but in use ... it is barren ... that is, not dexterous to be applied to the serious use of business and occasions. And therefore I make no more estimation of repeating a great number of names or

to £480 at my Landing in Ireland. Next to 13,060£ at finishing the Survey. And how after I gott my Land in Ireland and Estate in England &c, it was 3200£ at the King's Restoration &c. And so all along to this very day.

'Perhaps the like,' he concluded with satisfaction, 'hath not been seene.'[9] Petty's climb was indeed impressive—his annual income in 1685, when he composed his will, was £6,700.[10] 'Whatever becomes of me,' he wrote, 'I can leave such arguments of 50 yeares art and Industry as will be a credit to my children and friends.'[11] With this self-image went a certain coldness towards others less fortunate or industrious, as his will attested:

> As for legacys to the poor I am at a stand, as for beggars by trade & election I give them nothing, as for impotents by the hand of God the publique ought to maintain them as for those who have bin bred to no calling nor estate they should be put upon their kin[d]red As for those who can get no worke the magistrate should cause them to be imployed (which may be wel done in Ireland where is 15 acres of improvable land for every head) ... I am content that I have assisted all my poor relations & put many into a way of getting their own bread & have laboured on publique works & inventions, have sought out real objects of Charity, & doe hereby conjure all who partake of my estate to doe the like at their peril nevertthelesse to answer custome & to take the surer side I give 20£ to the most wanting of the parish wherin I die.[12]

Petty learned early to live by his wits, and had little patience for those who could or would not do likewise. His final act of charity was a grudging attempt to hedge his bets with pious custom—'to take the surer side'—and, apparently, nothing more.

Yet the unapologetic acquisitiveness so unattractive in the gouty Sir William of 1685 reflected Petty's humble origins. His first shilling came, he remembered, 'by 6d I got of a Country Squire for shewing him a pretty Trick on the Cards, which begot the other 6d fairly won at Cards.' Other, more honest tasks, brought further income:

> 6d was given (or rather paid) mee by Mother Dowling, who having been a sinner in her youth, was much relieved by my reading to her in the *Crums*

words upon once hearing ... than I do of the tricks of tumblers, funambuloes, baladines', namely, 'matters of strangeness without worthiness.' Bacon, *The Advancement of Learning*, Book Two, in Bacon (ed. Brian Vickers), *Francis Bacon* (Oxford: Oxford University Press, 1996), 229–230.

[9] Petty to Southwell, 12 June 1686, *PSC*, 211. A copy of Petty's will, dated 2 May 1685, is in BL MS Sloane 2903, ff.16–18. The will was also printed—with some important errors (on page iv 'Caen' is rendered 'Oxon', and on page xiii Petty's date of death is given as '1617')—in Petty, *Tracts; Chiefly Relating to Ireland* (Dublin: Printed by Boulter Grierson, 1769), iii–xiii.

[10] BL MS Sloane 2903, f.17r; Petty, *Tracts*, viii.   [11] *PSC*, 212.

[12] BL MS Sloane 2903, ff.17r–17v; Petty, *Tracts*, xi.

of Comfort, Mr Andrews' *Silver Watch Bell*, and *The plain man's pathway to Heaven*. The next 6d I got for an old Horace given (why do I say given?) or delivered mee by Len Green for often construeing to him in Ovid's *Metamorphoses* till my throat was soare.... My next Booty was 18d given mee by my Godfather, for making 20 verses to congratulate his having been made a Doctor in Divinity by some good Luck.

Probably in March of 1637, with a final shilling from his aunt, Petty began an apprenticeship on board a merchant ship trading between England and France. He soon put his capital to work there, too: 'This 4s 6d was layd out in France upon pittiful brase Rings, with coold glasse in them instead of diamonds and Rubies. These I sold at home to the young fellowes whom I understood to have sweethearts, for treble what they cost.' (The aunt, meanwhile, 'I repaid by a Bracelet bought in France for 4d, but judged to bee worth 16d.') Petty's memory games, card tricks, and cheap jewellery trade, which he supplemented with the sale of a couple of 'hair hatts', complete the portrait of a crafty young man on the make.[13]

The apprenticeship at sea, however, did not go smoothly. Petty discovered his extreme nearsightedness at a particularly inopportune time, having been asked by the ship's master to 'climb up the rope ladder, and give notice when he espied such a steeple … which was a landmark for the avoiding to a shelf; at last the master saw it on the deck, and they fathomed and found they were but a few foot water, whereupon … his master drubbed him with a cord.'[14] Others had different reasons for drubbing him. Petty's cleverness, an asset in his dealings with the rubes of Romsey, rubbed his shipmates (as it would many others) the wrong way, and he found himself unable 'to bear the envy of our Crew against Mee for being able to say my Compasse, shift my Tides, keep reckoning with my plain Scale, and for being better read in *The Seamen's Kalender*, the *safeguard of Saylers* &c, than Seamen of our Ship'. 'Having been ten months at sea,' Petty recalled, 'I broak my Leg, and was turnd a shoare'; bowing to the inevitable, he 'resolvd to quit the sea'.[15] At fourteen, he landed, alone and immobile, on the Normandy coast.

---

[13] Petty to Southwell, 14 July 1686, *PSC*, 216. The date of the apprenticeship cannot be established with certainty—Aubrey (242) records that it was in 'March' and Petty was 'about 15' when he 'began to play the merchant', but according to Petty, the apprenticeship lasted for ten months, and by March of 1639 he had been attending the University of Caen for some time—he lists writings from Caen for the years 1637 and 1638 in *PP*, 2:260. Further, Aubrey mentions a significant 'accident' before Petty turned fifteen. March 1637 thus seems to fit best.

[14] Aubrey, 245.   [15] *PSC*, 216–217.

This might seem to have been a low point. Yet in retrospect it was, as Aubrey remembered, 'the most remarkable *accident of life*, and ... the foundation of all the rest of his greatness and acquiring riches.'[16] Petty found himself in Catholic France at a time when English Protestants routinely identified the Pope with Antichrist; yet despite the obvious religious and linguistic differences, the town of Caen, where he wound up, would have been somewhat familiar. Like Romsey, Caen depended chiefly on the textile trade, and it enjoyed close trading connections with Southampton—which is, of course, how Petty found himself there in the first place. There was, further, a sizeable Huguenot community, many of whose members had personal connections in England, and relations between Catholics and Protestants were generally good—no doubt one influence on Petty's later ecumenism.[17] He was well treated, and during his recovery became something of a local celebrity, 'strangely visited by many' and known, with reference to his schooling, as '*Le Petit Matelot Anglais qui parle Latin et Grec.*' A farrier's wife, 'La Grande Jane', tended to his leg—for an écu, as he duly recorded; a further ten sous went to an apothecary and eight for some crutches 'of which I was afterwards cheated.' For income ('my Ring trade being understood and lost') a resourceful Petty fell back on '2 Cakes of Beeswax' apparently sent by his family, which he managed to turn to account 'upon the trade of playing Cards, white starch and hayre hatts, which I exchanged for tobacco pipes, and the shreds of Lether and parchment wherewith to size paper.' The proceeds of this variegated business, together with some ingratiating verses 'expressing my desires of returning to the Muses', earned him his next few years of education, at the Jesuit College of the University of Caen.[18]

Caen and the Jesuits

Caen, the 'Athens of Normandy', was an important intellectual centre, known for its medical faculty as well as for more humanistic scholarship—again, both Protestant and Catholic.[19] While little is known with certainty about Petty's time there, it was clearly an important moment

---

[16] Aubrey, 242.

[17] Noel Malcolm, *Aspects of Hobbes* (Oxford: Oxford University Press, 2002), 261.

[18] *PSC*, 217. Aubrey's claim that 'he was sometime at La Fleche in the college of Jesuits' (which Descartes had attended) is confused; there is nothing to suggest that Petty ever went there.

[19] Malcolm, *Hobbes*, 261, 281.

in his intellectual development. He wrote in his will that at fifteen years of age he had 'obtained the Latin, Greek, and French tongues, the whole body of common arithmetick, the practical geometry and astronomy, conducing to navigation, dialling &c. with the knowledge of several mathematical trades'.[20] According to Aubrey, 'Here [at Caen] he learnt the French tongue, and perfected himself in Latin, and had Greeke enough to serve his turn.'[21] While Aubrey is not invariably reliable, and Petty evidently had some mastery of both Latin and practical mathematics before his application to the Jesuits, it seems clear that he studied both arts and philosophy at the college. The mathematical component would be particularly important; by the age of twenty, so he later claimed, Petty had 'as much mathematicks as any of my age was known to have had'—and though some of this may have come from his pursuit of mathematical learning after he left Caen, much did not.[22] In 'A Collection of W. Petty's Severall Works and Writings since the Yeare 1636', which he drew up in 1671, Petty listed two pieces of writing from Caen which indicate the character of his studies: 'A Course of practicall Geometry and dialling', dated 1637, and a 'Cursus Rhetorices et Geographicae' from the following year.[23] Beyond these hints, direct evidence of Petty's doings among the Jesuits does not survive. Still, given the significance of this period for Petty's later work, some speculation is worthwhile.

Early modern academic culture is a vexed topic. A central theme of the history and historiography of the Scientific Revolution is a rigorous and relentless critique of academic teaching and scholarship. This went hand in hand with the polemical turn against 'scholastic' philosophy itself.[24] The proponents of various mechanical and experimental approaches to natural philosophy attacked this Aristotelian 'philosophy of the schools' as excessively abstract and speculative, removed from nature and useless for understanding it, deducing faulty conclusions from unprovable

[20] BL MS Sloane 2903, f.16r; Petty, *Tracts*, iv; *PSC*, 217. According to Aubrey (242), 'Here at Caen he studied the arts; at 18, he was (I have heard him say) a better mathematician than he is now.'

[21] Aubrey, 242. Hull claims that Petty 'supported himself in part by teaching navigation to a French officer and English to a gentleman who desired to visit England'; *EW*, xiv.

[22] BL MS Sloane 2903, f.16r; Petty, *Tracts*, iv.   [23] *PP*, 2:260.

[24] 'Scholasticism' here signifies the Christian philosophical teaching of most European universities, which focused on Aristotelian logic and natural philosophy and emphasized the construction of elaborate arguments based on knowledge of authoritative texts. See Jill Kraye, 'The Philosophy of the Italian Renaissance', in G. H. R. Parkinson (ed.), *The Renaissance and Seventeenth-Century Rationalism* (London: Routledge, 1993), 16–17.

assumptions and ignoring the concrete evidence of experience, obsessed with verbal sparring rather than knowledge of real things. The universities, correspondingly—and the Jesuit colleges, like nearly all universities in Europe, were formally committed to teaching some form of Aristotelian philosophy—were charged with inculcating worthless logic-chopping and inhibiting the investigation of the real world. (The story of a Jesuit philosopher refusing to look through Galileo's telescope, preferring to learn about nature from The Philosopher's books, is well known.[25]) The revolution in science would take place off campus, and old school lessons had to be unlearned before it could begin.

This is a fair picture of what some exponents of the new philosophy wrote in the heat of debate, but it does justice neither to the flexibility of the Aristotelian tradition—which influenced the new science and survived, for several decades, its impact—nor to the varied curricula pursued in the educational institutions of the time.[26] Nor, for that matter, were the 'new' philosophers uniformly or unambiguously committed either to inductive reasoning from experimental data or to the exclusion of hidden powers from explanations of natural phenomena.[27] The academic establishment was less monolithic and less hidebound than has sometimes been claimed. While Baconian and Hobbesian assaults on meaningless jargon would influence Petty, for example, it is likely that his Jesuit education predisposed him to this type of critique; certainly, he applied it to ancients and moderns alike.[28] Further, although one form or another of Aristotelian natural philosophy remained at the core of university teaching until new philosophies like that of Descartes began to displace it from 1640 on, there was plenty of variety within Aristotelianism and ample space within academia for new

[25] George Molland, 'Science and mathematics from the Renaissance to Descartes', in Parkinson, 120. The unreliable nature of early telescopes makes such refusals more comprehensible; see Mario Biagioli, Galileo, Courtier: The Practice of Science in the Culture of Absolutism (Chicago: University of Chicago Press, 1993), 169, 237–238.

[26] Joseph S. Freedman, 'Aristotle and the Content of Philosophy Instruction at Central European Schools and Universities during the Reformation Era (1500–1650)', Proceedings of the American Philosophical Society 137:2 (1993), 213–253, doubts the coherence of 'Aristotelian tradition' by the late sixteenth century. On the relationship between late Aristotelian and Cartesian natural philosophy, see Dennis Des Chene, Physiologia: Natural Philosophy in Late Aristotelian and Cartesian Thought (Ithaca: Cornell University Press, 1996).

[27] See for example Steven Shapin and Simon Schaffer, Leviathan and the Air-Pump: Hobbes, Boyle, and the Experimental Life (Princeton: Princeton University Press, 1985); Peter Dear, Discipline and Experience: The Mathematical Way in the Scientific Revolution (Chicago: Chicago University Press, 1995).

[28] Sharp (12) sees the Jesuits, especially Suarez, as a source for Petty's 'intense rationalism' and 'his strong belief in the need for verbal clarity and the formal definition of terminology as a prerequisite for discursive reasoning'.

work in such fields as medicine and mathematics—to name two areas
of importance to Petty.[29] What mattered was who ran the institution in
question.

Here the Jesuits were in their own class. Aristotelian or not, they hardly
stifled new learning: René Descartes and Marin Mersenne, two prominent
representatives of new philosophy in seventeenth-century France, attended
Jesuit schools, and Descartes at least sought Jesuit approval for his work.[30]
Several other leading European scholars of the period—the polymath
Athanasius Kircher, for example, and the astronomer and mathematician
Christophorus Scheiner—belonged to the Jesuit order themselves. Even
Bacon, who sharply criticized scholasticism and deplored the Church of
Rome, repeatedly praised the intellectual labours of the Society of Jesus,
regretting only that they served the wrong master. As scholars and as
teachers, 'partly in themselves and partly by the emulation and provocation
of their example', the Jesuits had 'much quickened and strengthened
the state of learning', combining scholarly discipline and submission to
authority in a manner Bacon greatly admired.[31] In the intellectual vanguard
of the Counter-Reformation, the Jesuits planned their curriculum with
consummate care and updated its contents regularly. Petty's shipmates had
done him a favour.

In theory, all Jesuit colleges followed the plan laid down in the *Ratio
atque Studiorum Societatis Jesu* of 1599 (drafts had been tested in 1586 and
1591).[32] This resembled the traditional university curriculum in outline, but
reflected important Renaissance modifications. In the medieval University
of Paris—the model for most northern universities—a seven-year arts and
philosophy course, ending in an MA, led to three years of advanced study
in theology.[33] In the Jesuit colleges (themselves modelled on Parisian
collèges de plein exercise where linguistic and philosophical studies were

[29] On medicine see Robert G. Frank, Jr., *Harvey and the Oxford Physiologists: A Study of
Scientific Ideas* (Berkeley: University of California Press, 1980); Andrew Wear, *Knowledge and
Practice in English Medicine, 1550–1680* (Cambridge: Cambridge University Press, 2000). On
mathematics see Mordechai Feingold, *The Mathematician's Apprenticeship: Science, Universities
and Society in England, 1560–1640* (Cambridge: Cambridge University Press, 1984). On the
changing status of mathematicians as against philosophers, and the boundary disputes that
ensued, see Biagioli.
[30] On Descartes's education at La Flèche, see Geneviève Rodis-Lewis (trans. Jane Marie
Todd), *Descartes: His Life and Work* (Ithaca: Cornell University Press, 1998), 8–23.
[31] Bacon, *Advancement*, Book One, in Bacon, *Francis Bacon*, 153, 133; Stephen Gaukroger,
Francis Bacon and the Transformation of Early-Modern Philosophy (Cambridge: Cambridge
University Press, 2001), 128–130.
[32] John E. Wise, 'Jesuit School Beginnings', *History of Education Quarterly* 1:1 (1961), 29–30.
[33] Richard Tuck, 'The Institutional Setting', *CHSCP*, 1:15.

pursued together), students followed a shorter, five-year arts sequence in Latin and Greek grammar, rhetoric, and literature, before moving on to a three-year course in philosophy—including logic, metaphysics, and physics, as well as pure and applied mathematics—in preparation for theology.[34] (Petty, who came to the college at a late age and was already capable in Latin, appears to have taken the last year of the arts sequence and the first, or perhaps the first two, of philosophy.) Jesuit pedagogy, too, was innovative. Teachers monitored pupils' progress through frequent 'recitations, disputations, memory lessons, [and] written compositions'; 'the love of learning was instilled by enticing young students with accolades and glory' in essay competitions and debates.[35] Petty's vigour in argument and habit of systematically weighing the pros and cons of a given proposal—reminiscent of the Scholastic *quaestio*, wherein a proposition is advanced with one set of reasons, objected to with another set, and accepted only once each objection has been answered—may have originated at Caen.[36]

The college shaped Petty's reading as much as his habits of thought; he would later list both Aristotle and the Spanish Jesuit Aristotelian philosopher Francisco Suarez among the sixteen 'most Sagacious men' of ancient or modern times.[37] This education had a deeply classical cast, likely reflected in a reading list Petty later drew up for his own sons to read from the ages of 14 to 18 (roughly Petty's age at Caen), which included such 'moderns' as Erasmus, Sir Edward Coke, Thomas Hobbes, and, on a lighter note, Molière, but also many more 'ancient' works: Justinian's *Institutiones*, Aristotle's *Rhetoric*, Cicero's *De Officiis*, the historical works of Julius Caesar, Sallust, Tacitus, Suetonius, and Josephus,

---

[34] Tuck, 18–19. For an example of this division of studies, see Freedman, Table Q (244).

[35] Wise, 30; Mordechai Feingold, 'Jesuits: Savants', in Feingold (ed.), *Jesuit Science and the Republic of Letters* (Cambridge, MA: MIT Press, 2003), 7–8. The 'Laws for Prizes' are in *JRS*, 59–61.

[36] Strauss, 25; Sharp, 12. Kraye's description (17) of the structure of Scholastic treatises parallels that of live disputations: 'works were divided and subdivided into propositions or questions; arguments for and against were laid out; a solution was reached; possible objections were raised and appropriate responses supplied.' Kraye suggests that 'this structure had the advantage of covering issues from all possible angles and ensuring that the opinions of a wide variety of ancient and medieval thinkers were aired, even if Aristotle's were the most frequently endorsed.'

[37] Petty to Southwell, 21 September 1685, *PSC*, 158. Petty names eight 'ancients' (four Greek and four Roman) and eight 'moderns' (four English and four not): Archimedes, Aristotle, Hippocrates, Homer, Julius Caesar, Cicero, Varro, Tacitus; Molière, Suarez, Galileo, Sir Thomas More, Sir Francis Bacon, John Donne, Thomas Hobbes, and René Descartes. Suarez was prominent in both metaphysics and political philosophy; see Stuart Brown, 'Renaissance Philosophy Outside Italy', in Parkinson, 81–83; Jose Ferrater Mora, 'Suarez and Modern Philosophy', *Journal of the History of Ideas* 14:4 (1953), 528–547.

and Virgil's *Georgics*.[38] Petty would later criticize scholastic bookishness, champion empirical natural philosophy, and produce an important tract on educational reform, but some of his more radical rhetoric should perhaps be taken with a grain of salt. Despite a real commitment to new kinds of learning, the education he planned for his children was probably not all that different from his own.

Indeed, it is likely that Petty's awareness of the 'new learning' has Jesuit origins. Despite their formal commitment to Aristotle, many Jesuit professors brought newer material into the classroom—or else read Aristotle, who often canvassed rival philosophies before presenting his own view, against the grain, drawing out these alternatives. Ancient atomic theories (which, like modern corpuscularianism, explained the characteristics of things by reference to their hidden substructure, in contrast to the Aristotelian doctrine of 'substantial forms', which explained each substance in terms of its particular essence), had found their way into Jesuit lectures by the early seventeenth century; waves of official injunctions against such doctrines from the 1630s on suggest that they had taken root in some colleges well before Petty's day.[39] Scholasticism itself spoke in many voices. The *Ratio studiorum* instructed professors of philosophy 'not [to] depart from Aristotle in matters of importance', but it also instructed them to criticize different traditions of interpretation impartially (though they 'should always speak favourably of St. Thomas' Aquinas) and to challenge The Philosopher himself where he departed from either 'the common teaching of the schools or, more serious still … the true faith'. There was latitude for discretion, even for those who went by the book.[40]

Most importantly, Jesuits produced their own 'new philosophy'. The 'neoscholasticism' of Francisco Suarez, for example—and Suarez remained

---

[38] 'Bookes for Charles & Henry, from 14 to 18 Years of Age', *PP*, 2:5. The paper is undated but was presumably written in the mid-to-late 1680s (Charles was born in 1673 and Henry in 1675). In its 'Rules of the Teacher of Humanities', the *Ratio studiorum* recommended daily readings from Cicero, 'especially those [works] that contain reflections on the standards of right living', and history readings from 'Caesar, Sallust, Livy, Curtius and others like them'; Virgil and Horace are recommended for poetry. See *JRS*, 79–80.

[39] Feingold, 'Jesuits', 27–29.

[40] *JRS*, 40–41. In accordance with the fifth Lateran Council, the Professor of Philosophy 'shall not attach himself or his students to any philosophical sect, such as the Averroists'—followers of the twelfth-century Islamic Aristotelian Averroes (Ibn Rushd), who denied the individuality of the soul—'the Alexandrists'—followers of the third-century Peripatetic Alexander of Aphrodisias, who denied its immortality—'and the like … but he should sharply question and minimize their authority because of these errors.' Yet professors were not to gloss over or ignore unorthodox philosophical ideas. In theology, by contrast, the vetting of unorthodox views was removed to a much higher level: the Provincial himself 'is to be especially careful that no one be appointed to teach theology who is not well disposed to the teaching of St. Thomas.' *JRS*, 3.

one of Petty's lifelong heroes—was an attempt to solve some of the same philosophical problems (the relationship between form and matter; the principle by which substances were individuated; the nature of being) that later yielded more famously 'modern' solutions from the likes of Descartes, Spinoza, and Leibniz.[41] Suarez tried to answer Renaissance critics of scholasticism and to incorporate some of the strengths and insights of humanist scholarship, furnishing an Aristotelianism updated for the seventeenth century. In so doing, he also sought to sever philosophical investigation from theology—in the teeth of St. Thomas, the Lateran Council, and the *Ratio studiorum* alike—renewing the notion of two separate 'truths', rational and revealed, which need not coincide.[42] This was of more than epistemological significance in an age when politics and religion were frequently fused and the allegiance of Catholics to papal authority, in particular, was seen to undermine their loyalty to Protestant rulers. The possibility of dividing spiritual from the secular allegiance afforded some hope that different denominations might peacefully coexist; in this regard Suarez was an important voice of moderation.[43] Whatever Petty's specific understanding of Suarez's work, the strict separation of reason from religion—and of spiritual from civil allegiance—would become crucial to his own.[44]

Probably the greatest Jesuit innovation was in mathematics. In the archetypical medieval curriculum, mathematical topics made up the

[41] On late scholastic natural philosophy see Patricia Reif, 'The Textbook Tradition in Natural Philosophy, 1600–1650', *Journal of the History of Ideas* 30:1 (1969), 17–32.

[42] Brown, 82; Mora, 535. The doctrine of 'double truth' was originally associated with Averroes and rejected by St. Thomas Aquinas; see Kraye, 18.

[43] In a British and Irish context the vehicle for such a distinction in the early seventeenth century was the 'Oath of Allegiance', which required Catholics to deny the Pope's temporal power to depose the King of England but which did not, as the 'Oath of Supremacy' applied to office-holders did, require them to deny the Pope's spiritual authority; Alan Ford, '"Firm Catholics" or "Loyal Subjects"? Religious and Political Allegiance in Early Seventeenth-Century Ireland', in D. George Boyce, Robert Eccleston, and Vincent Geoghegan (eds), *Political Discourse in Seventeenth- and Eighteenth-Century Ireland* (Basingstoke: Palgrave, 2001), 1–31. Izaak Walton included in his *Life of Dr. John Donne* a letter from the Bishop of Chichester stressing Suarez's moderate response to James I's *Apology for the Oath of Allegiance*, which, the bishop claimed, had been doctored by the Roman Inquisition to 'advance the Popes Supremacy' by stressing the papal power to authorize 'the Deposing, and then Killing of Princes'; Walton, *The Lives of Dr. John Donne, Sir Henry Wotton, Mr. Richard Hooker, Mr. George Herbert*, (4th ed., London: Printed by Tho. Roycroft for Richard Marriot, 1675), 6–7.

[44] Francis Bacon similarly warned philosophers and theologians alike not to 'mix things human with things divine'; Bacon (ed. and trans. Lisa Jardine and Michael Silverthorne), *The New Organon* (Cambridge: Cambridge University Press, 2000), 74. There is no evidence that Petty had read Bacon at this time, and every reason to think that Suarez influenced him in this respect. It seems that the Jesuits prepared Petty for Bacon.

quadrivium (arithmetic, geometry, astronomy, and music) that occupied
a place between the elementary *trivium* (grammar, logic, and rhetoric)
and the higher discipline of philosophy (itself preparation for advanced
study in medicine, law, or theology). The Jesuit *Ratio studiorum*, however,
elevated the *quadrivium*: pure and applied mathematical topics were taught
alongside, indeed as part of, philosophy.[45] This was a contentious move.
Combining mathematics with natural philosophy tampered with both the
traditional curriculum and the principled division of knowledge behind it.
Mathematics had usually been propaedeutic to philosophy, pedagogically
speaking; but it had also been subordinate to it in a more fundamental
sense, unable to provide the causal knowledge of natural processes that
characterized true science.[46] The Jesuit curriculum challenged this view.
It also raised the status of mathematicians, who now claimed equal rank
with philosophers within academic institutions (in the *Ratio* they were
'professors', not 'teachers', as those handling the *trivium* were called) and
in the learned world generally.[47] Many academic philosophers, naturally,
resented both encroachments.

This departure was largely the work of Christopher Clavius (1538–1612),
who bears mentioning here both as a pedagogue and as a scholar. His
1574 edition of Euclid's *Elements*, part of the sixteenth-century recovery
of ancient mathematical texts that paved the way for seventeenth-century
transformations, was Descartes's and perhaps Petty's textbook at college, and may also have been the book that converted Thomas Hobbes
to the deductive method of geometrical demonstration.[48] Clavius's influence on the *Ratio studiorum* was considerable. As a professor at the
Roman College from 1564 to his death, he was consulted on both early
drafts of the *Ratio*; as the only mathematics professor at the college

---

[45] The 'Rules of the Professor of Mathematics' appear after the 'Rules for the Professor of
Moral Philosophy' under the general 'Rules for the Professor of Philosophy'; *JRS*, 46. See also
Dear, *Discipline*, 35; Kristin Heitman, 'Hobbes, Wallis and Seventeenth-Century Mathematical
Method' (Ph.D. thesis, The Johns Hopkins Universty, 2000), 116–117.

[46] If true knowledge (*scientia*) was knowledge of causes, then pure mathematics—which
dealt with abstract relations rather than concrete causal processes—had no true knowledge to
offer. 'Mixed' mathematical subjects such as optics, astronomy or music, meanwhile, lacked the
homogeneity of *scientia*, since they drew their subjects from a variety of areas. See Heitman,
117–119; Dear, *Discipline*, 39.

[47] Galileo pointedly insisted on the title of 'Chief Mathematician *and* Philosopher' to the
Grand Duke of Tuscany; see Molland, 120.

[48] Heitman, 85–90. On Clavius see Dear, *Discipline*, 32–62; on his mathematical pedagogy,
see also Dennis C. Smolarski, 'Teaching Mathematics in the Seventeenth and Twenty-First
Centuries', *Mathematics Magazine* 75:4 (2002), 256–262.

before 1595, he likely determined the handling of his subject in the final version.[49] Though long dead by Petty's time and nowhere mentioned in his writings, Clavius thus shaped the young Englishman's mathematical training and thinking through his edition of Euclid, the guidelines for pedagogical practice set out in the *Ratio*, and his influence on the status of mathematics in the Jesuit curriculum vis-à-vis other branches of knowledge.

Some of this is spelled out in the *Ratio* itself. The three 'Rules of the Professor of Mathematics' paint a picture of what Petty would have experienced in the classroom:

(1) He should spend about three quarters of an hour of class time in explaining the elements of Euclid to the students of physics. After two months, when his students are somewhat familiar with the subject, he should add some geography or astronomy or similar matter which the students enjoy hearing about. This added material is to be given on the same day with Euclid or on alternate days.

(2) Every month, or at least every second month, he should have one of the students solve some celebrated mathematical problem in the presence of a large gathering of students of philosophy and theology. Afterwards, if he wishes, the solution may be discussed.

(3) Once a month, generally on a Saturday, the class period should be given over to a review of the subject matter completed that month.[50]

As this suggests, there was a strong emphasis on the public presentation of work, and students were encouraged to discuss their thinking with one another. As this also shows, the mathematics course combined the close study of Euclid's *Elements* with the exploration of 'mixed' mathematical disciplines—applied as opposed to pure mathematics—such as geography (to which the *Cursus Rhetoricae et Geographicae* in Petty's list of early works partly refers) or astronomy.[51] These mixed sciences, which applied mathematical principles to physical objects, were central not only to Clavius's attempt to raise the status of mathematics within the academy but also to the wider reorientation of science towards empirical observation and experience—a shift that was part and parcel of the 'Scientific Revolution' itself.[52] The application of mathematical reasoning to nonmathematical

---

[49] Smolarski, 'Teaching Mathematics', 257–259; Dear, *Discipline*, 33. [50] *JRS*, 46.
[51] *PP*, 2:260. Whether 'A Course of practicall Geometry and dialling' (which Petty lists for 1637) dates from before or during his time at the University of Caen is not clear.
[52] Dear, *Discipline*, 58–62.

subjects would become a defining characteristic of Petty's scientific as well as his political thinking.

Utrecht, Leiden, Amsterdam, and Paris

How Petty's career at Caen ended is unknown, and in fact the following several years of his life are something of a black hole. A convoluted passage in his will seems to suggest that he left for England in the latter part of 1638.[53] His list of writings, however, has him studying both rhetoric and geography (different courses, usually taken in different terms) during that year and lists 'A Systeme of Astronomy (Ptolemaical, Copernican)' for 1639, which, though grouped with works written in London, might reflect part of his mathematics course at Caen.[54] It is evident, at any rate, that he returned to England at some point either late in 1638 or in early 1639, and that shortly thereafter his mathematical learning earned him a position in 'the King's navy'—presumably an administrative post, given his poor eyesight.[55] This kept him in London, where, besides 'A Systeme of Astronomy', he apparently produced 'Severall drawings and paintings' in 1640, and 'An English Poem of Susanna and the Elders' in 1643.[56] It has been speculated that Petty met William Oughtred, perhaps the most prominent English mathematician then living, during these years, and it is possible that he now got to know another mathematician, John Pell, whose acquaintance would subsequently serve him well.[57] By the age of twenty, the energetic Petty 'had gotten up about three-score pounds, with as much mathematics as any of my age was known to have had.'[58] However, at just that moment, 'anno 1643, when the civil wars betwixt the king and parliament grew hot', he left England once more—this time with his brother Anthony in tow—to study medicine.[59]

Though prompted by political events, Petty's decision to study medicine abroad rather than at Oxford or Cambridge was a fairly conventional

---

[53] BL MS Sloane 2903, f.16r; Petty, *Tracts*, iv.

[54] *PP*, 2:260; Strauss, 25. The 'Copernican' component makes this less likely, assuming Petty's teachers followed the rules laid down for them; but if Descartes learned of Galileo at La Flèche there is no reason why Petty should not have done so at Caen. See Rodis-Lewis, 60.

[55] BL MS Sloane 2903, f.16r; Petty, *Tracts*, iv.   [56] *PP*, 2:260. None of these survive.

[57] Strauss, 26. There is no direct evidence, however, that Petty ever knew Oughtred personally.

[58] BL MS Sloane 2903, f.16r; Petty, *Tracts*, iv; Aubrey, 242.

[59] BL MS Sloane 2903, f.16r; Petty, *Tracts*, iv.

one for Englishmen of the time.[60] Medicine, like mathematics, was in a state of flux. Traditional medicine was characterized by Galenic humoral physiology, wherein health was identified as a balance between four essential bodily fluids or humours—yellow bile, blood, black bile and phlegm—whose relative predominance determined a person's 'complexion' and susceptibility to illness.[61] It was also marked by a strict intellectual and social division between learned physicians, expert in the managing the humours through the six 'non-naturals' (air, food and drink, sleep, exercise, evacuation, and emotional states), and much lower-status apothecaries and surgeons, who were licensed by their respective corporations in much the same way as ordinary tradesmen.[62] By Petty's time, challenges had appeared from a variety of directions: the Renaissance interest in anatomy (pioneered by Vesalius) encouraged physicians to undertake direct observation and learn some of the skills of the surgeon; the creation and refinement of alchemical approaches to medicine (first by Paracelsus and subsequently by van Helmont) directly opposed humoral theory; anatomical discoveries like Harvey's combined with mechanistic natural philosophies like Descartes's to encourage a view of the body as a machine. In England, however, into the 1640s at least, the old orthodoxies still reigned.[63]

Petty's medical training occasioned few autobiographical remarks. His will tersely noted that 'I went into the Netherlands and France for three years, and having vigourously followed my studies, especially that of medicine, at Utrecht, Leyden, Amsterdam, and Paris, I returned to Rumsey, where I was born, bringing back with me my brother Anthony, whom I had bred, with about 10£ more than I had carried out of England.'[64] As with Caen, we can speculate about the sort of studies

[60] William Harvey had studied under Hieronymus Fabricius at the University of Padua; Sir Thomas Browne preceded Petty at Leiden in the 1630s, by which time universities in France (especially Montpellier) and the Low Countries—where clinical and chemical medicine were coming into vogue—were increasingly common destinations for English medical students. See A. W. Sloane, *English Medicine in the Seventeenth Century* (Durham: Durham Academic Press, 1996), 75; Jeremiah S. Finch, *Sir Thomas Browne: A Doctor's Life of Science and Faith* (New York: Collier, 1961), 65–75.

[61] Mary Lindemann, *Medicine and Society in Early Modern Europe* (Cambridge: Cambridge University Press, 1999), 66–70.

[62] Lindemann, 66–70; Wear, 155–158, 216–217.

[63] On iatrochemistry, see Allen G. Debus, *The Chemical Philosophy: Paracelsian Science and Medicine in the Sixteenth and Seventeenth Centuries*, 2 vols (New York: Neil Watson Academic Publications, 1977); Wear, 351–473. On English medical reform, see Charles Webster, *The Great Instauration: Science, Medicine and Reform 1626–1660* (London: Duckworth, 1975).

[64] BL MS Sloane 2903, f.16r; Petty, *Tracts*, iv.

Petty pursued—though as he moved between four cities in the course of three years, his time and therefore his activities at any one institution are more difficult to account for, even hypothetically. His list of early works provides some hints, and his early encounter with alchemical medicine would turn out to be of immense significance to his political work later on. So, in a more general way, would his engagement with mechanical philosophy, which also began at this time. Perhaps most immediately important is that this period seems to mark Petty's entry into the kinds of intellectual networks that would sustain him over the next decade. Now, in Amsterdam, Leiden, and perhaps especially Paris, he forged some of his first significant intellectual relationships—significant less because they endured individually than because of the impact they had on his thinking and because of the doors they later opened. Intellectually and socially, he was on the way up.

About Petty's time in Utrecht it is hard to say anything definitive. If his recollection was correct, he went there sometime in 1643 and perhaps remained through the following spring—all else is speculation. However, probably in Utrecht, and certainly in Leiden, Petty came face to face with both eager proponents and vigorous opponents of Cartesian philosophy, the most divisive academic issue of the day.[65] Moving past sceptical critiques of traditional philosophy in search of a new basis for certain knowledge (the point of his famous *cogito, ergo sum*), Descartes posited a radical division between mind and matter and built upon it a scaled-back, materialist account of nature to replace the more layered, organic Aristotelian conception of purposive natural change: mechanical, mathematically expressible contact between inert extended bodies composed of concrete corpuscles, not the active tendency from potentiality to actuality inscribed in substantial forms.[66] Cartesianism further extended mathematical method to the study of nature—Descartes too had read Clavius at school—while banishing spiritual forces from it;

[65] In the absence of direct evidence from Utrecht, Sharp surmises (18–19) that Petty first encountered Cartesianism at Leiden. Yet if Petty did indeed go to Utrecht in 1643–44 as a student of medicine and philosophy, he would likely have encountered some of the leading participants in the debate.

[66] Gaukroger outlines the 'core theses' of mechanical philosophy as 'the postulates that nature is to be conceived on a mechanical model, that "occult qualities" cannot be accepted as having any explanatory value, that contact action is the only means by which change can be effected, and that matter and motion are the ultimate ingredients in nature.' Gaukroger, 'Descartes: Methodology', in Parkinson, 174. But Des Chene challenges the idea that mechanists held to any core tenets consistently; see also John Cottingham, 'Descartes: metaphysics and the philosophy of mind', in Parkinson, 201–234.

and around him extended a widening circle of 'physico-mathematicians'.[67] Petty certainly met some of these men later on in Paris, but it is tempting to think that Utrecht and Leiden were his real introduction.

It is intriguingly plausible. Petty, a student of medicine and philosophy, arrived in Utrecht, presumably, some time early in 1643; he was matriculated at Leiden the following May, on his twenty-first birthday.[68] Since 1641 Utrecht—which had only been a university since 1636—had been embroiled in an ugly battle between proponents of Descartes's philosophy and their critics, who sought to reimpose a strict Aristotelianism. Professor of medicine, Hendrik de Roy (Regius), who championed the theory of the circulation of the blood and defended Cartesianism in public debate, led the former. The latter were led by the university rector Gijsbert Voet (Voetius), who saw, in Descartes's method of 'hyperbolical doubt' (which leaves only the *cogito* as the basic certainty), a threat to religion. By the time Petty arrived—perhaps to study medicine under Regius, who had been forbidden in 1641 to teach anything else—Cartesian topics had been repeatedly banned. Argument raged on in Leiden, where a small community of Cartesians had formed, and where repeated attempts to stifle debate failed.[69]

It is among these Leiden Cartesians that Petty seems principally to have moved. Evidence comes from two letters Petty wrote to the mathematician John Pell, who, like him, had left England in 1643, taking a professorship in Amsterdam.[70] Like many other mathematicians of the time, Pell was interested in the problem of squaring the circle. Quadrature, or more precisely mathematicians' inability to perform quadrature, was important because the apparent incommensurability of curved and straight lines suggested a flaw in the methods of classical geometry—a flaw that became more embarrassing the more mathematicians claimed for their subject the status of a science and for themselves the status of natural philosophers.[71]

---

[67] The exclusion of occult forces from nature was originally directed not against Scholasticism but rather against Renaissance Neoplatonism and the theologically threatening idea that nature was itself active; see Gaukroger, 'Descartes', 175.

[68] *EW*, 1:xiv n.2; Rodis-Lewis, 172.

[69] On Regius, see Charles McCracken, 'Knowledge of the Existence of Body', *CHSCP*, 1:629; Erik Jan Bos, 'Regius, Henricus', *CHSCP*, 2:1459. On the reception of Cartesian philosophy in Leiden and Utrecht, see Theo Verbeek, *Descartes and the Dutch: Early Reactions to Cartesian Philosophy, 1637–1650* (Carbondale, IL: Southern Illinois University Press, 1992); Rodis-Lewis, 143–187.

[70] Christoph J. Scriba, 'Pell, John (1611–1685)', *Oxford DNB* <http://www.oxforddnb.com/view/article/21802>.

[71] Heitman, 233–234. See Paolo Mancosu, *Philosophy of Mathematics and Mathematical Practice in the Seventeenth Century* (Oxford: Oxford University Press, 1996).

In 1644, responding to a purported quadrature by the Danish mathematician Longomontanus, Pell penned a single-sheet refutation and
entrusted Petty with distributing it to various Leiden academics. That
Pell selected Petty, ten years his junior, may suggest that Petty's later
claims of mathematical proficiency were not as exaggerated as they might
otherwise sound. Or it may simply reflect Petty's being in the right place
at the right time. Either way, the people to whom Petty delivered Pell's
paper were an intriguing group, and give us at least some notion of Petty's
surroundings.[72]

Among them was Jacob Gool (Golius), who held chairs at the university
in both mathematics and oriental languages, had travelled to Morocco,
Syria, and Arabia, compiled an Arabic lexicon, and translated the medieval
Islamic astronomer al-Farghani; he was also an old friend of Descartes's.[73]
Petty had 'much discourse' with Claude de Saumaise (Salmasius), a
Huguenot 'polyhistor' described by one contemporary as 'a man from
whom one could cut three specialists'; lacking a university post, he was
referred to by Petty as 'Professor Honorarius'.[74] Another contact was
Frans van Schooten, a Cartesian mathematician based in Leiden and
an acquaintance of Pell's. One 'Mr. de Laet' was probably the Leiden
geographer (and Dutch West India Company director) Joannes de Laet,
who, as a cartographer, would have had a natural interest in geometry.[75]
Adriaan Heereboord, Professor of Philosophy at Leiden and a recent convert
to Cartesianism—he oversaw public debates of Cartesian principles in
Leiden during 1644, and later attempted to combine the Cartesian and
Aristotelian systems—likewise received Pell's work from Petty, as did
'Joncker' Cornelius van Hoghelande, whom Petty described as 'a Chymist
and Physician, Des Cartes his most intimate friend'.[76] Rounding out the
list of those who can be identified with a fair degree of certainty is Jan de

[72] Petty to Pell, 14/24 August and 29 August/8 September 1644; both letters are printed in
Fitzmaurice, 8–10.
[73] Marina Tolmacheva, 'The Medieval Arabic Geographers and the Beginnings of Modern
Orientalism', *International Journal of Middle East Studies* 27:2 (1995), 150–151; Rodis-Lewis, 64,
94, 172.
[74] Anthony Grafton, *Bring Out Your Dead: The Past as Revelation* (Cambridge, MA: Harvard
University Press, 2001), 185. Salmasius eventually took up a formal post at Leiden. His 1650
anti-regicide tract *Defensio regia pro Carlo Primo* famously provoked John Milton's 1651 *Defensio
Pro Populo Anglicano*.
[75] De Laet appears prominently in Patricia Seed, *Ceremonies of Possession in Europe's Conquest
of the New World, 1492–1640* (Cambridge: Cambridge University Press, 1995), 149–178.
[76] On Heereboord, see Christia Mercer, 'Heereboord, Adriaan', *CHSCP*, 2:1433. On
Hoghelande (or Hogelande), see Rodis-Lewis, 97; Stephen Gaukroger, *Descartes: An Intellectual
Biography* (Oxford: Oxford University Press, 1995), 295.

Wale (Walaeus), who, as Professor of Medicine at Leiden, was probably one of Petty's teachers. Trained as a Galenist, de Wale had recently begun teaching the Harveian theory of the circulation of the blood.[77] A certain 'Dr. Spanheim' was probably the Leiden Professor of Theology.[78] A Dutch 'Dr. Ryper' and 'an Englishman and mathematician', 'Dr. Wybord', remain, with 'divers others', unknown. Besides these, perhaps Petty also met Johannes de Raey, a young associate of Heereboord's and former student of Regius's who, like Petty, had moved from Utrecht to Leiden to study medicine and philosophy.[79]

Petty's list of early works includes an entry from 1644 entitled '*Collegium Logicum et Metaphysicum*', which suggests that he was more than a delivery boy for this Cartesian circle.[80] The paucity of sources, however, makes its influence on him as difficult to assess as it is to dismiss. Leiden oscillated uneasily between the traditional world of Aristotelian natural philosophy, Ptolemaic cosmology, and Galenic medicine, and the emerging world of Descartes, Galileo, and Harvey: a mechanical world set in an infinite universe, watched by God from afar. Neither was simple, comprehensive, or wholly consistent, and it is important not to exaggerate the incompatibility of elements from each. Petty's teachers, figures like Heereboord and de Wale, straddled old and new; eclecticism was inevitable and, often, principled.[81] Petty was probably never a Cartesian in any strict sense, and later rejected Descartes's 'phantasmaticall seeming philosophy' in favour of a more empirical path to knowledge. More important than doctrinal purity, however, was the range of possibilities that presented themselves.[82] His own education had included the classics, Aristotle, Ptolemy, and Galen. Yet he had also encountered innovations within the Aristotelian tradition as well as developments outside it, was acquainted with ongoing work in mathematics, and was in contact with some of the most important early proponents of Cartesian thought. This intellectual environment, creative, complex, and combative, threw open fundamental questions in all these areas, to be answered by people

---

[77] See Debus, 2:529.

[78] Arnaldo Momigliano, 'Ancient History and the Antiquarian', *Journal of the Warburg and Courtauld Institutes* 13:3/4 (1950), 299.

[79] In Leiden, van Schooten trained Christian Huygens, Johan de Witt and Johan Hudde, among others; the latter two would develop interests very similar to Petty's. See D. J. Struik, Review of J. E. Hofman, *Frans van Schooten der Jüngere*, *The American Mathematical Monthly* 70:9 (1963), 1030–1031. On de Raey, who had studied under Regius at Utrecht, see Christia Mercer, 'de Raey, Johannes', *CHSCP*, 2:1458.

[80] *PP*, 2:261. Petty noted that all his writings from his time in Holland were later 'lost at sea'.

[81] Gaukroger, *Bacon*, 28–36.   [82] Petty to Samuel Hartlib [early 1648], HP, 7/123/2a.

of ambition and ability—people like Petty—wielding new, physico-mathematical techniques.[83] Here, among the Cartesians at Leiden, Petty's scientific aspirations began.

The component of Petty's medical training that influenced his later work most profoundly was not mathematical or mechanical, however, but alchemical.[84] Chemical medicine, or iatrochemistry, posed a major challenge to the medical establishment. Beginning in the mid-sixteenth century with the chemical remedies and astral theories of the rather wild Philippus Theophrastus Bombastus Aureolus von Hohenheim (Paracelsus), and continuing with the more restrained Johan Baptiste van Helmont, iatrochemistry was an increasingly popular alternative to traditional Galenism. It dispensed with humoral theory, viewing diseases not as imbalances in patients' constitutions but as entities in their own right, with their own causes and cures. This focused attention on the preparation of medicines, and the plethora of potentially hazardous chemical remedies that resulted was no unmixed blessing. But it also directed attention to the body's own chemical processes, which were likened to chemical processes throughout nature.[85] Somewhat as mixed mathematics extended the principles of geometry to the physical world, iatrochemistry extended alchemical principles to the human body. Both shared a universalizing tendency that captured Petty's imagination.

Petty's iatrochemical training was apparently intensive. His list of early works includes for 1645 'An history of 7 monthes practise in Chymicall Laboratory', and although this was 'lost at sea', an alchemical reputation

[83] Of the ten people Petty later credited with the development of algebra—two ancients and eight moderns—at least three (Pell, Roberval, and Wallis) and perhaps six (adding van Schooten, Oughtred, and Descartes) were personal acquaintances; *PSC*, 321–322.

[84] There was no consistent distinction in the seventeenth century between 'alchemy' and 'chemistry'; see William R. Newman and Lawrence M. Principe, 'Alchemy vs. Chemistry: The Etymological Origins of a Historiographic Mistake', *Early Science and Medicine* 3:1 (1998), 32–65. Recent scholarship has emphasized both alchemy's complexity (it embraced a wide range of transformative processes, beyond 'gold-making') and its contribution to experimental method and corpuscularian matter theory. See Christoph Meinel, 'Early Seventeenth-Century Atomism: Theory, Epistemology, and the Insufficency of Experiment', *Isis* 79:1 (1988), 68–103; Principe, *The Aspiring Adept: Robert Boyle and His Alchemical Quest* (Princeton: Princeton University Press, 1998); Newman and Principe, *Alchemy Tried in the Fire: Starkey, Boyle, and the Fate of Helmontian Chemistry* (Chicago: University of Chicago Press, 2002); Newman, *Promethean Ambitions: Alchemy and the Quest to Perfect Nature* (Chicago: Chicago University Press, 2004); Newman, *Atoms and Alchemy: Chymistry and the Experimental Origins of the Scientific Revolution* (Chicago: University of Chicago Press, 2006). For a general discussion of alchemy's place in the Scientific Revolution, see Bruce T. Moran, *Distilling Knowledge: Alchemy, Chemistry, and the Scientific Revolution* (Cambridge, MA: Harvard University Press, 2005).

[85] Wear, 368–372. On Paracelsus, see Andrew Weeks, *Paracelsus: Speculative Theory and the Crisis of the Early Reformation* (Albany: SUNY Press, 1997).

stayed with him.[86] Who taught him is a mystery. There was at least one 'Chymist and Physician'—Hoghelande—among his Leiden contacts, and de Wale was close to François dele Boë (Franciscus Sylvius), a leading Helmontian who later set up an iatrochemical laboratory in Leiden—the first in any European university.[87] In 1645 Sylvius was in Amsterdam, but that does not rule him out: we know Petty was in Leiden from April or May of 1644, that he was in Paris from late 1645 and that he spent some of the intervening time with Pell, who was in Amsterdam.[88] He could easily have spent '7 monthes' in a 'Chymicall Laboratory' in Amsterdam during 1645, and it is plausible that he should have gone there to study with Sylvius on de Wale's recommendation. He may equally well have studied with Johann Rudolph Glauber, another alchemist then in Amsterdam, whose work Petty later admired.[89] It is impossible to know. What is clear is that Petty learned enough chemical medicine in the Low Countries to be regarded as competent in alchemical matters by other alchemists, and for his future work in political arithmetic to employ alchemical concepts idiomatically.

When Petty left for Paris, at the age of twenty-two, he had come a long way from the world of Romsey. Not yet a degreed physician, he was nevertheless, in Pell's estimation, 'a hopefull young man, who by countenance & counsel may become exceeding usefull'.[90] Fluent in French and Latin and competent in Greek, he had received from the Jesuits the elements of a classical education. At the same time, he was conversant with cutting-edge developments in mathematics, natural philosophy, and medicine, and familiar with at least some of the mathematicians, philosophers, and physicians behind them. He had received some training in iatrochemistry. Spurred on, no doubt, by his wider surroundings—the Dutch republic was still young, its constitutional arrangements subject to ongoing controversy—Petty had also begun to manifest other interests.[91]

---

[86] *PP*, 2:261.   [87] Debus, 2:529; Sloane, 81–82.

[88] A November 1645 letter to Pell from Petty (then in Paris) suggests that Petty had recently been with Pell in Amsterdam; Fitzmaurice, 7–8.

[89] For Petty's judgment of Glauber, see Hartlib's 'Ephemerides' for 1648, HP, 31/22/9a.

[90] Pell to Charles Cavendish, 15/25 November 1645, in Pell (ed. Noel Malcolm and Jacqueline Stedall), *John Pell (1611–1685) and His Correspondence with Charles Cavendish: The Mental World of an Early Modern Mathematician* (Oxford: Oxford University Press, 2005), 441.

[91] Malcolm (*Hobbes*, 41–43) comments on the intellectual backdrop of 'reason of State, Tacitism, religious toleration, the defence of unitary civil power, republicanism, Cartesianism, and Hobbesianism' which shaped a generation of Dutch thinkers—including not only Spinoza but also the future economic writers Johan and Pieter de la Court, both of whom spent time at the universities of Leiden and Utrecht in the mid-1640s. Petty was in part a product of the same environment.

Mention in his list of a 1645 'Collection of Frugalities of Holland' suggests a nascent concern with social and political matters: he noted 'Equall Tax' and 'Equall representation', low interest and high employment, and 'Tolleration', among other things.[92] In short, something of Petty's later range of intellectual interests is discernible, though nothing like his eventual combination of them could be guessed at from the evidence we have. With his introduction to Thomas Hobbes, it becomes less surprising.

Petty went to Paris in late 1645 on a mission from Pell: to secure from Hobbes a demonstration for the *Refutation of Longomontanus*.[93] There, the young medical student and the aging philosopher (Hobbes, born in 1588, was the almost exact contemporary of Petty's recently deceased father Anthony; his first major philosophical work, *De Cive*, appeared in 1642) quickly became friends.[94] Through the early part of 1646 Petty remained in Paris as something between Hobbes's amanuensis and his colleague. Here, through Hobbes, Petty met the leading lights of French corpuscularian philosophy and physico-mathematics (Marin Mersenne, Pierre Gassendi, Gilles de Roberval, and the Jesuit-educated Claude Mydorge), as well as important English royalists in exile, including Hobbes's patron and Pell's correspondent William Cavendish (Duke of Newcastle) and his brother Charles; their own philosophical circle included Margaret Cavendish (Duchess of Newcastle) and Kenelm Digby.[95] Although brief, these contacts plainly meant a lot to Petty. Decades later, dedicating his own blend of corpuscularianism and mixed mathematics to Newcastle, Pett would thank the Duke for his kindness '30 years ago' and recall how

> about that time in *Paris, Mersennus, Gassendy*, Mr. *Hobs*, Monsieur *Des Cartes*, Monsieur *Roberval*, Monsieur *Mydorge*…and your memorable Brother, Sir *Charles Cavendish*, did countenance and influence my Studies, as well by their Conversation as their Publick Lectures and Writings.[96]

---

[92] *PP*, 2:185–186, 261.

[93] Noel Malcolm, 'Hobbes, Thomas (1588–1679)', *Oxford DNB* <http://www.oxforddnb.com/view/article/13400>.

[94] Aubrey (242) records that Hobbes 'loved [Petty's] company', although the two do not seem to have remained in contact after Petty left Paris.

[95] For a comparison of Hobbes and Gassendi, see Tom Sorell, 'Seventeenth-Century Materialism: Gassendi and Hobbes', in Parkinson, 235–272. For the 'physico-mathematics' of the Mersenne circle, see Heitman, 130–131. On the Cavendish circle, see Lisa T. Sarasohn, 'Thomas Hobbes and the Duke of Newcastle: A Study in the Mutuality of Patronage before the Establishment of the Royal Society', *Isis* 90:4 (1999), 721–722.

[96] Petty, *The Discourse Made before the Royal Society the 26. of November 1674. Concerning the Use of Duplicate Proportion in Sundry Important Particulars* (London: Printed for John Martyn, 1674), sig. A8v–A9r. Though this suggests that Petty met Descartes in Paris, he cannot have done so: except for a brief visits to Paris in 1644 (when Petty was in Utrecht and/or Leiden),

Writing to Pell, Petty reported a good relationship with 'Father Mersen', whose empirical bent may have influenced Petty's later stress on the 'number, weight and measure' of things.[97] In this constellation of luminaries, however, it seems to have been Hobbes who shone brightest—or who had the most time for Petty. Petty continued his medical studies but took a turn from chemistry to anatomy, geared towards helping Hobbes with an English optical treatise commissioned by Newcastle.[98] The two read Vesalius together, and even performed dissections.[99] Petty, who 'then had a fine hand in drawing and figure-drawing' (recall the 'drawings and paintings' he is supposed to have done in 1640) 'drew Mr. Hobbes' optical schemes for him which he was pleased to like.'[100] The young man's medical training and steady hands would have been an obvious asset to Hobbes, and Petty's artisanal origins and practical bent were probably congenial.[101] There is even the possibility—strongly suggested by his work with the Hartlib circle in the years following—that Petty knew how to grind lenses, and had perhaps supported himself and his brother in this way while in the Low Countries. It is not surprising that Hobbes should have found in Petty an able assistant, and eager student, and an engaging companion.

Had Petty found a mentor? Whoever else he learned from, the only person whose 'disciple' he has ever been called is Hobbes.[102] If this is a little strong (Petty was never Hobbes's epigone), still the two were a good fit, personally, practically and intellectually. It has been suggested that Hobbes, like Petty, learned his Euclid from Clavius's edition, though later in life and in more dramatic fashion: finding the *Elements* lying open

and again in 1647 and 1649 (when Petty was in London and/or Oxford), Descartes was in the Low Countries throughout the 1640s. Petty may have encountered Descartes earlier, in Leiden or Amsterdam, but there is no evidence that he did. See Rodis-Lewis, 73.

[97] Finkelstein, 172–173.

[98] Petty's early works include a '*Cursus anatomicus*' dated to 1646 in Paris, as well as 'A discourse in Latin *De Arthriitide et Lue Venerea*'; *PP*, 261.

[99] Malcolm, *Hobbes*, 320.

[100] Aubrey, 242; *PP*, 2:261. A letter from Charles Cavendish to Pell, 1/11 November 1645, reported that 'Mr. Hobbes intends to publish as soon as he can a treatise of opticks; he hath done halfe of it, & Mr. Petit [i.e. Petty] hath writ it faire.' Pell, *Correspondence*, 434. Hartlib's 'Ephemerides' for 1655 contain a report from William Brereton that 'That Treatise of his [i.e. Hobbes's] Optica is to come forth by itself Dr Petty having made the diagrams vnto it.' Hartlib Papers, 29/5/33b. Hobbes's English optical manuscripts are in BL MS Harleian 3360.

[101] Hobbes's father was a failed curate from a family of clothiers, like Petty's. He fled assault charges when Hobbes was sixteen, dying, Aubrey wrote, 'in obscurity'; Malcolm, *Hobbes*, 1–3.

[102] Johnson (98) describes Petty as 'Essentially a disciple of Hobbes in his political theory'. Quentin Skinner adopts the same view in 'Hobbes's Disciples in France and England', *Comparative Studies in Society and History* 8:2 (1966), 153–167, reprinted in Skinner, *Visions of Politics*, 3 vols (Cambridge: Cambridge University Press, 2002), 3:308–323.

on a table during a visit to Geneva in 1630, Hobbes was immediately taken with it, and came to recognize in geometrical method the only source of certain knowledge.[103] For Hobbes and Petty alike, optics, the paradigmatic form of mixed mathematics, connected the man-made certainty of mathematics with God's physical Creation. For both, going further, this connection ultimately promised a mathematical science of politics and society. When Petty eventually did turn his hand to politics, he espoused both a view of sovereignty apparently derived from *De Cive*, which he perhaps read at this time, and an Erastian ecclesiology similar to Hobbes's. His views on language and psychology can similarly be classified as Hobbesian.[104] Yet Petty's political arithmetic—not least in its overt rejection of deductive geometrical demonstration, Hobbes's method of choice—deviated significantly from Hobbes's conception of what science should be, and despite lasting mutual regard, the two were rarely if ever in direct contact after Paris, even when Hobbes returned to England following the publication of *Leviathan* in 1651.[105] Hobbes's extension of mathematical method to politics was undoubtedly a key influence on Petty's later thinking. But it was neither the only such influence nor the decisive one. Petty's next move—to London and the world of the Hartlib Circle—was in many ways a radical change of direction.

Whatever the reason, it seems that things in Paris did not go quite as planned. Hobbes put the optical treatise on hold in the face of several succeeding distractions, including, after Petty's departure, a turn as mathematics tutor to the future King Charles II. His onetime patrons, the Cavendishes, found themselves increasingly short of money; for a time in 1648 Hobbes even became their creditor, temporarily 'buying' some of Newcastle's telescopes and microscopes to allow Newcastle to leave Paris and join a Royalist expedition.[106] Petty, too, went through a rough patch. Aubrey noted that 'he was driven to great straits for money, and I have heard him say, that he lived a week on two pennyworth (or three, I have

[103] Heitman, 85–90. It is possible that Hobbes had read Clavius even earlier, while cataloguing the Chatsworth library of his former patron, the Earl of Devonshire, in 1629; it contained various works by Clavius, including his edition of Euclid. See Malcolm, 'Hobbes', *Oxford DNB*.

[104] Finkelstein, 171, 175.

[105] Hobbes relayed his (very positive) opinion of Petty's 1674 *Discourse* via Aubrey rather than directly to Petty himself, and his tone suggests a strained, or at least distant, relationship: 'tell him that if I had seene his Booke before it went to the Presse I would not (as he thinks) haue hindred it, but done as the Society did, that is, vrg'd him to print it.' Hobbes to Aubrey, 24 February/6 March 1675/6, in Hobbes (ed. Noel Malcolm), *Thomas Hobbes: The Correspondence*, 2 vols (Oxford: Oxford University Press, 1994), 2:751. A copy is in BL MS Add. 72850, ff.134–135.

[106] See Sarasohn, 'Hobbes', 731.

forgotten which, but I think the former) of walnuts.'[107] It may be that this poverty, or some other trouble (Aubrey asked whether he was a 'prisoner' at some point), helped spur his return to England. Or it may be that he wanted to finish his degree—an MD from Oxford or Cambridge was still required for practicing in London—or to bring his younger brother Anthony home to Romsey, to see their mother and see to what little their father had left them. Whichever of these weighed most with Petty, he left Paris some time in the middle of 1646, bound for London.

[107] Aubrey, 242.

CHAPTER 2

The Making of a Virtuoso

At the age of twenty-three, Petty found himself in the thick of what we know as the Scientific Revolution. Friendly with Hobbes, versed in Cartesian philosophy, Harveian physiology, Helmontian iatrochemistry, and Jesuit mathematical scholarship, he could hardly have incorporated more of the new learning into his education than he did. Yet he remained, as well, the son of an artisan, with a keen interest in practical technique, whether in the anatomical experiments he performed with Hobbes or in the manual trades that supported his existence. Theoretically informed, Petty never lost this fundamentally practical bent, and over the course of the next several years he devoted himself to a series of practical projects alongside more obviously 'scientific' pursuits. This peculiar combination marked him and his work from this point onward, as he transformed himself from a student, assistant, and go-between into an experimental philosopher, physician, and 'improver' in his own right—in short, into the kind of multifaceted scientific figure known as a 'virtuoso'.[1]

This transformation was the work of a relatively brief period, roughly six years between his return to England from Paris in mid-1646 and his departure for Ireland at the beginning of 1653. But in this limited time, Petty's work—for he now began to produce work that was identifiably his own—encompassed an almost unbelievable range of fields, from practical mechanics to medicine to educational reform to experimental methodology to, very tentatively, politics. Little of it was printed (though his first printed

---

[1] Walter E. Houghton, Jr ties 'virtuosity' to high social status and a non-utilitarian orientation to nature (collecting curiosities rather than discovering laws or techniques): Houghton, 'The English Virtuoso in the Seventeenth Century: Part I', *Journal of the History of Ideas* 3:1 (1942), 51–73; Houghton, 'The English Virtuoso in the Seventeenth Century: Part II', *Journal of the History of Ideas* 3:2 (1942), 190–219. But the contrast between 'real natural philosophers' and 'gentlemen who played with science' is exaggerated—most of the Royal Society lay at neither end of this spectrum. Others see virtuosi simply as 'amateurs' with practical and theoretical interests in the study of nature; see Dorothy Stimson, 'Amateurs of Science in 17th Century England', *Isis* 31:1 (1939), 32–47. Webster, *Instauration*, gives the term a gentlemanly connotation yet links the virtuosi with the Hartlib Circle. Petty himself states that after receiving his MD from Oxford, he was 'admitted into the College of Physicians of London & into several clubs of the Virtuosi'; BL MS Sloane 2903, f.16r. Aubrey (243) describes the members of the Oxford 'experimental philosophy club' as 'virtuosi' without further qualification.

work appeared in 1648), but traces of it survive in dozens of manuscripts. In retrospect, Petty never became a major figure in the history of science, but in the 1640s he was as promising an experimentalist as anyone in his acquaintance—an acquaintance that included the likes of Robert Boyle. And although the years he now spent assiduously building a reputation for experimental and mechanical expertise, forming a scientific persona and a distinctively practical conception of science itself led to no epochal discoveries about nature, they would prove essential to his engagement with society.

The Hartlib Circle

After leaving Paris, Petty went first, his will tells us, to Romsey, and then, still in 1646, to Oxford, where 'in less than four years more I obtained my degree of M.D.'[2] In fact, though he did continue his anatomical studies through later 1646, and did receive his degree from Oxford in early 1650, he spent much of the intervening time in London, 'lodging next doore to the White Boare in Lothbury.'[3] There he joined the network of experimental natural philosophers, physicians, alchemists, and inventors linked to the Polish–German émigré Samuel Hartlib and known to posterity as the Hartlib Circle.[4] Like the Mersenne and Cavendish circles in Paris, the Hartlib Circle included a range of people from different countries with common philosophical interests, who shared correspondence and manuscripts (Hartlib published many of their works) and sought patronage for assorted projects of merit. Otherwise the Hartlibians were very different. They were socially diverse, ranging from the young aristocrat Boyle down to the impoverished utopian Gabriel Plattes, who literally dropped dead in a London street in 1644 after years of living hand-to-mouth.[5]

---

[2] BL MS Sloane 2903, f.16r; Petty, *Tracts*, iv.

[3] *EW*, 2:633. HP, 8/13/1a–2b is a 1646 'Cursus Anatomicus' listing topics in human and animal anatomy, attributed to Petty; see also Petty, 'In cursu Anatomico', BL MS Add. 72891, f.26. The Petty Papers contain several descriptions of diseases dating to 1646: see BL MS Add. 72891, ff.79–91, 202–207 and 256–257v. Petty mentions 'A discourse in Latin *De Arithridite et Lue Venerea* and *Cursus anatomicus*' in his list of works for 1646; *PP*, 2:261.

[4] The most comprehensive treatment remains Webster, *Instauration*. See also Mark Greengrass, Michael Leslie and Tim Raylor (eds), *Samuel Hartlib and the Universal Reformation: Studies in Intellectual Communication* (Cambridge: Cambridge University Press, 1994).

[5] Boyle's father was the second earl of Cork. See Michael Hunter, 'Boyle, Robert (1627–1691)', *Oxford DNB* <http://www.oxforddnb.com/view/article/3137>. A handwritten note in the BL copy of Plattes, *A Discovery of Subterraneall Treasure* (London: Printed by I. Okes for Iasper Emery, 1639), records that 'The Author of this booke died of meer want In the yeare 1644 at London.'

They focused more on practical science and 'improvement'—agricultural practices, mechanical devices, manufacturing techniques—than on systematic philosophizing. To varying degrees, they tended towards hard-line anti-episcopal Protestantism, or Puritanism. Their rise to prominence in the 1640s, no less than the Cavendish circle's removal to Paris, was a product of Parliament's victory in the Civil War.

As this suggests, Petty's move from Paris to London had political overtones: he exchanged the company of exiled royalists (and their Catholic hosts) for that of militant Protestants and Parliamentarians. Still, this contrast should not be pushed too far. Intellectual ties cut across political, confessional, and national boundaries, and though Petty might seem to be switching sides, there was a great deal of diversity within each grouping and many connections between the two. Pell, for example, was close to Charles Cavendish but knew Hartlib and later accepted a position under the Commonwealth; Pell's student William Brereton similarly associated with both groups.[6] Petty himself remained in contact with Cavendish through the end of the decade, and shared scientific news from Paris with Hartlib.[7] No cutting of ties was involved; during the turbulent 1640s (as was the case at the Restoration and again under James II) personal networks often outlasted political divisions. Petty was certainly capable of political conviction, but like so many political survivors of his generation he learned to hide it as prudence dictated. Joining the Hartlib Circle did not necessarily make him a radical or a Puritan, and given his later work it seems unlikely that he was either, at least more than superficially. That said, it was not the moderate Pell but Sir Cheney Culpeper, a radical Parliamentarian with an interest in alchemy, who first mentioned Petty to Hartlib in January 1647 as someone who might be of use.[8]

The overarching vision the Hartlib Circle pursued was immensely ambitious: nothing less than the 'universal reformation' of knowledge and society. Central to this was Sir Francis Bacon's notion of a 'great instauration' of experimental discovery and practical invention that would restore to mankind the knowledge and mastery of nature lost with exile from Eden.[9]

---

[6] Scriba, 'Pell, John', *Oxford DNB*; Anita McConnell, 'Brereton, William, third Baron Brereton of Leighlin (*bap.* 1631, *d.* 1680)', *Oxford DNB* <http://www.oxforddnb.com/view/article/39679>.

[7] Charles Cavendish to Petty, 7/17 April 1648, HP, 8/29/1a–2b.

[8] Webster, *Instauration*, 81 n.168; on Culpeper, see Mark Greengrass, 'Culpeper, Sir Cheney (*bap.* 1601, *d.* 1663)', *Oxford DNB* <http://www.oxforddnb.com/view/article/50336>.

[9] Bacon, *New Organon*, 221: 'For by the Fall man declined from the state of innocence and from his kingdom over the creatures. Both things can be repaired even in this life to some

But the Hartlibians brought to the great work of improvement a political and social radicalism alien to Bacon (Lord Verulam and Lord Chancellor of England). Many, like Culpeper, infused this with a millennial eschatology: a favourite Scriptural passage was Daniel 12:4: 'But thou, O Daniel, shut up the words, and seal the book, even to the time of the end: many shall run to and fro, and knowledge shall be increased.'[10] For both Bacon and the Hartlibians, however, the purpose of this increased knowledge was increased capacity for action. Bacon had conceived truth as productive; indeed, 'the discovery of products and results is like a warranty or guarantee of the truth of a philosophy.'[11] Real knowledge conferred power, and 'The task and purpose of human Power is to generate and superinduce on a given body a new nature or new natures': to master nature by transforming things for human benefit.[12] The Hartlibians gave Bacon's work a more demotic and sectarian cast, but they put something like this principle into action.

If there was any truly decisive intellectual influence on Petty during his first three decades, Baconianism—a set of methodological precepts and experimental aspirations more than a philosophical system—was it.[13] But assessing it as a single coherent source of ideas is a questionable operation. Bacon's work drew on Counter-Reformation scholarship that Petty encountered directly; thanks to the Jesuits, Petty may have been predisposed to certain 'Baconian' traits.[14] In Paris, Petty worked with Hobbes, who had been Bacon's amanuensis in his youth; in London, Bacon's work—which Petty did now read for himself—was also diffracted through the prism of Hartlibian reform. This last embraced a wide range of activities: the discovery of new devices and techniques for

---

extent, the former by religion and faith, the latter by the arts and sciences.' Man's prelapsarian knowledge of nature was associated with Genesis 2:19: 'And out of the ground the Lord God formed every beast of the field, and every fowl of the air; and brought them unto Adam to see what he would call them: and whatsoever Adam called every living creature, that was the name thereof.' Adam's language was thought to have reflected the true nature of the things he named; see Peter Harrison, *The Bible, Protestantism, and the Rise of Natural Science* (Cambridge: Cambridge University Press, 1998), 61.

[10] Webster, *Instauration*, 1–31. Bacon quotes Daniel 12:4 in *Advancement of Learning*, Book Two (Bacon, *Francis Bacon*, 184) and, in Latin, on the frontispiece to *Instauratio magna*: 'Multi pertransibunt & audebitur scientia'.

[11] Bacon, *New Organon*, 60.

[12] Bacon, *New Organon*, 102. Compare *New Organon*, 66: 'The true and legitimate goal of the human sciences is to endow human life with new discoveries and resources.'

[13] Gaukroger, *Bacon*, 222.

[14] Jorge Cañizares-Esguerra, *Nature, Empire, and Nation: Explorations of the History of Science in the Iberian World* (Stanford: Stanford University Press, 2006), 14–22.

agriculture, mining, and manufactures, and the promotion of schemes
for employing the poor; the discovery of new alchemical processes and
of new chemical medicines; the reform of education and the creation
of new academic institutions; the creation and collection of natural and
experimental histories and the design of scientific instruments; the reform
of scientific communications and of knowledge itself. Petty's multifaceted
background, quite as much as his expertise in any one area, made him a
natural fit for the Hartlib Circle. Hartlib described Petty to Boyle as 'a
perfect Frenchman, and good linguist in other vulgar languages besides
Latin and Greek [perhaps Dutch or German], a most rare and excellent
anatomist, and excelling in all mathematical and mechanical learning', a
young man of varied abilities and interests.[15]

Petty's early intellectual make-up is best read from the wide array of
work he now performed. Although any division is somewhat artificial,
for the sake of examination Petty's efforts can be sorted into six interrelated categories: invention and economic improvement, alchemical and
iatrochemical work, mixed mathematics, communications, experimental
methodology, and institutional reform. These categories reflect both the
different dimensions of the Hartlibian program and the peculiar combination of influences Petty was able to bring to bear within the Hartlibians'
Baconian framework. We are still a long way from the world of political
arithmetic, but we have arrived at the mindset that made it possible.

Agriculture and manufactures

The improvement of agriculture and manufactures, through the compilation of 'natural histories' of trades, the dissemination of information on
current best practices, and the invention of new devices and techniques,
was central to Hartlibian reform. Petty was well suited to this aspect
of the program, both as the son of an artisan and as a budding natural
philosopher in his own right. He rapidly adopted the Baconian outlook
of the reformers around him, pronouncing 'Verulam ... one of the chiefest
men for ... Reall Learning', a greater philosopher than More (whom Petty
yet admired as a statesman), and a greater man than Ralegh.[16] Among

---

[15] Hartlib to Boyle, 16 November 1647, in Boyle (ed. Michael Hunter, Antonio Clericuzio
and Lawrence Principe), *The Correspondence of Robert Boyle*, 6 vols (London: Pickering & Chatto,
2001), 1:63–64.

[16] *Ephemerides* 1649, in HP, 28/1/19b.

Hartlib's papers is an English translation, in Petty's hand, of a passage from Bacon's *New Organon* praising inventors:

> The Introduction of Noble Inventions seemeth to bee the Cheife of all humane actions, Which former Ages sufficiently Witnessed, Inasmuch as they attributed divine honours to such Inventours, Whereas they allotted onely the honour or title of Heroes to the well-deserving in ciuill affaires ... And truly whosoeuer shall well scan the Matter, hee shall find this Verdict of the Ancients to bee very just, For the Benefit of new Inventions may extend to all Mankind Vniversally but those the good of Civill atchievement can respect but some particular Cantons of Men, these latter doe not endure aboue a few ages, the former for euer, Moreouer the Reformation of States in civill affaires for the most part is not compassed without Violence and disturbances, But Inventions make all Men happy without either Injury or dammage to any one single person, Further New Inventions are as it were New Creations and are Imitacious of Gods owne Works.[17]

Nothing showed the primacy of invention better than Bacon's favourite trio of inventions, the magnetic compass, gunpowder, and the printing press, 'From whence have followed Innumerable Changes of things, so that no Empire, No Sect, nor no Constellation seemes to haue had a greater Influence upon humane [affaires] than these Mechanicall Inventions haue had.'[18]

Petty can hardly have aspired to invention on this epoch-making scale; his best-known inventions aimed more modestly at the reform of knowledge production and communications through innovations in existing technology. Nevertheless, the clothier's son was well aware of the role that less glamorous 'Mechanicall Inventions' could play in agriculture, manufactures, and commerce, and thus in the creation, if not of a new world, then at least of a reformed society:

> To provide for Poore, advance trade and make all manufactures flourish, England should bee endeavoured to bee made the shop of Europe and all manner of compendious ways invented wherby they may come to vndersel the Manufactores and commodities of all other Countrys. This would be better then to strengthen their monopolizing Corporations in ignorance and idlnes.[19]

---

[17] HP, 63/12a. See Bacon, *New Organon*, 99–100. Virtually the same translation, with the same omissions, appears in Cressy Dymock, *An Invention of Engines of Motion, Lately Brought to Perfection* (London: Printed by I. C. for Richard Woodnoth, 1651), sig. A2r–A2v.

[18] HP, 63/12b; compare Bacon, *New Organon*, 100.   [19] Ephemerides 1649, HP, 28/1/14b.

Criticizing (like many of his contemporaries) 'monopolizing Corporations' for restricting employment and resisting innovation, Petty sought England's economic advantage through maximal production, keeping goods plentiful and cheap, the poor occupied and the state strong.[20] This meant eradicating 'idleness' in the able-bodied population, but it also meant harnessing the power of 'art' by transmitting state-of-the-art knowledge and by creating new labour-saving technology—a paradox that was remarked upon at the time.[21]

Petty contributed to both strands. Hartlib's journals, the 'Ephemerides', are littered with Petty's opinions of artisans and products in an astonishing range of trades. His information ranged from simple evaluations of craftsmanship to anecdotal pictures of the life of a business or estimates of the scientific acuity of a tradesman:

> A clothiers servant did vndoe his Master by cutting always out so many yards out of the whole piece of cloth when it was made, having a neate way how to sew it vp. This was not perceived or found out by many years which made the Master to trie all manner of meanes how to better his cloth but could not which vtterly impoverished him. Petty.[22]

> Sweeting the Stationer in Popes-head alley hath invented a Motion that shall goe 2. or 3. months, which may been [sic] applied to clocks etc. It may be the same of part with Kochel…Hee is a very Learned Stationer and Mechanically-Mathmetical and a good Musician. Petty.[23]

> One Lawson is very excellent in making of Cabinets and Cases etc. which Art having kept private for some yeares amongst his Printesses and worke-men hee hath gotten a considerable estate by it and better then if hee should have had a Patent for it. But his men when they come to set vp for themselves hee intends to betake himself to something else. Petty.[24]

Petty sometimes went beyond the products or inventions themselves to their practical applications, experimental implications, or methodological shortcomings. At other times he supplied little more than an advertisement for a favoured artisan: 'Alcock the Watch-maker in Lumbard-street is the Man with all manner of Rarities to draw customers to himself'; 'Milles in Crutchet-Friars is very excellent also for Iacks'; 'One Boxe druggist in

---

[20] Finkelstein (60–73) points out that arguments for 'free trade' in the seventeenth century called for the expansion or redistribution, not elimination, of privileges.

[21] Gabriel Plattes, *A Discovery of Infinite Treasvre, Hidden Since the Worlds Beginning* (London: Printed by Iohn Legat, 1639), 75–76.

[22] Ephemerides 1648, HP, 31/22/4b.   [23] Ephemerides 1648, HP, 31/22/6a.

[24] Ephemerides 1649, HP, 28/1/27a–27b.

Cheape-side one of the best in all Europe.'[25] Petty's personal background in trade made his opinions worth having. The amount of advice he gave suggests that he spent a great deal of time among the tradesmen of London.

Bridging the 'philosophical' and 'mechanical' worlds, Petty cultivated his own status as an inventor. In July 1648 Hartlib reported Petty's 'New Invention ... for setting of Corne', apparently a kind of seed drill, 'able to doe all that which either Plats [i.e. Gabriel Plattes] or Demock [i.e. Cressy Dymock] vndertake by way of instrument.'[26] Dymock, like Petty, was a newcomer to Hartlib's circle; his 1651 *Invention of Engines for Motion*, which introduced his own machines using the same translation from Bacon quoted at the beginning of this section, described 'saving and multiplying Corn' as 'one of the chief and most substantial parts' of husbandry.[27] Plattes's 1639 *Discovery of Infinite Treasure*, the fruit of twenty-four years of 'observations and experiments', was probably the single most influential work on Baconian agricultural improvement.[28] Comparing his work to theirs, Petty placed his 'new method of Agriculture' at the forefront of the Hartlibian agricultural reform. (As if this were not ambitious enough for a twenty-five-year-old with no known experience of farming, he also promised Hartlib 'a certain Topica Agriculturae into which all the knowledge concerning that subject may bee most comprehensively referred.')[29] He quickly set to work testing his machine, and by mid-1649 boasted that a prototype 'hath fully succeeded and answered expectation' in trials on a friend's farm; another was set for further testing, perhaps in Romsey, where Petty went for two weeks in September, 'to see his Mother and to trie his engine for Corne-businesse.'[30]

More mysterious was Petty's 'Perpetuus Motus Invention'—perpetual motion being to 'mechanics' of the time what quadrature was to geometers.[31] An engine 'for drayning and lifting vp of great weights with celerity and speed', this could be used to make arable land out of waterlogged fen, perhaps to pump water from mines, and even to grind sugar-cane; all in

---

[25] Ephemerides 1649, HP, 28/1/36a; Ephemerides 1650, HP, 28/1/60a; Ephemerides 1649, HP, 28/1/2b.

[26] Ephemerides 1648, HP, 31/22/31a. This 'engine for planting Corne' also appears in Petty's list of 'works and writings' for 1648; *PP*, 2:261.

[27] Dymock, *Invention*, sig. A2r-A2v, 3. See Mark Greengrass, 'Dymock, Cressy (*fl.* 1629–1660)', *Oxford DNB* <http://www.oxforddnb.com/view/article/54119>.

[28] Webster, *Instauration*, 472; Plattes, *Infinite Treasvre*, sig. C2v; for Plattes's own seed drill see Plattes, *Infinite Treasvre*, 54–57; W.A.S. Hewins (rev. Anita McConnell), 'Plattes, Gabriel (*c.*1600–1644)', *Oxford DNB* <http://www.oxforddnb.com/view/article/22360>.

[29] Ephemerides 1648, HP, 31/22/31a.

[30] Ephemerides 1649, HP, 28/1/24b, 25b, 28b–29a.   [31] Dymock, 1–2.

all, Petty noted, 'a specimen of the greatest Art and Raritie that of all the 3 elements (Aire Fire Water) hath beene in this world.'[32] Similarly versatile was his 'Invention for brewing', a furnace not only for brewing but also for baking, smelting copper, and perhaps for boiling cane sugar (though Petty 'knows not whether there bee good store of combustible matter in Barbados') and curing tobacco.[33] Like the seed-drill, others, besides Petty, pursued these inventions—in this case, William Wheeler and Caspar Kalthoff. Wheeler was an extraordinarily wide-ranging inventor but also secretive and self-interested; Petty's apparent openness was a welcome contrast.[34] The Dutch engineer Kalthoff, on the other hand, was highly regarded and left a collection of model pumps and furnaces at the royal ordinance factory at Vauxhall, where he had worked under Charles I.[35] When Petty proposed a furnace Kalthoff thought impossibly large, Hartlib and his protégé Benjamin Worsley tried to put him off; Petty, beginning to show his trademark self-confidence, remained undaunted.[36]

Perhaps most significant, however, was an undated 'Phytologicall Letter' to Hartlib outlining the contents and purposes of an 'Essay which I propounded to you about Germination, or rather about a more perfect inquiry upon the whole subject of Vegetation.'[37] Befitting a work dedicated to both the advancement of knowledge and practical improvement, it was divided into 'Physicall' and 'Oeconomicall' parts and began, in Baconian fashion, with Petty's attempt 'to sett downe all the Phaenomena I could remember'. The most important phenomena cast light on the relationship between natural processes and artificial interventions. Petty noted, for example, 'That some earths are wholly barren' or 'wanted lust to conceive or bring forth any Plants of bigness'. Others 'had a Competent vigor & lust' and were 'perpetually conceiving ... though noe way assisted, sollicited, or impraegnated by the care Industry, designe or project of Man'. Yet, given fertile land, man might alter 'the disposition of its Lust' to produce a given crop.[38] Of plants

---

[32] Ephemerides 1649, HP, 28/1/9b, 11b. For an apparently similar engine, see Dymock, 8–12.

[33] Ephemerides 1649, HP, 28/1/3a, 8a, 11a, 13a.

[34] Webster, *Instauration*, 372–374. See William Wheeler, *A List of some of the Chief Workes which Mr. William Wheeler offereth to undertake* (Amsterdam: Printed by George Trigg, 1653); a similar 'Memo on Wheeler's inventions', possibly in Petty's hand, is in HP, 64/2/1a–4b.

[35] Webster, *Instauration*, 347–348, 364.

[36] Worsley to Petty, 15 June [1649], HP, 8/50/1a–2b. See also Worsley to Hartlib, 22 June 1649, HP, 26/33/1a–3b; Ephemerides 1649, HP, 28/1/3a, 18b.

[37] BL MS Add. 4292, ff.141–142v; see also HP, 8/22/1a–4b. No essay survives. The letter—only partially decipherable even with ultraviolet light—is discussed at length in Tony Aspromourgos, 'The Invention of the Concept of Social Surplus: Petty in the Hartlib Circle', *European Journal of the History of Economic Thought* 12:1 (2005), 1–24.

[38] BL MS Add. 4292, f.141r.

themselves, he noted, 'some … are great Travellers … and that [without] any Industry or care of Man' while others 'will admitt to be transplanted by Industry like the settling of new Collonies'; a few, however—like the cloves and nutmeg of the Spice Islands—had proved 'strickt Citizens, only of one Country or Place'.³⁹ He passed finally to 'Artificiall Phaenomena' aiming at

> the improving or alteration of Plants, by severall Media or Arts, either in their Colours, Od[ors], Figures, in their time of Ripening, times of Germination or budding, times of enduring or lasting, or to the extraordinary Increase of their Leaves or of their Flowers, or of their Roots, or of their Seeds, or … to the addition or suppression of their naturall tallnesse or growth with other like like curio[sities] & varieties[.]⁴⁰

The next step was to identify such 'true causes of vegetation' as 'may clearly resolve & fully Answer to all these both Naturall & Artificiall Phaenomena.' These might be drawn from 'Aristotles Hypothesis of the 4 E[lements] Or from Paracels[us] his 3. Principles of Salt, Sulphur, & Mercury, or from Des Cartes [principles?] of body, figure, or Motion; or … by some Magnetick or Astrologicall suppositions', or other principles yet to be discovered—only experimentation on seed, water, salt, earth, and heat would tell.⁴¹ Further observation would trace 'Causes accessory though less Principal', such as 'Aire' ('both simply, & attended with the Accidents of Light, wind, Thunder, Meteors, Blasting') and 'Dews', and assess 'The Operation & influence of the Sunn', moon, and 'other Coelestiall bodyes, and how these may be each of them tryed & their power sufficiently manifested.' By clarifying 'What … is reserved only for the Administration of Divine power & wisedome' and 'What Improvements are more obviously hopefull, Analogicall & Easy', Petty's natural history would conduce 'to understanding better the utmost possibility of Art & Industry.'⁴² The ultimate point, for Petty as for Bacon, was the superinduction of desirable qualities on things; the 'Oeconomicall' part of the essay would point up the applications of this hard-won experimental knowledge.

Alchemy and iatrochemistry

A similarly important dimension of the Hartlibian program was alchemical.⁴³ Today, 'alchemy' tends to conjure images of deluded gold-seekers

³⁹ BL MS Add. 4292, f.141r-v.   ⁴⁰ BL MS Add. 4292, f.141v.
⁴¹ BL MS Add. 4292, f.141v.   ⁴² BL MS Add. 4292, f.142r.
⁴³ Webster, *Instauration*, 384–402; Newman and Principe, *Alchemy*, 207–272.

chasing the Philosopher's Stone. Although much recent scholarship aims
at correcting this view, such imagery was commonplace in the seventeenth
century and earlier. Throughout the Middle Ages, alchemy had been
assailed as contrary to nature: either an impossible sham (of which
alchemists were both perpetrators and victims) or (as in Faust) a demonic
imposture.[44] Even those who acknowledged alchemy's claim to emulate
natural processes expressed reservations about it in practice. Bacon had
acknowledged that alchemy's 'ends or pretences are noble', and that
over the centuries alchemists had occasionally stumbled upon worthwhile
knowledge, but on the whole thought it a waste of time; Plattes, in similar
terms, wrote that 'though I affirme the Art of Gold making to be true, yet
I doe not affirme it to be lucrous [i.e. profitable] in these times.'[45] Serious
improvers had better things to do.

Alchemy, however, had no simple or universally agreed meaning. It is
difficult to distinguish in any consistent way between seventeenth-century
alchemy as the art of transmuting base metals into gold (*chrysopoeia*)
or silver (*argyropoeia*) and alchemy as the allegorical pursuit of mystical
truths (as in the Rosicrucian hoax), or, more importantly, between any
of these kinds of alchemy and what we would now call chemistry.[46]
Alchemical processes (distillation, sublimation, calcination, transmutation)
were involved in a range of operations that had little or nothing to do
with 'gold making'. Baking, brewing, dyeing, farming, metalworking,
and the natural processes these trades employed all depended on micro-
level material transformations that could be understood in alchemical
terms. Indeed, the ultimate goal of Baconian science, the superinduction
of qualities on substances for the benefit of mankind, was, from this
perspective, a generalized application of alchemical transmutation; for
Plattes,

> all treasure and riches are nothing but congealed vapours: for what is
> corne, and fruits, the chiefest of all riches, but the fatnesse of the earth;
> *Iacobs* blessing elevated by the heate of the Sunne, and turned into vapour
> by the helpe of the Vniversall spirit of the world, then drawne together
> by the Adamantine vertue of the Seeds, and Plants, and so congealed
> into the same forme? and what is Silke, Velvet, fine Clothes, &c. but the

[44] Newman, *Ambitions*.

[45] Bacon, *Advancement of Learning*, Book One, in Bacon, *Francis Bacon*, 143; Plattes, *Infinite Treasvre*, sig. C4r.

[46] Lawrence M. Principe and William R. Newman, 'Some Problems with the Historiography of Alchemy', in William R. Newman and Anthony Grafton (eds), *Secrets of Nature: Astrology and Alchemy in Early Modern Europe* (Cambridge, MA: MIT Press, 2001), 385–431.

vapours of Animalls congealed in the superficies of their bodies, where
the Animall heate was able to elevate them no further? ... [Even] Gold
that great Commander, is nothing else but the said fatnesse of the earth,
elevated by the said universall spirit, and after depuration congealed into
that splendorous Body.[47]

The difference between improvement and alchemy in the sense pertinent
here was not between reason and madness but between using one set of
chemical transformations to produce corn and another to produce gold.
True, the poor could eat corn and could be employed to grow it, while
'good gold may be extracted out of iron' only by 'a tedious, laborious, and
costly way' that produced 'no gaine, unless it be in conceite'; farming
was plainly more worthwhile than gold-making.[48] But in both cases,
wealth was created by 'congealing' the earth's treasure through a carefully
proportioned compound of the 'Terrestrial' and 'Aetheriall' natures mixed
together in it—in other words, alchemically.[49]

Alchemy in this broad sense was integral to the creation of wealth in
any trade that worked upon the minute qualities of materials, and essential
therefore to the social reformation the Hartlib Circle sought.[50] Seen
in this light, Petty's 'Brewing Invention' (which transformed substances
by applying heat) and his expertise in the dyeing trade (which did so by
applying chemicals) were as much a part of his alchemical contribution to
Hartlibian reform as was his training in Helmontian medicine. At the same
time Petty—and his brother Anthony—engaged in more conventionally
alchemical experiments. In early 1649, Hartlib related Petty's description
of flower-like patterns formed by 'The smoake or sooth of a certain flame
burning within a cucurbita'; 'His Brother', meanwhile, 'hath distilled all
manner of herbs into oiles wherby you may keepe all the year long a
Perpetual Garden of so many smels as you please.'[51] Later in the year
Petty himself was 'about experiments for fixing of sents', which included

[47] Plattes, *Infinite Treasvre*, sig. C3v–C4r.

[48] Plattes, *Subterraneall Treasure*, 25. Plattes wrote *Subterraneall Treasure* as a companion
volume to *Infinite Treasure*, devoted to mining and metallurgy.

[49] Plattes, *Infinite Treasvre*, sig. A4v–A5r.

[50] For some Hartlibians, *chrysopoeia* offered an alternative to debasement and thus an early
solution to the 'shortage of coin' later remedied by credit-money. See Carl Wennerlind, 'Credit-
Money as the Philosopher's Stone: Alchemy and the Coinage Problem in Seventeenth-Century
England', *History of Political Economy* 36 (2004), 235–262.

[51] Ephemerides 1649, HP, 28/1/5a, 9b. Petty's experimental production of floral patterns from
ash recalls contemporaneous attempts to demonstrate palingenesis (the reproduction of living
plants from their own ashes); see Harrison, 150–151, and Malcolm, *Hobbes*, 121–122. As a model
for understanding the process of resurrection, palingenesis played a role in reconciling Christian
doctrine and the new science through 'physico-theology'; Newman, *Ambitions*, 232.

comparing the rate at which different spirits evaporated.[52] Hartlib thought
Petty sufficiently versed in alchemical matters to translate Johan Rudolph
Glauber's *Furni novi philosophici*, a book on 'philosophical furnaces' by one
of the most prominent alchemists then living.[53] Petty declined, not for lack
of competence: he claimed 'that if hee had leisure and other accomodations
hee could teach his Brother Anthony a far more dispatching cheape easy
certain and delicate Way of distilling, then either is used ordinarily or
by any of Glauber his devices.'[54] Others agreed with him. According to
the Paracelsian physician Johann Brun, Petty's 'new way of distilling is
from some applications and advantages which he takes from his way of
Brewing far better then that of Glauberus.'[55] Petty was taken seriously
as an alchemical innovator, and his improvements and his alchemy were
intimately connected.[56]

This connection was, it should be emphasized, entirely standard. Hartlib
had originally qualified his mostly glowing description of Petty to Boyle
by admitting that the young man was 'not altogether a very dear Worsley',
referring to Benjamin Worsley, who linked Hartlib and Boyle with an
'Invisible College' of alchemical correspondents across Europe.[57] Petty
seems to have been regarded as something of an unknown quantity,
suspected of lacking the radical Worsley's devotion to the spiritual aspects
of the universal reformation—which was, as it happened, quite true. In
Worsley's absence, however (he was in the Low Countries between 1647
and 1649), Petty was encouraged to fill his role—for instance, as we

---

[52] Ephemerides 1649, HP, 28/1/14b.

[53] Charles Webster, 'Benjamin Worsley: Engineering for Universal Reform from the Invisible
College to the Navigation Act', in Greengrass *et al.*, 219.

[54] Ephemerides 1649, HP, 28/1/13b.

[55] Ephemerides 1649, HP, 28/1/14a. Brun, like Petty, gave medical advice to Robert Boyle;
he later took up medical practice in Cork; Webster, *Instauration*, 78, 81 n.166, 302.

[56] An entry in the Ephemerides for 1648 states that 'Lord Baltimore Governor of Virginia
[Cecil Calvert, second Baron Baltimore, was actually granted the charter to Maryland, of
which his brother and second son served as governors] ... came to Petty and discoursing about
many things professed very much to have read in all manner of Chymical Books de lapide
philosophorum [i.e. of the philosophers' stone] etc.' The episode remains mysterious, but
it is interesting that the Catholic proprietor of a colony promoting toleration should have
discussed alchemy with Petty at this early stage; Ephemerides 1648, HP, 31/22/5a. On Baltimore,
see Francis J. Bremer, 'Calvert, Cecil, second Baron Baltimore (1605–1675)', *Oxford DNB*
<http://www.oxforddnb.com/view/article/37257>.

[57] Hartlib to Boyle, 16 November 1647, in Boyle, *Correspondence*, 1:63–64. See Thomas
Leng, *Benjamin Worsley (1618–1677): Trade, Interest, and the Spirit in Revolutionary England*
(Woodbridge: Boydell and Brewer, 2008); Charles Webster, 'New Light on the Invisible
College: The Social Relations of English Science in the Mid-Seventeenth Century', *Transactions
of the Royal Historical Society*, 5th series, 24 (1974), 19–42; Antonio Clericuzio, 'New Light on
Bejamin Worsley's Natural Philosophy', in Greengrass *et al.*, 236–246.

have seen, in translating Glauber's work, a task which others including Worsley ultimately took on.[58] Petty and Worsley both turned alchemical instruments and processes to the practical end of improvement; Petty through his furnaces, Worsley through a scheme to manufacture saltpetre for use as a fertilizer.[59] The two eventually came to blows years later over which of them should survey Ireland, a battle in which Petty's whole relationship to the Hartlib Circle became hopelessly entangled. However, during the later 1640s Petty apparently seemed like a quite capable, if less experienced, less radical, and more mercenary, version of Worsley. Alchemy was their common denominator.

This connection carried over into medicine, for iatrochemistry too had a place in the universal reformation. Exile from Eden had not only meant the loss of Adam's perfect knowledge of creation, but had also put a term to man's existence, ushering in pain, disease, and death ('for dust thou art, and unto dust shalt thou return').[60] The advancement of natural and artificial learning promised to redress this alchemically.[61] Again, the distinction between medical and other sorts of alchemy is somewhat artificial; all relied on the same set of processes.[62] Thus Petty's 'new way of distilling' drew on 'his way of Brewing' but—according to Brun, a physician himself—competed with Glauber's furnaces, 'by help whereof many most excellent medicaments for the cure of most grievous and otherwise incurable diseases and effects may be prepared.'[63] Of course, Petty was also trained in non-chemical aspects of medicine; he conducted anatomical exercises with the assistance of his brother Anthony (whom he called 'as able an Anatomist as any is in all England'), and his best known contribution to medicine in this period was the institutional reform he proposed in his *Advice to Mr. Samuel Hartlib*, considered below.[64]

Mixed mathematics

Mathematics may seem to have little connection to the goals of Puritan reform. In fact, the various 'mixed' mathematical sciences, such as optics,

---

[58] John French's translation finally appeared in 1651. See Johann Rudolph Glauber (trans. John French), *A Description of New Philosophical Furnaces* (London: Printed by Richard Coats for Tho: Williams, 1651).

[59] See Webster, 'Light', 26; Slack, *Reformation*, 84; Newman and Principe, *Alchemy*, 238–239.

[60] Genesis 3:19.   [61] Webster, *Instauration*, 246–323.

[62] Webster, *Instauration*, 276–278.   [63] Glauber, sig. B1v.

[64] Ephemerides 1649, HP, 28/1/13a.

astronomy or astrology, and music, were of great concern to the Hartlibians. Optics especially, through the microscope and the telescope, improved fallen man's access to the Book of Nature that Adam, with his superior powers of sense, had once read with ease—giving renewed insight into God's creation, fostering appreciation of His providence, and yielding new tools for human advancement.[65] Bacon lauded both 'microscopes, lately invented, which … reveal the hidden, invisible small parts of bodies, and their latent structures and motions' and 'Galileo's great achievement, [the] telescope, with whose help we may open up and practice a closer approach to the stars, as if by ferries or dinghies.' These were prime examples of what he called 'instances that open *doors* or *gates*', tools 'that assist direct actions of sense.'[66] Once again, science could make good the losses incurred by original sin, rectifying and extending man's degenerate sensorium.[67]

Hartlib and his associates were aware of Petty's role in Hobbes's optical work, and Petty's possession of one of Hobbes's telescopes exercised a particularly powerful fascination, it seems, on Benjamin Worsley.[68] Visiting Amsterdam on alchemical business, Worsley compared some lenses he had bought in London with others ground by Cornelius Drebbel (an engineer and experimentalist whose work Petty admired) and by a former assistant of Drebbel's, Ahasuerus Fromanteel, who happened to be in Amsterdam at the time.[69] Fromanteel's lenses impressed Worsley:

> But because I heare neyther this, that I have, which cost me 25sh in London … nor any of this Sort, are so good as some that [are] made in France, and that Mr. Petty did assure me severall times, he had such a one, which he valewed as I take it at 3lb sterl. Mr Hobbs of Paris giving it to him. Lett me intreat you … to entertayne some talke with Petty about optickes grinding of glasses, & about these microscopes, & never leave solliciting of him, till you can [get] a sight of his; & which having let me beg of you, to gett one of Fromantills glasses to compare it with Pettyes, and if you find Mr Pettyes much to exceed Fromantills in goodnesse give Mr Petty from your selfe what price he will have for it, if he will by no meanes sell it, shew it to Fromantill & lett him take out the mold of the glasses … & grind such

[65] Harrison, *Bible*, 212–213.   [66] Bacon, *New Organon*, 170–171.

[67] Robert Hooke, *Micrographia* (London: Printed by Jo. Martyn and Ja. Allestry, 1665), sig. a1r–d1r.

[68] In 1655 Hartlib reported William Brereton's news that 'That Treatise of his [i.e. Hobbes's] Optica is to come forth by itself Dr. Petty having made the diagrams vnto it.' Ephemerides 1655, HP, 29/5/33b.

[69] Anita McConnell, 'Fromanteel, Ahasuerus (*bap.* 1607, *d.* 1693)', *Oxford DNB*, <http://www.oxforddnb.com/view/article/37435>.

that if it bee possible wee may advance this Art in England, & this excellent
& pleasurable Instrument so highly magnified by Peiresckius, Gassendus,
Kircherus & others & yet excelling … all their commendation.[70]

As this breathless passage indicates, Petty was, or was thought to be, in
possession of a valuable piece of technology, which he was to be coaxed
and cajoled into sharing at almost any price.

Petty's own optical expertise attracted a fair amount of attention. (He
may have learned to grind glasses as a way of paying for his studies in the
Low Countries.)[71] Early in 1649 Hartlib wrote that Petty 'hath … perfected
his Optical Glasses and hee can make or grinde all those Conical and
other figures which des Cartes hath wished' in his 1637 *Optics*, 'in so
much that working but one houre in a day (which hee purposed to doe
notwithstanding all his other Inventions or gaines) hee can get his living by
it.'[72] This never happened, but Hartlib later reported that Petty 'Shewed
mee his new glasses of Tubes which far exceedeth the hand Perspective
of Mr Sadler', apparently the Cambridge Platonist John Sadler, another
contact of Hartlib's.[73] He went on:

Hee [i.e. Petty] can make such as are both telescopes and microscopes. And
fit them for short-sighted eyes that they shall see as well as the other best
eyes. Hee hath a very singular good Telescope of 4. feete long that presents
in his Chamber to him the Grashopper vpon the Exchange pinnacle so
exactly and so neare as is wonderful … But hee is trying also for Instruments
of the Parabolical and other conical figures and hopes to go through stich[?]
with them. which if accomplished will above present wonders to our eyes as
if the Moone or stars lay before our feete.[74]

The reference to 'short-sighted eyes' recalls Petty's ill-fated apprenticeship
at sea. From a wider perspective, however, it was part of the great
neo-Baconian project of extending the powers of the senses.

[70] Worsley to Hartlib, 22 June 1648, HP, 8/27/2a–2b. 'Peiresckius' was Nicolas-Claude Fabri
de Peiresc (1580–1637), astronomer and coordinator of one of the largest scientific correspondence
networks of the seventeenth-century; 'Gassendus' was Pierre Gassendi, a close friend and client of
Peiresc's; 'Kircherus' Athanasius Kircher, another of Peiresc's protégés. On Peiresc's patronage,
see Lisa T. Sarasohn, 'Nicolas-Claude Fabri de Peiresc and the Patronage of the New Science
in the Seventeenth Century', *Isis* 84:1 (1993), 70–90.

[71] Strauss (28) suggests that Petty may have worked as a jeweller in Amsterdam, on the
strength of Petty's later composition of a 'Dialogue of Diamonds' (BL Sloane MS 2903,
ff.44–48; *EW*, 2:624–630).

[72] Ephemerides 1649, HP, 28/1/3a–3b.

[73] Richard L. Greaves, 'Sadler, John (1615–1674)', *Oxford DNB* <http://www.oxforddnb.com/
view/article/24459>; Webster, *Instauration*, 300, 308.

[74] Ephemerides 1649, HP, 28/1/5b.

This meant sight first and foremost, but could include other senses as well. In 1648 Petty was working on what he called 'the Musical Memorie' (*memoria musica* or *mnemonica musicalis*), which would allow children to remember notes 'without the helpe of a Booke.'[75] In 1649 Hartlib noted that 'Petty is also much labouring about the Art of Hearing to perfect that as well as of seeing', while in 1650 he wrote that 'Petty hath found out the way to make malliable Glasses as likewise a readier helpe to teach one to play the Viol'; the following year, thanks in large part to Hartlib and his connections, Petty would be appointed Professor of Music at Gresham College in London.[76] We can interpret Petty's earlier experiments with 'scents' along similar lines, as an attempt to sketch the limits of the human sense of smell, or to tailor nature to it by manipulating scents themselves. Analogously, in his later 'History of Dy[e]ing or Tinctures'—written for the Royal Society's own neo-Baconian 'History of Trades' project in 1662—Petty would preface his discussion of dyeing materials and techniques with a disquisition on the nature of colour and of light itself.[77] Sense and sensed went together.

Communications

Investigation, invention, and improvement were one side of the pro-gramme, communication—the production, reproduction, and dissemina-tion of all these inventions and improvements—quite another. Hartlib's own role as epistolary clearing-house and organizer shows both the im-portance and the limitations of individual 'intelligencers' in collecting and conveying the information that constituted the Scientific Revolution.[78] As Petty's appearances in the Ephemerides illustrate, Hartlib could bring a vast array of people and projects together, but he was quite unable to coordinate them all. Petty likened the resulting mess of overlapping and conflicting efforts to the chaos of the battlefield:

> [M]e thinkes the present condition of men is like a field where a battle hath beene lately fought, where we may see many leggs, and armes, and eyes lying here and there, which for want of a union and a soule to quicken and

75 Ephemerides 1648, HP, 31/22/3b.
76 Ephemerides 1649, HP, 28/1/6a; Ephemerides 1650, HP, 28/1/44b.
77 BL MS Add. 72897, ff.1–37; printed in Thomas Sprat, *The History of the Royal-Society of London, for the Improving of Natural Knowledge* (London: Printed by T. R. for J. Martyn, 1667), 284–306.
78 Dorothy Stimson, 'Hartlib, Haak and Oldenburg: Intelligencers', *Isis* 31:2 (1940), 309–326.

enliven them, are good for nothing but to feed Ravens; and infect the aire. So we see many Wittes and Ingenuities lying scattered up and downe the world, whereof some are now labouring to doe what is already done, and puslling themselves to reinvent what is already invented, others we see quite stuck fast in difficulties, for want of a few Directions, which some other man (might he be met withall) both could and would most easily give him; againe one man wants a small summe of mony, to carry on some designe, that requires it, and there is perhaps another, who hath twice as much ready to bestow on the same designe; but these two having no Meanes ever to heare the one of the other, the good Work intended and desired, by both parties doth utterly perish and come to nothing[.]⁷⁹

In the absence of 'some Generall Rande vouz' for the exchange of up-to-date information, labour and resources were continually wasted and the advancement of learning and improvement hindered.⁸⁰

The solution was to replace the overworked intelligencer with a more permanent and better-funded institution. Hartlib and others repeatedly proposed such an 'Office of Address'—a place where, as Petty put it, 'the wants and desires of all may bee made knowne unto all, where men may know what is already done in the businesse of Learning[,] What is already at present in doing, and what is intended to be done', for the sake of facilitating 'communication of designes, and mutuall assistance.'⁸¹ Such hubs were a standard component of projects for the advancement of learning, starting with Bacon's own description of 'Salomon's House' if not with More's *Utopia*, and continuing through the influential educational tracts of Jan Amos Komensky (Comenius) and John Dury.⁸² In Paris, the Paracelsian physician Théophraste Renaudot had already set up a 'Bureau d'Addresse' that collected the scattered thoughts of 'the Virtuosi of France' on everything from the first principles of matter and motion to 'the little Hairy Girl lately seen in this City', 'How long a Man may continue without eating', and 'Whether a Man or Woman be most inclin'd to Love.'⁸³ Despite this manic heterogeneity, Petty saw some such office as

⁷⁹ Petty, *The Advice of W.P. to Mr. Samuel Hartlib For The Advancement of some particular Parts of Learning* (London: [s.n.], 1647 [1648]), 2.

⁸⁰ Petty, *Advice*, 1.   ⁸¹ Petty, *Advice*, 1–2. See Webster, *Instauration*, 67–77.

⁸² Dury proposed that university librarians systematically augment their 'stock', maintain scientific correspondence, and give annual accounts of the 'profits' they had made in this 'trade'; Dury, *The Reformed Librarie-Keeper* (London: Printed by William Du-Gard, 1650), 15–24.

⁸³ Renaudot (trans. G. Havers), *A General Collection of Discourses of the Virtuosi of France, upon Questions of all Sorts of Philosophy, and Other Natural Knowledg* (London: Printed for Thomas Dring and John Starkey, 1664); Renaudot (trans. G. Havers and J. Davies), *Another Collection of Philosophical Conferences of the French Virtuosi, upon Questions of All Sorts; For the*

a crucial step not only towards scientific and educational reform, but also, later on, towards solving social ills (regional unemployment in England, insecurity of land title in Ireland) caused by too little information and political problems aggravated by too much. The idea endured in Petty's much later concern with statistics, the raw material of political arithmetic.

Petty also promoted scientific communications through scholarship. This included sifting, evaluating, and redacting existing works of natural history and philosophy—part of the work of the would-be Office of Address—as well as the translation of important philosophical or scientific texts into English. Hartlib spoke of him as 'a perfect Frenchman, and a good linguist in other vulgar languages besides Latin and Greek', and we have seen that he was considered a suitable candidate for the task of translating Glauber's alchemical work; the scrap of Bacon he appears to have translated into English may fall into the same category.[84] Whatever the case, he certainly did translate the Silesian physician and linguist Cyprian Kinner's brief pedagogical tract *Cogitationum didacticarum Diatyposis summaria*.[85] Printed in 1648, Petty's translation aimed both at making Kinner's ideas available in English and at raising English funds for the impoverished author, who was connected not only to Hartlib (who had helped to get the original Latin *Diatyposis* printed) but also to Comenius and his teacher Johann Heinrich Alsted.[86] In this small way, Petty helped sustain the far-flung network of European Protestant reformers; his own thoughts on education were correspondingly enriched.

His more noticeable efforts were mechanical. In March 1648 Petty announced his 'invention for double-writing': 'an Instrument of small bulke and price, easily made, and very durable, whereby any Man, even at the first sight and handling, may write two resembling copies of the same thing at once, as serviceably and as fast … as by the ordinary

---

Improving of Natural Knowledg (London: Printed for Thomas Dring and John Starkey, 1665). See Hugh Trevor-Roper, 'The Paracelsian Moment', in Trevor-Roper, *Renaissance Essays* (Chicago: University of Chicago Press, 1985), 188; Stephen Clucas, 'In Search of "The True Logick": Methodological Eclecticism among the "Baconian Reformers"', in Greengrass *et al.*, 52–53.

84 Hartlib to Boyle, 16 November 1647, in Boyle, *Correspondence*, 1:63–64; HP, 63/12a–12b.

85 Kinner (trans. Petty), *A Continuation of Mr. John-Amos-Comenivs School-Endeavours* (London: Printed for R.L., 1648). The translator is unnamed, but Kinner himself praised Petty; G. H. Turnbull, *Hartlib, Dury and Comenius: Gleanings from Hartlib's Papers* (London: Hodder & Stoughton, 1947), 433–434.

86 See Kinner, sig. A2r–A3v. On Hartlib's ties to other Protestant reformers, see Michal J. Rozbicki, 'Between East-Central Europe and Britain: Reformation and Science as Vehicles of Intellectual Communications in the Mid-Seventeenth Century', *East European Quarterly* 30 (1996), 401–419.

way.'[87] Designed for 'Lawyers and Scriveners ... Merchants, Intelligencers, Registers, Secretaries and Clarks', it could be used 'for Transcribing of rare Manuscripts, and preserving of Originals from falsification'. Unattractively yet understandably concerned to profit from his invention, Petty kept its workings secret even after receiving a fourteen-year patent from Parliament (awarded 7 March 1648), awaiting 'a competent reward'.[88] A *Declaration Concerning the newly invented Art of Double Writing*, devoted mostly to defending his recourse to exactly the sort of 'privileges' reformers often criticized, spoke of '20 persons of... credit, worth and judgement (most of them strangers to me)' who could 'impartially' confirm the machine's experimental success.[89] Yet Petty never found the contributors he sought, and as his self-imposed deadlines came and went the interest he had generated gave way to exasperation.[90] By May 1654 Hartlib, whose relations with Petty were already strained for other reasons, wished forlornly

> that Dr. Petty would show himself to the world by some rare piece or other. For since the non-performance or non-divulging of the invention of his double-writing, his credit is mightily impaired in England, and other nations, which have heard of it. Those, that know the way, which Mr. Wren doth use, say, his art of double writing is not worth a rush, for it can never be readily practised.[91]

[87] Petty, *Advice*, sig. A2r.

[88] Petty, *Double Writing* (London: [s.n.], 1647 [1648]). An undated, anonymous manuscript in the Hartlib Papers describes two such machines, one for merchants using paper, the other for scriveners using parchment. Both apparently worked by following the motions of the writer's hand with a second pen; HP, 71/7/3a–4b.

[89] Petty, *A Declaration Concerning the newly invented Art of Double Writing* (London: Printed by R. L. for R. W., 1648), 6–8. A 1647 draft of the announcement included a signed testimonial from ten sworn witnesses that Petty had produced 'two copies exactly resembling one another of the first Chapter to the Hebrewes in lesse time then another sufficient and professed Writer did one, the same beeing performed in a quarter of an hower.' ('Memo & Testimonial on Double Writing', HP, 71/7/3a–4b.) Most of the witnesses seem to have been 'mechanicks' of low status; one of them was the cloth trader and linguist Francis Lodwick (or Lodowyck).

[90] On receiving the patent Petty had promised (in *Double Writing*) that the 'Instrument shall be discovered unto Contributors, by the first day of *April*. 1649. at the furthest, or so soon before, as a competent reward shall be collected'. He later claimed to have approached both Parliament and the London livery companies without success, however (*Declaration*, 2–4, 8), and continued to seek patrons. In April 1648 Charles Cavendish thanked him for a letter describing the invention, but offered no subscription (Cavendish to Petty, 17 April 1648, HP, 8/29/1a); in June Petty dedicated the machine to Robert Boyle, 'hereby to oblige your noble and ingenious spirit so much the faster to continue your love and assistance to inventions' (Petty to Boyle, 21 June 1648, in Boyle, *Correspondence*, 1:71–73). No response survives.

[91] Hartlib to Boyle, 15 May 1654, in Boyle, *Correspondence*, 1:177. Later that year Hartlib noted Boyle's report of 'a fellow of Oxford who hath found out another double-writing, that hath not so many inconveniences in it as that of Dr. Petty or Wren' (Ephemerides 1654, HP, 29/4/30b).

With this final whimper, double-writing disappeared. Yet it was only one
of several related inventions. In 1648 Petty had also proposed what Hartlib
described as 'a new way of writing'—probably, since Hartlib compared it to
the work of the linguistic theorist, language teacher, and physician Joseph
Webbe, a new instrument for teaching children to write.[92] The following
year came the so-called 'instrumentum Pettii', an easy-to-use and portable
printing machine; Petty indicated that 'hee was about to print in it of
China Arabick and the like Letters which are not to bee had at all' and
even suggested a novel social purpose for the machine: the employment
of Oxford's purged royalist academics, 'deprived [by Parliament] of their
preferments and … enforced to become mechanical'.[93] This, too, came to
nothing when Petty's brother Anthony died that October, 'for it was it
seemes their designe by a secret practise of it to have gotten their living
by it.'[94] Yet as late as 1658, and from as far away as Frankfurt, Henry
Oldenburg (later the first Secretary of the Royal Society) heard tell of
Petty's 'commodious way of printing, called jnstrumentum Pettii, very
convenient to carry about'.[95] By then, however, Petty was in Ireland, his
mind on a very different set of problems.

Experimental methodology

The kind of practical work surveyed above encouraged in Petty an increasingly outspoken philosophical commitment to the experimental method
and to empirical epistemology, and he voiced many of the then current
criticisms of traditional Aristotelian learning. Take this passage, recorded
by Hartlib in 1649:

> The common and verbal Philosophies are of that nature that whosoever
> hath most witt will get the better of his Adversarie, but real experimental
> Learning is for Truth and wh[o]soever can make out by visible experiment
> that which hee vndertakes hee will evince that hee hath the truth. For
> all knowledge must bee brought before their true Iudges which are either
> demonstration or sense and experiment, the rest is meere wit or Rhetorick.[96]

[92] Ephemerides 1648, HP, 31/22/15a. On Webbe see Vivian Salmon, 'Webbe, Joseph
(d.c.1630)', in Oxford DNB <http://www.oxforddnb.com/view/article/28932>.
[93] Ephemerides 1649, HP, 28/1/28b–29a. According to Hartlib 'Hee [i.e. the printer] needeth
not dis-compose at all. And could compose as fast as one could write faire. And print of far
faster than in the ordinarie way even many Copies at once. It needeth not so long a learning as
the common ones.' Ephemerides 1649, HP, 28/1/31a.
[94] Ephemerides 1649, HP, 28/1/31a.   [95] Oldenburg to Hartlib, 18 July 1658, HP, 39/3/16a.
[96] Ephemerides 1649, HP, 28/1/10a.

Following Bacon, and fortified by Hobbes, whose stress on the limitations of language and 'Rhetorick' he adopted, Petty here portrayed scholastic philosophy as insubstantial 'verbal' games, academic in the worst sense and wholly unconcerned with 'real' learning or with 'Truth', which was to be found only by the sort of 'visible experiment' Petty now engaged in. These were hardly original points, but they were exactly those that an up-and-coming experimental philosopher would be expected to make. As Bacon had written of the scholastics: 'They defeat and conquer their adversary by disputation; we conquer nature by work.'[97]

Rather deeper was Petty's brief engagement with Henry More. More, ten years Petty's senior, was to be the most prominent of the academic theologians known as the Cambridge Platonists. He was also among the first English philosophers to take up the Cartesian cause, and, as such, an important proponent of at least one variant of the 'New Philosophy' as against the old Aristotelianism we have just seen Petty attack. Hartlib sought More out as a potential intellectual ally; indeed, it was through Hartlib that More began to correspond with Descartes, in 1648.[98] But, wholly taken with Descartes's rational, deductive natural philosophy, More disparaged the sort of experiments Hartlib's associates conducted as the work of narrow-minded, conceited, 'low Spiritts', incapable of providing the demonstrative certainty that Cartesianism promised and that alone made true knowledge possible.[99] It is a measure of Petty's philosophical standing—he certainly knew his Descartes and had met many of the other intellectual greats of the time, but he was still just twenty-five years old—that he appears to have been deputed to respond. The resulting letter to More, addressed via Hartlib, was the fullest statement of the role of experimental method in natural philosophy that he would ever write.

Petty began by acknowledging Descartes's superiority to the kind of 'common and verbal Philosophies' decried above. 'Monsieur Des Cartes', he wrote, 'hath indeed made vse of sensible principles such as are Matter, Locall Motion [that is, change of place], Magnitude, figure, situation &c. so that when hee speakes, it is possible to vnderstand what he meanes.' In this respect 'hee is much to bee preferd before the Common school philosophers, who indeed have Nothing else but words, & those such as are not ... the Images and Representatives of things'—as, for Hobbes,

<hr />

[97] Bacon, *New Organon*, 15–16.
[98] Sarah Hutton, 'More, Henry (1614–1687)', in *Oxford DNB* <http://www.oxforddnb.com/view/article/19181>.
[99] A. Rupert Hall, *Henry More: Magic, Religion and Experiment* (Oxford: Blackwell, 1990), 180–181; Webster, *Instauration*, 146–147.

they ought to be—'but words meerly chimaerical, signifying nothing, a language fitter to be vsed in another Imaginary phantasticall World, then in this reall one wherein wee are.' Impressive, too, was the demonstrative skill More had emphasized: 'out of these principles hee doth deduce soe Ingenious & well tuned hypotheses, that indeed hee solves the phaenomena of Nature by them much more probably and intelligibly, then can be done by the common way'; 'hee is also', Petty noted, 'accompted even by his adversaryes [Hobbes and Roberval among them] a most excellent Mathematician'.[100]

However, Petty's sly reference to the 'probable' nature of Descartes's 'Ingenious hypotheses' gave the game away, for the whole point of Cartesian deduction was that, like geometrical demonstration, its conclusions were certain and inescapable. Petty took a different view: 'I cannot thinke him soe excellent a philosopher as Mr More doth nor in the best way to bee soe', for

> I cannot beleeve his principles of philosophy to be firme, that stand upon such narrow feet as those few Experiments mentioned in his Works are, for it is not sufficient for Impositions [that is, hypothetical suppositions] to bee accompted Axioms, when they only solve a few phenomena by the help of a strong witt to drive them on, but if they bee true, they must solve all equally well, & that soe easily, as that meane capacity may bee able to foretell the Effects of nature by them before they happen, and consequently produce great & Noble pieces of art, tending to the happines of Mankind[.][101]

Petty rejected the premise that rational deduction alone provided certainty about the real world. The alternative view he proposed shows, in two respects, how very deeply he had immersed himself in the world of Hartlibian reform. First, any valid explanation of a natural process should not only be based on experiment but should, further, be easy, even for people of 'meane capacity', both to understand and to employ. Science, in short, should not be confined to a clever elite; any explanation that needed a 'strong witt' to drive it on was questionable for just that reason. Second, and related, science should serve a practical social purpose—it should produce not 'Ingenious hypotheses' but 'great & Noble pieces of art'.

Going full bore on the attack, Petty questioned not only Descartes's philosophy but also More's ability to judge its value. 'I beleeve that judicious Men versed in Multitudes & varieties of Experiments (though slibber sawce

---

[100] Petty to Hartlib [early 1649], HP, 7/123/1a.
[101] Petty to Hartlib [early 1649], HP, 7/123/1a.

ones)'—here he turned More's mockery of Cornelis Drebbel's 'slibber-sauce experiments' against him—'may better see the defects or vselesnes of Des Cartes his Philosophy then such as know noe more experiments, than what hee himselfe hath pickt out, and tells them of, to verify his owne Imaginations.'[102] As for Descartes and his celebrated works,

> I accompt him the best philosopher that knowes most of, & is best acquainted with nature's Workes, & knoweth how to rule them in order to the procurement of good to Mankind, wherefore God made them. Now whether or noe or how much des Cartes his philosophy conduceth hereunto, Wee may know by sence (that sure though slow guide) by Enquiring how much the Telescopes are mended, since the writing of his dioptricks; whether any man can foretell the weather by his discourse of Meteors? of what disease hath hee found out the certaine cure by his consideration of animalls; or what besides Notionall conjectures (though ingenious enough) hath hee reduced? Or who, that hath followed his principles, hath drawne any new usefull or pleasant art or reall conclusion from them? Till Monsieur Des Cartes hath approved himselfe a philosopher in this sence, I shall prefer Cornelius drebbel before him, though he understood no Latin[, as] one that hath done more though said lesse.[103]

This taunting reply suggests Petty's bitterness at More's tone (and particularly his mockery of Drebbel).[104] But it also points to fundamental philosophical differences regarding both the sources of human knowledge and the purposes of natural philosophy. Where Descartes speciously deduced a philosophical system from a handful of pet experiments and 'notional conjectures', Petty, following Bacon, laboured away on the ground, gathering the raw material of natural history; only vast amounts of such data, collected through an exhaustive experimental process (a process More derided), could justify the kind of inferences Descartes claimed to make.

Descartes neglected nature for intellectual parlour-games; More did not even know what real philosophy was. Their faults, Petty continued, were those of all over-zealous system-builders, whether in natural philosophy, alchemy, or medicine: 'I have wearied myself in running through Aristoteles, Galens, Campanellas, Helmonts Paracelsus & De[s] Cartes their

---

[102] Petty to Hartlib [early 1649], HP, 7/123/1a.

[103] Petty to Hartlib [early 1649], HP, 7/123/1b.

[104] Drebbel died in 1633, but Petty may have known his son-in-law, the mechanic and iatro-chemist Johann Sibertus Küffeler. See H.A.M. Snelders, 'Drebbel, Cornelis (1572–1633)', *Oxford DNB* <http://www.oxforddnb.com/view/article/8044>; Webster, *Instauration*, 78, 301–302, 388–390. Hartlib reported (Ephemerides 1649, HP, 21/1/5a) that Petty 'approves highly of the Optical MS. of Drebbels, being the true and only way to write Opticks which course himself intends to observe.'

Imaginary principles', but having turned once and for all to the life of experiment,

> I thinke that I better vnderstand Nature now, then when I puzled myselfe in their Bookes, although I doe not as yet pretend to have found out Axioms. I wish therefore that the great wits of these times would employ themselves in collecting & setting down in good order & Method all lucriferous [i.e. profitable] Experiments & not bee too buisy in making inferences from them till some Volumes of that Nature are compiled ... [I] never knew any man who had once tasted the sweetnes of experimental knowledge that ever afterward lusted after the Vaporous garlick & Onions of phantasmaticall seeming philosophy.[105]

Bacon himself had written that:

> the way the thing has normally been done until now is to leap immediately from sense and particulars to the most general propositions, as to fixed poles around which disputations may revolve; then to derive everything else from them by means of intermediate propositions; which is certainly a short route, but dangerously steep, inaccessible to nature and inherently prone to disputations. By contrast, by our method, axioms are gradually elicited step by step, so that we reach the most general axioms only at the very end; and the most general axioms come out not as notional, but as well defined, and such as nature acknowledges as truly known to her, and which live in the heart of things.[106]

Petty's recourse to a similar argument placed More and Descartes in the same camp as the scholastics Bacon addressed: all jumped too quickly to axioms far removed from experience. But, much more than the boiler-plate assault on scholasticism quoted earlier, it also reflected Petty's own experimental work and philosophical convictions. The autobiographical twist Petty gave his critique, the emphasis he placed on 'Lucriferous experiments' (experiments profitable both intellectually and materially), and the sheer confidence and vehemence of his tone all show that he had made Hartlib's empirical, experimental, and practical outlook very much his own. It was part declaration of solidarity with Hartlib, part declaration of independence from the 'Imaginary principles' that had dominated his education.

More's response was initially good-humoured, and he apologized for his reference to 'slibber sauce'.[107] But the Baconian and the Cartesian were

---

105 Petty to Hartlib [early 1649], HP, 7/123/1b–2a.   106 Bacon, *New Organon*, 16.
107 More to Hartlib, 12 March 1649, HP, 18/1/3b.

plainly talking past one another. Referring to Bacon's call (which Petty repeated) for histories of nature 'vexed' by human art, More admitted that he 'never could finde in my heart yett to vexe Nature', though he espoused the hope that there was 'rome enough, for both these Geniuses [Descartes and Petty, Bacon's proxy] to pitch their booths in, and open their shops, and shew their variety of Fare.'[108] Still, he complained that Petty 'vilifyes Des Cartes principles, by this contemptible title of Imaginary ones. [H]e might have called them rationall ones. Can himself produce sensible ones?'[109] As for Petty's cautious empiricism,

> I must confesse I haue not patience to wayt for experiments to embolden me to pronounce this Axiom. That the first and most generall Principles of Nature have more of Divinity and Majesty in them then ever to suffer themselves to be Hermetically imprisoned in some narrow neckd glasse, or like a iack in a box, to astartle the eyes of the vulgar at the opening of a Lidd … If Mr Petty can bring one instance out of his many experiments that thwarts Des Cartes his grownds I shall thanke him for it … But if he has not tryde enough yett to be able to rayse an axiom contradictory to these Principles, I would know gladly, when he thinkes he shall haue experienced enough for that purpose[.][110]

More claimed to 'account experience the basis of knowledge', but he was also 'confident, that there are so many known experiments upon record already, that nothing new can be hit upon' to prove or disprove Cartesian philosophy more 'than what is found out already'. This being so, 'there was more need of an Arckitectonicall witt, then of an Empiricks industry.'[111] The facts were in, and if Petty could offer no axioms of his own, then his attacks on Descartes were counterproductive.[112] As to the purposes of philosophy, for More 'the knowledge of the altissimes causes, is the very use of them, their contemplation and that more noble pleasure of the minde arising therefrom, is the fruict and profitt of them'; the vulgar 'Mr Petty would measure the worth of all Philosophy by what it can procure for your back, bed and bord.'[113] Mounting the pulpit at last, More

---

[108] See Bacon's 'Aphorisms on Compiling a Primary History' in Bacon, *New Organon*, especially 223–224. Petty's *Advice*, which More may have seen by this point, referred to 'the history of Trades' as a history 'of Nature vexed and disturbed.' (Petty, *Advice*, 26.)

[109] More to Hartlib, 12 March 1649, HP, 18/1/2a.

[110] More to Hartlib, 12 March 1649, HP, 18/1/2a–2b.

[111] More to Hartlib, 12 March 1649, HP, 18/1/2b.

[112] More later abandoned Cartesianism; see Hall, 146–167.

[113] More to Hartlib, 12 March 1649, HP, 18/1/2b. Bacon had written that 'The true and legitimate goal of the sciences is to endow human life with new discoveries and resources.' (*New Organon*, 66.)

denounced 'the highest heaps of Lucriferous experiments as he calls them' as 'but the ground of Luciferan knowledge, which the divine Light in just indignation may well thunderstrike and confound.'[114] There was nowhere further for this argument to go.

Universal reformation

Petty's confident handling of More probably rested on his first real publication, *The Advice of W. P. to Mr. Samuel Hartlib For The Advancement of Some Particular Parts of Learning*, which had appeared the year before and seems to have been well received.[115] As the title suggested, it was an explicitly Baconian work, taking its cue from Bacon's description of Salomon's House in the utopian *New Atlantis*.[116] This fictional institution was 'dedicated to the study of the Works and Creatures of God', 'Instituted … for the finding out of the true nature of all things (whereby God might have the more glory in the workmanship of them, and man the more fruit in the use of them)'.[117] It was, indeed, 'the very eye' of the whole kingdom of Bensalem.[118] In it were gathered natural and artificial specimens of all kinds, and all manner of means to emulate and manipulate nature: pits, towers, artificial lakes, gardens, brew-houses, kitchens, dispensatories, furnaces, 'perspective-houses', 'sound-houses', 'perfume-houses', and even 'houses of deceits of the senses'.[119] It sent 'merchants of light' around the world, gathering ideas and objects of interest, and employed a complex hierarchy of intellectual labourers to test and systematize existing knowledge, plan and conduct new experiments, and put the fruits of these experiments to practical as well as theoretical use.[120] As Bacon summed it up, speaking through the 'Father of Salomon's House', 'The End of our Foundation is the knowledge of Causes, and secret motions of things; and the enlarging

---

[114] More to Hartlib, 12 March 1649, HP, 18/1/3a.

[115] Petty, *Advice*. An undated, anonymous 'Remonstrance on William Petty's design for advancement of learning' (HP, 53/36/1a–2b) argued that most of Petty's suggestions were feasible. As late as October 1660, Hartlib apparently sent a copy of Petty's tract to his American correspondent John Winthrop; HP, 32/1/12a–12b.

[116] *The New Atlantis* was unfinished at Bacon's death in 1626, and first appeared in print as an addendum to his *Sylva Sylvarum: or A Naturall Historie* (London: Printed by Iohn Haviland and Augustine Mathewes for William Lee, 1628). It is reprinted in Bacon, *Francis Bacon*, 457–489.

[117] Bacon, *New Atlantis*, in Bacon, *Francis Bacon*, 471.

[118] Bacon, *New Atlantis*, in Bacon, *Francis Bacon*, 464.

[119] Bacon, *New Atlantis*, in Bacon, *Francis Bacon*, 480–486.

[120] Bacon, *New Atlantis*, in Bacon, *Francis Bacon*, 486–487.

of the bounds of Human Empire, to the effecting of all things possible.'[121]
The Hartlibians drew heavily on this idea—Plattes even wrote his own,
derivative, *Description of the Famous Kingdome of Macaria*—in which some
of the features and ambitions of the future Royal Society are discernible.[122]
What Petty did was to transform Bacon's utopian dialogue into a detailed
program of practical institutional reform.

Petty's interest in an Office of Address has been mentioned; the opening
pages of the *Advice* described how its staff would sift and collect 'all … Reall
or Experimental Learning' by 'perusing al[1] Books and taking notice of all
Mechanicall Inventions', compiling 'Out of all these Bookes one Booke or
great Worke … of many Volumes' that would establish (subject to annual
updates) what was known and what remained to be found out.[123] But the
bulk of the work set out three new institutions designed to revolutionize
education, the trades, and the sciences, especially medicine. First were
'*Ergastula Literaria*'—state-supported 'Literary work-houses' that would
provide 'all Children of above seven yeares old', regardless of resources, with
a new kind of practical education.[124] Building on established criticisms
of 'verbal' learning, Petty reasoned that 'since few children have need of
reading before they know … the Things they read of, or of writing, before
their thoughts are worth the recording', they should first of all 'be taught to
observe and remember all sensible Objects and Actions', both 'Naturall and
Artificiall'.[125] Only later would they study language, learning to write both
in the 'Common Way' and 'Swiftly and in Reall Character', as well as to use
double-writing; they would also study 'Artificiall Memory', drawing, 'the
Elements of Arithmetick and Geometry' (both intrinsically useful and 'sure
guides and helps to Reason'), and foreign languages.[126] The greatest stress
fell on vocational training, Petty insisting 'That all Children, though of
the highest ranke, be taught some gentile Manufacture'—poorer children
for obvious reasons, richer ones to become 'industrious in general' and to
avoid being 'cousened by Artificers' in later life. Mechanical, mathematical,

---

[121] Bacon, *New Atlantis*, in Bacon, *Francis Bacon*, 480.

[122] Gabriel Plattes, *A Description of the Famous Kingdome of Macaria* (London: Printed for
Francis Constable, 1641). This tract was long attributed to Hartlib himself; see Charles Webster,
'The Authorship and Significance of *Macaria*', *Past and Present* 56 (1972), 34–48.

[123] Petty, *Advice*, 2–3.　　[124] Petty, *Advice*, 3–4.

[125] Petty, *Advice*, 4. Echoing Kinner but perhaps also recalling his Jesuit schooldays, Petty
suggested 'That they use such Exercises whether in work, or for recreation, as tend to the health,
agility and strength of their bodies.'

[126] Petty, *Advice*, 5. Petty's curriculum incorporated his own 'new way of writing' and of
double-writing, Lodwick's universal character and Comenius's and Kinner's methods of language
teaching.

or chemical trades were especially recommended: making mathematical, navigational, chronological, or musical instruments; painting, engraving, or sculpting; cutting jewels and grinding lenses; both naval and land-based architecture; dyeing, 'Chymistry', and metallurgy; anatomy and gardening. This was to be a school for improvers.

The second institution Petty proposed was a 'Gymnasium Mechanicum or Colledge of Trades-men', a place where 'the Prime most Ingenious Work-man' in each trade could devote himself to improving his art. Selected tradesmen would live in the College rent-free, producing 'rare and exquisite pieces of Workmanship' and enjoying the benefits conferred by 'the Credit of being admitted into this Society,' including 'the quick sale which certainly they would have of their Commodities'. While the marketing dimension of the college would attract 'the very ablest Mechanicks' to seek admission, their concentration in the college would encourage 'new Inventions' and present 'the most effectual opportunities and meanes, for writing a History of Trades in perfection and exactnesse'—furthering the improvement of economy and society and furnishing 'Active and Philosophicall heads' with new means for the 'Interpretation of Nature' through experiment and observation.[127] The least fleshed-out part of Petty's *Advice*, the College was in some ways the most concrete. We have seen Petty surveying the inventive skills of mechanics in various trades and reporting his findings, however casually, to Hartlib, and we have watched him struggle with the tension between public benefit and private gain that invention involved. The state patronage of invention he here envisioned would solve this problem by fusing the interest of the tradesmen in making sales with the public interest in technological improvement. The Ergastula Literaria would create children capable of contributing to improvement; the Gymnasium Mechanicum would give adults a reason to do so.

The third of Petty's proposals, on the other hand, was both the most detailed and the closest to Bacon's *New Atlantis*. 'Within the walls' of the Gymnasium would be

> a Nos[o]comium Academicum [i.e. a teaching hospital] … a complete *Theatrum Botanicum*, stalls and Cages for all strange Beastes and Birds, with Ponds and Conservatories for all exotick Fishes … a Repositorie of all kind of Rarities Naturall and Artificiall pieces of Antiquity, Modells of all great and noble Engines, with Designes and Platforms of Gardens and Buildings. The most Artificiall Fountaines and Water-workes, a Library of Select Bookes, an Astronomicall Observatory for celestiall Bodies and

---

[127] Petty, *Advice*, 7.

Meteor[s], large pieces of Ground for severall Experiments of Agriculture, Galleries of the rarest Paintings and S[t]atues, with the fairest Globes, and Geographicall Maps of the best descriptions[.][128]

There would also, ideally, be a 'Chymicall Laboratorie, Anatomicall Theater, Apotheca, with all the Instruments and Furniture belonging to them'; in short, 'we would have this place to be the Epitome or Abstract of the whole world.'[129] Here was a second Salomon's House, hardly less utopian than the original.[130] Yet having laid out this universal epitome Petty quickly re-established a more pragmatic tone. Recognizing that 'such a work could not be brought to passe without much charge', and declining 'to frame Utopias', Petty proceeded to describe 'only such a Nosocomium, as may be made out of one of our old Hospitals, without any new donations or creeping to Benefactors, onely with a little paines taken by the Reforming hand of Authority.'[131] Drawing less on reading than on experience (in this case his experience of clinical medicine at Leiden), Petty once again focused on practical reforms within the reach, if not of individual improvers, then of the state.

The Nosocomium was described through its personnel. Besides a non-medical governing body of 'three or foure Curators', there were to be ten 'Ministers'—a Steward; a Physician, Vice-Physician, and Student; senior, junior, and apprentice surgeons; and senior, junior, and apprentice apothecaries—as well a number of nurses ('honest carefull ancient Widowes') fluctuating in proportion to the number of the sick.[132] This threefold division of the medical faculty reflected the traditional medical hierarchy, in which physicians were learned 'doctors', while surgeons and apothecaries were members of guilds like other tradesmen. Yet the Nosocomium was probably most remarkable for the proximity it established between all three, the cooperation it encouraged between them, and the neatly nested medical, pedagogical, and scientific functions they all, collaboratively, performed—perhaps a legacy of Petty's time in the United Provinces.[133] The Physician was to visit every patient twice a day,

---

[128] Petty, *Advice*, 8.   [129] Petty, *Advice*, 8–9.

[130] Petty further wished (*Advice*, 8) 'that a Society of Men might be instituted as careful to advance Arts as the Iesuites are to Propagate their Religion'.

[131] Petty, *Advice*, 9–10; see Webster, *Instauration*, 293–297.   [132] Petty, *Advice*, 10.

[133] Petty, *Advice*, 11. The Physician would receive £120 annually, the Steward £80, the Vice-Physician £50, the head 'Chirurgeon' and head Apothecary £60 each, the Student £25, the surgeon's and apothecary's 'mates' £20 each, their Apprentices £10 each, and the Nurses £4. On Dutch practice, see Harold J. Cook, *Matters of Exchange: Commerce, Medicine and Science in the Dutch Golden Age* (New Haven: Yale University Press, 2007), 150.

dictating each case history (in Latin) to the Vice-Physician; 'a Philosopher, skill'd at large in the Phaenomena of Nature', the Physician was further to ensure that the surgeons and apothecaries kept similar histories, to 'oversee ... the Preparation of all Chymical Medicaments', to direct all chemical, botanical, and surgical 'Enquiries and Experiments' and to keep up 'with all the Histories taken in the Hospitall, Laboratory, Anatomical Chamber, garden, &c.'[134] The Vice-Physician, besides assisting his chief by attending to patients, was to keep 'the History of Patients', augmented 'now and then' by reading but substantially filled out by 'the making of Luciferous experiments'.[135] The Student would follow a course of reading, observation, and experiment prescribed by the Physician, while helping the surgeons and apothecaries compile histories of their own.[136] Parallel relationships tied the master, junior, and apprentice surgeons and apothecaries, while the nurses watched the patients night and day, reporting 'all remarkable Accidents'—and changed the sheets.[137]

Above them all was the Steward. Naturally, he should be 'skill'd in Mathematicks; chifely in Arithmetick and keeping Accounts, measuring of Land, timber, board, Architecture, frugall contrivances and the like.'[138] But his real job was to foster 'the Advancement of Physick' by tracking the incidence of diseases, using the best tools then available:

> We desire he may be skill'd in the best Rules of Judiciall Astrology, which he may apply to calculate the Events of diseases, and Prognosticate the Weather; to the end that by his Judicious and carefull Experiments, the Wheat may be separated from the Chaffe in that Faculty likewise; and what is good therein may be applied to good uses, and the rest exploded. He shall keep a Journall of all notable Changes of Weather, and fertility of Seasons ... he shall take notice of the severall diseases ... which in each yeare have infected each Species of Annimals ... All which Particulars with the Epidemicall diseases befalling man, he may compare with the Aspects of the Celestiall bodies, and so examine the precepts delivered unto us by the Professors of that Art.[139]

Like alchemy, astrology now has an occult ring, and its presence in the middle of Petty's tract on scientific reform may seem incongruous. Yet no more than alchemy and chemistry had astrology and astronomy separated in the 1640s, and no more than alchemy was astrology, in some of its manifestations, incompatible with the new science Petty championed. Sir Christopher Heydon, the major English defender of astrology in the

---

134 Petty, *Advice*, 12–13.   135 Petty, *Advice*, 13.   136 Petty, *Advice*, 13–14.
137 Petty, *Advice*, 14–17.   138 Petty, *Advice*, 11.   139 Petty, *Advice*, 11–12.

early seventeenth century, used 'astronomy' and 'astrology' interchangeably
to describe the study of celestial motions and their effects, and he carefully
distinguished this study from witchcraft and prophecy, insisting that it
dealt exclusively with 'evident' or 'second causes in nature'—not the
secrets of Providence but the physical interactions of visible creation.[140]
In Petty's hands judicial astrology (opposed by Heydon to 'Speculative' or
'Theoricall' astrology, which focused on the motions of the stars rather
than their terrestrial effects) was a matter of empirical data-gathering and
the search for correlations—an attempt to cobble together, and make
practical use of, astronomical, meteorological, and medical statistics.[141] It
was effectively a predictive branch of mixed mathematics, and one with
potentially massive social as well as scientific significance; the Steward
was less an 'astrologer', in our pejorative sense of the word, than a
proto-statistician. What the apothecaries, surgeons, and physicians did for
individual bodies, he tried to do for the population at large.

   Only after outlining 'such Societies and Institutions, as we have thought
most fit for the advancement of Reall Learning' did Petty turn his
attention to books. Or rather, to one extraordinary book—the *Vellus
Aureum sive Facultatem Lucriferarum Descriptio Magna*, 'wherein all the
practiced ways of getting a Subsistence and whereby Men raise their
fortunes, may at large be declared.'[142] It would describe, with text and
illustrations, 'the whole Processe of Manual Operations and Applications
of one Naturall thing ... to another, with the necessarie Instruments and
Machines, whereby every peice [sic] of work is elaborated', 'the Mechanicall
reason of every Instrument Materiall and operation', the 'divers Wayes
and Methods' employed in each manufacture, and the 'Oeconomy' of each
profession:

> What seasons of the yeare are most proper to each Worke, which the
> best places and times to buy Materials, and to put off the Commodities
> when finished, how most thiftily to hire, entertaine, and oversee ser-
> vants and Workmen, how to dispose of every excrement and Refuse of
> Materials ... with all Cauteles, Impostures and other sleights good or bad,
> whereby men use to over-reach one another.[143]

---

[140] Christopher Heydon, *A Defence of Iudiciall Astrologie* (Cambridge: Printed by Iohn Legat,
1603), sig. ¶3r, 2, 5–6, 14–15, 17.
   [141] Heydon (2–3) distinguished between two branches of judicial astrology: general, which
concerned nations, and particular, which concerned individuals. See William R. Newman
and Anthony Grafton, 'Introduction: The Problematic Status of Astrology and Alchemy in
Premodern Europe', in Newman and Grafton, 13–14.
   [142] Petty, *Advice*, 17–18.   [143] Petty, *Advice*, 18–19.

Bacon had proposed a science capable of 'effecting ... all things possible';
the *Vellus Aureum* would be its textbook, a sort of *Encyclopédie* a century
early. But it would be more than that, too, and here we can see the distinct
and portentous twist Petty gave to the neo-Baconian advancement of
learning. If 'Reall Learning' was to have a lasting effect on the real world,
it could not begin and end, as the History of Trades often did, with a
catalogue of materials, techniques, and equipment. What the dyer's son
clearly saw—and what the young experimentalist was in a position to
say—was that practical science had also to embrace 'Oeconomy' (which
classically connoted 'household management'): not only the management
of production processes, but also the running of a business, the mastery of
the various markets involved, and, beyond all that, a knowledge of human
behaviour.

As this suggests, Petty had already begun to articulate more obviously
social, economic, and even political ideas. These ideas at first grew out of
the Hartlib Circle's notion of improvement, and carefully accommodated
the various mechanical creations the group produced; but they would
increasingly become objects of inquiry and endeavour in their own right. In
early 1649 Hartlib noted Petty's interest in identifying 'new Emploiments
etc or enterprises in which the Poore should bee invited or ordered to
worke', and 'which might also serve for the idle souldjery kept up in the
kingdom.'[144] Besides the scientific benefits of the schemes outlined in his
Advice (which included increasing 'the number of mixt Mathematicall Arts'
and the gradual discovery of those axioms More so impatiently demanded),
Petty promised to improve the fortunes of the commonwealth by reforming
the English population itself: educating children for improvement, training
apprentices more efficiently, and setting adults to work.[145] He outlined
not another Utopia but an achievable England, modelled partly on his
observations of the booming United Provinces and centred on the capacity
of policy to transform land and people alike:

We see that all Countries where Manufactures and Trades flourish, as
Holland, &c, become potent and rich. For how can it otherwise be? when
the Revenues of the State shall be encreased by new and more Customes,
all Beggars feeding upon the Labours of other men, and even Theeves and
Robbers (made for want of better employment) shall be set on work, barren
grounds made fruitfull, wet dry, and dry wet, when even hogs and more
indocile beasts shall be taught to labour, when all vile Materials shall be

turned to Noble uses, when one man or horse shall do as much as three, and every thing improved to strange Advantages.[146]

In early 1649—with the King's head on the block and anything possible—Petty even ventured to suggest 'an Expedient wherby the People or every individual Person may come to give their vote to any question put to them by Parliament within 3. Weekes', though this aimed at gauging public sentiment and defusing dissent on 'fundamental' matters rather than fostering democracy or collective action; Petty argued that 'The individual voting ... will leave no roome for any factions etc.'[147] Whatever its political valence, however, this kind of proposal shows Petty extending his interests from experimental philosophy and improvement to the mechanics of the society he wanted to improve.

At the same time, however, Petty also faced the immediate problem of finding a place for himself. Not always subtly, he tended to insert himself into his proposals. It is difficult not to see him, for instance, in the 'compiler' of the *Vellus Aureum*, who 'should be as young as sufficient Abilities will admit' and 'must be content to devote his whole life to this employment, one who ... hath the fire of Industry and the Alembick of a Curious and rationall head, to extract the Quintessence of whatsoever he seeth.'[148] Whether he had any real hope of success is another matter, although it may not have seemed completely unfeasible—an anonymous 'Remonstrance' on Petty's *Advice* argued that 'Neither the summes, time nor labour necessary thereunto doe exceed mediocrity, there beeing only wanting vnto them a propitious and wise Authority'—an authority that was still taking shape.[149] Hartlib, for his part, hoped that 'Mr Petty may also be set apart or encouraged for the advancement of experimental and mechanical knowledge at Gresham College in London' (Petty secured a post there two years later). Versatile as he was, however, Petty failed to make a living from his inventions. The death of his brother Anthony, in

---

[146] Petty, *Advice*, 22–23. In linking crime to unemployment Petty was probably following Sir Thomas More; see More (ed. George M. Logan and Robert M. Adams), *Utopia* (Cambridge: Cambridge University Press, 1989), 15–21. According to Hartlib, Petty thought 'Mores Vtopia a most excellent Booke, [and More] one of the best English-wits counted by Petty in all State affaires, as Verulam the other Chancellor was one of the chiefest men for other Reall Learning.' Ephemerides 1649, HP, 28/1/19b.

[147] He added, rather limply, that 'Let the forme of government be what it will it matters not so much as if only the Persons or Governours be holy and good. That is all in all.' Ephemerides 1649, HP, 28/1/10a–10b.

[148] Petty, *Advice*, 21. The same alchemical analogy occurs earlier (*Advice*, 18). Petty may, alternatively, have seen himself as a potential 'Vice-Physician' for the Nosocomium.

[149] HP, 53/36/1a.

October 1649, may have encouraged him to make a move. Taking on his cousin John Petty as an assistant for 'chemistry and anatomy' work, Petty went back to Oxford and to medicine.[150]

An academic interlude

He returned at an opportune time. Following the Royalist surrender of Oxford in 1646, the Puritan Parliament gradually ejected, first, those Anglican and royalist academics who refused to sign the anti-episcopal 'Solemn League and Covenant'—a nominally religious requirement that amounted to a political purge—and, later, those who refused the parliamentary 'Engagement'. Space was available for the politically reliable, and Petty used his connections to advantage.[151] He received his MD in March of 1650, and with help from the London parliamentarians Edmund Wylde and Captain John Graunt secured a lectureship in anatomy; later that year, supported by Hartlib and John Dury through Hartlib's patron, and chairman of the parliamentary Committee for the Universities, Francis Rous, he became a Fellow of Brasenose College.[152] His ascent was smooth and swift. Initially assisting the Professor of Anatomy, Sir Thomas Clayton—probably with the dissections that were said to disgust Clayton himself—in 1651 Petty took over the Professorship in his own right, rising at the same time from Fellow to Vice-Principal of Brasenose.[153] (He also, with Graunt's help, secured the Gresham Professorship of Music—a post that, by a strange coincidence, Clayton had also held.)[154] Petty had embarked on what looked to be a promising life in academia.[155]

Petty's advancement was not wholly a matter of politics. He had his influential friends, after all, in large part because of the considerable experimental work he had already done and the real contribution he was expected to make to the future reformation of knowledge and society.

[150] Strauss, 31–32.   [151] Webster, *Instauration*, 155.
[152] Sharp, 83–89; C. G. Lewin, 'Graunt, John (1620–1674)', *Oxford DNB*, <http:/www.oxforddnb.com/view/article/11306>; Webster, *Instauration*, 81–82, 153; Strauss, 31. Aubrey (242) suggested that Petty took up his fellowship in 1648, but Petty's will indicates that it followed his MD; BL MS Sloane 2903, f.16v; Petty, *Tracts*, iv. Petty's appearances in the Ephemerides for 1648, 1649 and even early 1650 suggest that he was still based in London. On Rous, see Colin Burrow, 'Rous, Francis (1580/81–1659)', *Oxford DNB* <http://www.oxforddnb.com/view/article/24171>.
[153] BL MS Sloane 2903, f.16v; Petty, *Tracts*, iv; see also Aubrey, 242; Barnard, 'Petty, Sir William', *Oxford DNB*.
[154] Lewin, 'Graunt, John', *Oxford DNB*; Webster, *Instauration*, 81–82.
[155] Barnard, 'Petty, Sir William', *Oxford DNB*.

Nor did moving to Oxford mean leaving the experimental life behind for a sinecure. Despite the poor reputation of academic philosophy among many reformers (awareness of this polemic surely tinged More's response to Petty's criticism of his 'Imaginary' principles), by the 1640s some elements of the new philosophy had begun to penetrate university teaching, and others were pursued by both faculty members and students in their spare time. Indeed, the Parliamentary purges themselves displaced some prominent academic natural philosophers, most notably the ageing physiologist William Harvey, discoverer of the circulation of the blood and a committed royalist. They also, necessarily, brought in a new generation, with scientific interests of its own. Whether or not this process reflected, as once thought, a conscious Parliamentary attempt to introduce a stronger scientific agenda, one result of the turnover was the creation of an Oxford 'Experimental Philosophy Club'.[156]

In many respects the Oxford club anticipated the later Royal Society. More than thirty future Fellows of the Royal Society were involved, representing a mixture of interests and backgrounds and including some of the great names of later seventeenth-century English intellectual life: Robert Boyle, Robert Hooke, and the young John Locke only came to Oxford after Petty had left, but the physicians Ralph Bathurst, Jonathan Goddard, and Thomas Willis, the mathematician John Wallis (soon to engage in a bitter debate with Hobbes over quadrature), the astronomer Seth Ward, and the polymathic Christopher Wren were all there. The club's figurehead was the natural philosopher and theologian John Wilkins, creator of a celebrated 'universal character', Warden of Wadham College, and later Bishop of Chester. Some became lasting friends of Petty's. Robert Wood, who had written a brief tract on the advantages of decimalization for Hartlib, would, like Petty, wind up in Ireland, playing a key role in circulating Petty manuscripts there during the early 1670s; the jovial Peter Pett, who rose to prominence as a naval administrator during the Restoration, also became a close friend, and would similarly help circulate Petty's papers in England later on. Between 1648 and his departure some time in 1651, Petty, 'beloved by all the ingenious scholars', hosted many of the club's meetings himself.[157]

His lodgings, located above an apothecary's shop, were convenient for the purpose. The club's activities included experiments in chemical medicine and comparative anatomy, probably including the gruesome but

---

[156] Webster, *Instauration*, 153–172.
[157] Aubrey, 242. For the club's membership, see Webster, *Instauration*, 166–167.

common practice of vivisection; at any rate, Petty somehow discovered, according to Hartlib, that 'The pulse of dogs is in the groines as in the most tendrest place.'[158] The group took up less bloody pursuits as well—lifting things 'by blowing of bladders', for instance, and experimenting with 'snow Candles', which, however, 'are more for curiosity then any real use.'[159] Petty announced in 1651 that 'The Club-men have cantonized or are cantonizing their whole Academia to taske mee to several Imploiments and amongst other's to make Medulla's [*medulla*, marrow] of all Authors in reference to Experimentall Learning.' The idea recalled Petty's suggestion in the 1648 *Advice* that all existing natural knowledge be sifted and summarized through the Office of Address, and Petty himself was now 'to write the History of Concoctions', reflecting once again his iatrochemical expertise.[160] Another, presumably related, project was the creation of 'an accurate Catalogue vpon Oxford library.'[161] Heterogeneity was the rule. Grand projects of transcendent significance rubbed elbows with transient curiosities. But that was simply the nature of mid-seventeenth-century science, 'cultivated by these virtuosi', as Aubrey put it, 'in that dark time.'[162]

Petty's official business, however, was now medicine. As assistant and then successor to Clayton he performed dissections and was responsible for giving regular anatomical lectures. It is hard to say how many lectures he actually gave, as he seems to have left Oxford during the first half of 1651, not very long after his appointment, but those that survive suggest that he applied the fruits of his Continental training to the full, transferring to the English scene the mechanistic physiology and chemical medicine he had picked up in Utrecht, Leiden, Amsterdam, and Paris.[163] Yet an undated 'Scheme for a Medical Essay' reveals a certain catholicity in Petty's approach which his later practice, in and beyond medicine, confirms. It included both 'Hippocrates & Galen (especially the former)' and 'Some new Theory of physiology and pathology'; both chemical 'pharmacy' and 'luciferous experiments' in 'Botanicks.'[164] Petty's real commitments, in medicine as in natural philosophy, were more methodological than doctrinal:

---

158 Ephemerides 1651, HP, 28/2/7a.

159 Petty to Hartlib, 16 December 1650, HP, 8/23/1a; Ephemerides 1651, HP, 28/2/5b.

160 Ephemerides 1651, HP, 28/2/5b.   161 Ephemerides 1651, HP, 28/2/6b.

162 Aubrey, 242–243.

163 Petty listed 'Six Physico Medicall Lectures' as having been written in 1649 and 'read at Oxford'; *PP*, 2:261; see Frank, 101–102.

164 *PP*, 2:167–168.

That as few as possible of insensible things, and such as cannot be examined by experiments, bee supposed.

That if there bee, their nature in all qualities may be described in a sensible manner.

That nothing bee supposed impossible or absurd.

That the supposition bee simple & short, & easily intelligible.

That it solve all the phaenomena.

That from it nothing may follow but what appears.

That as many such severall suppositions as possible may bee found out & the most suitable retayned.

That none of all the suppositions made upon divers matters may disagree and bee inconsistent one with another.

That having made suppositions of matters of many different natures, some principles bee afterwards drawne from them all, which were common to all the said suppositions and dispersed in them.

That we find out sensible effects which are produced of sensible and cleere causes, very like unto other sensible effects begott from insensible causes.[165]

Principles came from specific 'suppositions', not the other way around; it was success in particulars that mattered, not the vindication of generalities (whether Hippocratic, Galenic, Paracelsian, or Helmontian)—a point of view perhaps especially congenial to a practicing physician. In so far as Petty had a clear bias it was towards visible, testable, and 'easily intelligible' causal relationships. Chemical and mechanistic rather than humoral pathology and physiology may have lent themselves more readily to such observation in principle (though not always in practice), but observation, not theoretical principle, came first.

Petty's experimental endeavours thus continued. He was propelled to fame, however, neither by his natural philosophy nor by his medical teaching but instead by a bizarre accident—as he described it to Hartlib, 'a very miracle'—that took place in Oxford late in 1650, as he went to collect a cadaver for dissection.[166]

Upon the 14ᵗʰ day of December 1650, there was brought to the place of execution, one Anne, daughter of Wm. Greene of Steeple Barton in Oxfordshire, for having as was alledged murthered her owne new-borne infant, and there hung by the neck above ¼ of an hower. And while shee was

---

165 PP, 2:168.
166 Petty to Hartlib, 16 December 1650, HP, 8/23/1b. See Petty's 'History of the Magdalen: or The Raising of Anne Greene', printed in PP, 2:157–167.

hanging, divers friends of hers and standers by, some hung with their whole weight upon her, others gave her great stroakes on the breasts; and moreover a suoldier [sic] did the same severall tymes with his musquett. When shee was cutt downe and putt into the coffin (which was sent for her by those to whom her body was consigned to bee dissected [i.e. Petty himself]) and brought to the place where the said dissection was to bee made, and the coffin opened, she rattled in the throate; Whereupon a lusty fellow standing by stampt upon her breast and stomach severall tymes with his foot.[167]

When Petty returned to her with Willis in tow, however, she continued 'to rattle a little as before'. Having survived not only the hangman's rope but also the best efforts of a series of well-meaning friends and 'lusty fellows', the unfortunate Anne now faced the test of early modern medicine. The two doctors first 'wrenched open her teeth which were fast sett, and put in some strong waters'—which made her 'obscurely to cough or spitt'—and 'then wrenched open her hands, the fingers being also stiffly bent downe,' and spent fifteen minutes 'rubbing her extreme parts.' Before very long 'wee thought of letting her blood', and, 'The vayne beeing cut, shee bled so freely that having bled about 5 ounces, when we desired to stop, wee could not easily.' Once they had stanched the bleeding, the four of them (for now Bathurst and Henry Clerke, of Magdalen College, were also involved) gave her a concoction of rainwater, cinnamon, and sorrel, 'anointed her neck ... with spiritt of turpentine', applied plasters to her chest, and, for good measure, injected a 'healing and odoriferous clyster' (enema), finally putting her to bed with another woman, who was instructed to 'keep rubbing her lower parts gently', keeping her warm.[168]

The next week witnessed a cascade of clysters and cataplasms, juleps and suppositories, and even some ground mummy (a favourite iatrochemical ingredient also used in sympathetic or magnetic healing).[169] Whatever the effects of these attentions, the patient steadily improved. By the afternoon of the 14 December 'she breathed handsomely' and still later 'obscurely opened her eyes' and drank a little; the following morning 'shee began to

---

[167] *PP*, 2:157–158.   [168] *PP*, 2:158–159.

[169] Andreas Tentzel (trans. Ferdinando Parkhurst), *Medicina Diastatica or Sympatheticall Mumie* (London: Printed by T. Newcomb for T. Heath, 1653); Fludd, *Mosaicall Philosophy: Grounded upon the Essentiall Truth, or Eternal Sapience* (London: Printed for Humphrey Moseley, 1659); Helmont (trans. J. C.), *Van Helmont's Works: Containing his most Excellent Philosophy, Chirurgery, Physick, Anatomy* (London: Printed for Lodowick Lloyd, 1664). For specific applications see Nicholas Culpeper, *Culpeper's Directory for Midwives: Or, A Guide for Women. The Second Part* (London: Printed by Peter Cole, 1662), 51; *Chymical, Medicinal, and Chyrurgical Addresses made to Samuel Hartlib, Esquire* (London: Printed by G. Dawson for Giles Calvert, 1655), 91.

speake many words intelligibly'; on the 15th she ate some bread and by the
19th managed 'the leg and wing of a chick', though still unsteady on her feet.
Petty's surviving observations attest to his thoroughness: how and how
long she slept, how much and with what difficulty she ate, drank, urinated,
and excreted, where she was bruised, numb, swollen, or sore, how easily
she spoke and what she said—all was carefully noted. Partly for selfish
reasons (this was, after all, a unique medical event), the young professor was
especially interested in Anne's memory, noticing that she 'talked, as shee
certainly did in prison before her execution, of being patient and contented
with her sufferings &c.'; as Petty remarked to Hartlib, 'shee cannot remember how shee came out of Prison, how shee was hanged what shee said on
the Gallows (although she spake liberally)'.[170] It was 'as if there had been
merely a cessation of her life and that shee had gone on where shee left of
before.'[171] (A later pamphlet, using a metaphor worthy of Petty, compared
her 'to a Clock whose weights had been taken off a while, and afterwards
hung on again.')[172] Well aware of Anne's scientific interest, Petty noted
that 'My endeavours in this businesse have bettered my reputation.'[173]

   This was an understatement. The resurrected Anne Greene became a
cause célèbre far beyond the circles of the virtuosi. 'Thousands of people',
Petty wrote two days after the hanging, 'come from all parts to admire the
great and powerfull hand of God.'[174] At least three pamphlets appeared in
short order. Two (William Burdet's *A Wonder of Wonders*, which appeared
in January 1651 and was 'witnessed by Dr. Petty', and the mostly identical
Declaration from Oxford, of Anne Greene) featured a vivid woodcut of Anne
by turns on the scaffold (a soldier hitting her with the butt of his musket
and another man pulling her down by the feet), in bed with the woman
Petty had instructed to warm her (proclaiming 'Behold Gods Providence'),
and beneath the scaffold, kneeling in prayer.[175] The burden of both was
the miraculous action of the divine hand in the business; both supplied
Anne with a lengthy and suitably pious scaffold speech. The third, Richard
Watkins's sensationally titled but altogether more highbrow *Newes from
the Dead*, focused more on the work of the doctors and the legal merits of
Anne's case, and dedicated over twenty pages to more than forty mostly

---

[170] *PP*, 2:161; Petty to Hartlib, 16 December 1650, HP, 8/23/1b.   [171] *PP*, 2:162.

[172] Richard Watkins, *Newes from the Dead* (Oxford: Printed by Leonard Lichfield for Thomas
Robinson, 1651), 5.

[173] Petty to Hartlib, 16 December 1650, HP, 8/23/1b.

[174] Petty to Hartlib, 16 December 1650, HP, 8/23/1b.

[175] W. Burdet, *A Wonder of Wonders* ([London: J. Clowes], 1651); *A Declaration from Oxford,
of Anne Green* (London: Printed by J. Clowes, 1651).

awful poems from assorted Oxonians, including Christopher Wren.[176] In
all three pamphlets Anne—who had claimed all along not to have known
she was pregnant, and whom Petty and others supported in arguing
that the child had been stillborn—appeared both as suffering innocent
(vindicated by the providential death of her employer and persecutor,
Sir Thomas Read, within days of her pardon) and as cautionary tale (she
had not killed her child, but she had allowed herself to be seduced).[177]
Dr Petty, meanwhile, became at once God's agent, the girl's saviour, and
medicine's champion.

A rising star

It was probably no coincidence that he left Oxford soon afterwards. He
left few comments on the universities in general or Oxford in particular,
but his attitude to book-learning and verbal philosophy, as opposed to
real experiments and the discovery of visible causes, suggests a certain
uneasiness with the business of academia, which his background in
trade may have exacerbated. Perhaps, too, he found it insufficiently
lucriferous for a man of his practical gifts; he could certainly make
more money as a physician in London—and his medical reputation
could hardly be any higher than it was immediately following the Anne
Greene episode—while pursuing his scientific interests back among the
Hartlibians and as Professor of Music at Gresham College. Whatever
combination of things pushed or pulled him, Petty went, joining the Royal
College of Physicians and going into private practice, apparently with
great success. Looking back on his life, he would tell Southwell that, had
he never meddled with Irish land, 'I could Anno 1656 have returned into
England and been at the top of practice in Oliver's Court, when Dr Willis
was casting waters at Abingdon Markett and the Cock Lowre [Dr Richard

---

[176] Watkins, *Newes*. (I refer to the second impression.) Petty and the other physicians thought
a stillbirth probable, and found it 'not improbable' that Anne had been unaware of her pregnancy
before excessively 'violent' work induced the miscarriage. The sudden death of Sir Thomas
Read (who had led the prosecution and whose grandson, Jeffrey Read, was the father) they
admitted as 'possible' evidence of her innocence. See 'Anne Greene's Petition', in *PP*, 2:164–167;
Watkins, *Newes*, 6–7. Many of the poems, predictably, belaboured classical allusions (Orpheus
and Euridice, Castor and Pollux); others adopted a bizarrely misogynistic humour ('Women in
this with Cats agree, I think,/Both Live and Scratch after they'have *tip't the Wink*'; 'Well, for
this trick Ile never so be led/As to believe a Woman, though shee's dead').

[177] Anne married and had three children, dying in 1659; Laura Gowing, 'Greene, Anne
(*c*.1628–1659)', *Oxford DNB* <http://www.oxforddnb.com/view/article/11413>.

Lower, a prominent Restoration physician who had been a student at Oxford in Petty's time there] but an Egge.'[178] Brashness aside, the claim seems plausible.

At the same time, he was expected to ring in great changes at Gresham College, an Elizabethan institution devoted to public lectures that had seen better days. Besides his 1648 *Advice*, Petty probably authored a proposal in 1649 for the reform of the College itself.[179] This suggested scrapping three of the seven original lectureships (those in Divinity, Civil Law, and Rhetoric) as unnecessary; 'when Bookes treating of almost all Matters [are] in plenty and abundance', he reasoned, only subjects that permitted 'ocular demonstration' and dealt with 'sensible' rather than 'intellectual' things required public lectures.[180] Such were Physics (including 'Anatomicall Operations' and 'chymistry'), Geometry (including 'surveying of Lands' and 'Fortification'), Astronomy (including 'Dialling, Navigation & Geography'), and—Petty's job—Music:

> The Professor of Musick need not so much teach his Auditors actually to play or make as to explain the grounds thereof, to teach men to know the differences and distances of Tones, the Natures of concord and Discords, the Nature of sounds and sounding bodies, the Reasons of the fabric and figure of all Musicall Instruments, Not omitting Enquiries after the Meanes to better hearing answerable to what hath been happily done for the advantage of sight.[181]

All were described with special attention to their capacity for visible demonstration and practical application; music, in particular, was also connected to the improvement of the human senses. Removing divinity, law, and rhetoric would open up space for lectures investigating magnetism, optics, practical chemistry ('the Nature of all the Materials and Ingredients and applications of them ... made by Dyers, Tanners, leather dressers, Wool workers, Potters, Metallmen, Timber workers, Soapboylers and such like trades'), and mechanics.[182] This was entirely of a piece with Petty's earlier work, and must have made him a natural candidate to reform Gresham College along Hartlibian lines. Yet in the end he spent even less time in London than he had in Oxford. He got as far as writing some lectures on music (whether he delivered any of them is doubtful) but soon left Gresham, which doddered on into the Restoration, increasingly

[178] Petty to Southwell, 13 July 1686, *PP*, 214.
[179] Printed in Webster, *Instauration*, 548–551.   [180] Webster, *Instauration*, 549.
[181] Webster, *Instauration*, 550.   [182] Webster, *Instauration*, 550–551.

marginalized.[183] In September 1652, on the strength of both his personal connections and of his own rapidly rising medical reputation, Petty was appointed Physician-General to the Cromwellian Army in Ireland.

Before we proceed to re-examine Petty's time in Cromwellian Ireland, however, it is worth reflecting for a moment on his place in his world. A physician (thanks to Anne Greene, a very well-known physician), the holder of academic posts in medicine and music, and a contributor to nearly every aspect of the Hartlib Circle's project of universal reformation, Petty was much more than a peripheral scientific enthusiast or hanger-on. His inventions may not have amounted to much in the end, but the same can be said for most of the very similar inventions that others of the time produced—the other perpetual motion machines, the other double-writing instruments, and so on, not to mention the still more celebrated universal characters or symbolic languages put forward by Petty's friends Francis Lodwick (a witness to his demonstration of double-writing) and John Wilkins, as well as by Mersenne and later Leibniz.[184] Like so many other efforts of early science, Petty's attempts matter not because they lived up to the wild promises he made for them but because they show us the new kinds of scientific practice—experiment, eye-witnessing, sworn testimony, and (less endearingly but no less enduringly) the defence of intellectual property—that the Fellows of the Royal Society would later employ in the investigation of nature and that Petty himself would extend to society. Petty was part of what scientific community there was, struggling with the same problems other experimentalists and improvers faced. Out of these struggles would come their natural, and his social, science.

His diverse efforts reflected a coherent and consistent idea of how science should be done and what its proper purposes were. However one interprets his pursuit of the lucriferous—and he did little to hide its pecuniary aspect—there can be little doubt about his commitment to experiment or his focus on its social and economic applications. Science

[183] His 1671 list of writings includes 'Severall Musick Lectures' as having been written in 1650, but there is no reference to their having been read; *PP*, 2:261.

[184] In 1647 Lodwick published a proposal for a universal character, drawing on mathematical and medical symbols for the 'hieroglyphical representation of words'; Lodwick, *A Common Writing* (London: Printed for the author, 1647), sig. A2r-A2v. He was interested in Petty's double-writing and later proposed to translate Petty's 1674 *Discourse ... Concerning the Uses of Duplicate Proportion* into 'the real character'; Petty was honoured, but 'doubt[ed] of its acceptance in the world.' (Petty to Aubrey, 29 May 1678, BL MS Egerton 2231, f.90.) See Vivian Salmon, 'Lodwick, Francis (*bap.* 1619, *d.* 1694)', *Oxford DNB* <http://www.oxforddnb.com/view/article/37684>; Michael Losonsky, 'Language and Logic', in Donald Rutherford (ed.), *The Cambridge Companion to Early Modern Philosophy* (Cambridge: Cambridge University Press, 2006), 179–180.

should be empirical, practical, and profitable; its workings should be visible, testable, and accessible to the average intelligence. It should be, in some sense, collaborative. Petty's sharp reaction to Henry More was as much personal as it was philosophical; in fact, it was personal *because* it was philosophical, for the conception of science Petty articulated was a direct extension of the philosophical persona he was building for himself: the cautious experimentalist, humble about axioms, averse to speculation, but committed to improvement. In the details of this improvement we can begin to see elements of political arithmetic. Alchemical concepts would make 'the transmutation of the Irish into English' thinkable; a mixed-mathematical approach to both the senses and the world they worked on would ultimately yield the 1674 *Discourse ... Concerning the Uses of Duplicate Proportion* (which spoke of 'political arithmetic' and 'geometrical justice'); even judicial astrology, deployed in the *Nosocomium Academicum* as a sort of proto-statistics, would influence Petty and Graunt's quantitative demography; the plebiscite scheme, and indeed the whole project of institutional reform in the 1648 *Advice*, was just the beginning of a lifelong interest in the mechanics of society. Without all this, political arithmetic would not have been possible. Without Ireland, it would not have been necessary.

CHAPTER 3

Surveying Ireland

The unsetling of a Nation is an easy work, the setling is not ...[1]

At the age of twenty-nine, Petty had a promising medical career ahead of him, 'among the Chief, in the chief City of a Nation.'[2] He enjoyed a fair reputation among his scientifically-minded contemporaries at Oxford and in London, and shared with them a range of natural-philosophical interests that a successful medical practice in the capital might well support. Yet on 10 September 1652, the young doctor, still technically Professor of Anatomy at Oxford and of Music at Gresham College, landed at Waterford, as the new Physician-General of the English army in Ireland. The move was not an obvious one. Ireland was a proverbially wild country, torn by a decade of brutal fighting, barely subdued by Cromwell's army. There was hardly any scientific community to speak of, certainly no philosophical club or experimental society, and little of the urban wealth a famous young doctor might hope to tap. Indeed, looking back in later years, Petty would often claim that he would have been better off, at least financially, if he had never left London. Yet the next eight years, from his landing in Ireland to King Charles II's in England, in many ways, were the making of Petty. He arrived in Ireland a physician and experimentalist. He became the director of a major, state-supported scientific project—the 'Down Survey' of Ireland—which was also at the core of the Cromwellian land settlement. Deriving bureaucratic power from his scientific expertise, he at last became—for a moment—the sort of Baconian technocrat he had described in his *Advice* to Hartlib. Yet he also became a wealthy landowner, a man with the means to pursue his ideas with or without

---

[1] Vincent Gookin, *The Great Case of Transplantation in Ireland Discussed* (London: Printed for I. C., 1655), 29.

[2] Petty, *Reflections on some Persons and Things in Ireland* (London: John Martin, James Allestreye, and Thomas Dicas, 1660), 17.

patronage or office. Finally, he gained a stake in Ireland's political and economic fate. In short, he became the person who would create political arithmetic.

From science to politics?

Petty had been offered the post of Physician-General early in 1652, by Major-General John Lambert, 'a favourer of ingeniouse and usefull arts' named Lord Deputy of Ireland when the incumbent, Henry Ireton, died, in November 1651. However, when Parliament refused to renew Lambert's commission as 'Lord Deputy' ahead of his departure for Ireland in May 1652—offering him the title of 'Commander-in-Chief' instead—he baulked, and in July Charles Fleetwood was appointed in his place. Petty, having meanwhile 'fixed his thoughts uppon that designe for Ireland, found acceptance with the Lord Ffleetwood alsoe', and went along.[3] Ireland was not the losing proposition it might seem. Petty's salary as physician to the army, as well as to Fleetwood and his family, was a generous £1 daily; he would, further, be allowed to continue private practice on the side.[4] The position carried a certain prominence; Fleetwood was Oliver Cromwell's son-in-law, and Petty's medical duties brought him into contact with 'the Generals and the Officers Families, even their Wives Children and Servants'—an elite clientele.[5] In other words, it was a sound professional move, secured, once again, by Petty's parliamentarian connections, and by his medical reputation post-Anne Greene.[6]

It also gave Petty a chance to pursue, on a modest basis, some of the sorts of administrative reforms outlined in his *Advice* of 1648:

> The said Dr had not been landed two moneths, but, observing the vast and needlesse exspense of medicaments, and how the Apothecary-Generall of the Army, with his three asistants, did not spend their time to the best advantage; did forthwith, to the content of all, with the State's bare disbursement of about £120, save them five hundred pounds per annum of their former charge, and furnished the army, hospitalls, garrisons, head quarters, &c., with medicaments, without the least noise or trouble, reducing that afaire to

[3] Petty, *History*, 1; Barnard, 'Fleetwood, Charles, appointed Lord Fleetwood under the Protectorate (c.1618–1692)', *Oxford DNB* <http://www.oxforddnb.com/view/article/9684>; D. N. Farr, 'Lambert, John (bap. 1619, d. 1684)', *Oxford DNB* <http://www.oxforddnb.com/view/article/15939>.

[4] Petty, *Tracts*, iv; BL MS Sloane 2903, f.16v.   [5] Petty, *Reflections*, 126.

[6] Petty, *History*, 1.

a state of easiness and plainness, which before was held a mistery, and the
vexation of such as laboured to administer it well.[7]

Petty's move, then, was as much an outgrowth of his earlier interests
as it was a break with his former surroundings. There were quite a few
Hartlibians scattered about Ireland already: Robert Boyle's family seat was
at Lismore, in Waterford; Benjamin Worsley had occupied various offices
in the country since 1651 and was now Surveyor-General of confiscated
Catholic estates; Gerard Boate, a Dutch physician, had been compiling
material for a natural history of Ireland before his death in 1650, at which
point his brother Arnold, a Biblical scholar, took it up (dying in 1653); Miles
Symner, who helped prepare the Boates' work for publication, became
Professor of Mathematics at Trinity College in 1652; the agricultural
improver and alchemical enthusiast Robert Child, who planned a natural
history of his own, had settled at Lisneygarvey, in Antrim, in 1651. Robert
Wood would follow Petty to Dublin in 1656, while another Oxonian,
the physician and chemist Jonathan Goddard, had preceded Petty as
Physician-General.[8]

Petty was thus able to continue his experimental pursuits in good
company. He seems in particular to have become closer to Robert Boyle,
though only gradually. A letter from Petty to Boyle in early 1653 addressing
the latter's too assiduous reading (which, Petty thought, encouraged
hypochondria) combined medicine, methodology, and flattery in equal
parts:

> [A]lthough you read 12 hours per diem … you shall really profit by no
> more of what you read, then by what you remember, nor by what you
> remember, but by so much as you understand & digest, nor by that, but
> by so much as is new unto you, and pertinently set down. But in 12 hours;
> how little … can you … advantage yourself by this laborious way? How little
> of true history doe our books contain? how shy is every man to publish any
> thing either rare or usefull? How few opinions do they deliver rationally
> deduced, but from their own principles? and lastly, how few doe begin
> their tedious systems from principles possible, intelligible, and easy to be
> admitted?

[7] Petty, *History*, 1–2.
[8] Webster, *Instauration*, 293; Hunter, 'Boyle, Robert', *Oxford DNB*; Charles Webster (rev.)
'Worsley, Benjamin (1617/18–1677)', *Oxford DNB* <http://www.oxforddnb.com/view/article/
38153>; Stephen Clucas, 'Child, Robert (1613–1654)', *Oxford DNB* <http://www.oxforddnb.com/
view/article/53661>; E.I. Carlyle (rev. Michael Bevan), 'Wood, Robert (1621/2–1685)', *Oxford
DNB* <http://www.oxforddnb.com/view/article/29890>; Malcolm Oster, 'Goddard, Jonathan
(bap. 1617, d. 1675)', *Oxford DNB* <http://www.oxforddnb.com/view/article/10857>.

On the other side, what a stock of experience have you already in most things? What a faculty have you of making every thing you see an argument of some usefull conclusion or other? How much are you practiced in the method of cleere and scientifical reasoning? How well doe you understand the true use and signification of words...So well are you accomplisht in all these particulars that I safely persuade myself...that you can draw more knowledge and satisfaction from two hours of your own meditation, then from 12 hours endurance of other mens loquacity.[9]

Hartlib had advised Boyle not to 'complain of that barbarous (for the present) country, wherein you live', but 'to make a right use of yourself...towards Dr. Child, Mr. Worsley, Dr. Petty, major [Anthony] Morgan (not to mention others)', who 'would abundantly cherish in you many philosophical thoughts, and encourage you...to venture even upon diverse choice chemical experiments, for the advancement both of health and wealth.'[10] By April 1654, Boyle was conducting anatomical experiments with the 'ingenious' Dr Petty.[11] Petty had meanwhile been working on a number of mixed mathematical and mechanical projects, including 'certain musical and dialing anatomies' and 'some rare piece about the Irish harp.'[12]

Ireland had interested the Hartlib Circle, as a group, since the 1630s at least.[13] Initially this was an outgrowth of the same Protestant internationalism that tied the London circle to scholars in central Europe like Comenius, Alsted and Kinner—James Ussher, Archbishop of Armagh and one of Protestantism's brightest lights, had helped both Comenius and John Dury to promote their ideas before Parliament. Other bishops of the Church of Ireland, such as William Bedell of Kilmore and John Richardson of Ardagh, though themselves English by birth and education, were likewise 'crucial components of the Irish section of the Hartlib Circle.'[14]

---

[9] Petty to Boyle, 16 April 1653, in Boyle, *Correspondence*, 1:142–3.

[10] Hartlib to Boyle, 28 February 1654, in Boyle, *Correspondence*, 1:159.

[11] Boyle to Clodius, April/May 1654, in Boyle, *Correspondence*, 1:167.

[12] Hartlib to Boyle, 15 May 1654, in Boyle, *Correspondence*, 1:177; Ephemerides 1654, HP, 29/4/9a; see also Ephemerides 1655, HP, 29/5/55b–56b; Wood to Hartlib, 10 June 1656, HP, 33/1/3a–3b.

[13] T. C. Barnard, 'The Hartlib Circle and the Origins of the Dublin Philosophical Society', *Irish Historical Studies* 19:73 (1974), 56–71; Barnard, 'The Hartlib Circle and the cult and culture of improvement in Ireland', in Greengrass *et al.*, 281–297; Barnard, *Cromwellian Ireland: English Government and Reform in Ireland, 1649–1660*, (2nd ed., Oxford: Oxford University Press, 2000).

[14] Elizabethanne Boran, '"Propagating Religion and Endeavouring the Reformation of the Whole World": Irish Bishops and the Hartlib Circle in the Mid-Seventeenth Century',

The Church of Ireland's intellectual leadership guaranteed it a role in the Universal Reformation, even as its geographical position—an embattled outpost of Protestantism in the midst of a hostile and dangerous Catholic population—mirrored that of its Continental brethren in Bohemia and the Palatinate.

As a large, sparsely populated, and poorly developed English colony, Ireland was itself the focus for some of the reformers' most ambitious schemes. For decades, Hartlib and his friends had sought a physical space to put their ideas into practice: an 'Antilia', 'Christianopolis', or 'Macaria', a utopian settlement that might model, and ultimately transmit, spiritual and material improvement. In the 1620s, Lithuania had looked plausible; later on, New England or Virginia seemed more promising; now, in the wake of Cromwell's reconquest, Ireland beckoned.[15] Civilizing Ireland accordingly became a Hartlibian as much as a Cromwellian concern.[16] An undated manuscript in the Hartlib Papers outlined a massive 'Vniversity of London' with eleven component colleges, including not only those 'For an Office of Address', 'For Advancement of Vniversal Learning', and 'For Verul[a]mian-Experimental Philosophy', but also seminaries 'For Conversion or Correspondency of Jews', 'For Conversion or Correspondency of Greeke Churches', and 'For Plantations and Conversion of the Gentiles'; second on the list was 'a Seminary for Ireland', or 'Irish College', apparently meant to spearhead the conversion of the unregenerate population of Ireland.[17]

Most, however, focused less on converting the Irish than on improving, by expropriating, their land. Here, the terms of the Cromwellian land settlement—which promised to repay both government creditors (or 'adventurers') and soldiers in debentures for vast amounts of land confiscated from Irish Catholics—were of crucial importance. As early as 1649 Petty witnessed John Holland's pledge 'to give for good vses of Arts out of his Irish Adventures five hundred Acres'; a decade later he advised Robert

in Vincent P. Carey and Ute Lotz-Heumann (eds), *Taking Sides? Colonial and Confessional Mentalities in Early Modern Ireland: Essays in Honour of Karl Bottigheimer* (Dublin: Four Courts Press, 2003), 165–184.

[15] Hartlib was especially influenced by the alchemist and Rosicrucian Johann Valentin Andreae; Rozbicki, 401–419; Donald R. Dickson, 'Johann Valentin Andreae's Utopian Brotherhoods', *Renaissance Quarterly* 49:4 (1996), 760–802; Hugh Trevor-Roper, 'Three Foreigners: The Philosophers of the Puritan Revolution', in Trevor-Roper, *The Crisis of the Seventeenth-Century: Religion, the Reformation, and Social Change* (New York: Harper & Row, 1967), 219–271.

[16] Webster, *Instauration*, 67–77, 225–231; Barnard, *Ireland*, 216–226.

[17] 'A Catalogue of all the City Vniversities ex [Chronologiam?] Alstedj', HP, 47/9/20a–21b.

Wood on the purchase of confiscated Irish land on Hartlib's behalf.[18] The reformers might use Irish land themselves, or they might put the proceeds from its sale towards setting up an Office of Address.[19] In either case they meant to reap the fruits of Cromwell's victory and to incorporate a new, Protestant Ireland into their wider reform programme. As John Beale wrote to Hartlib, 'I conceive the Plantation of Ireland with English, who would bee good examples to stir up a lazy people to abhor their idlenes, & to enrich themselves & that soyle would bee of much concernement to us.'[20] Wood sounded a similar note: 'The country considered impartially is in it selfe a brave country beyond what the English generally will ever be perswaded to imagine & wants nothing but an industrious people'.[21]

Nothing illustrates these hopes—and the attitude to the Irish that generally underpinned them—so well as the project for a natural history of Ireland, which occupied several members of the circle, Petty included, throughout the 1640s and 1650s.[22] Its most tangible result, the Boate brothers' incomplete *Irelands Naturall History*, appeared in 1652.[23] Gerard Boate's agenda was clear from the outset: natural history was the essential foundation of husbandry, 'the most profitable' branch of human science and 'the Head spring of all ... native Commerce and Trading'; knowledge and improvement of nature, in turn, freed man both from material want and the 'yokes of Vanity'; liberty and learning advanced together, towards salvation. The book's dedicatees, Oliver Cromwell and Charles Fleetwood, had themselves been 'very eminent Instruments [in] the breaking of our yoakes', and Boate looked forward to the plantation of Ireland with English, Dutch, and Bohemian Protestants.[24] The book made clear that the bog-draining, wood-clearing, mine-digging English had been the 'introducers of all good things, in Ireland'. The Irish, 'one of the

---

[18] Ephemerides 1649, HP, 28/1/31b; Wood to Hartlib, 20 April 1659, HP, 33/1/54a–b.

[19] Wood to Hartlib, 8 April 1657, HP, 33/1/13b.

[20] Beale to Hartlib (undated), HP, 52/166b.

[21] Wood to Hartlib, 27 May 1657, HP, 33/1/15b.

[22] See notes and queries in HP, 25/3/1a–b, 31/17/6a–7b, 62/45/1a–7b, and letters to Hartlib from Thomas Field from 1654 (31/14/1a–4b) and Robert Wood from 1656 and 1657 (33/1/3a–4b and 13a–16b). See also T. C. Barnard, 'Miles Symner and the New Learning in Seventeenth-Century Ireland', *Journal of the Royal Society of Antiquaries of Ireland* 102:2 (1972), 129–142, and Patricia Coughlan, 'Natural history and historical nature: the project for a natural history of Ireland', in Greengrass et al., 298–317.

[23] Gerard Boate, *Irelands Naturall History* (London: Printed for John Wright, 1652); reprinted in James Hewitt Lifford (ed.), *A Collection of Tracts and Treatises Illustrative of the Natural History, Antiquities, and the Political and Social State of Ireland, at Various Periods prior to the Present Century*, 2 vols (Dublin: Alexander Thom & Sons, 1860–1861), 1:1–148.

[24] Boate, 3–7; compare Dury, 'Memo on Protestant exiles and Commonwealth trade' (c. 1653), HP 53/6a–b.

most barbarous Nations of the whole earth', had answered them 'with unthankfulness, hatred, and envy, and lately [in 1641] with a horrible and bloody conspiracie, tending to their utter destruction'.[25]

For English Protestants, Ireland was both an important front in seventeenth-century religious geopolitics—a reservoir of popishness and barbarism, a dangerous backdoor for a Catholic invasion of Britain, and a drain on England's military and fiscal resources—and a store of valuable land and potentially useful population, blessed with natural ports and a strategic location. For the Hartlibians, Ireland's transformation from a weak point to a source of strength required much the same improvement of agriculture and manufactures, encouragement of trade, institutional innovation, and spiritual reform they promoted in England. In this sense, Petty had simply moved from one theatre of Universal Reformation to another. What differed were the political and social circumstances he now inhabited. For the reformation of Ireland would happen in the teeth of the majority of the population: its agents and beneficiaries would be English Protestants, and it would rest foursquare on a foundation of conquest. Not all the Hartlibians were as stridently anti-Irish as Boate (certainly Petty was not), but most agreed that systematic improvement implied extensive state support and thoroughgoing Protestant plantation—in a word, colonization. The land settlement was the key. In this light it is no wonder that Petty should have involved himself in it. Yet by taking on a task that was at once both technical and political, he moved from the familiar confines of experimental natural philosophy into a more social science, and a more political career.

Unsettled Ireland

When Petty arrived in Ireland, England's mission on the island was five centuries old, having begun with the ramshackle invasions of Anglo-Norman feudal lords under Henry II in the 1160s and 1170s. The results had not, to date, been happy. Driven by internal rivalries and the need for allies, by Irish resistance—which reduced the sphere of English influence to the fluctuating 'Pale' around Dublin—and by the simple facts of their geographical and demographic situation, these early conquerors had, over the course of generations, mixed with the 'mere' Irish population. They took on Irish allies, married into Irish families and adopted Irish

[25] Boate, 95–96 and 102–103.

customs, so that—as the poet and planter Edmund Spenser put it in 1596—'the most parte of them are degenerated and growen almost mere Irishe' themselves.[26] Worse, these 'Old English' (or 'English-Irish') had mostly remained Catholic after the Protestant Reformation.[27] This further compromised their usefulness in Anglicizing Ireland and called their own allegiance into question at a time when—given the assassinations of William the Silent of Holland in 1584 and Henry IV of France in 1610, and the 1605 Gunpowder Plot against the English King and Parliament—Catholics were seen as king-killing zealots, their worst treasons forgiven, if not commissioned, by their murderous Pope. In Ireland as in much of Europe, religion came to trump, indeed to define, nation. The Old English, in Protestant eyes, were a dangerous fifth column.[28]

'New English' Protestant plantation in Munster from 1585 and Ulster from 1609—already the focus of extensive Scottish Presbyterian immigration—threatened Irish and Old English property and status alike.[29] The Old English stayed loyal during the Nine Years War (1594–1603), but their political influence steadily waned, the English government content to follow the New English in lumping all Catholics together. By the outbreak of rebellion in Ulster, late in 1641, with Civil War in England imminent, they had little to hope for from Crown or Parliament and thus little to lose by joining their coreligionists in what Protestants saw as 'an universal defection and general revolt,—wherein not only all the meer Irish, but almost all the old English, that adhered to the Church of Rome, were totally involved.'[30] The rest of the decade witnessed a three-way struggle between royalists, parliamentarians, and a Catholic confederate association divided in both leadership and aims. While a poorer, northern, more clericalist group (associated more with the Gaelic Irish and with Rome) pushed for the wholesale restoration of Catholicism and greater political independence, a wealthier, southern, more royalist wing (associated

[26] Edmund Spenser (ed. W. L. Renwick), *A View of the Present State of Ireland* (London: Eric Partridge Ltd at the Scholartis Press, 1934), 62.

[27] Fynes Moryson (ed. Graham Kew), *The Irish Sections of Fynes Moryson's Unpublished Itinerary* (Dublin: Irish Manuscripts Commission, 1998); John Temple, *The Irish Rebellion: Or, an History of the Attempts of the Irish Papists to Extirpate the Protestants in the Kingdom of Ireland* (London: Printed by R. White for Samuel Gellibrand, 1646; London: R. Wilks, 1812).

[28] Aidan Clarke, *The Old English in Ireland, 1625–42* (Dublin: MacGibbon and Kee, 1966).

[29] William J. Smyth, *Map-making, Landscapes and Memory: A Geography of Colonial and Early Modern Ireland, c. 1530–1750* (Cork: Cork University Press, 2006), 54–102.

[30] Temple, *Irish Rebellion*, 25.

more with the Old English) had less ambitious goals.[31] Between 1649 and 1652—with the English royalists defeated, King Charles dead, and the confederates split—Cromwell's armies reconquered the country in a campaign notorious then and since for its brutality.

Intra-Catholic divisions meant little to the victors. Even more than the Civil War in England, the conflict in Ireland conflated religious, political, and national distinctions: Irish and Catholic were interchangeable terms, either one implying guilt. The settlement planned for the country reflected this both in its harshness and in its categorical presumption that Irish Catholics—until proven innocent—were guilty not only of rebellion, but also of something like genocide. The original Ulster rebellion of October 1641 had sparked widespread violence against English Protestants, which, combined with the effects of cold, hunger, and disease on those turned out of their homes and stripped of their possessions, resulted in several thousand deaths. As bad as things were, they were rumoured to be much worse: escaped survivors claimed that Catholics had slaughtered 154,000 Protestants, while Sir John Temple's *The Irish Rebellion* (1646)—which quickly became, and long remained, the standard Protestant history—suggested a figure of 300,000.[32] Papists had launched a war of extermination, and nearly succeeded; that could not be allowed to happen again. Protestant plantation—long a haphazard series of semi-private initiatives—must be secured on a firmer footing, even if this meant uprooting the Catholic population altogether.

That was the basic idea behind the Cromwellian land settlement. As early as 1642 Parliament had passed the first 'Adventurers' Act', according to which £1 million borrowed from London adventurers to pay for an invasion of Ireland, would be repaid with debentures for 2.5 million acres of profitable Irish land confiscated from the rebels. In the event, fewer lenders came forward than hoped, and their money was in any case spent on fighting the king in England rather than the Irish. But subsequent acts

---

[31] Micheál Ó Siochrú, *Confederate Ireland, 1642–1649: A Constitutional and Political Analysis* (Dublin: Four Courts Press, 1999), 245, plays down the ethnic dimension of the split; but see James Scott Wheeler, *Cromwell in Ireland* (Dublin: Gill and Macmillan, 1999); Smyth, *Map-making*, 148.

[32] See Smyth, *Map-making*, 116–117. Petty thought Temple's figures impossible; his own estimate of 37,000 massacred is now generally seen as itself too high, although Wheeler (225–226) regards it as plausible. Petty thought that 112,000 Protestants and 'about 504,000 of the *Irish* perished, and were wasted by the Sword, Plague, Famine, Hardship and Banishment' in the first year; Petty, *The Political Anatomy of Ireland* (London: Printed for D. Brown and W. Rogers, 1691), 18.

renewed and extended the same principle, so that by 1653 confiscated Irish land was supposed to pay back not only a decade's worth of adventurers' loans but several years of soldiers' arrears as well—in all, £2.5–3 million in government debt.[33] The criteria for confiscation were accordingly broad, stipulating, as Petty later summarized them:

> That Irish papists who had never been for the Rebells or King should lose Nothing. That English or Protestants who had not assissted the Parliament should lose a part. That Irish of that Kind should lose a greater part, & should have the Equivalent of what they were to retain in Connaught. & That all other plebeian Irish & papists should go free.[34]

In principle this punished all those, Protestant or Catholic, unable to prove their 'constant good affection' to Parliament since 1641—no mean feat. In practice, however, English Protestants were often allowed to 'compound', retaining some or all of their estates in exchange for a fine (which, in many cases, was never collected).[35] The vast majority of confiscated lands were Irish Catholic-owned: 10,000 lost their estates, though few even of those eligible claimed their compensation in Connacht.[36]

The massive dislocation of Irish landownership helped clear the way for a systematic recolonization, though the war, too, had done its share. A decade of fighting, intermittent famine, and latterly the plague—which raged throughout the period of Cromwell's invasion—may have killed off a third or more of the prewar population of perhaps 1.8 million. Of those that survived, 35,000–40,000 soldiers were allowed to leave and take up service in Continental Europe (roughly 20,000 had already gone during the 1640s), while between 15,000 and 25,000 men, women, and children were transported to English colonies in the West Indies and Virginia.[37] Besides the horrific human toll, the land itself was wrecked, stocks destroyed, and trade at a standstill.[38] From the ashes, however,

---

[33] Smyth, *Map-making*, 167; see also Karl S. Bottigheimer, *English Money and Irish Land: The 'Adventurers' in the Cromwellian Settlement of Ireland* (Oxford: Oxford University Press, 1971).

[34] Petty, 'A smale History of the Rebellion of Ireland with some Questions thereupon' (1686?), BL MS Add. 72884, f.58r–v.

[35] Smyth, *Map-making*, 170; Kevin McKenny, 'The Seventeenth-Century Land Settlement in Ireland: Towards a Statistical Interpretation', in Jane Ohlmeyer (ed.), *Ireland from Independence to Occupation, 1641–1660* (Cambridge: Cambridge University Press, 1995), 181–200, esp. 192–194.

[36] Smyth, *Map-making*, 161.   [37] Smyth, *Map-making*, 160.

[38] Raymond Gillespie, *The Transformation of the Irish Economy, 1550–1700* (Dundalk: Studies in Irish Economic and Social History 6, 1991; rpr., 1998), 39–40.

a new and more secure plantation would rise. Soldiers and adventurers were to settle estates in a great band of ten counties, stretching across Ireland from Antrim in the northeast to Limerick and Waterford in the south. By later 1653, Connacht itself was supposed to become a sort of reservation, a new Cromwellian policy calling for the entire Irish Catholic population to be 'transplanted' there and penned in by Protestant buffer zones along the seacoast and the west bank of the Shannon—though only perhaps 45,000 actually moved during the allotted time-frame of July 1653–May 1654, after which the plan was eventually dropped.[39] Yet even as the transplantation of Catholics sputtered, the expropriation of their land continued.

The great unknown was the land itself. The terms of the settlement required that forfeited land not only be precisely measured and subdivided into suitable tracts but also that its quality be assessed. With the exception of a part of Connacht covered by the 'Strafford' survey of 1637, none of the relevant information was available in 1653—by which time disbanded soldiers joined anxious adventurers in clamouring for their land. In September of that year the 'Act for the Satisfaction of Adventurers and Soldiers' called for three new surveys: one to establish by 'inquisition' the current boundaries, quality and ownership of the forfeited lands; another to 'admeasure' specific holdings in preparation for their reallocation; and a third to measure the borders, or 'surrounds', of the much larger baronies in which the estates were located.[40] The last, known as the 'Gross Survey', began almost immediately, but failed to distinguish between profitable and unprofitable land, feeding fears that there was too little of the former to cover the state's debts. To remedy this, in early 1654 the survey by inquisition, known as the 'Civil Survey' since it was directed by civil authorities ('courts of survey' operating in consultation with 'juries' of locals), began to gather written descriptions of the lands and their improvements—only to reignite the fury of the soldiers and adventurers when it became clear that the Gross Survey had underestimated the amount of profitable land available. By mid-1654 it was clear that both a precise admeasurement and a standardized assessment of the lands in question were needed. It was at this point that Petty entered the fray, to propose a survey of his own.

[39] Smyth, *Map-making*, 161, 168–169.
[40] See Petty, *History*, xiii; Smyth, *Map-making*, 170–172; J. G. Simms, 'The Civil Survey, 1654–6', *Irish Historical Studies* 9:35 (1955), 253–263.

The Down Survey in theory

After political arithmetic, Petty's greatest claim to fame since the seventeenth century has been the Down Survey.[41] Yet just how Petty came to intervene in the Cromwellian land settlement is hardly obvious. Surveying was a well-established trade, with its own technical literature, instruments, procedures, and practitioners, and it is worth asking why Petty felt able to propose his own solution to what was, essentially, a surveying problem, albeit one with wider repercussions. The answer probably lies partly in his conviction, evident from his earlier inventions, that the right empirical method could make up for an ignorance of traditional practices. On the other hand, Petty's artisanal background and formal training in mixed mathematics, of which surveying was one form, no doubt gave him the confidence to wander into—so to speak—uncharted territory. Above all, perhaps, was a certain ambition, at once philosophical and personal, luciferous and lucriferous. For his solution to the settlement's problems, a new survey of his own devising, to be executed under his own direction, became not only the foundation of his personal fortune but also, arguably, the greatest single state-supported scientific project of its day. Petty never got his Nosocomium Academicum; he got the Down Survey instead.

In mid-1654 Petty approached the Surveyor-General—his old Hartlibian associate, Benjamin Worsley—with some criticisms of the ongoing surveys, which, as disbanded soldiers demanded their land, were causing more than technical headaches. Rebuffed, Petty sharpened his criticisms and extended his attack to Worsley himself, 'who, having been often frustrated as to his many severall great designes and undertakings in England, hoped to improve and repair himselfe uppon a less knowing and more credulous people'.[42] He questioned Worsley's religious

---

[41] Few episodes of Petty's life are as richly documented. Between late 1659 and early 1660, he himself wrote 'A Briefe Account of the most materiall Passages relatinge to the Survey managed by Doctor Petty in Ireland, anno 1655 and 1656', printed in Petty, *History*, xiii–xvii; he simultaneously compiled the weighty *History*, reproducing scores of documents; in 1660 he printed his polemical *Reflections upon some Persons and Things in Ireland*. The most thorough study remains Y. M. Goblet, *La Transformation de la géographie politique de l'Irlande dans les cartes et essais anthropogéographiques de Sir William Petty*, 2 vols (Nancy: Imprimerie Berger-Levrault, 1930), especially 1:257–351. In English, see Smyth, *Map-making*, 166–197; J. H. Andrews, *Shapes of Ireland: Maps and their makers 1564–1839* (Dublin: Geography Publications, 1997), 118–152; Fitzmaurice, 23–68; Sharp, 110–145; Strauss, 54–65.

[42] Petty, *History*, 2.

shifts: he had become an increasingly (and, in the army, fashionably) radical Protestant sectarian. He also, more seriously, challenged Worsley's scientific credentials, and in particular his 'flights to become suddenly rich, as by the *Universal Medicine, Making of Gold, Sowing of Salt-Peter*'—'alchemical' schemes in the pejorative sense of the word. (It is worth noting, in passing, that Petty lumped in with these pseudo-scientific get-rich-quick schemes Worsley's economic ideas, in particular the '*Universal Trade*' he argued for in *The Advocate*.)[43] The mutual hostility that now exploded was at once personal, philosophical, and political.

Petty found six major problems with Worsley's handling of 'the Geometricall Survey of Ireland'. '1st, there was paid for admeasurements twelve times *pro ratâ* more than ever was given before ... 2ndly. The manner of admeasurement was such as noe man could examine whether it was well or ill performed. 3dly. The said admeasurement ... was but a meer vitiation [i.e. modification] of the countries estimate, which might be had for nothing'. Fourth—and most absurd to modern eyes—surveyors were paid not by the length of the 'surrounds' they measured, but rather by the volume of land the surrounds enclosed (forty-five shillings per thousand acres). This bore no constant relation to the linear distance the surveyors covered; indeed, 'by so much the more paines they tooke, by soe much less wages they had.' Fifth, 'there was neither due tryall of artists or instruments, neither good instructions before hand, nor examinations afterwards'—a criticism of Worsley's administration of a collaborative scientific endeavour that harks back to the 1648 *Advice*. Finally, surveyors were paid only for *profitable* land they surveyed: unprofitable land within the surrounds they measured was deducted from the total acreage and thus from their pay. As Petty realized, this gave the surveyors a vested interest in exaggerating the proportion of profitable land and 'begat infinite jealousies and discontents in the army', whose debentures were inevitably devalued.[44] On top of all this, the survey might take a decade or more to complete. Soldiers unable to settle their claims were forced to sell their debentures at huge discounts—thus taking a fraction of their due pay. Their 'discontents' understandably grew.

Petty developed his proposal during the summer of 1654 and presented it to the government in September. It offered an ambitious solution to the problem posed by the terms of the soldiers' settlement (the adventurers, for

[43] Petty, *Reflections*, 89, 107; see Benjamin Worsley, *The Advocate* (London: Printed by William Du-Gard, 1651).
[44] Petty, *History*, xiii, 2–3.

now, went their own way) and a bold model for state-supported scientific
work. Yet in its narrowly technical aspects—surveying equipment and
techniques of measurement—it differed little from earlier surveys; Petty
was, in his own words, 'rather a contriver of the way and method how
many surveyors should worke, then a surveyor myselfe'.[45] His innovations
were, instead, organizational.[46] First, he suggested that the different aims
of the different surveys be combined:

> that the whole land should be measured both accordinge to its civill bounds,
> viz., by barronyes, parishes, townelands, ploughlands, balliboes, &c., and
> alsoe by its naturall boundings by rivers, ridges of mountaines, rockes,
> loughes, boggs, &c.; as answeringe not only the very ends of satifyinge
> the adventurers and souldiers then in view, but all such other future ends
> whatsoever as are usually expected from any survey.[47]

As they measured, surveyors would distinguish six categories of unprofitable and profitable land ('wood, bog, mountaine, arable, meadow, and
pasture'); they would also 'add and sett out such auxiliary lines and lymits
as may facilitate and ascertaine the finall subdivision'.[48] In short, one
survey would measure, map, assess, and subdivide all the land confiscated
for the army.[49] The soldiers could have their land as soon as the army had
worked out the relevant apportionments. The state would have a complete
picture of Irish geography. From a scientific standpoint, meanwhile, the
survey would exemplify a new approach to empirical natural history, based
(unlike Boate's, or indeed any earlier work) on the extensive, systematic,
and precise measurement, observation, and classification of the land itself. Hartlib was quick to recognize the role this might play in Ireland's
improvement.[50]

Finally, Petty promised, 'provided the allowance might be somewhat
extraordinary', to complete the entire survey in thirteen months. If the

---

[45] Petty, *History*, 294.
[46] Petty claimed (*History*, 17) 'That he had, by a more distinct, methodicall, and comprehensive
ffield booke; by removing some entanglement in the card wherein the needle playes; by
exterminating the use of triangles and intermixt multiplication ... much facilitated the whole
practice of surveying.' He likely used William Leybourn, *The Compleat Surveyor* (London: Printed
by R. and W. Leybourn for E. Brewster and G. Sawbridge, 1653); Irma Corcoran, *Thomas Holme,
1624–1695: Surveyor General of Pennsylvania* (Philadelphia: American Philosophical Society,
1992), 40. Leybourn argued, in Petty-esque fashion, that a modified plain table could do the
work of several other standard instruments. Petty's originality lay in his division of labour; see
Goblet, 1:252–258.
[47] Petty, *History*, xiv.   [48] Petty, *History*, 9.
[49] These had been separate tasks under the old plan; it was because all this information was
now put down on the surveyors' maps that the 'Down Survey' was so named; Petty, *History*, 14–15.
[50] Ephemerides 1655 and 1656, HP, 29/5/31b, 43b, 55b, 58b, and 60b. See Sharp, 134–135.

survey itself was ambitious, this timetable was incredible; Worsley told
Petty that twenty years would be needed.[51] But Petty's confidence was
based on a radical reorganization of the work involved, and it is here
that both the project's deep roots in Baconian science and its remarkable
anticipation of later practice are most striking. Petty recognized that professional surveyors 'are commonly persons of gentile and liberall education,
and theire practise esteemed a mistery and intricate matter ... and withall,
the makeinge of theire instruments is a matter of much art and niceity'.
A survey of the sort he planned, besides taking a long time, could be
prohibitively expensive. The answer was a new division of labour:

> The said Petty, consideringe the vastnesse of the worke, thought of dividinge
> both the art of makeinge instruments, as alsoe that of usinge them into many
> partes, vizt., one man made onely measuringe chaines, vizt., a wire maker;
> another magneticall needles, with theire pins, vizt., a watchmaker; another
> turned the boxes out of wood, and the heads of the stands on which the
> instrument playes, vizt., a turnor; another, the stands or leggs, a pipe maker;
> another all the brasse worke, vizt., a founder; another workman, of a more
> versatile head and hand, touches the needles, adjusts the sights and cards,
> and adaptates every peece to each other.

At the same time, 'scales, protractors, and compasse-cards, beinge matters
of accurate division' were ordered from London, along with the paper
and field-books the surveyors would use. Just as Adam Smith's imaginary
manufacturer did for pin-making, Petty broke down the intricate apparatus
of surveying into simple, standardized parts that Dublin and London
tradesmen could supply in quantity.[52]

Once the equipment was ready, the task itself was likewise split up:

> He divided the whole art of surveying into its severall parts, viz.: Ffield
> worke; 2, protracting; 3, casting [the maps]; 4, reducing [the surveyors' work
> to a finished form]; 5, ornaments of the mapps; 6, writing fair bookes;
> 7, examination of all and every the premisses [i.e. verifying the foregoing
> work]; withall setting forth, that for the speedier and surer performance he
> intended to imploy particular persons uppon each specie [i.e. each kind of
> job], according to their respective fittness and qualifications.[53]

The 'principall division of this whole worke' was the physical measurement
of the land. This was not only arduous in itself but also dangerous given
the survey's purpose, which was, after all, the expropriation of Catholic
estates, many still occupied by their original owners. It required 'certayne

[51] Petty, *History*, xiv.   [52] Petty, *History*, xiv–xv, 17.   [53] Petty, *History*, 17.

persons, such as were able to endure travaile, ill lodginge and dyett, as allsoe heates and colds, beinge also men of activitie, that could leape hedge and ditch, and could also ruffle with the severall rude persons in the country, from whome they might often expect to be crossed and opposed.' Here Petty turned to the soldiers themselves, 'many of whom, having been bread to trades, could write and read sufficiently for the purposes intended.' Given some basic training in the use of their instruments and some rules of thumb for judging the quality of land (and paid by linear distance measured rather than by the area or value of the land enclosed), a thousand of these men, though 'not of the nimblest witts', were more than capable of performing the basic tasks assigned them.[54] Petty's organization would take care of the rest:

> men saw … how I had facilitated and regulated the whole Art, that I had divided the whole practice into several parts, and committed each to such Actors as were respectively most fit for it, how I provided a double proportion of Workmen and Instruments to prevent emergent hinderances, and had the examination performed under my own Eye … I say … men saw, how by a little better contrivance and method, and a little more diligence and asiduity I was like to perform my undertaking, and to gain more for my work *pro ratâ* then the *Vulgus* of ignorant, immethodical, loytering, disunited, emulating and contentious Surveyors (especially the vastness of the work being considered) could ever do.[55]

The right method could simplify—and exploit—the most arcane art.

The Down Survey in practice

In practice, things were more complicated. Worsley, who remained Surveyor-General, put up a stern fight against the new survey, and allied himself with a number of radical Protestants in the army against Petty's more moderate backers. The personal animosities of the actors involved reflected broader alignments in the politics of the Irish settlement, and eventually of the Commonwealth itself. Although Petty got a hearing for his idea in September 1654, it was 11 December before a contract was signed, and February 1655 before the work really began.[56] His own payment was in principle generous, but whereas he had originally offered to complete the survey (and pay for its employees and equipment) for either a lump

[54] Petty, *History*, xv–xvii, 17–18, 46–50.   [55] Petty, *Reflections*, 106–107.
[56] Petty, *History*, 18–46.

sum of £30,000 or at a rate of £6 per thousand acres (whether profitable or unprofitable, so as to avoid imputations of bias), in the end he was paid, as the earlier surveyors had been, according to the quality as well as the acreage of the land: £7 3s 4d per thousand acres of profitable land, £3 per thousand otherwise.[57] This did eventually lead, as he had feared, to charges that he had overestimated the amount of profitable land. In the mean time the government advanced funds to him irregularly, one or two thousand pounds at a time, so that a great deal of equipment and pay came at first out of his own pocket.[58]

Petty orchestrated the survey from Dublin Castle, with the help of his cousin John Petty and Thomas Taylor, who helped examine the surveyors' work and oversaw the engraving of the maps.[59] The surveyors themselves, scattered across Ulster, Leinster, and Munster, faced considerable difficulties on the ground. Visible agents of the recolonization effort, they naturally attracted resistance. In Wicklow, eight of them were captured, given a mock court-martial, and killed by Irish 'tories'—apparently the worst but probably not the sole example of violence against Petty's army of soldier-surveyors.[60] Quite apart from such physical dangers, the soldiers had a difficult task. They had trouble distinguishing profitable from unprofitable land in any consistent way.[61] The 'mearsmen' on whom they depended for knowledge of local boundaries were usually (to Worsley's consternation) Catholics, and thus both reluctant to help and liable to be driven away by transplantation.[62] Petty had been compelled to pay off the surveyors Worsley had employed on the older surveys, initially at his own rates but later on at their original, much higher, salaries.[63] Some, he thought, were 'Spies' for Worsley.[64] Some of his own surveyors sold the equipment he had furnished and abandoned their posts.[65]

Despite all this, the greatest problem was, ironically, the survey's rapid progress. Originally, Petty had undertaken to demarcate the new subdivisions immediately after having measured the land, so that the confiscated estates could be redistributed almost as soon as they had been surveyed. But the army only began supplying information about apportionments from May 1655, months after the survey began, and, more

---

[57] Petty, *History*, 7–8, 26–27.   [58] Petty, *History*, 30, 53.

[59] With Petty's help, John became Surveyor-General of Ireland in 1662; Taylor became his deputy. See Andrews, 127–130; Smyth, *Map-making*, 174; Goblet, 1:92.

[60] Smyth, *Map-making*, 54–55.

[61] Petty, *History*, 93–101 (see also 117), includes a letter on this point from two Kerry surveyors.

[62] Petty, *History*, 20–21, 118, 123.   [63] Petty, *History*, 50–51.

[64] Petty, *Reflections*, 53.   [65] Petty, *History*, 122.

to the point, months after surveyors had moved on from the areas in question. From late 1655, fresh waves of disbanded soldiers (as well as the wounded, and widows and orphans of the dead), aware that earlier surveys had underestimated the amount of land available, demanded satisfaction of their claims.[66] Petty found himself swamped with 'orders upon orders, exceeding thicke, to make ready the surveyes ... of the lands forthwith to be sett out to the forces', often in areas long since surveyed but never subdivided. He was consequently forced to send men back to perform the missing subdivisions 'when the mearers were fled, the surveyors dead, the marks on the land worn out, the ratts had eaten the originall plotts, and a new interest risen up, for shewing different meare[s] at the subdivision from what were showen at the first admeasurement.'[67] Though there was little he could do about it, Petty bore the brunt of the blame.

The survey was nevertheless completed by the beginning of March 1655, and by any standard it was a major accomplishment. Petty's surveyors had measured over 2,200,000 acres of land (1,809,613 acres of profitable forfeited land, 132,489 of unprofitable, 262,159 of Crown or Church land, and 33,274 of commons). The linear distance covered, he claimed, was 'enough to have encompassed the world neer five tymes about.' (He would augment this claim throughout his life—by 1687 it was eight times, not five.)[68] And, as he was not shy to remind both his employers and his rivals, 'what they were told to be above seven years work', he had 'dispatcht in one'.[69] Worsley continued to make trouble, however, successfully dragging out the evaluation of Petty's work from March into May 1656. The payment of Petty's fees, which amounted to over £16,800—and which included the costs of the equipment and the personnel under him—was still another matter. Beginning in early 1657, Petty commuted as much of his unpaid salary as possible into land debentures, and purchased still more with the pay he had received—acquiring perhaps 10,000 acres or more in various parts of the country in 1657 alone.[70] Petty was careful to secure permission for his purchases, but the conflict of interests they implied would inevitably come back to haunt him.

---

[66] Petty, *History*, 43, 66–80.   [67] Petty, *History*, 42.

[68] Petty, *History*, xvii, 150–151. Elsewhere Petty claimed only to have measured only 'as much Land-line ... as would have neer four times begirt the whole Earth in its greatest Circle'; Petty, *Reflections*, 12. But by the last years of his life the distance grew considerably, from 'measuring the whole world ... neer 6 times about' to 'the equivalent to eight times about the world'; Petty to Robert Southwell, 31 July 1686 and 13 October 1687, *PSC*, 223, 294.

[69] Petty, *Reflections*, 13.   [70] Petty, *History*, 2.

Even once fair copies of the survey books and maps had been delivered to the Surveyor-General's office and the contract cancelled, in December 1657, Petty's work was far from over.[71] But it is worth considering for a moment what he had accomplished in terms of where he had begun—that is, seeing the Down Survey as a Hartlibian project.[72] For, however temporarily, the survey realized exactly the kind of collaborative, state-supported scientific endeavour Petty's *Advice* (or Plattes's *Macaria* or Bacon's *New Atlantis*) had outlined. In his letter to Henry More, Petty had insisted that 'real learning' should be both useful and accessible even to people of 'mean capacity'; the Down Survey not only showed 'that what those formal Glorioso's cryed up for a mystery, was nothing beyond the reach of a mean capacity within a few moneths time', but also put the mean capacities of hundreds of men under the more skilled direction of a few for the eminently practical purpose of measuring and dividing up a country. It may seem odd to compare a land survey with a body of philosophical writing. But that contrast is precisely the point, for the question Petty had raised with More was what sort of thing natural philosophy was—whether it was a closed intellectual system or a cumulative, experimental, and practical advancement of learning; whether it was something that a single 'strong witt' could grasp or that many hands must assemble; whether it changed one's picture of the world or remade the world itself. No less than his letter to More or his *Advice* to Hartlib, Petty's Down Survey answered this question in favour of the latter. And unlike the Nosocomium, the Office of Address or Salomon's House, the Down Survey—the scientific instrument of a military government—*did* transform a society.

Yet if the survey was Petty's greatest Hartlibian project, it also ended his association with the Hartlib Circle as a group. His run-ins with Worsley may have made this inevitable, and certainly set the tone. In April 1657, Robert Wood wrote to Hartlib that an unnamed third party was hoping to set up an Office of Address in Dublin, adding that 'I have given him the best general directions ... & Dr. Petty had given him a Catalogue of such particulars, as more nearly concerne the present trade of Ireland.'[73] But by this point 'the rich doctor' was clearly suspect.[74] Petty had been involved

[71] Petty, *History*, 182–183.

[72] Michael Hunter, *Science and Society in Restoration England* (Cambridge: Cambridge University Press, 1981), 25.

[73] Wood to Hartlib, 8 April 1657, HP, 33/1/13b.

[74] See Hartlib to Boyle, 8 December 1657, in Boyle, *Correspondence*, 1:243; see also Ephemerides 1656, HP, 29/5/58b, where Hartlib notes that Petty was estimated to have made £7,000 from the survey.

since the late 1640s with Hartlib's plan to invest Irish land debentures in an Office of Address or some type of college; now, although he was better-placed than ever to ensure the plan's success, he was no longer wanted. Worsley complained that Petty was somehow 'diverting' revenues for the project 'and under the notion of the states care to put himself into the management of it', and Hartlib wrote to Boyle wishing that Petty would keep out.[75] When the project eventually fell through, Hartlib blamed Petty. Writing to Boyle in August of 1658—having just seen Petty in person—he complained that 'Dr. Petty hath taken away above two hours from me, which should have been devoted to your service.'

> Most of the time was spent in telling the contrivance of his great design, upon which he was resolved to spend two thousand pounds, not doubting but that he would be a good gainer in the conclusion of it. The design aims at the founding of a college or colony, of twenty able learned men, very good Latinists, of several nations, that should teach the Latin tongue (as other vulgar languages are learnt) merely by use and custom. This, with the history of trades, he looks upon as the great pillars of reformation in the world. I wish you could handsomely present unto him, how he hath defeated me of two hundred and fifty pounds a year ... by undermining that more universal design of learning, upon which I have been made to hope these two years.[76]

Petty tried to win Boyle and Hartlib back, lamenting that Worsley had 'sown tares', imploring them to 'suspend your judgment of me' and promising to 'demonstrate the causes and necessity of the most malign action I am taxed with'.[77] But they no longer trusted him, whether because of his involvement with debentures or simply because of the way he had advanced his interest at Worsley's expense. As often happened, Petty's mixture of public service and private gain got him into trouble.

Office, influence, faction

The survey was accepted in May 1656; Petty's 'next service and suffering', starting in July, 'was in the distribution and setting forth of the lands soe

[75] Hartlib to Boyle, 1 June 1658, in Boyle, *Correspondence*, 1:278–280.

[76] Hartlib to Boyle, 10 August 1658, in Boyle, *Correspondence*, 1:286–287. It was Petty's behaviour rather than his ideas that bothered Hartlib, who retrospectively praised Petty's plan for a 'Glottical College'; see Hartlib to Evelyn, [February?] 1660, in Evelyn (ed. William Bray), *Diary and Correspondence of John Evelyn, F.R.S.*, 4 vols (London: Henry G. Bohn, 1862), 3:132–133.

[77] Petty to Boyle, 17 February 1658, and Hartlib to Boyle, 16 April 1659, in Boyle, *Correspondence*, 1:254–255 and 336–338.

by him admeasured.'[78] Together with Myles Symner and Vincent Gookin (a political pamphleteer descended from a Protestant planter family), Petty was appointed to a commission charged with subdividing and distributing the army's land to officers and soldiers. It was a difficult position, and in practice it fell to Petty alone. Gookin, having been elected to Parliament, left Ireland almost as soon as he had been appointed, while Symner, 'foreseeing the danger of incurring ... the armyes causeless hatred', kept out of the business as much as possible, 'Soe that the daily directing of neer fourty clerks and calculators, cutting out worke for all them, and giving answers as well to impertinent as pertinent questions, did lye chiefly uppon the Doctor'.[79] At the same time the Council of State entrusted Petty and Worsley with extending the original Down Survey to those baronies set aside for the 'adventurers' and the Commonwealth itself, as well as to lands which had been 'irregularly' set out to particularly importunate soldiers in 1653 and 1654—in effect, a whole new survey on roughly the same scale as the original, completed in the spring of 1658.[80]

Petty's execution of the surveys earned him the status of an expert on the intricacies of the land settlement, at a time when the settlement was the focus of Irish politics. His offices multiplied:

> My experience arising from the management of the Survey, brought me to be one of the Commissioners for setting out Lands to the Army. That employment [brought me] to be one of the Clerks of the Councell (the one third part of the business of that Office, during my Employment in it, consisting of Orders, References, &c. concerning Lands, The Niceties whereof where not obvious to every man [)] All these Employments together, gave me the opportunity, to let the Lord Deputy see, I was ... able to serve him as Secretary.[81]

As was only natural, however, this very 'plurality of offices', and the influence it implied, 'multiplyed Envy almost from every Body'.[82] It suggested, further, a degree of control over the specifics of the settlement that understandably made Petty the focus of the soldiers' various complaints:

> [H]ee became the Robin Goodfellow and Oberon of the country; for, as heretofore domestique servants in the countrey did sett on foot the opinion of Robin Goodfellow and the ffairies, that when themselves had stole junketts, they might accuse Robin Goodfellow for itt; and when themselves had been

[78] Petty, *History*, 184.   [79] Petty, *History*, 208.
[80] Petty, *History*, 52–53; Smyth, *Map-making*, 190–191; Goblet, 1:231–232.
[81] Petty, *Reflections*, 109.   [82] Petty, *Reflections*, 110.

revelling at unseasonable houres of the night, they might say the fairies danced ... in the same manner severall agents of the army [i.e. the soldiers' representatives in the Army Council, which decided apportionments], when they could not give a good accompt to those that entrusted them, to say Dr Petty was the cause of the miscarriage was a ready and credible excuse.[83]

Being the public face of the settlement meant becoming the scapegoat for its shortcomings—'he was reputed the author of whatever displeased any man'.[84]

This suffering tone would become a trademark of Petty's autobiographical commentary, but there was some truth to his complaint. We have seen how his rivalry with Worsley affected his relations with Hartlib and Boyle, but the antagonism had a deeper political dimension. Petty had arrived in Ireland in 1652 under Lord Deputy Fleetwood, as physician to an English army that included a large number of Protestant sectaries (Independents, Baptists, or—later on—Quakers) and staunch republicans. The expulsion of the Long Parliament and Oliver Cromwell's creation as Lord Protector in 1653 seemed to many of these a *de facto* restoration of monarchy. This, combined with restrictions on sectarian worship, tensions between the sects themselves, and frustration with the land settlement, aroused considerable opposition in the army. Whether unwilling or unable, Fleetwood did little to contain the increasingly explosive situation, so that in 1654 Cromwell sent his son Henry to investigate. Henry returned the following year as his father's *de facto* lieutenant (he became Lord Deputy in 1657), charged with containing the sects and seeing the settlement through. Petty became his secretary.[85]

As Fleetwood's role diminished and the army sectarians' political power eroded, Petty—professedly 'a votary neither to any one particular sect or superstition ... nor to any one Faction or party'—found himself caught up in a wider struggle over the shape not only of the Irish settlement but of the English government as well.[86] His antagonists before, during, and after the survey—the most important of whom, besides Worsley himself, were Colonel Richard Lawrence and Sir Hierome Sankey—were Baptists, still attached to Fleetwood and critical of the

[83] Petty, *History*, 209; *Reflections*, 112–116.   [84] Petty, *History*, 208.
[85] See Peter Gaunt, 'Cromwell, Henry (1628–1674)', *Oxford DNB* <http://www.oxforddnb. com/view/article/6764>; Robert W. Ramsey, *Henry Cromwell* (London: Longmans, Green and Co., 1933).
[86] Petty, *Reflections*, 118–119.

Protectorate and of Henry Cromwell.[87] His supporters, on the other hand, were more moderate in their religion and more pliant in their politics; like Petty himself, they quickly attached themselves to the new Lord Deputy. Sir Anthony Morgan, who had helped get the Down Survey approved by the army, had started the Civil War as a Royalist, but served Ireton, Fleetwood, Henry Cromwell, and eventually Charles II equally well; he also shared some of Petty's scientific interests and was connected to the Boyles.[88] Sir Hardress Waller, an army officer and (having signed Charles I's death warrant) regicide, was another of Petty's backers—as well as his future father-in-law—and was linked by marriage to Cromwell's family.[89] Vincent Gookin, Petty's co-commissioner and friend, belonged to an established Protestant planter family, was allied with the Boyles, and served as an MP in several successive Parliaments during the Protectorate; he also replaced Worsley as Surveyor-General in 1658.[90] Such was Petty's network; his battles became theirs, and theirs his.

Transplantation and transformation

Petty had unpleasant dealings with Worsley and, a little later, Sankey, but the dispute that most deeply influenced his subsequent thinking about Ireland apparently involved him only indirectly. This was the 1655 pamphlet debate between Gookin and Lawrence over the proposed 'transplantation into Connacht': the forced removal of various categories of Irish Catholics from their homes in Ulster, Leinster, and Munster across the Shannon. The army and the Protestant sects—would-be new planters who took a very hard line towards the Irish—supported the plan with special enthusiasm. Petty's initial thoughts on the matter were shaped by his survey work: the transplantation made Catholic mearsmen scarce. It is possible, though far from certain, that he went beyond this in discussions with Gookin; a later list of writings includes a 1654 'discourse against

[87] *Reflections*, 88–89, 155–156; Webster, 'Worsley, Benjamin', *Oxford DNB*; Toby Barnard, 'Lawrence, Richard (d. 1684)', *Oxford DNB* <http://www.oxforddnb.com/view/article/16184>.

[88] See Patrick Little, 'Morgan, Sir Anthony (1621–1668)', *Oxford DNB* <http://www.oxforddnb.com/view/article/19216>.

[89] See Patrick Little, 'Waller, Sir Hardress (c.1604–1666)', *Oxford DNB* <http://www.oxforddnb.com/view/article/28557>.

[90] See Patrick Little, 'Gookin, Vincent (c.1616–1659)', *Oxford DNB* <http://www.oxforddnb.com/view/article/11008>.

the Transplantation into Connaught'.[91] Whatever the nature or extent of Petty's contribution, Gookin's arguments against the transplantation, which reflected both his family's experience as planters in Ireland and his own reading and thinking on the subject, influenced Petty's later work in a way few others did. They set the political agenda for 'the transmutation of the Irish into English', and thus to an important degree for political arithmetic itself.[92]

In *The Great Case of Transplantation in Ireland Discussed*, Gookin opposed the transplantation as unjust and futile. Although Irish 'national blood-guilt' putatively justified it, many had been wholly ignorant of the deeds of the 'bloudy rebels'; still more had been led into rebellion by their priests or pushed by their lords. The leaders of the rebellion were either dead already or on the Continent, and as 'for the poor Commons, the Sun never shined (or rather not shined) upon a Nation so completely miserable'—defeated and impoverished, they were no threat to the English. Only a tiny proportion of those nominally required to transplant, further, had even begun to move.[93] But his most compelling arguments were less about justice or logistics than about England's own interests. First, transplantation stored up trouble for the future:

> continuing the Irish Papists, or making them turn Atheists, the knitting again like Worms their divided septs and amities which are now cut in sunder, the entailing barbarousness upon them by such a consociation for ever, the giving them power to rebell again by crouding them all together, and will, by the great injury they conceive they have in this action.[94]

Second, it would do immediate harm to English interests in the country. For one thing, 'The Revenue of Contribution of *Ireland* is generally raised out of Corn, and the Husbandmen of that Corn are generally Irish, the removal therefore of these necessarily infers the failure of that'. More

---

[91] *PSC*, 2:261.

[92] Ted McCormick, '"A Proportionable Mixture": Sir William Petty, Political Arithmetic, and the Transmutation of the Irish', in Coleman A. Dennehy (ed.), *Restoration Ireland: Always Settling and Never Settled* (Aldershot: Ashgate, 2008), 123–139; Patricia Coughlan, 'Counter-currents in colonial discourse: the political thought of Vincent and Daniel Gookin', in Jane H. Ohlmeyer (ed.), *Political Thought in Seventeenth-Century Ireland: Kingdom or Colony*, (Cambridge: Cambridge University Press, 2000), 56–82; Sarah Barber, 'Settlement, Transplantation and Expulsion: a Comparative Study of the Placement of Peoples', in Ciaran Brady and Jane H. Ohlmeyer (eds), *British Interventions in Early Modern Ireland* (Cambridge: Cambridge Universty Press, 2005), 280–298. Fitzmaurice (31) asserts that Petty co-authored Gookin's first pamphlet, but I know of no direct evidence for this.

[93] Gookin, *Great Case*, 6–7, 13, 25.   [94] Gookin, *Great Case*, 26–27.

important, Irish labour was vital to successful plantation in general, and (paradoxically) the land settlement in particular:

> The Souldiers lately disbanded (especially the private Souldiers) have neither Stock, nor Money to buy Stock, nor (for the most part) skill in Husbandry: But by the labours of the Irish on their Lands, together with their own industry, they may maintain themselves, improve their Lands, acquire Stock, and by degrees inure themselves sutably to that course of life: But the transplantation of the Irish leaves these poor mens proportions of Land totally wast[.][95]

The same went for established planters, for urban patricians, and for the merchant class: English prosperity required Irish labour.

Irish labour, in turn, meant mixed settlement—which would both necessitate and facilitate the transformation of the Irish from 'blinded Papists, bloody Rebels' into 'good Protestants, honest Subjects'.[96] Gookin was sanguine: while it was true, as Lawrence pointed out, that mixture had led the Old English to degenerate, 'even that likewise seems to add weight to this expectation, because whatever inducements perswaded the English formerly to turn Irish, the same more strongly invite the Irish now to turn English.' Specifically, 'The Irish numbers (now so abated by Famin, Pestilence, the Sword, and Forein Transportations) are not like to overgrow the English as formerly, and so no fear of their being obnoxious to them hereafter: but being mixed with, they are likelyer to be swallowed up by the English, and incorporated into them'.[97] As Gookin elaborated in *The Author and Case of Transplantating the Irish ... Vindicated*, 'the *English* are what the *Irish* were; rich, high, powerfull, &c. the *Irish* what the *English* were, poor, few, &c.' And, because

> they are few, the *English* many; we may overspread them, and incorporate them into our selves, and so by an onenesse take away the foundation of difference and fear together; we may breed up their youth, habituate them to our customs, cause a disuse of their Language: we have opportunities of communicating better things unto them, and probabilities they may be received, the Priests being gone that did harden, and affliction on them which may soften[.][98]

Gookin confidently predicted that, provided the English abandoned transplantation, allowed mixed settlement, and encouraged conversion through

---

[95] Gookin, *Great Case*, 15–16.   [96] Gookin, *Great Case*, 31.

[97] Gookin, *Great Case*, 19, 21–22.

[98] Gookin, *The Author and Case of Transplanting the Irish into Connaught Vindicated* (London: Printed by A. M. for Simon Miller, 1655), 41.

missionary work, 'a few Centuries will know no difference present, fear none to come, and scarce believe what were pass'd.'[99]

Lawrence was scandalized. In *The Interest of England in the Irish Transplantation, Stated*, he claimed that the transplantation was not an indiscriminate punishment—thanks to various qualifications to the original act, it directly affected only 'Proprietors and men in Arms'—but a precaution for future settlement, made necessary by 'the most horrid, causless Rebellion and bloudy Massacre that hath been heard of, in these latter ages of the World'. Further—and somewhat at odds with his claim that the transplantation was targeted at specific groups—he made clear that 'the Offendors' were 'not particular persons or parties of the *Irish* Nation ... but the whole *Irish* Nation it self, consisting of Nobility, Gentry, Clergie, and Commonalty', their united aim 'to root out and wholly extirpate all *English* Protestants from amongst them'.[100] Mixed settlement was out of the question; 'by their promiscuous and scattered inhabiting amongst the *Irish* who were in all places far the greater number, and in most a hundred to one,' Protestants were 'even as sheep prepared for the slaughter'. Instead:

> I would propose (as essential to the security of the *English* interest and people in *Ireland*) That the *English* inhabitants in that Nation should live together in distinct Plantations or Colonies, separated from the *Irish*; And (so far as the natural advantages of the Countrey, or their own ability will afford it) to maintain Frontier Garrisons upon Lines or Passes, for the security of every Plantation; And to admit no more *Irish* Papists (that they had not eminent grounds to believe were or would be faithful to the *English* interest) to live within them, than what they might have ... visibly at their mercy and dispose when any new disturbance shall arise[.][101]

With adequate support from England, these compact, pure colonies could in time 'make these three Provinces wholely *Brittish*, and thereby enable the *English* Interest in *Ireland* to support itself.'[102] The transplanted Irish would be destroyed as a nation, their territorial organization disrupted, their septs and lordships fatally weakened—though as individuals, compensated for their material losses with Connacht estates, they would barely be inconvenienced.[103] A new, British Ireland would no longer be a 'grave and place of destruction to *English* men (as hetherto)' but 'a nurserie and

[99] Gookin, *Great Case*, 21–22.
[100] Richard Lawrence, *The Interest of England in the Irish Transplantation, Stated* (Dublin: Printed by William Bladen, 1655), 13.
[101] Lawrence, 17–18.   [102] Lawrence, 27.   [103] Lawrence, 22.

breeder of *English*, not onely to supply its own use, but to serve the Interest of *England* elswhere, if occasion should be.'[104]

From Gookin's perspective, Lawrence's hard-line approach, justified or not, was completely misguided because it failed to address the economic basis of settlement. Pronouncing transplantation 'essential' in view of Irish barbarism, Lawrence—an army officer with no experience of Ireland prior to the war—willfully ignored the role Irish labour played in English plantation. In fact, beyond assuring his readers that the 'Irish Nation' as such would be destroyed by transplantation, he said virtually nothing about the fate of the Irish at all. Instead, he imagined a purely English Ireland, a model colony from which the native population simply vanished. As optimistic as Gookin's rival vision of assimilation might seem, by contrast, it was at least grounded in recognition of the fact that, without a massive, unforeseen influx of English settlers, English landlords needed Irish labour. The task that faced the government was not displacing the Irish but securing their loyalty and industry, something best done by encouraging social mixture, religious conversion, and, eventually, assimilation. When he came to write his own proposals for Ireland, Petty would considerably refine Gookin's understanding of what assimilation meant and which mechanisms promoted it, stretching methods and borrowing concepts familiar from his natural-philosophical training and scientific work. But his goal in so doing—the transmutation of the Irish into English—was, in essence, Gookin's, and his pursuit of that goal was based on a reading of Irish economic and social reality that resembled, if it did not derive from, Gookin's own.

Petty on trial

While the transplantation petered out much as Gookin had expected, Petty stuck to the work of survey and distribution, the clerkship of the Council, and his work as Henry Cromwell's secretary—which was, politically speaking, hazardous enough. In May 1658, shortly after the survey of the adventurers' lands was complete, Henry sent Petty to London to try to convince the adventurers' representatives at Grocers' Hall to coordinate their settlement with the army's, using his own surveys.[105] While in London, Petty doubled as Henry's go-between, conveying

104 Lawrence, 28.
105 Petty, *History*, 211; Henry Cromwell to Thurloe, 5 May 1658, in *CSP Thurloe*, 7:114.

confidential communications to the Lord Protector's Secretary of State, John Thurloe, to his close adviser Baron Broghill (Robert Boyle's brother, Roger, later Earl of Orrery), and even to Fleetwood himself. As Henry wrote to Broghill, Petty was 'one, unto whom your lordship may safely communicate such things, as your leisure and indisposition will not permit you to write yourself'—indeed, it was Petty who carried over the Irish army's formal submission to the authority of the new Protector, Richard Cromwell, after Oliver's death.[106] He was a valuable servant in a turbulent time.

By the same token, he was an increasingly convenient target for Cromwell's enemies. 'When the Dr came into England, he found himselfe out run by a libell sent from Ireland', charging him with mismeasuring the army's and adventurers' lands and evidently designed by Petty's foes to scuttle the negotiations. Thurloe wrote to Henry that he 'sett nothing by' the paper 'after soe good a character given of the person by your excellency; and my freedome with him since that will, I trust, evince it to hym'.[107] The accusations affected the adventurers, however, who worried 'they have a very unmeet physicion; not that the Dr wants braines or policy, they much more feare his integrity'; at the outset of their discussions, Petty found them disposed to rely on their own surveys and distributions rather than his. He eventually secured a hearing for his proposals, however, and following a debate at the end of August the adventurers agreed that his survey was better. They appointed him to oversee its application to the distribution of their lands, paying him 1½d per acre for so doing.[108] A unified land settlement was at last coming together, at least on paper, with Petty in charge of both halves; the surveys complete, the distribution was set out by the end of the year. Yet Petty's political troubles were just beginning.

In July, a new 'strange libell' against him, the first of several, had surfaced back in Dublin.[109] By the time he arrived back in Ireland to defend himself, in January 1659, the stakes involved in the political squabbling around him were higher than before. Oliver Cromwell's death the previous September had further loosened the Protectorate's hold on the army and the sects; Richard, who succeeded his father with Henry's backing, attracted none of the personal loyalty that Oliver had inspired.

[106] Henry Cromwell to Thurloe, 5 May 1658; Henry Cromwell to Fleetwood, 5 May 1658; Henry Cromwell to Broghill, [May] 1658, in *CSP Thurloe*, 7:114–115. See also Henry Cromwell to Fleetwood, [June 1659], in *CSP Thurloe*, 7:684.

[107] Thurloe to Henry Cromwell, [July] 1658, *CSP Thurloe*, 7:282.

[108] Petty, *History*, 227–237.   [109] Petty, *History*, 257.

Petty continued his role as go-between, delivering letters from Henry to the new Protector, and he deepened his involvement still further when, with Gookin's help, he was elected in two different ridings (eventually sitting for West Looe, in Cornwall) to the Protectorate Parliament of 1659—part of Richard's effort 'to have such chose as are of peaceable and healing spirits'.[110] The attacks on Petty became accordingly more extreme. Letters surfaced accusing him of plagiarizing work from the Civil Survey, of shortchanging soldiers seeking land; even his religion—a revealing target—was 'rationally conjectured' to be suspect. Rumours that Henry Cromwell planned to sacrifice him made the adventurers suspicious, his tenants slow to pay rent and 'himselfe ... discouraged from improving his estate'. Under pressure, the Lord Lieutenant and Council subjected the army distribution to the oversight of a new committee.[111] Finally, in April 1659, Petty received notice of proceedings against him in Parliament.[112] He was summoned to London to defend himself once more.

Sir Hierome Sankey, a Baptist adherent of Fleetwood and now an MP, brought half a dozen charges against Petty:

1) That he the said Doctor had received Great Bribes.

2) That he had made a Trade of buying Debenters in vast numbers against the Statute.

3) That he had gotten vast summes of Money, and Scopes of Land by Fraud.

4) That he had used many foul Practices, as Surveyour and Commissioner, for setting out Lands.

5) That he and his fellow Commissioners, had placed some Debenters in better places than they could claime, denying Right to others.

6) That he and his fellow Commissioners had totally disposed of the Armies Security; the Debt still remaining chargable on the State.[113]

Compelled to answer by Parliament, Petty took his seat on 19 April and launched his defence two days later. He denied all of the charges, and noted their lack of specificity. Far from profiting illegally, he claimed to

---

[110] Henry Cromwell to Richard Cromwell, 18 September 1658; Thomas Clarges to Henry Cromwell, 11 December 1658, in *CSP Thurloe*, 7:400–401, 559.

[111] Petty, *History*, 257–267.   [112] Petty, *History*, 289.

[113] Petty, *A Brief of the Proceedings between Sr. Hierom Sankey and Dr. William Petty* (London: [s.n.], 1659), 1. The 'Articles of Misdemeanours' are reproduced in Petty, *History*, 290–291.

have lost money; what payment he had received was strictly accounted for in his contract. His land purchases had taken place after his survey work was done, and he had been careful to secure 'exspress and legall leave to buy more debentures then I did'; 'As for necessitating [others] to sell, I conceive that was not possible ... The debentures I bought were of such men as bought to sell again.'[114] Taking the offensive, Petty appealed to the competence of his superiors—including, with stinging irony, some of Sankey's own associates:

> itt seems a foule reflection, not only uppon the present Lord Lieutenant [i.e. Cromwell], but uppon the late Lord Deputy Ffleetwood, and alsoe uppon the Councill, the surveyor [i.e. Worsley], auditor, receiver, and Atturney-Generall ... that they should bee soe frequently and soe grossely cousenned by me of such vast summes; not is it less arrogance for any one stranger in these affaires [i.e. Sankey], not famouse for his sagacity, to smell out those frauds and cousenages, which soe many ministers of State, acting in their proper spheares, could not.[115]

Finally, he stood upon the evidence of his own undisputed scientific and practical accomplishment:

> Sir, if I have not been in a dream these three or four yeares, and drunk with selfe conceit, the practises I have used, both as surveyor and Commissioner, are such as I can glory in, that is to say, to have admeasured ... twenty-two countyes inn thirteene monenths time ... to have done this by the ministery of about one thousand hands, without any suit of law ... to have maintained this survey stiff and stanch against the impugnation of some thousand diligent find-faults ... to have assigned satisfaction for above twenty thousand debentures in such a way as hath admitted of no chopping and changing afterwards, and soe as a slight coppy out of our booke is accepted in courts of justice as a good evidence, meerly by virtue of the naturall justice and validity whereuppon it stands.[116]

Sankey was not so much refuted as outclassed. He responded by sneering at Petty's 'starcht studied speech', but his own was rambling, repetitive, and vague; he had trouble keeping the attention of the House and was finally asked to come back when he had put some specific charges in writing.[117] Petty spent another week in London awaiting further

114 Petty, *History*, 292–4. Petty's speech is reproduced in Petty, *History*, 292–298.
115 Petty, *History*, 295.   116 Petty, *History*, 295–296.
117 Petty, *History*, 298–300; Petty, *Reflections*, 70–74.

proceedings, but was back in Ireland when a new set of eleven articles appeared.

Politics and science

By then, the Protectorate was at an end. While Petty was defending himself in Parliament, the army had forced Richard out. In Ireland, Hardress Waller led a mini-coup preventing the Lord Lieutenant from sending troops to intervene, and when Petty returned to London in June, he carried with him Henry's letter of acquiescence to the restored Rump Parliament. In Ireland Petty had been convinced all along that Sankey's attempt 'to pull me down' had been but 'a small beginning to pull down the Government it self'. Now this had come to pass: Richard and Henry Cromwell were prisoners, and Petty faced the future alone. Nothing ever came of Sankey's eleven articles; the Rump was itself brought down by a second military coup in October, while a second Irish coup in December put Waller temporarily in charge. This prolonged period of uncertainty just before the Restoration of the Stuarts proved important for the development of Petty's political thinking. It was then, in late 1659 and early 1660, that he published an anonymous *Brief Account* of the April proceedings, compiled his massive *History of the Cromwellian Survey*—which bore out his claims by reproducing a vast array of documents relating to the survey—and composed his polemical *Reflections on Some Persons and Things in Ireland*, cast in the form of letters between himself and a couple of anonymous friends from Oxford days. It was then, too, that Petty briefly frequented the 'Rota Club', a political discussion group centred on the republican political theorist James Harrington, best known as the author of *Oceana*. The fruits of these engagements belong to the next chapter, but Petty's initial thoughts on his, and the Protectorate's, political troubles are worth a brief examination.

Historians differ on the merits of Sankey's charges. It is clear enough that Petty gained a great deal from his work—he admitted to a profit of £9,000, while Aubrey reported that his Irish estates were worth £18,000 per annum before the Restoration and that even after the retrenchments of the 1660s, when his income was less than half that, Petty could, 'from Mount Mangorton in the county of Kerry, behold 50,000 acres of his own land.'[118] It is also clear that whatever legal barriers were in place

---

[118] Aubrey, 244; Petty, *Tracts*, v.

could hardly prevent conflicts of interest where one man was surveyor, distributor, and planter. Petty undoubtedly profited from the privileged information he alone commanded.[119] However, it is not so clear that he abused his power in the way Sankey suggested. His genuine conviction that the attacks on him were part of a larger movement against the Protectorate is credible not only because of the people involved but also because that is how Henry Cromwell saw them. Writing to Thurloe before Petty's speech in Parliament, Cromwell anticipated Petty's own defence ('Hee has curiously deluded mee these foure yeares, if he be a knave'), and noted in particular that 'The activeness of Robert Reynolds,' a Hampshire MP opposed to Richard's acceptance as Protector, 'and others in this business, shews, that Petty is not the only marke aimed at'.[120]

Petty's material gains, licit or not, were the vital basis for the freedom he enjoyed throughout the rest of his life to pursue his ideas, but the politics behind his prosecution was hardly less significant for the shape those ideas took. He stressed throughout his *Reflections*—a more explicitly discursive document than the *History*, which deviated only occasionally from a neutral narrative tone—not only that his enemies were the state's, but also that the difference between them was that whereas he was simply 'obedient to my present visible Governours' (a Hobbesian sentiment), they were united by their sectarianism. Yet:

> I would not have you think that I conceive these Gentlemens, (I mean those called Anabaptists,) their Opinions concerning Baptisme or other Speculations … to be the cause of their distasting me, no more then I believe, That 'tis some contrariety in the nature of Wool and Leather, which makes the Clothiers and Weavers, Tuckers and Taylors in a Town I know, so spightful against the Tanners, Curriers, Shooemakers, and Glovers of the same, and that the one are against the other in all matches for Foot-ball, Wrestling, Quaits, Nine-pins, &c. But rather there being the Seeds of discord and contention sown in the very nature of Man since his fall, I think that their own depraved nature … was the cause of what they did.

Religious differences were 'no other than the Marks and Ensigns of the disagreeing parties', masks for the tendency to discord inherent in post-lapsarian man—a point Petty would ultimately apply to Catholics as well

---

[119] Petty himself (*Reflections*, 131–132) indicated the possibilities for fraud his position presented.

[120] Henry Cromwell to Thurloe, 11 April 1659, in *CSP Thurloe*, 7:651. See C. H. Firth (rev. Sean Kelsey), 'Reynolds, Sir Robert (1600/01–1678)', *Oxford DNB* <http://www.oxforddnb.com/view/article/23434>.

as dissenting Protestants.[121] Yet there was more to this than Christian resignation. Man's depravity had regular effects, which the state would do well to heed. Again, Petty wrote:

> 'twas not as Anabaptists that they have so often in this kind troubled the State, themselves, their Neighbours, and Me: But as Separatists from another form, in more visible repute and vogue, in which sense I conceive that even Cathedrall Protestants [i.e. Anglicans] were [h]eretofore as much, and no otherwise troublesome to the preflourishing Papists, and so will the Quaker be to the Anabaptists themselves. Besides, whoever departs from a comonly received Religion ... must be of a jealous discontented, and withall of a busie inquisitive temper, the which will carry him to question and scruple every other thing as well as the *Creed* of his Country[.]

At this point his analysis became almost sociological, contrasting the inquisitive personalities and 'Confederate' habits of 'separatists' of any stripe with the complacency of 'such, who lazily believe as the Church believes, never prying into the Prerogatives, nor scanning the Commands, either of their Civil or Ecclesiastical Magistrates.'[122] He spoke not of the content of belief—indeed, his tone here became astonishingly blithe—but of the natural, predictable behaviour of people in groups: of majorities and minorities. At issue was not salvation in the next life but stability in this one. Here were the beginnings of a political science.

Petty's recourse to man's fall in his explanation of sectarian politics recalls Bacon's own hope—influential among the Hartlibians, as we have seen—that the advancement of learning might restore Adam's knowledge of nature. In fact, Petty's analysis of Anabaptist opposition both to his own work and to the state on whose behalf he performed it can be seen, like the Down Survey itself, as a logical, if not exactly obvious, outgrowth of his Hartlibian activities. Implicit in Petty's account of the Baptist faction's motivations was the notion that there were natural laws behind political no less than physical phenomena, laws that might be discovered and—again, no less than those governing the motion of inert objects—employed by human art for human benefit. As Petty himself put it, explaining why he had 'wandered out of the study of Medicine, with those other Mathematical, Mechanical and Natural Exercises, in which I was once a Busie-body' in the first place, 'I hoped hereby to enlarge my Trade of Experiments from Bodies to Mindes, from the motions of the one, to the manners of the other, thereby to have understood passions as well as

---

[121] Petty, *Reflections*, 90–91.   [122] Petty, *Reflections*, 92–93.

fermentations, and consequently to have been as pleasant a Companion to my ingenious friends, as if such an intermission from Physicks had never been'.[123] His background in mechanical philosophy and physiology, not to mention his association with Hobbes, no doubt predisposed him to view the passions of human minds, like the motions of human bodies, as rule-governed and thus subject to scientific inquiry. But his scientific and political experience in Cromwellian Ireland supplied the empirical basis for his first serious reflections on the subject.

Of course, it did much more than that. The Down Survey is chiefly known neither because of its contribution to the development of political arithmetic nor even because of its innovative division of labour, but because it was the rock upon which successive Acts of Settlement founded two centuries of 'Protestant Ascendancy' in Ireland. It enabled the redistribution of approximately 8,400,000 acres of land from Catholic to Protestant owners—transforming Ireland's social geography and cementing English colonial domination of the island. Irish Catholic landownership, roughly 80 per cent in 1600 and still nearly 60 per cent in 1641, was reduced to 22 per cent in 1688; the Cromwellian settlement, and its instrument, Petty's survey, made that difference.[124] Behind these numbers lay a still wider and longer-term social and economic transformation: the enclosure and improvement of lands, the extension of infrastructure and commercial networks, the reorientation of agricultural production to the demands of the (English) market, and the growth of trade. Petty's survey, which reduced the Irish estates to standard units of size and gradations of value, and whose progress fed speculation in land debentures, commodified Irish land—just as Gookin's pamphlets, which played down national and religious differences, emphasized the commodity status of Irish labour. Colonization and commercialization went hand in hand. Petty, and the tendencies his work both aided and embodied, changed Ireland.

Ireland, by the same token, changed Petty. At age twenty-nine he had been a callow young physician, fresh from Oxford. At thirty-six he was a wealthy landowner, the protégé of Henry Cromwell and the architect of the Irish land settlement. Even by mid-seventeenth-century standards, his rise was meteoric. Yet he retained many of his old concerns and at least a few of his old friendships. In fact, the most striking feature of Petty's life between 1652 and 1660 may be the way he adapted existing interests and skills to new tasks. The Down Survey was both a radical novelty in an Irish context and a logical extension of Petty's Hartlibian projects.

[123] Petty, *Reflections*, 15.   [124] Smyth, *Map-making*, 377.

Likewise, his extension of experimental philosophy from bodies to minds was at once a departure and a continuation. Most important, as far as the development of political arithmetic is concerned, the consideration of socio-economic relationships Petty was shortly to embark upon was not so very far removed from the analysis of sectarian behaviour he put forward in his *Reflections*, which was itself cast at least partly in Baconian terms. His position, on the other hand, had changed dramatically. He had become what we would call an expert—an officeholder, but one whose claim to authority derived less from his office than from his experience and technical abilities. More than that, he had acquired enough wealth to remain an expert out of office. He was beginning to fashion himself into something new: a political arithmetician.

CHAPTER 4

Science and Policy in the Restoration

Formation of government is the creation of a political creature after the image of a philosophical creature, or it is an infusion of the soul or faculties of a man into the body of a multitude.[1]

By 1660 Petty's writing already suggested both the naturalistic approach to social and political problems and many of the motivating concerns that would mark political arithmetic. Yet he only started to write political arithmetic a decade later, and he did so in part with purposes framed and tools forged after the Restoration. Perhaps the most important of these was the idea of population, not merely as a productive or political resource endowed with good or bad characteristics but also as an object of precise quantitative knowledge and calibrated manipulation. Elements of this were visible in the 1648 *Advice* (which applied judicial astrology to public health) and 1659 *Reflections* (which linked the behaviour of sectaries to their minority status); the mid-1650s debate over the transplantation into Connacht, too, had involved the problem of settling different proportions of different kinds of people securely. But only with John Graunt's 1662 *Natural and Political Observations … upon the Bills of Mortality*—a work Petty helped produce—was population reduced to the kind of 'number, weight, and measure' political arithmetic employed.[2] Likewise, political arithmetic's treatment of economic questions both on Petty's Interregnum work and on his 1662 *Treatise of Taxes and Contributions*, itself directed towards the familiar goal of 'universal Reformation'.[3] Reformation remained a matter of invention as well as legislation, and under the auspices of the

---

[1] James Harrington (ed. J. G. A. Pocock), *The Commonwealth of Oceana* and *A System of Politics* (Cambridge: Cambridge University Press, 1992), 273.

[2] Graunt, *Natural and Political Observations, Mentioned in a following Index, and made upon the Bills of Mortality* (London: Printed by Thomas Roycroft for James Martyn, James Allestry, and Thomas Dicas, 1662).

[3] Petty, *A Treatise of Taxes and Contributions* (London: Printed for N. Brooke, 1662), 9.

new Royal Society, Petty's mechanical career reached its peak. At the same time, thanks to James Harrington, among others, Petty's notion of 'policy' and its relationship to science changed significantly.

This was also the decade when 'Dr Petty' became 'Sir William'—a coffee-house regular, the friend of Pepys and Evelyn and the occasional guest of Charles II, the Duke of York, and the Duke of Ormond; and when, at the advanced age of forty-four, he married and started a family. Finally, these were the years that set the political stage for political arithmetic: the harsh religious uniformity imposed at the Restoration, the disasters of mid-decade (war with the Dutch from 1664, the plague of 1665, the Great Fire of London), mercantilist measures against Irish trade, and, at decade's end, the growing perception that a Francophile, Catholicizing court threatened English freedom, Protestant supremacy, and—not the least of Petty's concerns—the Irish land settlement. Petty entered the Restoration with the outlook that governed political arithmetic and many of the materials that went into it. Only at the end of the decade, prompted by a gathering sense of political crisis, mobilizing new social connections, and armed with a new way of thinking about human collectivities and a conception of 'natural' policy that linked the art of government to the practice of natural philosophy, would Petty consolidate his extension of Baconian science from bodies to minds and from inert objects to living populations.

Surviving the Restoration

The Restoration of the monarchy, consummated by Charles II's entry into London in late May 1660, ended nearly two years of political turmoil following Oliver Cromwell's death. What it would mean for Petty was not immediately clear. As a servant first of Parliament and then of the Protectorate, he was obviously vulnerable to the royalist reaction. Yet as Ireland's surveyor he was insulated both by his expertise and by the peculiarity of the Irish situation. The complexity of the conflicts of the 1640s, which at various stages had most Irish Catholics—as well as some Protestants—pitting themselves against both Parliamentarian and Royalist forces, precluded any simple revocation of the Cromwellian settlement. The settlement itself was less acceptable to Catholics, rebel and royalist alike, than to Protestants, whether Royalist or Parliamentarian; thanks to the active trade in land debentures, established 'Old Protestant' planter families, not Cromwellian soldiers, grabbed most of the confiscated land. After a December 1659 coup put Charles Coote and Roger Boyle (Baron Broghill), leading representatives of the Old Protestant interest, in charge of Dublin Castle, an Irish Convention met in February 1660 and offered its submission to Charles. This set the wheels in motion for the English Convention Parliament, which voted to restore the king on 1 May. Thus the beneficiaries of the Cromwellian settlement in Ireland became the founders of the Stuart Restoration.[4]

We last saw Petty in London, fending off Baptists with his *Reflections on some Persons and Things in Ireland*. The printing, distribution, and reception of the *Reflections* occupied him on and off throughout 1660, as its purposes widened from confuting Worsley and Sankey to justifying the survey and its architect to a new regime. Petty's correspondence with his cousin John—who acted as his all-purpose agent and informer in Dublin—shows the political survivor working at full tilt. The book went to press in early January 1660; by late February ten copies were on their way via John Petty to Coote, Broghill, and Hardress Waller, among others; not three weeks later a further forty-five followed, and more would come.[5] Petty's strategy apparently worked: 'I am glad to heare my books Rellish so well', he wrote John at the end of March; his antagonists were now 'laught all over the nacion.'[6]

Yet while the political order remained unsettled Petty worried 'that few of us shall keep our lands'.[7] He also worried about the impression his politicking made, and in his *Reflections* defended his conduct towards his former patron. 'I finding the Lord *Henry Cromwell* to be a person of much Honour and Integrity to his trust, as also of a firm faith and zeal to God and his Church, and withall to have translated me from a stranger into his bosome', Petty wrote, 'I did (as in justice and gratitude I was bound) serve him faithfully and industriously'.[8] Acknowledging all Henry had done for him, Petty stressed that he had made sacrifices of his own. 'I was his Secretary without one penny of reward, I neglected my own

[4] Tim Harris, 'Restoration Ireland—Themes and Problems', in Dennehy, 2. See Aidan Clarke, *Prelude to Restoration in Ireland: The End of the Commonwealth, 1659–1660* (Cambridge: Cambridge University Press, 1999), and Toby Barnard, 'The Protestant Interest, 1641–1660', in Ohlmeyer (ed.) *Ireland from Independence*, 218–240; regarding the settlement in particular see Karl Bottigheimer, 'The Restoration Land Settlement in Ireland: A Structural View', *Irish Historical Studies* 18:69 (1972), 1–21; Kevin McKenny, 'The Restoration Land Settlement in Ireland: A Statistical Interpretation', in Dennehy, 35–52.

[5] Petty to John Petty, 3 and 28 January, 21 and 28 February and 8 and 20 March 1660, BL MS Add. 72850, ff.4–5, 9–10, 15–19.

[6] Petty to John Petty, 31 March 1660, BL MS Add. 72850, f.43r.

[7] Petty to John Petty, 31 March 1660, BL MS Add. 72850, f.43r.

[8] Petty, *Reflections*, 119–120.

private affaires to promote his ... and I serv'd his friends *caeteris paribus*, before his enemies.' So that Henry 'should not be jealous of me, I became as a stranger to other Grandees ... when he was shaken I was content to fall; I did not lessen him to his Enemies to magnifie my self.' Petty had not abandoned Henry. But with Henry's fall the relationship—a political marriage—had come to a natural end:

> I never promised *to live and die* with him, which is the common Phrase; Yet I did stay to see his then interest which I had espoused, dead and buried, Esteeming that then, and when a convenient time of mourning was over, That If I should marry another Interest, and be as fixt unto it as I had been to his, I should do no more then I alwayes in his prosperity told him I would do, if I saw occasion.[9]

This may not sound like a very profound loyalty, but whatever its romantic deficiencies it was both practical and honest given the circumstances. In fact, Petty continued to defend Henry's interests well after the Restoration.[10]

Indeed, Petty's ability to help both himself and his fallen friends depended on courting those in power. He awaited the king's return in May 1660 with resignation: 'Let Nature Worke, Things must have their Vicissitudes, They must Ebbe & flow.'[11] But on a personal score the transition proved unexpectedly smooth. In August Petty wrote to his cousin that 'I have a little interest in my Lord of Ormond [James Butler, Marquis (later Duke) of Ormond, soon Lord Lieutenant of Ireland] Insomuch as hee was pleased Voluntarily to say that Hee had espoused me for his friend and would make mee the King's Servant.' At the same time, he sounded a note of caution: 'You cannot Imagine What selling of places there is, what advantages taken of holding by beneplacitum, & how the having been of the parlaments party is a sufficient Malè se gessit.'[12] After Charles's 'Gracious Declaration' of 30 November 1660 confirmed the adventurers' and soldiers' claims, Petty was more optimistic, and in early February 1661 he enjoyed a lengthy audience with the king.[13] He

---

⁹ Petty, *Reflections*, 120.

¹⁰ In February 1661 Petty persuaded Charles II to confirm Henry's claims, and he (and Robert Wood) continued to act on Henry's and his widow's behalf for many years: BL MS Add. 72850, ff.29v, 116–117, 147–150.

¹¹ Petty to John Petty, 22 May 1660, BL MS Add. 72850, f.64r. John Graunt wrote John Petty on 26 May 1660 that describing the King's reception at Dover 'would seem more like a Romance, then a History' (BL MS Add. 72850, f.66); Petty simply noted that 'his Ma[jes]ty was heartily rec[eive]d in London.' Petty to John Petty, 29 May 1660, BL MS Add. 72850, f.68r.

¹² Petty to John Petty, 8 August 1660, BL MS Add. 72850, f75r.

¹³ Petty to John Petty, 4 and 22 December 1660, BL MS Add. 72850, ff.96 and 100–101.

seized this opportunity to justify his work for the Protectorate: 'I was since my last with the King, hee seemed earnest enough to speake with mee, I began with a small prologue, among other things telling him, that I never accepted of any trust out of desire or designe to doe him harm, nor had I ever broken any to do him service'. Charles, however, was more interested in Petty's science than his politics:

[B]ut the King seeming little to mind apologies as needlesse replied [But Dr, why have you left of your Enquiries into the Mechanick of Shipping?] In briefe hee held mee ½ an hower before 40 lords upon the philosophy of shipping, loadstones, [shreevd?] guns, the feathering of arrowes, the vegetation of plants the history of trades &c, about all which I discoursed Intrepidè and I hope not very contemptibly. In fine Wee parled faire & not without cleere signes of future good acceptance.[14]

Before Petty could finish the letter, 'the Marquis of Ormond met mee and told mee hee had expresse Order to bring mee to the King' once again.[15]

The first meeting had gone well. Two weeks later, Petty reported that he 'was this day private with the King halfe an hower in his closet. I thinke super totam Materiam That I am in the State of grace to say No More.' Crucially, 'I am also one of the Commissioners' charged with overseeing the settlement. 'I heare Knights swarme', he added, 'I think I could bee a knight also'.[16] In late March he pronounced himself 'not much apprehensive' about the land settlement: 'There will be a terrible scramble and much begging of Estates, but my opinion is that most of the Orders will come to nothing at long runn.'[17] A week later, he rejoiced at 'The Kings acknowledgement of mee by actions Words & his gracious letters, by my ancient right to my lands by the declaration and Instruccions', as well as 'by my being in the Commission & by my presence' in the Irish Parliament—a useful defender of Protestant land claims, he was elected MP for Inistioge in Kilkenny.[18] Before leaving England he was indeed knighted, on 11 April. Sir William Petty's 'good acceptance' appeared complete.

The Gracious Declaration proved too good to be true. Bowing to Protestant lobbying, it confirmed the adventurers' and soldiers' claims—in

---

[14] Petty to John Petty, 5 February 1661, BL MS Add. 72850, f.26r. The second set of square brackets is Petty's, marking a quotation.

[15] Petty to John Petty, 5 February 1661, BL MS Add. 72850, f.26v.

[16] Petty to John Petty, 19 February 1661, BL MS Add. 72850, f.29.

[17] Petty to John Petty, 23 March 1661, BL MS Add. 72850, f.37.

[18] Petty to John Petty, 30 March 1661, BL MS Add. 72850, f.114v. He had also been returned for Enniscorthy, in Wexford; Barnard, 'Petty, Sir William', Oxford DNB.

practice, securing Old Protestant gains from the debenture trade. To the horror of Catholics and royalists, it thus made the Cromwellian settlement the starting point for any readjustments. But the readjustments were massive: Catholics innocent of rebellion were to be reinstated, as were royalists in service before 1649 and various individual nominees. Worse, Charles granted land freely to assorted favourites, starting with his brother James, Duke of York. The 1662 Act of Settlement put the Declaration into effect, establishing a Court of Claims that judged most of the Catholic landowners it heard innocent; within a year Parliamentary outrage forced its suspension, the vast majority of claims still pending.[19] There was clearly not enough land to go around. Finally, in 1665, an Act of Explanation cut the Gordian knot, compensating innocents and royalists by forcing Cromwellian claimants to retrench their estates by a third. The legislation was largely complete, but the lawsuits were just beginning.[20]

Having taken up his seat in Dublin, Petty returned to London in August 1661 to negotiate the terms of the Bill of Settlement.[21] He succeeded in ensuring that 'reprisals' to the dispossessed were to be drawn first from unallotted lands, and the Act confirmed his own holdings as of 7 May 1659. However, the Court of Claims quickly found many more innocents than unassigned land could compensate. Petty, like many others, lost a considerable portion of his estate in 1663, and a further third following the Act of Explanation two years later. (Aubrey, though not the most reliable source, estimated that Petty's rental income declined from £18,000 per annum in 1659 to £7,000–£8,000 — still a comfortable living.)[22] Even after all this, a dispute over quit-rents with the farmers of the Irish revenue dragged on for years. This near-constant litigation did produce some colourful episodes. One of Petty's friends' favourite stories came out of a 1661–1662 dispute with Sir Alan Brodrick (an old royalist and now Surveyor-General), over lands in Limerick. Here is John Evelyn's version:

> He is, besides, courageous; on which account, I cannot but note a true story of him, that when Sir Aleyn Brodrick sent him a challenge upon a difference betwixt them in Ireland, Sir William, though exceedingly purblind, accepted the challenge, and it being his part to propound the weapon, desired his

---

[19] In June 1663, Petty sent the Earl of Anglesey a list of 'Reasons why 3/5 of all the Lands belonging Anno 1641 to Irish Papists should be forfeited'; BL MS Add. 72878, ff.74–75.

[20] On contemporary and later attitudes to the settlement, see Michael Perceval-Maxwell, 'The Irish Land Settlement and its Historians' and Coleman A. Dennehy, 'The Irish Parliament, 1661–1666', in Dennehy, 19–34 and 53–68 respectively.

[21] Fitzmaurice, 125–139.   [22] Aubrey, 244; Petty, *Tracts*, v; BL MS Sloane 2903, f.17.

antagonist to meet him with a hatchet, or axe, in a dark cellar; which the other, of course, refused.[23]

Petty accepted a second challenge years later, after differences with the revenue farmers moved him to give one of their men, a certain Colonel Vernon, a public caning—though, again, no actual duel resulted.[24] Such high-spirited moments aside, however, Petty's legal wrangles were a time-consuming, costly, and counterproductive headache.

Harrington and natural policy

Petty's attention was turned from mechanical invention and experimental philosophy to the problems of administration—from bodies to minds—by his deepening involvement in Ireland's politics. Yet he brought to his political thinking much the same empirical approach, and indeed some of the same reforming aims, developed in his scientific work. The Survey itself—and the maps whose production Petty pursued at great expense from late 1659 into 1661 (his atlas, *Hiberniae Delineatio*, would appear only in 1685)—was both a political instrument and, ideally, part of a new-model natural history that put precise measurement and exhaustive observation in the service of a neo-Baconian vision of improvement.[25] Indeed, it was a political instrument *because* it was a natural history. Petty's 'Phytologicall Letter' to Hartlib had proposed a natural history of plants that would facilitate their manipulation. This natural history, in the same way, would extend both knowledge and control of Ireland.

Before and after the Restoration, Petty developed a number of schemes designed to extend or duplicate his Irish survey, among them the so-called '1659 Census' of Ireland, now recognized as abstracts of the 1660 and 1661 Irish poll tax returns.[26] Assisted in 1661 by his cousin John (now

---

[23] Evelyn, 2:102–103. Evelyn retold the story when giving a description of Petty's life to William Wotton: Evelyn to Wotton, 12 September 1703, in Evelyn, 3:394–395. Aubrey (243, 246–247) mistakenly identifies Petty's antagonist as Sir Hierome Sankey; see Fitzmaurice, 151–152.

[24] Fitzmaurice, 176–178.

[25] See Petty's correspondence with John Petty, who communicated with Thomas Taylor on his behalf: BL MS Add. 72850 ff.9–10, 26, 37, 39–40, 57–58, 72–73, 75–76, 82–83; Petty, *A Geographicall Description of the Kingdom of Ireland* (London: Published by Francis Lamb, 1685) and *Hiberniae Delineatio* (London: [s.n.], 1685). The production of the Down Survey maps, the barony maps and the atlas is discussed in Goblet, 1:270–325 and 2:1–177.

[26] Seamus Pender (ed.), *A Census of Ireland, circa 1659* (Dublin: Irish Manuscripts Commission, 2002). See William Smyth's introduction to the book, 'Wrestling with Petty's Ghost: The

Deputy Surveyor-General), John's assistant (and Down Survey veteran) Thomas Taylor, Robert Wood, and others, and making use of his own Parliamentary position, Petty tried to gather the kind of social and demographic information that would complete his picture of Irish society. He outlined what he wanted in a letter to John shortly after the latter's appointment:

> Now you have beaten up your drums and have hands enough, let there bee made a generall catalogue of all the barronyes in each county, of the parishes in each barony & all the usual denominacions in each parishe as they appear in any of your 53, or 64-civill survey[s] or in our owne admeasurement Whether the same bee forfeited or not, church crowne Hospitall schoole land &c.

> Let there bee also lists of all the proprietors, protest[an]t or papist as they stand in any of the said surveyes. Let these bee ranged also according to Provinces countys baronyes parrishes & denominacions. Let other lists of the same bee made I mean as well of lands as proprietors alphebetically. With a number of reference to the other liste.

> These are great Works but I conceive tis in Effect done, in our Abstract bookes ...[27]

The resulting 'census', though incomplete, remains a major source of information concerning the shape of Irish society in the wake of the Interregnum. It tabulated, for each place in each parish in each barony, the number of proprietors, the names of the more important ('Tituladoes'), and the numbers of English (or 'English & Scots') and Irish; it then listed the 'Principal Irish [sometimes '& Scotch'] Names' in each barony and gave the total number of proprietors, English and Irish.[28] It testified to Petty's goal of a complete picture of Ireland's physical, social, and political geography.

It also hinted at a turn to economic questions. Yet Petty's new enthusiasm for such topics as taxation, trade, employment, and money originated in and remained tied to his scientific and political concerns, as his 1661 proposal for a 'Registry of Lands, commodities and Inhabitants', an economic

Origins, Nature and Relevance of the So-Called "1659 Census"', iii–lxii; Smyth, 'Society and Settlement in Seventeenth Century Ireland: The Evidence of the "1659 Census"', in William J. Smyth and Kevin Whelan (ed.), *Common Ground: Essays on the Historical Geography of Ireland, Presented to T. Jones Hughes, M.A., M.R.I.A.* (Cork: Cork University Press, 1988), 55–83.

[27] Petty to John Petty, 19 March 1661, BL MS Add, 72850, f.35r.

[28] The census apparently judged between English and Irish on the basis of names alone, as occasional uncertainties reveal: the lists for the Barony of Toome in County Antrim, for example, includes 'Brownes not all Irish, 12', and the question 'Cunningham, query whether Irish, 6'; Pender, 7.

'Office of Address', illustrates.[29] Some such registry was a commonplace solution to Ireland's economic problems; Robert Wood proposed one himself in 1661.[30] Wood's land registry—like Petty's—would certify titles and record encumbrances, encouraging plantation by restraining fraud in the land market, promoting credit by making real property acceptable collateral, and facilitating trade by redressing a currency shortage. But for Petty, unlike Wood, the instrument had much wider scientific and political purchase: it would show the king 'whether his People (that is the Naturall and true riches of his Kingdome) multiply or diminish, grow richer or poorer', revealing 'The Impediments as well of Forraigne Commerce as of Domestick plantation and manufacture' and facilitating both equitable taxation and effective government: 'when wee have a cleere view of all persons and things, with their powers & familyes, wee shall bee able to Methodize and regulate them to the best advantage of the publiq and of particular persons.'[31] It was not just a useful regulation; it was a tool of scientific government, a way of methodizing both policy and people.

In this respect, Petty's thinking reflected not just his natural-philosophical background and his Irish concerns but also the more recent influence of James Harrington. Best known for his 1656 *Oceana*, Harrington blamed the turmoil of the Civil War and Interregnum on the widening distribution of landownership since the sixteenth century, which had impoverished the nobility and given commoners property without representation, fatally destabilizing the monarchy. Power naturally followed landed property: 'such ... as is the proportion or balance of dominion or property in land, such is the nature of the empire.'[32] Without restrictions on land transfers, no form of government would survive for long. He therefore advocated an 'equal commonwealth' whose 'foundation' was an 'agrarian law' restricting the accumulation of land and maintaining the balance of property in the people, and whose 'superstructure' was the rotation of office, which relieved political passions through the regular use of the ballot.[33] A constitution framed in accordance with the natural laws of politics could make a commonwealth 'immortal, seeing the people, being the materials, never

---

[29] BL MS Add. 72878, ff.36–44v, printed in *PP*, 1:77–90. The registry remained a pet idea of Petty's throughout the 1670s an 1680s; BL MS Add. 72865, ff.24–28 and 72880, ff.42–45v.

[30] HP, 33/1/73a–74b. See also an anonymous 'Proposall ... in order to the Setlement of all mens estates in Ireland', dating from 1678–1682, in Bodl. MS Carte 53, f.6. For an argument against similar registries in England, see Fabian Philipps, *The Reforming Registry* (London: Printed by Tho. Newcomb for the author, 1662). Philipps's tract had been written in 1656.

[31] BL MS Add, 72878, ff.36–44v; *PP*, 1:77–90.   [32] Harrington, *Oceana*, 11.

[33] Harrington, *Oceana*, 21, 101, 114, 123.

dies, and the form, which is motion, must without opposition be endless.'[34] A constitution that neglected the agrarian law or put a stop to rotation would dissolve the polity in faction.[35]

Harrington propagated his ideas in print and through the discussions of the 'Rota' club, which met in late 1659 and early 1660 at Miles's Coffee House in New Palace Yard on the River Thames Embankment.[36] These debates challenged both monarchy and godly conceptions of the commonwealth such as John Milton's and attracted the satire of royalist pamphleteers; one such, purporting to offer *The Censure of the Rota Upon Mr Miltons Book, Entituled, The Ready and Easie way to Establish A Free Common-wealth*, caricatured both the intellectual energy and the formality of Rota meetings, which included putting proposals to the ballot:

> it is our usuall custom to dispute every thing, how plain or obscure soever, by knocking Argument against Argument, and tilting at one another with our heads (as Rams fight) untill we are out of breath, and then refer it to our wooden Oracle the *Box*; and seldom anything, how slight soever, hath appear'd, without some Patron or other to defend it.[37]

Or, as Henry Stubbe—later a virulent critic of the Royal Society—put it, 'A question here, though nere so rude,/Is so belabourd, and so tewd [?],/And into sundry pieces hewd.'[38] In these meetings Petty took an active and critical part. Samuel Pepys's diary entry for 10 January 1660 records a trip 'to the Coffee-house, where … a great confluence of gentlemen', including Harrington and Petty, enjoyed 'admirable discourse till 9 at night.'[39] Aubrey later recalled that 'Sir W. Petty was a Rota man, and troubled Mr James Harrington with his arithmetical proportions, reducing politics to numbers.'[40]

---

[34] Harrington, *Oceana*, 99.   [35] Harrington, *Oceana*, 123.

[36] See H. M. Höpfl, 'Harrington, James (1611–1677)', *Oxford DNB* <http://www.oxforddnb.com/view/article/12375>.

[37] J.H., *The Censure of the Rota Upon Mr Miltons Book, Entituled, the Ready and Easie Way to Establish a Free Common-Wealth* (London: Paul Giddy, Printer to the Rota, 1660), 3. 'J. H.' is meant to suggest James Harrington. Milton's book had first appeared earlier in the year: Milton, *The Readie & Easie Way to Establish a Free Commonwealth* (London: Printed by T. N. for the Author, 1660).

[38] Henry Stubbe, *The Rota: Or, News from the Common-Wealths-Mens Club* (London: [s.n.], 1660), [1].

[39] Pepys (ed. Robert Latham and William Matthews), *The Diary of Samuel Pepys*, 11 vols (London: G. Bell and Sons, 1970–1983), 1:14.

[40] Aubrey, 247.

As with Hobbes's influence on Petty, so with Harrington's: points
of contact are not proofs of discipleship. Interestingly, however, Petty's
most 'Harringtonian' manuscript—undated but probably produced during
the Rota's run—was a scheme of government couched as a critique of
Hobbes.[41] It began by taking Hobbes to task for the questions he had
asked in weighing monarchy against republican government: which may
better 'endow its … sons with riches'; which punishes innocent men more
often; in which do 'citizens possess more liberty'; whether 'matters of
state' are best discussed by many or by few.[42] Petty proposed a new set of
questions, which approached the form of state from a more empirical and
practical standpoint:

1) Is it possible looking at historical events, to imply that democracies
   last longer than monarchies; smashed or dissolved neither by internal
   inactivity nor by outside force?

2) Whether the citizens are usually both universally and individually wealthier? Whether they perish more rarely through hunger and need; whether
   they seek new colonies and whether they are enlisted in a mercenary army?
   Whether more often than not fraud and robbery occur in a monarchy
   than during popular rule? Whether the mechanical arts flourish more so
   in one state or the other? Or whether useful inventions are more frequent
   in one state or the other?

3) Whether also a greater number of citizens is able to be conscripted in
   an army of a monarchy or a democracy, for both defensive and offensive
   purposes?

4) Whether the same number of parents may produce more offspring in
   exactly the same time? Further, whether more people join the state than
   leave it?

Finally, which was 'more pleasant to human nature', and what administrative difference did it make?[43]

The first question has an especially Harringtonian ring, and, rather
than answering, Petty spent the remainder of the paper outlining an ideal
state along Oceanic lines, paying particular attention to the administrative

---

[41] BL MS Add. 72898, ff.89–92; *PP*, 2:35–39. The original is in Latin; an English translation
(used here) appears in Frank Amati and Tony Aspromourgos, 'Petty *contra* Hobbes: A Previously
Untranslated Manuscript', *Journal of the History of Ideas* 46:1 (1985), 127–132. Harris tentatively
dates the paper to the 1660s. Given its Harringtonian flavour, and since Petty's administrative
speculations took a monarchical turn with Charles II's return, it seems likely to date more specifically from the period of political uncertainty during which the Rota met (i.e., between October
1659 and February 1660), when it might have functioned as the basis for a coffee-house debate.
[42] Amati and Aspromourgos, 129.   [43] Amati and Aspromourgos, 129–130.

and electoral divisions of the population.[44] None of this made Petty a republican (any more than Hartlib made him a Puritan, or Leiden a Cartesian); the paper seems designed to provide an evening's discussion at Miles's, and no more. However, it does show Petty deeply engaged with Harrington's thinking at the very moment his own thoughts were turning to economic and political topics.

Like Hobbes, but at a more critical time, Harrington showed Petty a bridge—or, rather, two bridges—between natural philosophy and the business of the state. First, Harrington's notion of the balance of property underlined the connection Petty had already begun to draw between quantification and government, while recasting it in economic rather than straightforwardly political terms. Second, and more importantly, Harrington saw the relationship between political possibilities and natural constraints in terms closely analogous to those in which Petty himself, following Bacon, saw the relationship between nature and art. The statesman, like the natural philosopher, respected nature's dictates:

> To make Principles or Fundamentals, belongeth not unto Men, unto Nations, nor unto humane Laws. To build upon such Principles or Fundamentals as are apparently laid by GOD in the inevitable necessity or Law of Nature, is that which truly appertaineth unto Men, unto Nations and unto humane Laws. To make any other Fundamentals, and then build upon them, is to build Castles in the Air.[45]

Both the statesman and the philosopher, however, built upon these natural foundations, and what they built mattered. Just as a drainage pump could make bog land productive, so a well-formed government 'maketh evil men good.'[46] In a grotesque but revealing piece of imagery, Harrington compared the workings of a rightly ordered commonwealth to those of a Roman carnival pageant:

> I saw one which represented a Kitchin, with all the proper Utensils in use and action. The Cooks were all Cats and Kitlings, set in such frames, so ty'd and so ordered, that the poor creatures could make no motion to get loose, but the same caused one to turn the spit, another to baste the meat, a third to scim the pot, and a fourth to make green-sauce. If the Frame of your Commonwealth be not such as causeth every one to perform his

[44] Amati and Aspromourgos, 130–132.
[45] Harrington, *Aphorisms Political* (London: printed by J. C. for Henry Fletcher, 1659), 12.
[46] Harrington, *Aphorisms*, 2.

certain function as necessarily as this did the Cat to make green-sauce, it is not right.[47]

The mechanism of the commonwealth could not violate the laws of nature any more than a pump could, but both harnessed natural forces to create effects nature alone would never produce. A perpetual-motion machine constructed by men schooled in natural principles, the commonwealth *improved* its materials, human and non-human alike. Petty did not put down science to take up political economy—the tasks of government and of natural philosophy, as he understood them, simply merged. Over the next decade or so, by fits and starts, he developed a framework for policy that combined social analysis and natural knowledge to improve both the human multitude and its natural surroundings.

Graunt and the natural and political observations

The first half of 1662 saw the appearance not only of Petty's *Treatise of Taxes* but also of John Graunt's *Natural and Political Observations … upon the Bills of Mortality*, still regarded as the bible of statistical demography. Graunt's work significantly influenced Petty (who oversaw production of an expanded fifth edition in 1676) and has even been attributed to him.[48] Briefly, there seems no reason to deny Graunt's authorship and every reason to think Petty helped. The two were old friends with common interests who habitually shared their thoughts; at the very least, Petty furnished data from Romsey and shaped the book's treatment of medical questions. On the other hand, the book handled statistics more adeptly than Petty's later work, and it is unclear why Petty would dissemble writing something he obviously admired.[49] Several of Petty's friends claimed it was his—Robert Southwell congratulated Petty for printing his 1683 *Observations on the Dublin Bills of Mortality* under the name of 'the Observator on the London Bills', which Southwell took as a public

[47] Harrington, *A Discourse upon This Saying: The Spirit of the Nation is not yet to be trusted with Liberty* (London: Printed by J. C. for Henry Fletcher, 1659), 12.

[48] *EW*, 317–318. On the authorship question, see C. H. Hull, 'Graunt or Petty?', *Political Science Quarterly* 11:1 (1896), 105–32; M. Greenwood, 'Graunt and Petty', *Journal of the Royal Statistical Society* 91:1 (1928), 79–85; Ian Sutherland, 'John Graunt: A Tercentenary Tribute', *Journal of the Royal Statistical Society*, Series A, 126:4 (1963), 537–556; D. V. Glass, 'John Graunt and His Natural and Political Observations', *Proceedings of the Royal Society of London* 19:1 (1964), 63–100; P. D. Groenewegen, 'Authorship of the *Natural and Political Observations upon the Bills of Mortality*', *Journal of the History of Ideas* 28:4 (1967), 601–602.

[49] Pearson, *History of Statistics*, 38–40; Reungoat, 33–42.

acknowledgement that 'the spiritt of Sir William Petty and not of John Graunt [had] presided' in the earlier work.[50] This 'admission' is at best ambiguous, however, and everywhere else—including subsequent letters to Southwell—Petty consistently spoke of the 1662 book as Graunt's.[51] That his friends' claims postdated Graunt's conversion to Catholicism, impoverishment in the Great Fire of London, and death in 1674 casts further doubt on their value. Southwell's disparagement of 'Poore John' in 'his purgatory'—in his demographic work 'The good man was ... like a dwarfe mounted on an Elephant'—establishes little besides genteel Protestant contempt for a lowly Catholic tradesman.[52]

In a sense, it hardly matters whether Petty wrote or merely contributed to, used, and expanded Graunt's *Observations*. More important is that the fusion of science and policy the work effected through its creation of population as an object of both mixed-mathematical knowledge and systematic regulation was of a piece with Petty's conception of a trans-formative natural philosophy. Graunt's dedication to Lord Robartes, Lord Privy Seal (and later, briefly, Lord Lieutenant of Ireland), suggested 'That it doth not ill become a *Peer of the Parliament* or *Member of his Majesties Council*' to consider the economic, political, and public health concerns raised by the weekly bills of mortality.[53] Graunt addressed Sir Robert Moray, then President of the Royal Society, at greater length:

> The Observations which I happened to make ... have faln out to be both *Political* and *Natural*, some concerning *Trade* and *Government*, others

[50] Southwell to Petty, 28 November 1682, *PSC*, 112; Petty, *Observations upon the Dublin-Bills of Mortality, MDCLXXXI, and the State of that City* (London: Printed for Mark Pardoe, 1683). Evelyn wrote in 1675 that Petty 'is the author of the ingenious deductions from the bills of mortality, which go under the name of Mr. Graunt'; Evelyn, 2:104. In a letter to Robert Boyle, John Beale referred to 'Sir W: Pettys notes on the Bills of Mortality'; Beale to Boyle, 16 February 1681, in Boyle, *Correspondence*, 5:242–243. Writing to Pepys, John Houghton, F.R.S., cited Petty 'in Graunt's Observations'; Houghton to Pepys, 13 July 1702; Pepys (ed. J. R. Tanner), *Private Correspondence and Miscellaneous Papers of Samuel Pepys, 1679–1703*, 2 vols (London: G. Bell & Sons, 1926), 2:263–265. But Pepys himself said nothing, while Aubrey attributed the *Observations* to Graunt; Aubrey, 243.

[51] Petty to Southwell, 4 March 1679, 20 August 1681 and 25 December 1686, *PSC*, 69, 92, 248. Petty included 'Observations on the Bills of Mortality' in his later list of writings (strangely, for 1660 rather than 1662), but this need not imply outright authorship; the list also included a 1654 'discourse against the Transplantation into Connaught', possibly indicating that Petty contributed to Vincent Gookin's work, and 'Letters &c between the Protector and the Ch. Govr. Of Ireland' that Petty simply delivered. See *PP*, 2:261–262.

[52] Southwell to Petty, 28 November 1682, *PSC*, 112. Newton used a similar figure in an opposite way when he claimed to stand 'on the shoulders of giants'—alluding to the socially inferior (and hunchbacked) Robert Hooke. (I owe this point to Mordechai Feingold.)

[53] Graunt, sig. A2v.

concerning the *Air, Countries, Seasons, Fruitfulness, Health, Diseases, Longevity*, and the proportions between the *Sex* and *Ages* of Mankind. All which (because Sir *Francis Bacon* reckons his Discourses of *Life* and *Death* to be *Natural History* ... I am humbly bold to think *Natural History* also[.][54]

Graunt's 'Pamphlet' belonged both to the state, 'so far as it relates to *Government* and *Trade*' and, 'as it relates to *Natural History*, and, as it depends upon the *Mathematicks* of my Shop Arithmetick', to the Royal Society—that 'Privy Council for *Philosophy*' and 'Parliament of *Nature*' whose '*Expeditions* against the Impediments of Science' mirrored the movements of armies and navies around the world.[55]

Before we come to the Royal Society, however, it is important to grasp both the role natural knowledge might play in policy and the *kind* of natural knowledge involved. Weekly bills of mortality for London's parishes had first appeared during a plague outbreak in 1592 and had been printed regularly since 1603, another plague year. Despite the wealth of data they contained, however, they had so far functioned only as fodder for conversation and to help wealthy Londoners 'judg of the necessity of their removal' from the city in plague time. Taking 'a view of the whole together', and 'comparing ... one *Year, Season, Parish*, or other *Division* of the City, with another', Graunt aimed 'not only to examine the Conceits, Opinions, and Conjectures' he had framed—that is, to test his hypotheses with statistics—but 'further, to consider what benefit the knowledg of the same would bring to the World'.[56]

In a dozen chapters he did just that, highlighting conclusions of particular interest or surprise and stressing throughout the policy implications of his demographic findings. He established that London's population was growing despite the fact that its death rate exceeded its birth rate, sparking not only a comparison of urban and rural air from a medical point of view but also a discussion of rural-urban and interurban mobility, a possible object of regulation.[57] He also found that 'few starve of the many that beg':

the vast number of Beggars, swarming up and down this City, do all live, and seem to be most of them healthy and strong; whereupon I make this Question, Whether, since they do all live by begging, that is, without any kind of labour; it were not better for the state to keep them, even although they earned nothing? That so they might live regularly, and not in that Debauchery, as many Beggars do; and that they might be cured of their bodily Impotencies, or taught to work, &c. each according to his condition

---

[54] Graunt, sig. A3v.   [55] Graunt, sig. A4r.
[56] Graunt, 1–2.   [57] Graunt, 41–46.

and capacity; or by being imployed in some work (not better undone) might be accustomed and fitted for labour?[58]

The observation of an apparently natural demographic pattern—the high proportion of 'sturdy beggars', idle but healthy—revealed a space for the state to step in and improve the population it governed, instilling habits of industry in the able-bodied unemployed. Comparable observations prompted reform proposals dealing with everything from plague regulations, to economic policy, to the size of parish churches.[59]

Along the way, Graunt commented on the limitations of his data and of the methods used to collect it, treating the bills as a collaborative scientific project that might be, with a little thought, improved. He sought a better fit, for example, between the categories that the bills included (such as male and female fatalities) and excluded (such as marriages) and the ostensible or potential purposes the data might serve.[60] Given that the bills included not only such heterogeneous causes of death as 'Affrighted', 'Bleeding', 'Childbed', 'Drowned', 'Executed', 'French-Pox', 'Grief', and 'Itch', but also categories whose explanatory value was virtually nil—'Kil'd' by several Accidents', for instance, or simply 'Suddenly'—a little standardization could go a long way.[61] Graunt also questioned the criteria by which numbers were assigned to certain categories. The old women employed by parishes as 'searchers', whose reports were the original source of the data, might be relied upon where causes of death were 'but matters of sense', such as stillbirths; verifying cases of plague, however, was notoriously difficult and required 'other Ratiocinations' than mere searchers could give.[62] Like the Down Survey, the bills of mortality required a coordinated and rationalized division of scientific labour to realize their full theoretical and practical potential.

Like the Down Survey, too, the *Observations* were indeed both natural and political: what the survey did for land, statistics did for population. Asking himself the purpose of 'all this laborious bustling and groping', Graunt compared his work favourably not only with 'the Art of making Gold' (a matter of arcane secrecy, useful only to a few) and the 'voluminous Transcriptions' of traditional philosophy but also with the self-interested politics of the day—for 'whereas the Art of Governing, and the true *Politicks*, is how to preserve the Subject in *Peace* and *Plenty* ... men study only that part of it which teacheth how to supplant and over-reach

---

[58] Graunt, sig. A2v, 19.   [59] For the last, see Graunt, 57–58.
[60] Graunt, 12.   [61] Graunt, 9.   [62] Graunt, 13.

one another'.[63] Graunt, instead, envisioned an 'honest harmless *Policy*' grounded in a thorough knowledge of 'the Land, and the hands of the Territory'. This meant not only a survey of 'the *Geometrical* Content, Figure, and Situation of all the Lands of a *Kingdom* ... according to its most natural, permanent, and conspicuous Bounds' and the 'accidentall, or extrinsick' features, such as proximity to markets, that impinged on land values, but also a census of the population by 'Sex, State, Age, Religion, Trade, Rank, or Degree, &c.' Such knowledge had obvious economic uses; if consumption patterns were better known, for example, 'Trade might not be hoped for, where it is impossible.' Its applications extended well beyond the economy, to balancing 'Parties and Factions both in *Church* and *State*.'[64] A full survey of the state's natural, demographic, and economic situation would reveal the full range of constraints upon and opportunities for human action—whether art, as for Bacon, or policy, as for Harrington. It would enable the 'good, certain, and easie Government' of lands and hands alike.[65]

Universal reformation and the *Treatise of Taxes*

Historians of economics regard Petty's *Treatise of Taxes*, which appeared a few months after Graunt's *Observations*, as his first and most important contribution to the development of political economy, and it unquestionably contains his most sophisticated attempt to explain economic relations and processes in theoretical terms.[66] Yet the *Treatise* was a call not for theoretical economics but for the 'universal Reformation of what length of time hath warped awry' in government. Something of a companion piece to the *Observations*, it combined a Harringtonian notion of natural policy, a Hobbesian view of sovereignty, and an approach to population borrowed from Graunt in promoting economic, social, and political reforms still described in essentially Hartlibian terms.[67] It was an organic outgrowth of his earlier interests that led Petty into uncharted territory.

Unlike Graunt's book, Petty's had an Irish dimension; moved to write by 'the *Duke of Ormond*'s going Lord Lieutenant into *Ireland*' and hoping for a share of the Irish customs farm, Petty argued that Ireland, underpopulated and bearing the heavy burden of an occupying army, needed

---

[63] Graunt, 72.   [64] Graunt, 72–74.   [65] Graunt, 74.
[66] Aspromourgos, 'Life', 345. See Johnson, 97–108; Finkelstein, 107–129. Appleby uses the *Treatise* as the main source for Petty's views.
[67] Petty, *Treatise*, 9; see Finkelstein, 117–118.

not only an infusion of trade and people but also an understanding of 'the nature and measure of Taxes and Contributions'.[68] The stars had aligned for reform to begin: Ormond 'takes the great Settlement in hand, when *Ireland* is as a white paper, when there sits a Parliament most affectionate to his Person, and capable of his Counsel, under a King curious as well as careful of Reformation; and when there is opportunity, to pass into Positive Laws whatsoever is right reason and the Law of Nature.'[69] But if Ireland was a blank slate, its reformation was inseparable from England's. The *Treatise* appeared just as the English Parliament granted Charles a hearth tax, which Petty's arguments may have helped establish, and the preface spoke of how 'The employing the Beggars in *England* ... will make the Wool and Cattle of *Ireland* vend the better', attracting settlers and trade, increasing revenues and widening the tax base while lessening the need for an army.[70] Above all, finding and pursuing 'natural' policies was essential for both kingdoms: '*res nolunt male administrari* ... things will have their course, nor will nature be couzened'.[71]

The *Treatise* began with an enumeration of 'the several sorts of Publick Charges'—defence, administration, the church, schools and universities, poor relief, and infrastructure. Even in this preliminary list, the goals of reform inflected Petty's analysis: the universities, he acknowledged, were in fact mostly funded by 'the Donations of particular men', but they would rightly *become* 'a publick Charge' *if* they could be reformed 'to furnish all imaginable helps ... towards the discovery of Nature in all its operations'.[72] His ensuing account of 'the Causes which encrease and aggravate' these expenditures made the connection between quantification and reformation clearer still. First among these was 'the unwillingness of the people to pay them; arising from an opinion, that by delay and reluctancy they may wholly avoid them' and the popular suspicion that taxes were excessive, inequitable, and perhaps illegitimate in the first place—aggravated, interestingly, by the inconvenience of paying taxes in

[68] Petty, *Treatise*, sig. A2r-A3r; Barnard, 'Petty, Sir William', *Oxford DNB*.

[69] Petty, *Treatise*, sig. A4r.

[70] Petty, *Treatise*, sig. A3r; C. D. Chandaman, *The English Public Revenue, 1660–1688* (Oxford: Oxford University Press, 1975), 77–78. A ballad directed against the Hearth Tax may refer to Petty's poor eyesight: 'But was this done, my *Gracious Liege*, for You?/No, though at first it might make a shew,/As *Painted Projects* use, t'inhance Your Rents,/Their Subtle Sconces moulded worse intents/Than pur-blin'd Eyes discover'd; for they sought/Either by *Farming* what their *Brokage* wrought,/Or by their *Agents* to ingratiate/Your *Smile* for whom they did negotiate.' Richard Brathwaite, *The Chimney Scuffle* (London: [s.n.], 1662), 8.

[71] Petty, *Treatise*, sig. A4r.   [72] Petty, *Treatise*, 1–3.

cash at fixed times rather than 'in commodities, at the most convenient seasons'.[73]

False opinion cut both ways. Revenues suffered not only from a combination of 'Scarcity of Money' and 'Fewness of people, especially of Labourers and Artificers', but also from 'Ignorance of the numbers, Wealth and Trade of the people,' which caused 'a needless repetition … of new additional Levies' and multiplied expenses:

> An Offensive Forreign War is caused by many … personal distastes coloured … with publick pretences … but that the common encouragement unto them particularly here in *England* is a false opinion, that our Countrey is full peopled, or that if we wanted more Territory, we could take it with less charge from our neighbours, then purchase it from the *Americans*; and a mistake, that the greatness and glory of a Prince lyeth rather in the extent of his Territory, then in the number, art, and industry of his people, well united and governed.[74]

Civil wars were likewise the products of false opinions, whether by 'the punishing of Believers heterodox … with loss of life, liberty, and limbs' instead of 'tolerable pecuniary mulcts' or by 'the peoples fancying, that their own uneasie condition may be best remedied by an universal confusion'. (Petty added, perhaps addressing Harrington, that the 'Causes of Civil War are also, that the Wealth of the Nation is in too few mens hands', not too many.)[75]

The nation's troubles reflected the mistaken beliefs of both rulers and ruled—including, as for Hobbes, beliefs about sovereignty, rights, and religion, but most often and most reparably beliefs about numbers. The solution was an advancement of quantitative learning. Accurate and up-to-date knowledge of lands and hands would be more than a mere reference point to prevent mistakes; it could educate both prince and people about their respective needs and duties. More fundamentally, this proto-political anatomy would enable the state to reshape—to methodize—the population. Like Graunt, whom he perhaps influenced in this regard, Petty called for parishes to be standardized, even suggesting that clerical celibacy be restored to cut costs.[76] Universities, too, could be scaled back if

---

[73] Petty, *Treatise*, 4. Petty encountered similar problems collecting rents on his own estates, and suggested to his cousin John 'that if tenants can pay in cattle, twere best to take such rather then nothing.' Petty to John Petty, 20 March 1660, BL MS Add. 72850, f.18r.

[74] Petty, *Treatise*, 4–5, 16–17.   [75] Petty, *Treatise*, 5–6.

[76] Petty, *Treatise*, 8. Petty later rejected clerical celibacy as a hindrance to 'full peopling' and an example of unnatural policy. His embrace of it here may reflect sympathy with Graunt's providentialist interpretation of the sex ratio, which appeared to provide a surplus

only enough divinity, law, and medical students were admitted to supply the number of clergymen, lawyers, and doctors the population required.

The professions themselves should be thoroughly reformed: divinity through the standardization of parishes, law through the land registry (which would clarify property rights and reduce lawsuits).

> As for Physicians, it is not hard by the help of the observations which have been lately made upon the Bills of Mortality, to know how many are sick in London by the number of them that dye, and by the proportions of the city to find out the same of the Countrey; and by both, by the advice of the learned Colledge of that Faculty to calculate how many Physicians were requisite for the whole Nation, and consequently, how many students in that art to permit and encourage; and lastly, having calculated these numbers, to adoptate a proportion of Chyrurgeons, Apothecaries, and Nurses to them, and so by the whole to cut off and extinguish that infinite swarm of vain pretenders unto, and abusers of that God-like Faculty[.][77]

Once the correct proportions between the professions and the population were fixed—in the first instance, by filtering Graunt's data through a series of multipliers—mortality statistics for each of the faculties could be used to adjust recruitment year by year. The same should be done for the trades:

> by good Accompts of our growth, Manufacture, Consumption, and Importation, it might be known how many Merchants were able to mannage the Exchange of our superfluous Commodities with the same of other Countreys: And also how many Retailers are needful to make the subdistributions into every Village of this Nation, and to receive back their superfluities.[78]

People not needed elsewhere should be engaged in the only truly productive sectors, 'Husbandry and Manufacture.' Those unable to find employment should be kept busy by public projects—'no matter if it be ... to build a useless Pyramid upon *Salisbury Plain*, bring the Stones at *Stonehenge* to *Tower-Hill*, or the like', so long as it 'keep their mindes to discipline and obedience'.[79] Population, like land, was both a natural constraint and an economic and political resource; government, accordingly, became a matter of calibration and improvement. Taxation—the cause of so much trouble when poorly handled—was, properly used, both a source of revenue and

of men—natural bachelors, as it were—who could devote themselves to priestly or military pursuits without slowing population growth or undermining monogamy. See Graunt, 47–52.

[77] Petty, *Treatise*, 9.   [78] Petty, *Treatise*, 11.

[79] Petty, *Treatise*, 11–13. See James H. Ullmer, 'The Macroeconomic Thought of Sir William Petty', *Journal of the History of Economic Thought* 26:3 (2004), 401–413.

an instrument of fundamental social reform. It could turn the state itself into a sort of Nosocomium.

Pursuing this point led Petty into what we now consider economic theory. He began by exploding false opinions—the 'Ignorance of the Number, Trade, and Wealth of the people' that caused the prince to levy inefficient taxes, and the ignorance of economic relationships that caused the people to resist legitimate levies:

> Men repine much, if they think the money leavyed will be expended on Entertainments, magnificent Shews, triumphal Arches, &c. To which I answer, that the same is a refunding the said moneys to the Tradesmen who work upon these things; which Trades though they seem vain and onely of ornament, yet they refund presently to the most useful: namely, to Brewers, Bakers, Taylours, Shoemakers, &c.[80]

Taxes did not remove wealth from the people, since government spending worked its way back to them, sooner or later, through the network of exchanges, or 'commutations', that made up the economy. The first problem was to levy tax in such a way as to interfere as little as possible with business. This raised the question of money, since 'scarcity of coin' was among the causes of resistance. Petty argued that 'there is a certain measure, and proportion of money requisite to drive the trade of a Nation, more or less than which would prejudice the same.' Too little money drove up interest and hindered trade; too much caused inflation. The necessary amount was linked positively to 'the bigness of the payments' the nation made and inversely with 'the frequency of commutations'—here Petty pioneered the notion of the velocity of circulation—which itself depended on a mixture of law and custom. Further, 'where there are Registers of Lands ... and where there are Depositories of the τα χρυσα, as of Metals, Cloth, Linnen, Leather, and other Usefuls; and where there are Banks of money also, there less money is necessary to drive the Trade.'[81] Understanding circulation, the government could manipulate the effective supply of money through banks and its velocity through payment periods, fitting the form of its exactions to the nation's economic life.[82]

The second and more important problem, and the object of great debate when Petty wrote, was how to create a just, effective, and 'proportionable' tax. At his Restoration, Charles was still expected, as medieval monarchs had been, to 'live of his own' off the revenues of Crown

[80] Petty, *Treatise*, 15.   [81] Petty, *Treatise*, 17–18.   [82] Ullmer, 405, 408.

lands, supplemented by 'ordinary' supply from indirect taxes: customs and excise, the new hearth tax of 1662, and assorted licence fees and duties. These were insufficient, but direct taxes, considered 'extraordinary', faced tougher scrutiny. The two most substantial were the subsidy (which taxed property at a fixed rate and was subject to massive evasion) and the more productive but unpopular assessment (which assigned a target yield and then divided the burden). The latter was especially contentious both as a Commonwealth innovation and because it fell disproportionately on land; although it theoretically targeted both 'realty' and 'personalty', the former was easier to assess.[83] Designing a proportionable tax was thus not simply a matter of canvassing the different types of levy available; it also meant locating the sources of value for both land and other forms of wealth and finding a way to measure and compare them.

Starting with a chapter on the assessment, considered as a tax on rent, Petty attempted just this. He began by defining the natural rent of land in terms of the average value of the surplus the land produced over and above costs:

> Suppose a man could with his own hands plant a certain scope of Land with Corn, that is, could Digg, or Plough, Harrow, Weed, Reap, Carry home, Thresh, and Winnow so much as the Husbandry of this Land requires; and had withal Seed wherewith to sowe the same. I say, that when this man hath subducted his seed out of the proceed of his Harvest, and also, what himself hath both eaten and given to others in exchange for Clothes, and other Natural necessaries; that the remainder of the Corn, is the natural and true Rent of the Land for that year; and the *medium* of seven years, or rather of so many years as makes up the Cycle, within which Dearths and Plenties make their revolution, doth give the ordinary Rent of the Land in Corn.[84]

He then defined the specie value of the rent in parallel terms:

> Let another man go travel into a Country where there is Silver, there dig it, Refine it, bring it to the same place where the other man planted his Corn; Coyne it, &c. the same person, all the while of his working for Silver, gathering also food for his necessary livelihood, and procuring himself covering, &c. I say, the Silver of the one, must be esteemed of equal value with the Corn of the other.

As with corn and silver, so also with all other commodities: 'the foundation of equallizing and ballancing of values' lay in comparing the surpluses of

[83] Chandaman, 138–142.   [84] Petty, *Treatise*, 24–25.

each produced by equal amounts of labour applied to land over equal periods of time.[85] Petty thus arrived at his 'theory of value':

> all things ought to be valued by two natural Denominations, which is Land and Labour, that is, we ought to say, a Ship or garment is worth such a measure of Land, with such another measure of Labour; forasmuch as both Ships and Garments were the creatures of Lands and mens labours thereupon; This being true, we should be glad to finde out a natural Par between Land and Labour, so as we might express the value by either of them alone as well as or better then by both, and reduce one into the other as easily and certainly as we reduce pence into pounds.[86]

In sum, 'Labour is the Father and active principle of Wealth, as Lands are the Mother'.[87] A par between the two would be a sort of universal character or natural language of value: it would make all forms of wealth immediately commensurable.

Petty's pursuit of such a unitary measure took him in circles; land and labour remained irreducible. His notion of surplus, however, reflected a new understanding of social and economic development with implications for the larger reformation he pursued. The relative contributions of land and labour to value varied not only from commodity to commodity—labour's share increasing with each additional refinement—but also, correspondingly, from society to society. His discussion of unemployment suggested that the more developed the country, the more people—and the more kinds of people—a given amount of land, improved and worked intensively by a decreasing proportion of the population, would support:

> If there be 1000. men in a Territory, and if 100. of these can raise necessary food and raiment for the whole 1000. If 200. more make as much commodities, as other Nations will give either their commodities of money for, and if 400. more be employed in the ornaments, pleasure, and magnificence of the whole; if there be 200. Governors, Divines, Lawyers, Physicians, Merchants, and Retailers, making in all 900. the question is, since there is food enough for this supernumerary 100. also, how should they come by it?[88]

Agricultural surplus was the original cause of the division of labour in society, and the surpluses continuously generated by productive improvements in both agriculture and trades drove its continuing elaboration.[89]

---

[85] Petty, *Treatise*, 25.   [86] Petty, *Treatise*, 26.   [87] Petty, *Treatise*, 49.
[88] Petty, *Treatise*, 12–13.   [89] Aspromourgos, 'Invention'.

This process of differentiation impinged on every aspect of society, culture, and government:

> As a Kingdom encreaseth and flourisheth, so doth variety of things, of actions, and even of words encrease also; for we see that the language of the most flourishing Empires was ever the most copious and elegant, and that of mountainous Cantons the contrary ... as the actions of this Kingdom encreased, so did the Offices ... and on the contrary, as the business of the Offices encreased, so did the difficulty and danger of discharging them amiss decrease proportionably[.][90]

The production of a surplus freed more and more of the population from agriculture and triggered an ever-increasing refinement not only of goods and ideas but also of social roles. In its sweeping view, this sketch of social differentiation through history foreshadowed the stage-development theories of the high Enlightenment. Its form, however, recalled the naturalistic account of one specific type of differentiation, religious sectarianism, that Petty had sketched in his 1659 *Reflections*. Both described processes that obeyed natural laws and had natural roots (in the soil and in Adam's degenerate seed) but that also, by the same token, had social and political effects. These processes were to be studied and, ultimately, governed.

Taxes thus served both fiscal and social goals, which though ideally allied were nevertheless often distinct. Their uneasy relationship is captured in the curious dual sense in which Petty used the term 'proportion' to refer to both objective economic circumstances and normative demographic adjustments. Taxing proportionably to raise revenue without incurring resistance, on one hand, meant taxing according to wealth, allowing people to maintain their current positions relative to one another. Taxing proportionably to effect 'reformation', on the other hand, meant favouring productive or useful groups and taxing the idle or troublesome—deliberately manipulating the relative sizes and positions of the social groups in question. Petty's discussion of specific taxes silently maintains this bifurcation, of which he was perhaps only dimly aware; while his discussion of the assessment prompted an investigation of the origins and measures of value—the basis for an objectively proportional tax—other chapters pursued a normative proportionality that might or might not be congruent with maximizing public revenues or promoting private wealth. Lotteries, for instance, would fund bridges or highways

---

[90] Petty, *Treatise*, 56.

while serving a moral function as 'a Tax upon unfortunate self-conceited fools' who mulcted 'themselves in general, though out of hopes of Advantage in particular'—turning private vices into public benefits.[91] Reduced and reapportioned tithes would pay for the state church and compel it to reform the parish system.[92] Benevolences (effectively forced loans), in contrast, raised revenues but 'may divide a whole Nation into parties, or at least make the strength of Parties too well known' or else 'disguize the same', hindering government either way.[93] Petty's pet proposal, the hearth tax—an 'accumulative excise' proportioned to consumption—was valuable both for its 'Naturall Justice' and because it 'engages to thrift'.[94]

This tension between taxation as a mirror of the existing distribution of wealth and as a tool of social reform was in fact a common feature of contemporary economic argument. It particularly marked debates over the customs, the strategic use of which is often labelled 'mercantilism'—though the term has drawn criticism for imposing a false coherence on thinkers with divergent views.[95] Insofar as it was coherent, mercantilism identified national wealth and strength with a favourable balance of trade, brought about by minimizing imports (particularly of finished or luxury goods) and maximizing exports. In this vein, Petty thought duties on exports should be minimized to ensure domestic producers had subsistence, allow exporters a 'reasonable profit' and to keep prices competitive in foreign markets; correspondingly, he supported import duties high enough to promote domestic substitutes and restrain the use of 'Superfluities tending to luxury and sin'.[96] Yet he was against banning either exports of raw materials or imports of finished goods for the sake of propping up failing domestic industry. 'Prohibition of Importations ... needs not be, until they much exceed our Exportations', and then it would be a matter of 'making sumptuary Laws, and judicious use of them *pro hic & nunc.*' As for raw exports:

> The Hollanders having gotten away our Manufacture of Cloth, by becoming able to work with more art, to labour and fare harder, to take less fraight,

[91] Petty, *Treatise*, 45–46.   [92] Petty, *Treatise*, 58–62.   [93] Petty, *Treatise*, 46–47.

[94] Petty, *Treatise*, 73–75. Petty defined 'accumulative excise' in as 'Taxing many things together as one' at the end of the production process, rather than taxing materials repeatedly at different stages of production and thus forcing people to pay 'double or twice for the same thing'.

[95] Chandaman, 9–36. On mercantilism, see Eli F. Hecksher (trans. Mendel Shapiro), *Mercantilism*, 2 vols (London: George Allen & Unwin, 1934); D. C. Coleman (ed.), *Revisions in Mercantilism* (London: Methuen, 1969); Lars Magnusson, *Mercantilism: The Shaping of an Economic Language* (New York: Routledge, 1994).

[96] Petty, *Treatise*, 36–37.

Duties and Ensurance, hath so madded us here in *England*, that we have been apt to think of such extraordinary fierce ways of prohibiting Wool and Earth to be exported [and used by the Dutch to make cloth for sale in England], as perhaps would do us twice as much harm as the losse of our said Trade.

Rather than trying to turn back the clock or stop the flow of trade, England should shift its idle lands and hands to tillage and fisheries, or else 'draw over a number of their choice Workmen, or send our most ingenious men thither to learn'.[97] This was at odds with thinkers like Worsley—one of the architects of the 1650 Navigation Act—whose *Advocate* ('That frippery and Longlane of thredbare notions concerning Trade', as Petty called it) had suggested that it was simply through 'want of … Care' in England, and 'not our Neighbor's singular Industrie above us' that the Dutch had captured the trade.[98]

That said, Petty's general view of England's economic prospects and his specific recommendations echoed those of contemporary and earlier writers at many points. Like countless others alarmed by the social dislocation commercial society had brought since the sixteenth century, he believed in wage ceilings and sumptuary laws.[99] Like the mercantilist writers of his own century—Thomas Mun (who wrote in the 1620s but whose works remained in vogue through the 1660s) is a prominent example—he believed in pursuing a favourable balance of trade, and if necessary in restricting consumption to achieve it. Mun's view that 'we ought not to auoid the importation of forraine wares, but rather willingly to bridle our owne affections to the moderate consuming of the same' matched Petty's position.[100] Mun, too, had said that 'when more treasure must be raised than can be received by the ordinary taxes, it ought ever to be done with equality to avoid the hate of the people', and that 'the riches or sufficiencie of euery Kingdome, State, or Common-wealth' had two sources—'the

[97] Petty, *Treatise*, 40–41.

[98] Petty, *Reflections*, 107; Worsley, 8–9. On Worsley's role in the Navigation Act, see Steven C. A. Pincus, *Protestantism and Patriotism: Ideologies and the Making of English Foreign Policy, 1650–1668* (Cambridge: Cambridge University Press, 1996), 47–49; Charles Webster, 'Benjamin Worsley', 231–32.

[99] Petty, *Treatise*, 33–34, 37. On arguments for wage ceilings, see Edgar S. Furniss, *The Position of the Laborer in a System of Nationalism: A Study in the Labor Theories of the Later English Mercantilists* (1921; New York: Augustus M. Kelley, 1965).

[100] Thomas Mun, *A Discovrse of Trade, from England Vnto the East-Indies* (London: Printed by Nicholas Okes for John Pyper, 1621), 56. See also Mun, *England's Treasure by Forraign Trade* (London: Printed by J. G. for Thomas Clark, 1664), 27–30. Mun wrote *England's Treasure* c.1623, but it appeared in print only in 1664.

one is naturall, and proceedeth of the Territorie it selfe: the other is artificiall, and dependeth on the industry of the Inhabitants.'[101] Both men worried about the effects of wealth on occupational distribution.[102] Mun's argument that prohibiting bullion exports and manipulating the exchange rate violated the 'true causes and effects' of economic relations suggests a still more fundamental similarity.[103] For Mun as for Petty, finally, framing economic policy—which both compared to medicine—required recognizing both how trade naturally worked and 'how much Art doth add to Nature'.[104]

Yet if the *Treatise* had a great deal in common with earlier economic writing, and influenced subsequent work, it was not primarily a product of this tradition. What Petty's extensive overlap with Mun (among others) shows is not that Petty was actually an economic writer all along but rather that his goal of a universal reformation of society and government, derived from his background in natural philosophy, was congruent with much that had been and was still being written on economic questions—something more evident still in *Political Arithmetick*. This appears even in Petty's treatment of trade barriers, which he approached as 'neither Merchant nor Statseman [sic]' but rather 'as an idle Philosopher'.[105] He rejected import prohibitions against Dutch manufactures not only as harmful to English trade but also, and more fundamentally, because such barriers violated both the course of nature and the advancement of learning. Inviting Dutchmen over or sending Englishmen to learn their 'art' was 'the more natural way, then to keep that infinite clutter about resisting of Nature, stopping the windes and seas, &c.'[106] Petty here invoked a conception of the dynamic relationship between human art and nature, between the advancement of learning and the improvement of the material world, that was conspicuously compatible with Mun's views but that derived directly from Bacon.[107]

Perhaps the most obvious Baconian legacy in the *Treatise* was the massive advancement of empirical learning Petty's analysis of value would require if it were to have any practical application. The chapter on the assessment called for surveys dealing with 'the intrinsick Values of Land'

---

[101] Mun, *Treasure*, 165–166; Mun, *Discovrse*, 49–50.   [102] Mun, *Treasure*, 31.

[103] Mun, *Treasure*, 108.   [104] Mun, *Treasure*, 143, 175.

[105] Petty, *Treatise*, 36, 41.   [106] Petty, *Treatise*, 41.

[107] Similar overlaps litter the *Treatise*. The chapter on monopolies, for example, noted their role in protecting fledgling trading companies (one of Mun's arguments), but only after treating patents for inventions, including an emotive and evidently autobiographical digression on the difficulties inventors faced; Petty, *Treatise*, 55.

(including 'the Figures, Quantities, and Scituations of all the Lands', their civil and natural boundaries, quality, and products) and also covering such 'extrinsick or accidentall' factors as 'the multitudes of people living near this land', their 'luxurious or frugal' way of life and their 'Civil, Natural or Religious Opinions'.[108] His chapter on the poll tax, likewise, suggested that 'good and multiform Accompts' be kept of the population.[109] This massive gathering, sorting, and sifting of data—a sort of combined natural history, Down Survey, and '1659 Census' of England—required a collaborative effort and state backing:

> it will be objected, that these computations are very hard if not impossible to make; to which I answer onely this, that they are so, especially if none will trouble their hands or heads to make them, or give authority for so doing: But withall, I say, that until this be done, Trade will be too conjectural a work for any man to employ his thoughts about; for it will be the same wisdom in order to win with fair Dice, to spend much time in considering how to hold them, how much to shake them, and on what angles they should hit the side of the Tables, as to consider how to advance the Trade of this Nation[.][110]

This did more than simply put economic analysis on an empirical footing. As economic policy became a matter of scientific investigation, the state—the agent of policy—became a scientific agent as well, promoting growth through mechanical improvements and institutional innovations while extending its own knowledge and power through surveys and censuses. In proportion as policy was seen to be a matter of knowing and manipulating nature, politics became a branch of Baconian natural philosophy.

There was thus scientific substance to Petty's Harringtonian stress on promoting natural policies and dispensing with the unnatural. Usury laws were one example of 'the vanity and fruitlessness of making Civil Positive Laws against the Laws of Nature'.[111] Currency debasement, a hardy perennial of crown finance, was another—'a sign that the State sinketh, which catcheth hold on such Weeds as are accompanied with the dishonour of impressing a Princes Effigies to justifie Adulterate Commodities, and the breach of Publick Faith, such as is the calling a thing what it really is not.'[112] Things, not words, were what counted. In fact, the unnatural policy discussed at greatest length in the *Treatise* was not an economic policy at all, but the punishment of religious heterodoxy. Petty believed

---

[108] Petty, *Treatise*, 31–32.   [109] Petty, *Treatise*, 44.   [110] Petty, *Treatise*, 34.
[111] Petty, *Treatise*, 30.   [112] Petty, *Treatise*, 71.

with Hobbes that the sovereign had the right to impose a religion, but argued 'in consequence of our opinion, [That Labour is the Father and active principle of Wealth, as Lands are the Mother] that the State by killing, mutilating or imprisoning their members do withall punish themselves; wherefore such punishments ought (as much as possible) to be commuted for pecuniary mulcts, which will encrease labour and publick wealth.'[113] Besides reducing the labour force, harsh punishments 'spreadeth the Pseudodoxies', for such was the nature of schism. Moderate fines, on the other hand, would allow genuinely heterodox believers to live in peace while weeding out opportunistic 'Hypocrites' who 'abuse holy religion to cloak and vizzard worldly ends'—respecting and yet restraining human nature for the good of the state.[114] Taken together, the natural policies Petty pushed for would create an industrious, thrifty, and loyal population. Government itself became a collaborative scientific enterprise, half Down Survey and half Nosocomium. '[A]s wiser Physicians tamper not excessively with their Patients, rather observing and complying with the motions of nature, then contradicting it with vehement Administrations of their own; so in Politicks and O[e]conomicks the same must be used'.[115] When Petty referred, a decade later, to political arithmetic and political anatomy as 'political medicine', this is what he meant.

The Royal Society and its limitations

While Petty's approach to 'Politicks and Oeconomicks' employed new forms of social analysis, it did so within the natural-philosophical framework he had developed during the Interregnum. Just as then, Petty meanwhile pursued a range of other scientific projects, now under the aegis of the newly created Royal Society. The Society received its Royal Charter in April 1663, but had begun in November 1660, when an assortment of old Hartlibians, Oxford Philosophical Society veterans and others—Petty, Boyle, Wilkins, and Wren among them—met to discuss 'founding a college for promoting of physico-mathematical learning'.[116]

[113] Petty, *Treatise*, 49.   [114] Petty, *Treatise*, 50.   [115] Petty, *Treatise*, 41.

[116] Thomas Birch, *The History of the Royal Society of London for Improving of Natural Knowledge, from Its First Rise*, 4 vols (London: A. Millar, 1756–1757), 1:3–4. On the origins and early years of the Royal Society, see P. M. Rattansi, 'The Intellectual Origins of the Royal Society', *Notes and Records of the Royal Society of London* 23:2 (1968), 129–143; A. Rupert Hall and Marie Boas Hall, 'The Intellectual Origins of the Royal Society—London and Oxford', *Notes and Records of the Royal Society of London* 23:2 (1968), 157–168; Michael Hunter and Paul

They decided to convert their occasional discussions at Gresham College into formal weekly meetings, to pay a regular subscription for membership and to solicit royal backing. Petty's audiences with Charles bear witness to the vogue experimental science enjoyed at court, and though never financed by the crown the Society initially attracted a large and socially (if not always intellectually) impressive membership at the outset.[117] It promised institutional permanence for experimental philosophy: a venue for demonstrations, an audience for discoveries, a centre for collaboration and coordination. Yet after a flurry of activity in the first few years, attendance dwindled, committees dispersed, and dues fell into arrears. Even in its first years, further, it could not accommodate Petty's projects as the Hartlib Circle once had.

Petty's participation suggests the scope of the Society's interests. In December 1660, he, William, Viscount Brouncker (the Society's President), Sir Robert Moray, and Boyle were instructed 'to prepare some questions, in order to the tryal of the quicksilver experiment upon Teneriffe'.[118] In April 1661 he was 'to inquire in Ireland concerning the petrification of wood, the bernacles, the variation of the compass, the trial of the quicksilver experiment [again], and the ebbing and flowing of a brook'; in May he, Boyle, and Jonathan Goddard were 'to consult concerning the nature of gravity'.[119] January 1662 brought 'observations on the vibration of pendulums', February the evaluation of 'a paper concerning music' as well as Graunt's *Observations*, and May the examination of water-works and dyers' pumps.[120] The presentation, vetting, and publication of projects were considerably more formal than in Hartlib's circle, and Petty's relative status was higher. (He could also make politically helpful connections by sponsoring new members: in 1662 he sponsored Sir George Lane, the Duke of Ormond's secretary and a clerk of the English Privy Council; in 1664, Sir Winston Churchill, one of the commissioners appointed to implement the Act of Settlement and later the Act of Explanation in Ireland.)[121] The range of projects was, however, familiar.

B. Wood, 'Towards Solomon's House: Rival Strategies for Reforming the Early Royal Society', *History of Science* 24:1 (1986), 49–108.

[117] On the Society's membership, see Michael Hunter, *The Royal Society and Its Fellows, 1660–1700: The Morphology of an Early Scientific Institution*, (2nd ed., London: British Society for the History of Science, 1994).

[118] Birch, *History*, 1:4.   [119] Birch, *History*, 1:20, 22.

[120] Birch, *History*, 1:74–76, 84.

[121] See Toby Barnard, 'Lane, George, first Viscount Lanesborough (1620–1683)', *Oxford DNB* <http://www.oxforddnb.com/view/article/58510>; Paul Seaward, 'Churchill, Sir Winston

As with the Hartlib Circle, too, certain overarching goals gave some structure to the Society's heterogeneous interests. Most obvious was the characteristically Baconian 'History of Trades' project—an attempt to gather, by observing and talking to actual tradesmen, concise yet comprehensive studies of a wide range of crafts, thereby to improve both trade and science.[122] In early 1661 Petty and John Evelyn submitted lists of likely trades, and Petty was desired 'to deliver his thoughts on the trade of clothing' shortly thereafter. The Irish Parliament intervened, however, and the resulting history 'Of making cloth with sheeps wool' appeared only in late November, by which time Petty had been assigned an 'account of dy[e]ing' as well (this appeared in May 1662).[123] Delays aside, Petty's two histories may be taken as models of the sort of work aimed at. The first offered a step-by-step description, in forty-five numbered paragraphs, of the materials and techniques involved in processing wool. Drawing analogies between similar stages in different trades, Petty sought 'the very essence or *ratio formalis*'—the key mechanical 'ingenium', point, or trick—of each step. (The *ratio formalis* of spinning, for instance, was 'a series of continual twistings and interposings, wh[i]ther things are joyned or fastened to each other singly').[124] As if still debating Henry More, Petty defended the scientific merit of such gritty detail:

> I have been perhaps too long in describing the minutiae of very ordinary and small operations; but I hope no philosopher will despise this, no more than he would the anatomy of a mouse or frog; for as small, and as common, and

(*bap.* 1620, *d*. 1688)', *Oxford DNB* <http://www.oxforddnb.com/view/article/5406>. Petty also sponsored the Yorkshire gentleman John (later Sir John) Brooke, or Brookes, and the physician William Hoare, both in 1662, as well as John le Gassick (also apparently a doctor) in 1673; in 1675 he unsuccessfully proposed the Yorkshire physician William Simpson. See Hunter, *Royal Society*, 59, 68. An undated letter from Petty to Brooke (BL MS Add, 72850, ff.309–310v) mentions works that suggest a shared interest in natural history (and a date of c.1671): John Ogilby, *America: Being the Latest and Most Accurate Description of the New World* (London: printed by Thomas Johnson for the author, 1670); Arnaldus Montanus (trans. Ogilby), *Atlas Japannensis* (London: printed by Thomas Johnson for the author, 1670); Montanus (trans. Ogilby), *Atlas Chinensis* (London: printed by Thomas Johnson for the author, 1671).

[122] Walter E. Houghton, Jr. 'The History of Trades: Its Relation to Seventeenth-Century Thought: As Seen in Bacon, Petty, Evelyn, and Boyle', *Journal of the History of Ideas* 2:1 (1941), 33–60; Kathleen Ochs, 'The Royal Society of London's History of Trades Programme: An Early Episode in Applied Science', *Notes and Records of the Royal Society of London* 39:2 (1985), 129–158.

[123] The history 'Of making cloth with sheeps wool' is printed in Birch, *History*, 1:55–65; the 'Apparatus to the History Of the Common Practices of Dying' in Sprat, *History*, 284–306. A manuscript of the former is in BL MS Sloane 2903, ff.26–38v; one of the latter, dated 1 May 1662 and entitled 'The History of Dying or Tinctures', is in BL MS Add. 72897, ff.1–37. See Sharp, 171–179. The 'Apparatus' was delivered to the Society a week later: Birch, *History*, 1:83.

[124] Birch, *History*, 1:56.

as cheap as these are, I do not doubt but the invention of them was very difficult and curious at the first.

'I say,' he continued, 'to perform all these compounded operations with some simple regular motion ... is not contemptible, nor easy for a very inventive wit, without deep and long meditations to excogitate.'[125] What was second nature to a tradesman was mechanical philosophy to Petty.

The 'Apparatus to the History Of the Common Practices of Dy[e]ing' was sketchier, possibly because its design, or rather that of the unwritten history it mapped out, was more ambitious and more systematic. An enumeration of materials and ingredients was still central, but the nineteen instances of colouration that Petty listed now embraced both artificial processes (such as marbling paper) and natural phenomena. Further:

> it were not incongruous to begin the History with a Retrospect into the very nature of Light it self (as to inquire whether the same be a Motion or else a Body;) nor to premise some Theorems about the Sun, Flame, Glow-worms, Scales of some Fishes, the dashing of the Sea, stroaks upon the eyes, the *Bolonian* Slate (called by some the Magnet of Light) and of other light and lucid bodies.[126]

Petty classified and discussed dyestuffs according to their mineral, animal, or vegetable origins, apparently as a short-cut to the mechanical *ratio formalis* (now the active chemical ingredient—the 'fatty earthy particles' or 'saline substances') of each, before giving a 'synoptical' list of materials and their applications.[127] He closed with a set of 'General Observations upon Dy[e]ing' that promised ultimately 'to shew how any Colour assigned may be superinduced upon any kind of Material.'[128] Here the history of trades was literally the history of how simple physical motions and chemical combinations added up to transformative processes, enabling human art to superinduce desirable natures on natural substances—the old Baconian aim. (The history of dyeing and the *Treatise of Taxes*—which promised to superinduce industry, thrift, and loyalty on human populations through simple, natural policies—appeared in the same month.) Yet despite Petty's evident enthusiasm and the formation of a sizeable committee, the History of Trades program petered out by the later 1660s.

Petty's other major contribution to the early Royal Society was his 'Double-Bottom', 'sluice', or double-hulled ship—a sort of catamaran designed to outsail conventional commercial and naval ships alike, bearing

---

[125] Birch, *History*, 1:60.   [126] Sprat, *History*, 284.
[127] Sprat, *History*, 287–295.   [128] Sprat, *History*, 306.

greater sail and drawing less water while requiring a smaller crew.[129] When and how Petty first became interested in the subject is not entirely clear. In December 1660 the Royal Society asked him and Christopher Wren 'to consider the philosophy of shipping', while Charles II raised the matter with him in February 1661; later that year Petty 'proposed divers things for the improvement of Shipping' including 'a versatile keel that should be on hinges' and 'sheathing ships with thin lead', to the Royal Society.[130] He evidently saw in shipping a way to advance natural philosophy, commerce, and power while impressing the king—he wrote to Charles in April 1661 that 'there was no greater, no more stately, no more useful, nor more intricate engine in the World than a Ship, nor no inanimate thing coming nearer than it to the nature of an Animal' and 'that if I could attain truly to understand a Ship, I did even therein comprehend 1000d things more of excellent use & should advantageously exercise myself in the whole Doctrine of Number Weight & Measure.'[131]

He first mentioned his design for a 'double bottomed cylindrical vessel' in a letter to Brouncker, sent from Ireland and read at the 12 November 1662 meeting of the Society; 'he was desired to prosecute this invention, and to give farther notice of the success thereof upon the trial of the vessel at sea.'[132] He did both. With help from Sir John Clotworthy, Viscount Massereene (a major Irish landowner and one of the moving spirits behind the Restoration), Petty quickly built his first prototype, the *Invention*, and kept the Society appraised of his progress through frequent letters to Graunt (a Fellow thanks to his *Observations*) and Brouncker.[133] King Charles took an early interest, and the Society appointed a committee of five Fellows (Massereene, Sir Anthony Morgan, Peter Pett, Robert Southwell, and Petty himself) to discuss the design with fourteen outsiders with shipbuilding or sailing experience.[134] Examining plans and a 2.5-foot scale model of the vessel, 'most of the company, and especially the seamen,' expressed concerns about the strength of the structure but also 'saw in her the causes of out-sailing any thing already in use'. Petty responded to their worries but stressed that both objections and answers based on

---

[129] Sharp, 242–250; Fitzmaurice, 108–114. Strauss (115–117) dismisses it as a mere hobby.

[130] Birch, *History*, 1:7, 65–66; Evelyn, 1:379.

[131] Petty to Charles II, 11 April 1661 (extract), BL MS Add. 72894, ff.1–2.

[132] Birch, *History* 1:124.

[133] Sean Kelsey, 'Clotworthy, John, first Viscount Massereene (*d.* 1665)', *Oxford DNB* <http://www.oxforddnb.com/view/article/5709>; RSL Letterbook P.1, ff.28–37; Birch, *History*, 1:124, 131, 141, 167, 180, 183–192, 206, 287, 310.

[134] Sir Robert Moray to Petty, 16 December 1662, BL MS Add. 72850, ff.124–125.

mere plans and models 'may be thought conjectural' next to the testimony of experiment.[135]

In fact a public trial had taken place before the committee's report even appeared, in January 1663; racing against one of the king's barges, a 'large black pleasure-boat' and a man-of-war's boat, Petty's *Invention* won handily.[136] He soon built a second prototype, the *Invention II*. Reading Petty's letters with Graunt at the coffee house that summer, Pepys (a naval administrator as well as a Fellow of the Royal Society) had a keen eye for the ship's advantages. 'It is about 30 Ton in burden and carries 30 men with good accomodation'—'more men, with better accomodation by half, then any other ship' of similar size, plus 'ten guns of about five Tons weight.' It was also fast, having 'this month won a wager of 50£ in sailing between Dublin and Holyhead with the pacquett-boat, the best ship or vessel the King hath there': 'In their coming back from Holyhead, they started together; and this vessel came to Dublin by 5 at night and the pacquet-boat not before 8 the next morning; and when they came they did believe that this vessel had been drownded or at least behind, not thinking she could have lived in that sea.'[137] Pepys quickly became a fan of both ship and architect. In August he, Graunt, and Sir Anthony Deane (a prominent shipwright opposed to the Double-Bottom) argued over the vessel's merits, 'even to some passion on both sides almost.' In mid-October Pepys heard 'that Sir W. Petty and his vessel are coming, and the King intends to go to Portsmouth to meet it'; in December he went to the coffee house to meet Graunt and Petty himself, 'with whom I talked and so did many, almost all the house there, about his new Vessell; wherein he did give me much satisfaction in every point that I am almost confident she will prove an admirable invention.'[138]

The Double-Bottom provided the public and the court with an unusual spectacle and raised Petty's profile accordingly. In December 1664 Charles II and his brother James, Duke of York, attended the launch of the third prototype, the *Experiment*, as Evelyn and Pepys looked on.[139] Such a high profile cut both ways, however, and Petty's attempt to hire sailors to take the *Invention II* back from Dublin to London provoked a 360-line burlesque:

> Then first of all this famous Model
> Sprung from a mathematick Nodelle,

---

[135] Birch, *History*, 1:183–189; copies of the report and related material are in BL MS Add. 72852, ff.23–38v.

[136] Birch, *History*, 1:189–192.   [137] Pepys, *Diary*, 4:256–257.

[138] Pepys, *Diary*, 4:262–263, 334, 437.   [139] Evelyn, 1:379; Pepys, *Diary*, 5:353.

Who Honour saw, alltho dim sighted,
And was for fair Inventions Knighted.
He was one of those Learned Fellows,
That rais'd the Maiden from the Gallows,
To shew the Power of Phisicks Art,
When hang'd to make her live, and fart.
He who had many Acres got,
By measuring of Land a Spot.
How that should be the Art doth there lye,
For some doe say he measur'd fairly.

...

This knight not full of twittle twattle,
But bookish as was Aristotle,
To gaine the Name of a Philosopher,
An hundred Books did turn and toss over,
And his cold Fingers ends did blow, soe
To become a Virtuosoe.
In Studdy thus much Time he spent
Some new unheard of thing t'invent;
A thing not found since the Creation,
A spicke-span new Art of Navigation.

(Having taken his idea from a child's paper boat, Petty built his ship; but before it could sail he had to convince the sailors' wives to let their men go. This he did by getting them drunk.)

Thus he at last did Sailors gett,
With Mony, good Words, good Ale, and Wit.
Castor and Pollux now's on the Ocean,
And the Knight gaping for promotion,
Whose Fame shall everlasting be,
Whilst there is sailing on the Sea,
Whilst there are Men that love green Sallads,
Whilst there is burlisque Verse, or Ballads.[140]

Though seasoned with reflections on Petty's Irish career, the poem typifies the popular attitude to a great deal of experimental science. As Robert Southwell remarked to Henry Oldenburg (Secretary to the Royal Society), 'Our Noble Architect Sir Wm. Petty, who has found out a new way,

---

[140] 'In Laudem Navis Geminae E Portu Dublinij ad Regem Carolum IIdum Missae' ['In praise of the twin-hulled boat sent from the port of Dublin to King Charles II'] (1663), in Andrew Carpenter (ed.), *Verse in English from Tudor and Stuart Ireland*, (Cork: Cork University Press, 2003), 390–401.

to find out a new World, goes on cheerfully in fortifying his matchlesse Engine against two great Enemyes[:] the Sea, and the Multitude.'[141]

Shipwrights, too, were suspicious of an interloper in their midst. Peter Pett (a navy commissioner, not to be confused with his cousin Sir Peter) told Pepys that the Double-Bottom was 'the most dangerous thing in the world if it should be practised in the world'; once adopted by other nations, it would ruin English trade and naval power. For Sir Anthony Deane it simply 'must needs prove a folly'. Pepys attributed these comments to self-interest, however, and in general Petty's colleagues took a warm interest in his work. As Oldenburg wrote to Robert Boyle, 'all those, I think, that are wellwishers to the improvement of naval Architecture, wish good successe to this brave attempt.'[142] Royal Society propagandist Thomas Sprat punningly described the ship as

the most considerable *Experiment*, that has been made in this Age of *Experiments*: if either we regard the great charge of the work, or the wonderful change it was likely to make it *Navigation*, or the great success, to which this first *Attempt* was arriv'd. Though it was at first confronted with the doubts, and Objections of most *Seamen* of our *Nation*, yet it soon confuted them by *Experience*.[143]

It was a thirty-ton example of everything experimental science should be.

The reasons for its failure are therefore all the more interesting. The most obvious one was the loss of the *Experiment* during a storm in the Bay of Biscay in the spring of 1665. Evelyn reported that Petty 'was censured for rashness', though he and several others also noted that the same storm had sunk a fleet of conventional ships as well—'so that', as Sprat put it, 'the Ancient Fabricks of *Ships* have no reason to triumph over that new *Model*, when of threescore and ten sail that were in the same storm, there was not one escap'd to bring the News.'[144] Yet, well before this there were signs of trouble. Petty and Massereene fought over control of the first prototype, for which Massereene had helped pay.[145] Just as the second

[141] Southwell to Oldenburg, August 1663, BL MS Add. 72852, f.45r.

[142] Oldenburg to Boyle, 27 October 1664, in Boyle, *Correspondence*, 2:103. See also Hooke to Boyle, 18 July 1663, in Boyle, *Correspondence* 2:367.

[143] Sprat, *History*, 240. Sprat's castigation of Samuel Sorbière's observations of England illustrates the Double-Bottom's public visibility: 'For, he says, that *the double-bottom'd Vessel has two Masts in the Front*, when every *Sculler* on the *Thames* knows it has but *One*.' Sprat, *Observations on Monsieur De Sorbier's Voyage into England* (London: Printed for John Martyn and James Allestry, 1665), 112–113.

[144] Evelyn, 2:102; Sprat, *History*, 240. Sprat claimed that seventy ships had been lost in the storm, Evelyn fifteen.

[145] Fitzmaurice, 111–112.

ship seemed to be proving itself, in May 1663, the Royal Society informed Petty 'that the matter of navigation being a state concern was not proper to be managed by the Society', though he was free to discuss his invention with individual members 'for his private satisfaction'.[146]

The court proved equally fickle. For Charles, science, though interesting, was essentially an amusement—as Pepys witnessed during a visit to Whitehall in February 1664:

> Thence to White-hall, where in the Dukes chamber the King came and stayed an hour or two, laughing at Sir W Petty, who was there about his boat, and at Gresham College [i.e. the Royal Society] in general. At which poor Petty was I perceive at some loss, but did argue discreetly and bear the unreasonable follies of the King's objections and other bystanders with great discretion—and offered to take oddes against the King's best boats; but the King would not lay, but cried him down with words only. Gresham College he mightily laughed at for spending tyme only in weighing of air [referring to Boyle's air-pump experiments], and doing nothing else since they sat.[147]

This was hardly promising, and the response at lower levels of government, too, was mixed. Pepys was a consistent believer, having questioned Petty closely and inspected the *Experiment* in person, while Sir Thomas Clargues, impressed by the *Invention II*'s success against the pacquet-boat, suggested to Secretary of State Sir Henry Bennet that the king have one or two Double-Bottoms built.[148] Ormond may have been more typical: he was intrigued by the design but did not pretend to understand it.[149] Sir Winston Churchill—whose election to the Society Petty had sponsored—simply remarked that, like the Irish settlement (founded on the twin Acts of Settlement and Explanation), Petty's ship 'may hold in fair weather but never in a storm.'[150] In a sense, there was no definitive state position, just a series of individual reactions shaped by personal tastes and interests, Petty's arguments and demonstrations, popular reports and court wit, none of which meant anything without royal initiative. The Royal Society's corporate response, on the other hand, was to throw Petty on the mercy

[146] Birch, *History*, 1:249. See George N. Clark, *Science and Social Welfare in the Age of Newton* (2nd edn., Oxford: Oxford University Press, 1970), 15–16. The Society repeatedly deferred publication of Petty's account of the ship; Birch, *History*, 2:40, 42.

[147] Pepys, *Diary*, 5:32–33. Charles was not alone: the French ambassador De Cominges described Petty's ship to Louis XIV as 'la plus ridicule et inutile machine que l'esprit de l'homme puisse concevoir'; see Pepys, *Diary*, 5:25 n.1.

[148] Pepys, *Diary*, 5:24–25; Clargues to Bennet, 25 July 1663, *CSPI 1663–1665*, 187.

[149] Ormond to Charles II, 1 August 1663, *CSPI 1663–1665*, 191–192.

[150] Churchill to Bennet, 25 July 1663, *CSPI 1663–1665*, 185.

of Charles's court by defining navigation as state business—and this despite having asked Petty 'to consider the philosophy of shipping' in the first place.

Too much an *arcanum imperii* for the Society to manage, yet too much an experimental novelty for the court to take seriously, the Double-Bottom fell between two stools not because it was bad science or bad policy but because it fused science and policy in a way neither political nor scientific institutions were prepared to accommodate. This suggests the limitations of the Royal Society for Petty's purposes. True to its Interregnum roots, the group embraced Baconian method. But it proved incapable of compelling or sustaining the collaborative effort needed to realize even the more anodyne components of Bacon's vision, such as the History of Trades. Given its royal connections and politically mixed membership, further, it dodged more divisive topics whenever possible. This meant avoiding speculation about ultimate causes (which had theological implications) and instead reporting observable phenomena.[151] But it also meant keeping the more radical social and political applications of science—so central to the Hartlibian program and to Petty's reading of Bacon's natural philosophy—at arm's length.[152] Whether the Double-Bottom was genuinely too sensitive politically or simply a cause of bothersome arguments among the Fellows, it was more than the Society could handle. For Petty's larger projects, the state, whatever its shortcomings, was ultimately the only option.

Politics in the later 1660s: towards political arithmetic

The Double-Bottom was the last of Petty's large projects before political arithmetic. Even after its failure, however, he continued to attend Society meetings, though these became fewer and further between. In March 1665 the Society put him on a committee 'to consider the improvement of artillery' (apparently not such a state concern as navigation); in April he and others were 'desired to suggest experiments for improving chariots'; in June—as the plague was beginning to spread through London—he reviewed and approved Graunt's additions for a new printing of the *Observations*; by August he had escaped the city to ride out the plague

[151] Peter Dear, 'Totius in Verba: Rhetoric and Authority in the Early Royal Society' *Isis* 76:2 (1985), 145–161; Barbara J. Shapiro, *A Culture of Fact: England 1550–1720* (Ithaca: Cornell University Press, 2000), 163–165.
[152] But see Slack, *Reformation*, 87–88.

at Durdans, the home of Sir William Berkeley, near Epsom in Surrey.[153] Passing through, Evelyn found him living there with John Wilkins and Robert Hooke, 'contriving chariots, new rigging for ships, a wheel for one to run races in, and other mechanical inventions' and enthused that 'perhaps three such persons together were not to be found elsewhere in Europe, for parts and ingenuity.'[154] Such mechanical inventions, together with a familiar range of other experiments, continued to occupy Petty on and off for the rest of his life. But with the exception of a second 'fit of the Double-Bottom' in the early 1680s, which ended no better than the first, they never again approached the scale of the sunken *Experiment*. Instead, amid the distractions of the land settlement, estate-related lawsuits, and political upheaval, Petty returned little by little to the problems of economic, social, and political reformation first considered in the *Treatise of Taxes*.

The Second Anglo–Dutch War, which broke out in 1664, prompted Petty's second piece of economic writing, the brief *Verbum Sapienti* (printed only in 1691, as an appendix to *The Political Anatomy of Ireland*). Like the *Treatise*, *Verbum Sapienti* stressed the importance of taxing equitably—this time, to pay for the war—and of the utility of various 'Computations' to that end. The work's main distinction for historians of economics is that these computations began to resemble national accounting: as before, Petty called for calculations of the extent and value of the nation's land, housing, shipping, and livestock (its 'Estate'). But the greater part of the nation's wealth lay in 'the Value of the People' themselves, as a source of earnings: 'although the Individuums of Mankind be reckoned at about 8 years purchase; the Species of them is worth as many as Land, being in its nature as perpetual, for ought we know.' (This phrasing recalls Harrington's claim that 'the people, being the materials' of the commonwealth, 'never dies'.)[155] If Petty had refined his method, his goal of an industrious and obedient population was clearer than ever. Considering the plague, he coldly remarked that it did not discern 'between the well and the ill-affected to Peace and

---

[153] Birch, *History*, 2:24, 30, 57, 63. The new edition of Graunt's work included an Appendix making use of Dublin mortality bills, which Petty probably furnished; *EW*, 398 nn.1–2. In a letter to Brouncker from Dublin (written apparently in October 1662), Petty mentioned that 'When I first landed here, some matter presented itselfe whereuppon to make observation uppon Ireland, not unlike those which Mr Graunt made upon the London Bills of Mortality,' adding that 'I have done so much upon it, as hath cost me some pounds, but not so much as is worth more than a bare mention.' Petty to Brouncker, [29 October 1662], RSL Letterbook P.1, ff.22–25.

[154] Evelyn, 1:419; Evelyn to Lord Viscount Cornbury, 9 September 1665, in Evelyn, 3:167.

[155] Petty, *Verbum Sapienti*, 7–8 [*Political Arithmetick*, sig. P4r–v]; Harrington, *Oceana*, 99.

Obedience, or between the *Bees* and the *Drones*', so that 'the Loss is proportionable to the Benefit we have by them that survive.' Considering 'The Causes of irregular taxing', he now blamed an excessive focus on the 'past Effects' of labour—the nation's nonhuman 'Estate'—as against its 'present Efficiencies', as well as 'A fallacious tenderness towards the poor … interwoven with the cruelty of not providing them work, and indulging Laziness in them'.[156]

Verbum Sapienti said little about another economic challenge: protectionism in the English Parliament, directed against Irish trade. Following on from the Navigation Acts of 1651 and 1660, the 1663 Staple Act removed privileges and protections formerly accorded to Irish ports—excluding them from direct trade with English colonies and restricting their trade with Europe—and imposed tariffs on Irish cattle imported to England, which English landlords blamed for falling rents. This was a considerable blow to Irish landowners, Petty among them, but though Ormond and Arthur Annesley, Earl of Anglesey (vice-treasurer and receiver-general of Ireland and one of the framers of the Restoration land settlement) protested, little could be done. When a bill for the complete prohibition of Irish cattle was proposed in the Parliament of 1665—held at Oxford to avoid the plague—they made a concerted effort to mobilize a stronger opposition. Relocating from Durdans to Oxford, Petty joined the fight. Together with Edward, Lord Conway (a member of Ormond's privy council) and Boyle, he lobbied first Lord Arlington and then the Solicitor-General, Heneage Finch; finally he was permitted to address a Parliamentary committee directly.[157]

English landlords proved too strong in the end, and the bill became law in 1667. But the struggle against it, which lasted well into the 1670s, cast Petty once again in the role of Irish (as well as economic) expert. He and others argued that the bill was based on a false assumption: Irish cattle were not to blame for falling rents; 'Want of money, want of people, want of health, and want of peace', in Heneage Finch's words, were more likely causes. Further, while a cattle ban would help a small number of English landowners, it would harm many more: a sizeable proportion of Irish cattle went to England not for immediate consumption but rather to be fattened on English farms. English consumers would face artificially inflated prices. Navigation between England and Ireland, now a 'nursery of seamen',

---

[156] Petty, *Verbum Sapienti*, 8–9, 15–16 [*Political Arithmetick*, sig. P4v–P5r, P8r–v].
[157] *CSPI 1663–1665*, 652. See Carolyn A. Edie, 'The Irish Cattle Bills: A Study in Restoration Politics', *Transactions of the American Philosophical Society*, New Series, 60:2 (1970), 1–66.

would languish. Finally, harming the interests of New English landlords would set back not only plantation in Ireland but also the reformation of the Irish themselves. Finch summarized the point:

> Wee have long complained that Ireland could never be civilized, and tis most certaine that till they become an Industrious people they never wilbee soe. But this is a way to make them as Barbarous as ever, for if you turne all their Cattle upon their hands, you will make them Lazy, for foode wilbee soe cheap, as noe man neede to Labour for it.[158]

The only alternative would be for Ireland to pursue markets outside England, and this is exactly what happened. (In 1666 Petty himself sent Ormond's son, Lord Ossory, some tentative 'Considerations upon the design of carrying cattle alive to Rotterdam from Ireland'.)[159] Over the following decade, Ireland replaced live cattle with victualling and related exports (butter, tallow, hides) as well as wool, underselling English suppliers in Europe and the non-English Atlantic—and threatening a new alignment of Irish and Continental interests.[160]

Although the Cattle Act was a small part of the crisis that produced political arithmetic, arguments against it crystallized English anxieties about the industry and the loyalty of Ireland's population in a revealing way. As we have seen, fear of Irish barbarity was an old theme by the 1660s, revived by the events of 1641. Yet arguments against the Cattle Acts linked this barbarity less with Catholicism or Irishness than with the idleness produced by cheap and plentiful food. Again, deprecations of Irish economic and social arrangements went back to Giraldus Cambrensis and were entirely compatible with religious or ethnic bigotry. What is interesting about their appearance at this point, however, is that they now coincided with Petty's comments in the *Treatise of Taxes* and *Verbum Sapienti* about the idleness and ungovernability of the *English* population. The smaller the explanatory role ethnicity or religion played in accounting for Irish barbarity—and since the Cattle Acts were the target, there was every reason to play these causes down—and the larger the role played by bad (or unnatural) policy, the more Ireland's and England's troubles tended to converge. In both countries, the problem was to instil and maintain

---

[158] Finch's speech is in TCD MS 1180, ff.15–18. For related arguments see TCD MS 1180, ff.19–22, 27–30, 44–45, and 47–50 ('Sir Wm. Petty's Argument about the Restraint on Irish Cattle Urging it a disadvantage to England', 1673) and Petty's printed broadside, *Some of the Observations made by W.P. Upon the Trade of Irish Cattel* (London: [s.n.], 1673).

[159] Bodl. MS Carte 40, ff.555–556v.

[160] Edie, 'Irish Cattle', 41–42; but see also Gillespie, 45–47.

industry and loyalty in the governed; in both, the solution was good (or natural) social and economic policy. Put together, Petty's arguments in the *Treatise* and *Verbum Sapienti* and his allies' criticism of the Cattle Act implied that Irish rebelliousness and English idleness were similar problems with similar—indeed, linked—solutions. Political arithmetic would make this point explicit.

As important as the Cattle Act itself was the factionalism and religious politics it reflected, which pitted the bill's sponsor, the Duke of Buckingham, against the Lord Chancellor, Clarendon. The Cattle Act hurt Ormond, Clarendon's ally, but Buckingham's real aim was removing Clarendon from office and securing greater toleration for Protestant dissent than the strict High Church settlement (known as the 'Clarendon Code') allowed.[161] Clarendon was dismissed and exiled in 1667, done in by the compounded disasters of the Great Fire of London (at first blamed on Catholics) and defeat at the hands of the Dutch; the religiously diverse 'Cabal' ministry rose in his place.[162] Ormond fell in early 1669, replaced first by a Presbyterian and then by a Catholic sympathizer.[163] The 1670 Treaty of Dover charted England's new course: in exchange for subsidies enabling him to govern without Parliament, Charles would support Louis XIV against the Dutch and (according to a secret clause) convert to Catholicism. A Declaration of Indulgence and the Third Dutch War followed early in 1672.[164] By that time Irish Catholics, led by Richard Talbot (future Earl of Tyrconnell) had succeeded in getting Charles to review the terms of the land settlement.[165] Everywhere, it seemed, the Restoration settlement—both the religious settlement in England and the land settlement in Ireland—was nearing collapse. Dutch victories, French money, and Irish lobbying threatened Protestant freedom in England and authority in Ireland; 'popery and arbitrary government' loomed.[166] It was in the midst of this crisis that political arithmetic emerged.

---

[161] Edie, 'Irish Cattle', 17, 26–27; John Miller, *Charles II* (London: Weidenfeld and Nicolson, 1991), 142–174; Miller, *Popery*, 91–107.

[162] The 'Cabal' was named for its members: Clifford, Arlington, Buckingham, Ashley, Lauderdale.

[163] See J. I. McGuire, 'Why Was Ormond Dismissed in 1669?', *Irish Historical Studies* 18:71 (1973), 295–312. John, Lord Robartes succeeded Ormond as Lord Lieutenant in 1669 and was succeeded in April 1670 by John, Baron Berkeley, who served until 1672.

[164] Miller, *Charles II*, 175–219; Miller, *Popery*, 108–120.

[165] Anne Creighton, ' "Grace and Favour": The Cabal Ministry and Irish Catholic Politics, 1667–1673', in Dennehy, 141–160.

[166] Harris, *Restoration*, 85–135.

Paterfamilias, planter, political arithmetician

Before we turn to political arithmetic, however, it is worth taking another look at the man who wrote it. When Petty wrote the *Treatise of Taxes* he was nearing forty years old; the Down Survey behind him, he had extensive estates, a comfortable income, and an established reputation—for good and ill—in England and Ireland and in political as well as scientific circles. A seasoned political survivor, he had served the Commonwealth, the Protectorate and now the restored monarchy, coming full circle, in a sense, since leaving Paris in 1646. A knight, sometime MP, and expert on the Irish settlement, he devoted more and more of his time to defending his holdings in Ireland and their legal and political underpinnings. (His list of writings includes a single entry for 1667: 'Lawsuits.')[167] When not busy with his estates, in Parliament, or pitching his projects to a bemused court audience, he moved in overlapping circles of old Hartlibian acquaintances, fellow Fellows of the Royal Society, and political contacts—chatting in the coffee house with Graunt or Hooke, showing Pepys around the Double-Bottom, or, as in 1665, escaping the plague-stricken city to tinker with carriages or ploughs in the countryside—before heading up to Oxford and more politics.

The nearly fifty-year-old Petty who wrote *The Political Anatomy of Ireland* and *Political Arithmetick* at the beginning of the next decade was in many ways little changed: still a Fellow of the Royal Society, still a coffee house regular, and still, above all, determined to keep every shred of Irish land he could, cudgelling his foes in public if necessary. But he was now over a decade out of office, and his last great project, the Double-Bottom, had ended a costly and humiliating failure, dropped by the Royal Society and mocked at court. On the other hand, he had a new family, having married Elizabeth Fenton (widow of an Irish planter, Sir Maurice Fenton, and daughter of Petty's old associate Sir Hardress Waller) in June 1667. Their first three children died in infancy, but Charles (born 1672), Anne (1673) and Henry (1675) would all survive childhood.[168] (A natural daughter, Frances, born in 1664, was raised by her mother and

---

[167] *PP*, 2:262.

[168] 'Papers concerning Sr. W: P & his Lady's Family, Expences, Occurrences, Children's Education &c', BL MS Add. 72857, ff.75–76. Surprisingly, the first child mentioned, named Mariana, was 'borne at Merns [?] in france & buried at [forges?] neere Angiers Anno 1668', suggesting that Petty and Elizabeth visited France shortly after their marriage. I know of no other reference to such a visit. At least one of Elizabeth's pregnancies resulted in a miscarriage—Petty wrote Southwell in 1677 that she 'has not recovered the ill consequences ... to this day'; Petty to Southwell, 3 April 1677, *PSC*, 23–24.

resurfaced only later.) Evelyn's diary gives some notion of the changes marriage wrought:

> When I, who knew him in mean circumstances, have been in his splendid palace, he would himself be in admiration how he arrived at it; nor was it his value or inclination for splendid furniture and the curiosities of the age, but his elegant lady could endure nothing mean, or that was not magnificent. He was very negligent himself, and rather so of his person, and of a philosophic temper. 'What a to-do is here!' would he say, 'I can lie in straw with as much satisfaction.'[169]

Elizabeth, 'an extraordinary wit as well as beauty, and a prudent woman', gave Petty more than children and a home decent people would visit.[170] She facilitated his work in important if often invisible ways, managing their estates when other business demanded his attention and bringing him new social connections, among them her cousin Sir Robert Southwell, who became Petty's closest friend and unofficial archivist. This was a matter of personal ties and left few textual traces, but when Petty embarked on political arithmetic such ties would be crucial.

It is also worth looking again at how Petty's science had developed in the decade before political arithmetic. Rooted in his reading of Baconian natural philosophy, filtered through his encounter with Harrington, his work with Graunt and the lingering influence of his earlier education, Petty's pursuit of a new kind of systematic social knowledge (or even of a large-scale mechanical project like the Double-Bottom) ultimately confirmed the turn towards the state signalled earlier by the Down Survey. An individual farmer or brewer could use a new seed drill or furnace; a solitary philosopher could do great things with a microscope. But no individual could use the kind of knowledge Graunt and increasingly Petty generated: knowledge of populations, their numbers, their qualities, their relationships. Only the state could use it, to frame policies that would improve its natural resources and deal with social processes themselves anchored in human nature—religious dissent, resistance to unequal taxation, and so on. Only the state, for that matter, could produce it, gathering data as its agents taxed the people and its church christened, married, and buried them. Universal reformation meant scientific government; for that, science itself had to become social. Yet the result was not exactly social science, in the sense of analysis of society for its own sake. As Petty had told Henry More, speculation was

---

[169] Evelyn, 2:103; Petty to Southwell, 7 November 1676, *PSC*, 8.   [170] Evelyn, 2:102.

nothing without application. Knowledge was power, or else it was not real knowledge. Petty's extension of Baconian natural philosophy from bodies to minds would terminate not in economic analysis but in social engineering: a science of natural policy directed to the improvement of lands and hands.

'The Description and Excellency of the Double-Keel Vessel'. (Royal Society Library, EL/Pɪ/34a. © Royal Society Library.)

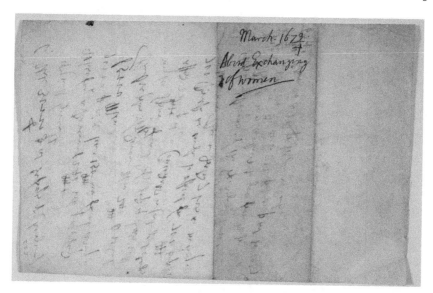

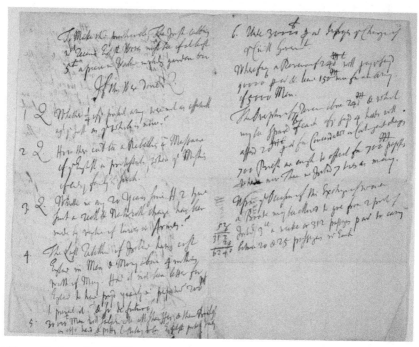

'About Exchanging of Women' (1674).

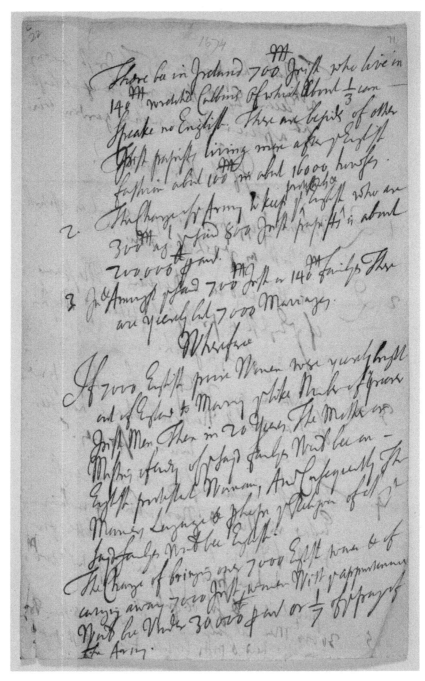

'About Exchanging of Women' (1674). (British Library Additional MS 72879, ff. 71, 71v–72, and 72v. © British Library.)

'Sir William Petty' by and published by John Smith, after John Closterman. Mezzotint, 1696. (National Portrait Gallery D11978. © National Portrait Gallery, London.)

CHAPTER 5

The Transmutation of the Irish

[S]ince Bodies, having but one common Matter, can be differenc'd but by Accidents, which seem all of them to be the Effects and Consequents of Local Motion, I see not why it should be absurd to think that (at least among Inanimate Bodies) by the intervention of some very small *Addition* or *Substraction* of matter (which yet in most cases will scarce be needed,) and of an orderly *Series of Alterations*, disposing by degrees the Matter to be transmuted, almost of any thing may at length be made Any thing[.][1]

English in *Ireland*, growing poor and discontented, degenerate into *Irish*; & *vice versa; Irish*, growing into Wealth and Favour, reconcile to the *English*.[2]

U p to this point, we have followed Petty's life and work, with special reference to the elements of both that would shape his political arithmetic. From here the stress falls on political arithmetic as Petty developed, circulated, and modified it over the course of his remaining sixteen years. Petty's life was in some ways more settled than before. He was now a family man, giving his children as much attention as he was able—often, to be sure, at long distance; he spent about two-thirds of his time in Ireland, where he set about attempting to improve his estates, but was frequently in London, sometimes for sustained periods.[3] In other ways little had changed. Lawsuits continued to be an unprofitable distraction, as did attempts to improve his estates; much of Petty's attention in the later 1660s and early 1670s was absorbed by his attempt to set up an ironworks on his Kerry land, a project that not only failed but also incurred considerable financial and political costs.[4] Despite this, however, he managed to work on a variety of experiments and inventions, designing new carriages for

[1] Robert Boyle, *The Origine of Formes and Qualities* (Oxford: Printed by H. Hall for Ric: Davis, 1666), 95–96.

[2] Petty, *Political Anatomy*, 112.

[3] Brief absences in London aside, Petty was in Ireland from early 1666 to late 1673, mid-1676 to early 1681 and mid-1683 to mid-1685; *EW*, 1:xv–xxx.

[4] Toby Barnard has examined Petty's landowning career in a series of articles: Barnard, 'Sir William Petty, His Irish Estates and Irish Population', *Irish Economic and Social History* 6

the hilly terrain of Kerry and even suffering once more 'the fitts of the Double-Bottome' in the 1680s. He never completely gave up his hopes of pursuing his projects in an institutional framework: together with Hooke and others he attempted to reform the Royal Society in the early 1670s, and a decade later he helped set up the Dublin Philosophical Society, serving as its first President. Meanwhile, he doggedly pursued state patronage for his projects or, better, an office for himself—though with limited success.[5]

Political arithmetic, on the other hand, grew and changed dramatically as Petty adjusted it to the vicissitudes of English commercial and military strength in Europe, and political and economic stability in England and Ireland. Tracing these developments hardly means leaving Petty behind. If the importance of context is one reason for this, the form political arithmetic took is another. The *Treatise of Taxes* aside, *Political Arithmetick* and *The Political Anatomy of Ireland*, both largely written during 1671 and 1672, would prove to be Petty's two most important books.[6] It is misleading to read them this way, however. Neither was printed, or even intended for print, in Petty's lifetime. Both circulated as manuscripts among a select group of people whose positions in or near the upper levels of government in England and Ireland might enable them to *use* Petty's ideas. Along with these two manuscripts, Petty produced a mass of smaller tracts—often no more than two to four folios each—few of which saw print but many of which circulated in a similar way. Another chapter deals with Petty's use of what has been termed 'scribal' publication and the social network that facilitated it. But, in assessing what Petty wanted *Political Arithmetick* and *Political Anatomy* to do, it is important to bear in mind that we are dealing not with polished treatises designed for a wide readership but rather with a collection of policy proposals meant for the eyes of a powerful few.

Nature, economy, and population

Petty's proposals came in the midst of a crisis over the threat of popery and arbitrary government that had been mounting since the disintegration

(1979), 64–69; 'Sir William Petty, Irish Landowner', in Hugh Lloyd-Jones, Valerie Pearl and Blair Worden (eds), *History & Imaginaton: Essays in Honour of H. R. Trevor-Roper* (London: Duckworth, 1981) 201–217; 'Sir William Petty as Kerry Ironmaster', *Proceedings of the Royal Irish Academy* 82C:1 (1982), 1–32.

[5] Petty to Southwell, 19 April 1683, *PSC*, 117.

[6] Petty, *Political Arithmetick* (London: Printed for Robert Clavel and Henry Mortlock, 1690); Petty, *Political Anatomy*. Manuscripts of the former are in BL MS Add. 21128 and 72865, ff.50–92, NA SP 9/2/1, RSL MS 366 Ex.I.4, and TCD MS 544; a copy of the latter is in BL MS 21127.

of the hard-line Anglican Restoration settlement and the rise of the Cabal ministry. Catholic influence at court, and policies that both favoured and imitated France, threatened English Protestant liberty. The French alliance codified in the 1670 Treaty of Dover, followed over the next few years by a contentious (and soon withdrawn) Declaration of Indulgence for religious dissent, an unpopular war with the Dutch, and the revelation that the king's brother and heir, the Duke of York, was a Roman Catholic brought these fears to a crescendo. Popery and arbitrary government were as much a threat to property as to religion. Even before the Third Anglo-Dutch War began, the system of raising credit upon redeemable 'orders' (created to finance Charles's previous war against the Dutch) had spiralled out of control, provoking a suspension of payments—the infamous 'Stop of the Exchequer'—in 1672.[7] War harmed trade, and England appeared to many to be on the wrong side. Finally, a resurgent Irish Catholic lobby, led by the future Earl of Tyrconnell, convinced Charles to review the land settlement. The government was insolvent, its policies unpopular, and religious faction on the rise.

Fear for England's church, state, and trade generated a considerable literature, much of it targeting France. Among writers on economic questions, however, considerable attention focused—particularly before French victory seemed assured—on the disproportionate wealth and power of the United Provinces, and on the ways England might emulate the Protestant republic. It was this discussion that engaged Petty and tied *Political Arithmetick* to the broader corpus of 'economic writings' of the period. Still less than the *Treatise*, however, was *Political Arithmetick* simply an economic tract. Both Petty's overlaps with and departures from contemporary and earlier writing on Dutch and English economic rivalry show the emergence of a framework for discussing political economy that was not only compatible with, but for Petty inseparable from, a Baconian understanding of the relationship between art, or policy, and nature. Petty's natural-philosophical approach to policy meshed with strands of thinking already commonplace in economic writing. This enabled him to speak to economic writers, but it did not reduce his message to economics.

Explaining the contrast between the wealth of the United Provinces and their turbulent history and limited resources had long been a standard task for English economic writers. A common approach focused on 'situation'—roughly, the location, natural features, and resources of a

---

[7] Chandaman, 224–228.

place. In the *Advocate*, Petty's old rival Worsley denied the Dutch any 'extraordinarie advantage in matter of Trade, either through their Countrie, its Situation, or otherwise', stressing instead 'the manner of their Care, and of the Government that is among them, and the meer vigilancie of the Method observed by them'.[8] Most gave situation more weight. For John Keymor, the Dutch fused sound policy with the exploitation of natural advantages—England's: '[T]hey take Herrings in his Majesties Seas', he wrote, 'and here sell them, and carry away most fine gold'; not satisfied with that, they 'make laws to cross and hinder us in our own Sales'.[9] The fishery promoted shipping, and shipping extended their dominance to corn, wine, salt, timber, wool, cloth, lead, and tin: 'they make the Commodities of other Kingdoms serve their turns, to set their Ships and People on work, wherewith they inrich and strengthen themselves, to the admiration of all Nations.'[10] John Smith picked up on the same theme: 'The *Hollanders* have not ... any other means to rise to this greatness of Wealth and Trade, but by betaking themselves to Fishing', inhabiting 'a Spot of Land, which doth not afford them any Commodities.' Yet their 'constant labour, and unwearied industry' had turned England's natural advantages into the basis of their own supremacy. 'Fish, and the Fishing-Trade ... hath encreased their Shipping and Wealth, that now they have lengthned their power all over the World'.[11]

'Situation' entangled art and nature much as Baconian natural philosophy and Harringtonian political science did. It had both harmed and helped the Dutch; driven to sea by their narrow, barren territory, they mastered their new element, overcoming their own natural poverty by exploiting England's (and Ireland's and Scotland's) natural wealth.[12] In a sense, their success was the result of artifice, but this artifice was itself a natural response to their situation. The obvious question was, as Tobias Gentleman wrote: 'what may we his Majesties Subjects do ... having in

---

[8] Worsley, 10–11.

[9] Keymor, *John Keymors Observation Made Upon the Dutch Fishing, About the Year 1601* (London: Printed for Sir Edward Ford, 1664), 3. Keymor's *Observation* was written c.1601 but remained in manuscript until the 1664 edition. See also Keymor, *A Cleare and Evident Way for Enriching the Nations of England and Ireland, and for Setting Very Great Numbers of Poore on Work* (London: Printed by T. M. & A. C., 1650), 6.

[10] Keymor, *Observations*, 2–4; *Way*, 2–4, 8.

[11] Smith, *The Trade & Fishing of Great-Britain Displayed* (London: Printed by William Godbid, 1661), 11–12.

[12] Not everyone thought Dutch territory *was* barren. William Aglionby thought Holland 'a terrestrial Paradise for its Meadows and pleasant fields', though 'there are very few plow'd grounds, considering the vast numbers of people that must be fed'; Aglionby, *The Present State of the United Provinces of the Low-Countries* (London: Printed for John Starkey, 1669), 220.

our own Countreys sufficient store of all necessaries to accomplish the like business?'[13] Keymor answered: 'the scituation of *England* lieth far better ... to serve the Southern, East, and North-east Regions then they, and hath far better means to do it, if we bend our course for it.' It was time 'to turn the stream of Riches raised by native Commodities, into the natural Channel from whence it hath been a long time diverted'.[14] Smith summarized:

> The scituation of our Country is such, that for the convenience of all kind of Marts the world hath not the like, and being feared between the North and South, so that it is fix'd, as it were, by Art and Nature, the fittest Staple for both Northern and Southern Commodities.

> Secondly, our Ports and Harbours are fairer and safer ... and more in number throughout the Three Kingdoms, than any Country in Christendom can boast of.

> And then thirdly, which exceedeth, we have valuable Commodities, as to the quantity and quality of them, such as are the inriching of all those that trade with them.

> So that if we are not our own Enemies, and will but be a little industrious ... we shall within few years have the greatest power at Sea, and make our selves Master of all Trades; and the *Hollanders* a servant to that Wealth and Power, of which at present he is the sole Master.[15]

Dutch 'Art and Industry' had triumphed over nature's limitations, yet in a *natural* way, by exploiting the opportunities given to them. Blessed by nature, English art could surely do better still. Similar ideas informed less ephemeral works. Thomas Mun's *England's Treasure by Forraign Trade* complained about Dutch encroachments on English waters and discussed Genoa's changing fortunes in terms of situation.[16] Samuel Fortrey—one of the few authors Petty cited by name—commented in *England's Interest and Improvement* that '*Holland* hath not much of its own store ... and yet by their industrious diligence in trade' they succeeded; as for England, 'by the bounty of nature and divine providence, this nation doth not onely equal any neighbour-countrey, but far excels in all the most profitable advantages.'[17] Like 'art' and 'nature', 'situation' was a flexible term. It provided a way of talking about the possibilities of human action

[13] Gentleman, *The Best Way to make England the Richest and Wealthiest Kingdome in Europe* (London: [s.n.], 1660), 1.

[14] Keymor, *Way*, 4, 16.   [15] Smith, *Trade*, 13.   [16] Mun, *Treasure*, 22–24, 128–132.

[17] Fortrey, *England's Interest and Improvement* (Cambridge: Printed by John Field, 1663), 2–3. Petty mentioned Fortrey's 'ingenious Discourse of Trade' in *Political Arithmetick*, 109.

in material circumstances—like human nature, it could be invoked to constrain or to open up options, to explain or criticize past choices and customs, and to account for the successes and failures of policy.

Although inescapable, situation was not inexorable. Its very constraints provoked human industry to work against (yet with) it; today's situation was in part the effect of human effort upon yesterday's situation. Sir William Temple captured this ambiguity in his *Observations upon the United Provinces*: 'as *England* shows in the beauty of the Countrey, what Nature can arrive at, so does *Holland* in the number, greatness, and beauty of their Towns, whatever Art can bring to pass.'[18] The Dutch had grown strong 'by the improvements of Industry, in spight of Nature'; but that very industry had natural causes: 'no State was ever born with stronger throws, or nurs'd up with harder fare, or inur'd to greater labours or dangers in the whole course of its youth; which are circumstances that usually make strong and healthy bodies; and so this has proved'.[19] Situation here overlapped with Harrington's idea of 'constitution'—at once a constraint upon and a creation of human activity—for the hardships Temple meant were both environmental and political. As Petty's Royal Society colleague William Aglionby put it, 'The situation of this noble *Province* is such, as if Nature intended it for the generall Martt of *Europe*', while 'that difficult exercise of their nonage not only promoted their *growth*, by necessarily exciting the Industry natural to that Nation, but likewise contributed to render the *Constitution* of the State it self more robust and athletic.'[20] Natural situation and political circumstance together forged the character of state and population.

Specific policy proposals show further points of contact between Petty's background and the economic writing of the time. Josiah Child's *Brief Observations Concerning Trade* argued that 'the means whereby [the Dutch] have thus advanced themselves' were 'in a great measure imitable ... by us of this Kingdom of *England*'; among them were the use of experienced merchants 'in their greatest *Councils of State and War*'; 'Their giving great incouragement and immunities to the Inventors of New Manufactures, and the Discoverers of any New Mysteries in Trade'; 'The education of the Children, as well Daughters as Sons', particularly in '*Arithmetick* and Merchants Accounts'; their 'employment of their Poor'; 'Their use

[18] Temple, *Observations upon the United Provinces of the Netherlands* (London: Printed by A. Maxwell for Sa. Gellibrand, 1673), 198.

[19] Temple, *Observations*, 197, 68 [N.B. the pagination of the 1673 edition runs 1–80 and then 65–255; I refer to the second page 68].

[20] Aglionby, 116, 233.

of BANKS'; 'Their *Toleration of different Opinions in matters of Religion*', which attracted immigration; and their use of 'PUBLICK *REGISTERS* of all Lands and Houses'. Last and most important was *'the lowness of Interest of Money with them'*, which was, as Child virtually yelled, 'THE CAUSE OF THE PROSPERITY AND RICHES OF ANY NATION'.[21] Petty differed with Child over interest rate legislation, but much of the rest recalled the aims of the Hartlib Circle, if not Petty's own observations of the Netherlands.[22] More strikingly, Child echoed Petty's vision of a methodized population:

> It is (I think) agreed on by all, That *Merchants, Artificers, Farmers of Land,* and such as depend on them … *viz. Seamen, Fishermen, Breeders of Cattle, Gardners, &c.* are the three sorts of People which by their study and labour do principally, if not onely, bring in Wealth to a Nation from abroad; other kinds of People, *viz. Nobility, Gentry, Lawyers, Physicians, Scholars* of all sorts, and *Shopkeepers*, do onely hand it from one to another at home.[23]

Child proposed nothing so ambitious or invasive as the quota system for the professions Petty had outlined; still, he hoped that 'abatement of Interest … will adde new life and Motion to those most profitable Engines of the Kingdom', the artisans, merchants, and husbandmen who produced the nation's wealth.

For Child, as for Petty, good policy would reshape the population. Here, again, the Dutch were past masters. Keymor described how 'they make their Landmen Seamen, their Seamen Fishermen, their Fishermen Marriners, Marriners Merchants, and of their Merchants Statesmen, to govern and make their Country prosper by long experience.'[24] The idleness and immobility of the English and Irish provided a baleful contrast:

> The people of *Ireland*, and round about the Coasts of *England*, after they have been at Sea and brought home their Vessels full of Fish, will not go to Sea again for more till those be spent and they in debt, till necessity compells them, unless it be some few, and they prosper, yet they are loath to take too much, lest it should be too cheap, for they never seek other Markets but their own … This is the life of these people where great riches is to be gotten.[25]

---

[21] Child, *Brief Observations Concerning Trade, and Interest of Money* (London: Printed for Elizabeth Calvert and Henry Mortlock, 1668), 3–6, 10.

[22] In 1673 Child wrote to Petty directly, hoping 'to convince you of the Verity, reasonableness and use of these conjectures'; Child to Petty, 15 October 1673, BL MS Add. 72850, f.132r.

[23] Child, 16.   [24] Keymor, *Observation*, 6.   [25] Keymor, *Observation*, 10.

Taking proper advantage of England's situation meant creating a population willing and able to improve and exploit it, a population resembling the Dutch. The right policies, fitted to England's situation, could do this. And such policies, no matter how dramatically they intervened in society, would be 'natural', in the dual sense that nature would have paved the way for them and that from them desirable consequences would naturally follow. Concluding his case for interest rate regulation, Child quoted 'the excellent, Sir *William Petty*'s Observation' in the *Treatise of Taxes*: '*Res nolunt male Administrare* [sic]: Nature must and will have its course'.[26]

Political arithmetic

Quite when Petty began working on what he came to call 'political arithmetic' is not certain. His earliest surviving references to it, in two letters written in December 1672, suggest that by that point the idea was well established in his head, if not on paper. 'I have a world more of Political Arithmethik', he informed Southwell. Writing to Arthur Annesley, Earl of Anglesey, he elaborated slightly, describing his activities as either 'Matters of recreation' ('such things as I exercised my self with before the age of 20'), 'Business' (including projects 'to rectifie double charge in the Exchequer ... To contest with proud Beggars, and ... to provide imployment for 300 usefull artisans and beggars', perhaps on his Kerry estates) or 'Mixt': 'The last sort are, Politicall Arithmetick [and] the Politicall Anattommy of Ireland whereupon I thinke depends The Politicall Medicine of that Country'.[27] Whatever the exact occasion, *Political Arithmetick*—written and circulated alongside *The Political Anatomy of Ireland*, but with wider application—approached the Dutch conundrum from the perspective of the 'philosopher' Petty thought himself to be. The parallel between situation's relationship to policy and nature's relationship to art enabled him to articulate Baconian methodology in a language economic writers understood.

Political Arithmetic's form and rhetoric suggest that it was provoked in particular by Roger Coke's *Treatise Wherein is Demonstrated, That the Church and State of England, Are in Equal Danger with the Trade*

---

[26] Child, 16. Petty did not agree with Child on the legislative issue, but each appealed to nature in exactly the same way to justify his position.

[27] Petty to Southwell, 7 December 1672, BL MS Add. 72858, f.58; Petty to Anglesey, 17 December 1672, BL MS Add. 72858, f.73.

of It and its companion, *Reasons of the Increase of the Dutch Trade*, which appeared together in 1671.[28] Coke identified population loss as the root cause of English decline, and his Treatise blamed several misguided but reversible policies—'The Law against Naturalization', 'The Peopling of the American Plantations', the Navigation Act, and the Irish Cattle Act—and castigated corporations, the poor law, and the excessive number of retailers.[29] Directly or indirectly, each hurt population, upon which the nation's wealth and strength depended, endangering church and state (by hurting their revenues) as well as trade. As usual, the Dutch had the answers. Their 'Men labour more industriously in Trade' under fewer restrictions. 'The Dutch build ships for Navigation more conveniently than the English' and thus 'acquire more Forein Commodities' and 'vend more domestic Manufactures in Trade'. Children 'of both Sexes' learned geometry, and their government was 'more Conversant in Trade'. 'The Dutch freely entertain men of all Nations' on equal terms.[30] These and other policies maximized both the quantity and the quality of the Dutch population.

Coke's list of Dutch policies, though more comprehensive than most, was essentially familiar, and like other writers—perhaps even more so—Coke emphasized art's capacity to supplement nature's limitations: 'though God in his infinite wisdom … created and disposed the Universe; yet without humane Understanding he did never build a House, Ship, or make Bread, or Cloth, &c. but those things come to pass only by humane Art and Industry.'[31] What set his treatises apart, and what most likely drew Petty's attention and ire, was their structure. Inspired by Plato and Euclid, Coke presented his arguments as a series of geometrical proofs: definitions, petitions, and axioms followed by propositions and theorems.[32] He expressed the hope that this 'Method of Reasoning (which heretofore hath been deemed impracticable, unless in Mathematicks, nor was it ever observed in those studies) may in some measure recreate and

---

[28] Coke, *A Treatise Wherein Is Demonstrated, That the Church and State of England, Are in Equal Danger with the Trade of It*, and *Reasons of the Increase of the Dutch Trade* (London: Printed by J. C. for Henry Brome and Roger Horn, 1671). The two treatises (labelled *I* and *II*) were printed together and paginated continuously. Coke had published a version of his argument the year before: Coke, *A Discourse of Trade* (London: Printed for H. Brome and R. Horne, 1670). Petty appears to have read the later work.

[29] Coke, *Treatise*, 1–76.   [30] Coke, *Reasons*, 106–107.   [31] Coke, *Treatise*, sig. B1v.

[32] Coke cited Plato's use of geometry in the epistle dedicatory and opened his preface by stating that all virtue, knowledge, and reason 'is begotten from prae-existing or fore-knowledge'; a 'Premonition to the Reader' following the preface explained the principles of geometrical demonstration with examples from Euclid. Coke, *Treatise*, sig. A4r, B1r, C3v–C6v.

delight you.'[33] It would also confer an aura of logical necessity on Coke's arguments. In a manner different from yet reminiscent of Hobbes's, Coke offered a political geometry. *Political Arithmetick* was Petty's reply.

First, Petty questioned Coke's pessimistic 'Perswasions' that rents were falling, bullion scarce, unemployment rife ('and yet that the Land is under-peopled'), '*Ireland* and the Plantations in *America* … are a Burthen to *England* … the *Hollanders* are at our heels … the *French* grow too fast upon both … and finally, that the Church and State of *England*, are in the same danger with the Trade of *England*'.[34] Next, he set out his own 'Method of Reasoning' in terms that recall his letter to More:

> The Method I take to do this, is not yet very usual; for instead of using only comparative and superlative Words, and intellectual Arguments, I have taken the course (as a specimen of the Political Arithmetick I have long aimed at) to express my self in terms of *Number, Weight*, or *Measure*; to use only Arguments of Sense, and to consider only such Causes, as have visible Foundations in Nature; leaving those that depend upon mutable Minds, Opinions, Appetites and Passions of particular Men, to the Consideration of others: Really professing my self as unable to speak satisfactorily upon those Grounds (if they may be call'd Grounds), as to foretell the cast of a Dye; to play well at Tennis, Billiards, or Bowles, (without long practice,) by virtue of the most elaborate Conceptions that have ever been written *De Projectilibus & Missilibus*, or of the Angles of Incidence and Reflection.[35]

Political arithmetic reflected Petty's long-held conception of natural philosophy. Like all real science, it was practical, not theoretical. It was rooted in common experience and visible causes rather than the 'Minds' or 'Opinions' of 'particular Men'. (The appetites and passions of human collectivities, which were subject to naturalistic interpretation, were another matter.) It was inductive and probable rather than deductive and certain.

Paradoxically, Petty's invocation of 'number, weight, and measure', combined with his connection to Hobbes and his collaboration with Graunt, has obscured some crucial implications of view of science for political arithmetic. One was that the accuracy or precision of the actual numbers Petty used was much less important than the possibilities for action that the *kinds* of figures he employed—demographic proportions in particular—opened up. In a manuscript dialogue of the 1660s, Petty

---

[33] Coke, *Treatise*, sig. A4r.   [34] Petty, *Political Arithmetick*, sig. a1v–a2r.
[35] Petty, *Political Arithmetick*, sig. a3v–a4r.

had defended the use of rough estimates in a variety of practical contexts, using imagery close to that of *Political Arithmetick*:

> B: I see you that ayme at so much cleernes & certainty are forced sometimes to fly to estimate & opinion.
>
> A: yes and to lott too; for in … representing a Man's face … the most Mathematical Limner useth no scale nor Compasses but measures properties both of lines and angles by the estimat of his Eye. Upon the Violin there are no frets or divisions upon the Neck but by estimate & yet the music [is] intended to bee exact. Those that play best at Tennis & billiards use no instruments for the angles of Incidence & Reflection … Wherefore there is more exactness in the conjectures of some Mens hadn & Eyes then in Measures or weights.[36]

As far as possible 'wee must stick to Number Weight & Measure'; but where the number of variables exceeded 'our senses & Instruments', 'the Estimate bona fide made by those of greatest practise & Experience must bee made use of'. *Political Arithmetick* took a similarly pragmatic line:

> Now the Observations or Positions expressed by *Number, Weight*, and *Measure*, upon which I bottom the ensuing Discourses, are either true, or not apparently false, and which if they are not already true, certain, and evident, yet may be made so by the Sovereign Power, *Nam id certum est quod certum reddi potest* [For that is certain which may be made so], and if they are false, not so false as to destroy the argument they are brought for; but at worst are sufficient as Suppositions to shew the way to that Knowledge I aim at.[37]

Another implication, increasingly obvious in later parts of *Political Arithmetick, The Political Anatomy of Ireland* and subsequent manuscripts, was that the purpose such numbers served was not just actuarial, but 'political' in a transformative sense—not simply to describe the nation's lands and

[36] Petty, 'How all persons & Things may contribute proporti[onally] to their Government & defense', BL MS Add. 72865, ff.7–8. Harris dates the manuscript to the 1660s.

[37] Petty, *Political Arithmetick*, sig. a4v. Mary Poovey suggests that Petty's printed works threw a veil of putatively 'impartial' numbers over private interests, helping thereby to create 'the modern fact'. This ignores Petty's manuscript circulation, underestimates his political ambition and overestimates both his need for duplicity and his ability to succeed in it. While Petty denied 'faction' or 'party'—bywords not for interest *tout court* but for politically divisive interest in particular—he frankly avowed the political 'argument' of his numbers, an argument for union (against party). His personal stake in the policies he promoted was common knowledge—especially among those to whom he directed his manuscripts. See Poovey, *A History of the Modern Fact: Problems of Knowledge in the Sciences of Wealth and Society* (Chicago: University of Chicago Press, 1998), 120–138; see also Margaret C. Jacob, 'Factoring Mary Poovey's *A History of the Modern Fact*', *History and Theory* 40 (2001), 280–289.

hands but to show the sovereign how to manipulate them. Hence the assertion that where the numbers failed, the 'Sovereign Power', conceived in Hobbesian terms as unitary and supremely powerful, would make them good. Yet political arithmetic was no Hobbesian science. According to *Leviathan*, 'The skill of making, and maintaining Common-wealths, consisteth in certain Rules, as doth Arithmetique and Geometry; not (as Tennis-play) on Practise onely: which Rules, neither poor men have the leisure, nor men that have had the leisure, have hitherto had the curiosity, or the method to find out.'[38] Petty's own tennis metaphor turned Hobbes on his head: bothering with abstract deductions was like calculating the motions of a tennis ball from the sidelines. The point was to win the game.

For Petty as for many others, Dutch experience was exemplary. Yet the first chapter of *Political Arithmetick*, arguing 'That a small Country and few People, by its *Situation*, *Trade*, and *Policy*, may be equivalent in *Wealth* and *Strength*, to a far greater People and Territory', embedded familiar elements of English economic writing in an unusually systematic discussion of what might, to paraphrase Adam Smith, be called the nature and causes of the wealth—and strength—of nations.[39] Stealing a page from Hobbes, Petty posited a state of nature, a 'first Plantation' at the beginning of history. At this stage, he thought, 'the Original and Primitive difference holds proportion as Land to Land'—that is, 'upon the first Plantation, the number of Planters was in Proportion to the quantity of Land'. All things being equal, population (and thus, assuming primitive circumstances, wealth and strength) should be evenly distributed across equal areas; 'wherefore, if the People are not in the same proportion as the Land, the same must be attributed to the Scituation of the Land, and to the Trade and Policy of the People superstructed thereupon.' In fact, neither wealth nor strength was evenly distributed, as a series of ratios illustrated: French land area was to Dutch as seven or eight to one, yet Amsterdam was one-third the size of Paris, its buildings worth half as much and the Dutch fleet nine times the size of the French. It followed 'that this difference of Improvement in Wealth and Strength, arises from the Situation, Trade, and Policy of the places respectively'.[40]

---

[38] Thomas Hobbes (ed. Richard Tuck), *Leviathan* (Cambridge: Cambridge University Press, 1991), 145.

[39] Smith, *An Inquiry into the Nature and Causes of the Wealth of Nations*, 2 vols (London: Printed for W. Strahan and T. Cadell, 1776).

[40] Petty, *Political Arithmetick*, 3–4, 10.

Political Arithmetick used this threefold framework both to compare and explain the present wealth and strength of nations and to delineate the scope of effective policy in the future. It began with the Dutch. 'Many Writing on this Subject', Petty wrote,

> do so magnifie the *Hollanders* as if they were more, and all other Nations less than Men (as to the matters of Trade and Policy) making them Angels, and others Fools, Brutes and Sots ... whereas I take the Foundation of their atchievements to lie originally in the Situation of the Country, whereby they do things inimitable by others, and have advantages whereof others are uncapable.[41]

Fertile Dutch soil permitted dense settlement, which reduced the cost of administration and defence and favoured 'mutual assistance in Trade.' The land was flat, making wind power easier to harness and further magnifying the effects of labour. Most important, Holland was perched between the sea and three navigable rivers. This not only rendered the country naturally defensible but also facilitated access to distant markets, allowing the Dutch to shift from agriculture to manufacturing and commerce. It promoted the development of fisheries and hence of shipping, encouraging the Dutch to visit 'all parts of the World, and to observe ... what each people can do, and what they desire, and consequently to be the Factors, and Carriers for the whole World of Trade.'[42]

'Situation hath given them Shipping, and Shipping hath given them in effect all other Trade'.[43] Trade conferred a second set of benefits, including an 'abundance of Silver, Gold, and Jewels'.[44] Yet Petty dwelt on the demographic changes underpinning these profits. 'Husbandmen, Seamen, Soldiers, Artizans and Merchants, are the very Pillars of any Common-Wealth', he wrote; 'all the other great Professions, do rise out of the infirmities, and miscarriages of these'. The *Treatise of Taxes* had distinguished husbandmen and artisans, whose numbers should be maximized, from members of the professions, whose numbers should be tied to the needs of the population. Now, Petty drew attention to a new group: 'every Seaman of industry and ingenuity, is not only a Navigator, but a Merchant, and also a Soldier ... because he is familiarized with hardship and hazards, extending to Life and Limbs.' In terms of his contribution to national wealth, further, 'a Seaman is in effect three Husbandmen'.[45] Petty's concern with sailors echoed contemporary economic literature, much of which focused on

---

[41] Petty, *Political Arithmetick*, 10.   [42] Petty, *Political Arithmetick*, 11–15.
[43] Petty, *Political Arithmetick*, 21.   [44] Petty, *Political Arithmetick*, 18.
[45] Petty, *Political Arithmetick*, 17–18. See also BL MS Add. 72865, ff.6–13.

fisheries and (reflecting balance-of-trade theory) long-distance commerce. But beyond that, seamen played a role in *Political Arithmetick* like that of soldiers in the Down Survey: a mobile, mutable, industrious population endowed with basic skills, pillars of national wealth and strength—political arithmetic's ideal subjects. Situation, and the trade that situation made possible, naturally maximized the number of such subjects in the Dutch population. Dutch success reflected no special intelligence or virtue; given similar natural surroundings and advantages, any nation could do the same.

Even when Petty turned to 'the effects of their Policy, superstructed upon these natural advantages', nature remained paramount. Noting that 'The *Hollanders* were one hundred years since, a poor and oppressed People, living in a Country naturally cold and unpleasant; and were withal persecuted for their Heterodoxy in Religion', he traced the origins of Dutch industry to a mixture of environment and historical circumstance:

> From hence it necessarily follows, that this People must Labour hard, and set all hands to Work: Rich and Poor, Young and Old, must study the Art of Number, Weight, and Measure; must fare hard, provide for Impotents, and for Orphans, out of hope to make profit by their Labours: must punish the Lazy by Labour, and not by crippling them: I say, all these particulars, said to be the subtile excogitations of the *Hollanders*, seem to me, but what could not almost have been otherwise.

All the various policies other writers singled out were in this sense just the natural consequences of the Dutch situation: 'Liberty of Conscience, Registry of Conveyances, small Customs, Banks, Lumbards, and Law Merchant, rise all from the same Spring, and tend to the same Sea; as for lowness of Interest'—Child's hobby-horse—'it is also a necessary effect of all the premisses, and not the fruit of their contrivance.'[46]

Yet even if good policies were ultimately nature's instruments, they still proximately depended on human effort; even if unnatural policies were doomed to fail, fallible statesmen might still pursue them. Thus the natural logic of Dutch policies was worth grasping. Petty gave particular attention to the reasons for liberty of conscience. Historically, 'They themselves broke with *Spain*, to avoid the imposition of the Clergy.' Sounding a little like Max Weber, Petty noted that 'Dissenters ... are for the most part, thinking, sober, and patient Men, and such as believe that Labour and Industry is their Duty towards God.'[47] Further, 'The

[46] Petty, *Political Arithmetick*, 21–22.
[47] Max Weber (trans. Talcott Parsons), *The Protestant Ethic and the Spirit of Capitalism* (1930; London: Routledge, 2001). Petty's argument, however, was about nonconformity in general.

Hollanders observe that in *France* and *Spain* ... the Churchmen are about one hundred for one, to what they use or need', their numbers swollen in the fight against heterodoxy. Trade multiplied useful seamen; uniformity created 'superfluous' clerics.[48] He speculated that trade might even depend on the global phenomenon of religious dissent: 'it is to be observed that Trade doth not (as some think) best flourish under Popular Governments, but rather that Trade is most vigorously carried on, in every State and Government, by the Heterodox part of the same, and such as profess Opinions different from what are publickly established'. 'Banians' in the Mughal Empire, Christians among the Ottomans, Jews in Turkey, Italy, and Portugal, Protestants in Catholic Europe, Dissenters in Protestant countries, even Catholics in Ireland, 'where the said *Roman* Religion is not authorized'—everywhere, 'the Heterodox part of the whole' drove trade out of all proportion to its size and political power. '[I]t follows, that for the advancement of Trade, (If that be a sufficient reason), Indulgence must be granted in matters of Opinion.'[49]

Petty did not explain the connection between dissent and trade, but he emphasized that heterodoxy was universal and inevitable, for the same reason given in the *Reflections* in 1659—the nature of post-lapsarian man. He now expressed this, however, in terms of demographic proportion: 'They believe that if 1/4 of the People were Heterodox, and that if that whole quarter should by Miracle be removed, that within a small time 1/4 of the remainder would again become Heterodox some way or other, it being natural for Men to differ in Opinion in matters above Sense and Reason.'[50] Dutch policy recognized that 'Heterodoxy most abounded' where uniformity was pursued, and that any human population naturally produced a certain proportion of dissenters, regardless of history or intentions. One may doubt whether Petty thought that Dutch policymakers consciously grasped this or that the heterodox proportion was naturally fixed at any one fraction of the total population. Either way, liberty of conscience was less important as the key to Dutch economic success than as a model of natural policy—a policy that built upon nature (whether situation or human nature), avoided meddling in matters of opinion, and, by letting nature work, improved the population and strengthened the state.

Just as Dutch toleration exemplified the power of natural policy, French and Spanish intolerance illustrated the perils of pushing against

---

[48] Petty, *Political Arithmetick*, 23–24.   [49] Petty, *Political Arithmetick*, 25–27.
[50] Petty, *Political Arithmetick*, 24–25.

nature—a bloated, expensive clergy and an exiled population of industrious Protestants (in the French case) and Jews (in the Spanish). Petty continued to criticize France in the third chapter of *Political Arithmetick*, focusing on Louis XIV's attempts to build up his navy. The chapter title said it all: '*France* cannot by reason of natural, and perpetual Impediments, be more powerful at Sea, than the *English*, or *Hollanders*'.[51] Like Dutch advantages, French impediments began with geography but ended with demography. France had 'no Ports able to receive large windward Vessels, between *Dunkirk* and *Ushant*'; the Atlantic ports, meanwhile, were difficult to defend.[52] Territory shaped population. Petty estimated France's fleet at 150,000 tons, 'and consequently not above fifteen thousand Seamen, reckoning a Man to every ten Tun.'[53] Recruiting seamen took time, and depended on the number of experienced seamen available to train new men—itself a function of situation and trade, not liable to the whims of policy alone:

> Besides it is three or four years at a *medium*, wherein a Seaman must be made; neither can there be less than three Seamen, to make a fourth, of a Landman: Consequently the fifteen thousand Seamen of *France*, can increase but five thousand Seamen in three or four years, and unless their Trade should increase with their Seamen in proportion, the King must be forced to bear the charge of this improvement[.][54]

Given these constraints, 'the King of *France*, neither hath, nor can have men sufficient, to Man a Fleet, of equal Strength to the King of *England*.'[55] Nature would not be cozened.

Turning at last to England, Petty argued 'That the People and Territories of the King of *England* are naturally near as considerable for Wealth and Strength, as those of *France*.'[56] He did not base this implausible claim on precise numbers; he admitted that Louis XIV controlled more territory than Charles II and estimated France's population at 13.5 million, as against 9.5 million in Britain and Ireland, 10 million counting overseas colonies and factories.[57] The key, rather, was a notional sense of proportion and a kind of *qualitative* demography. First, 'both Princes have more Land, than they do employ to its utmost use'; the ratio of hands to lands was more important than the absolute number of either.[58] Second, not all hands were equal: 'Although it be very material to know the number of

51 Petty, *Political Arithmetick*, 51.   52 Petty, *Political Arithmetick*, 53–54.
53 Petty, *Political Arithmetick*, 56.   54 Petty, *Political Arithmetick*, 60.
55 Petty, *Political Arithmetick*, 54.   56 Petty, *Political Arithmetick*, 64.
57 Petty, *Political Arithemtick*, 75.   58 Petty, *Political Arithmetick*, 65.

Subjects belonging to each Prince,' Petty wrote, 'yet when the Question is concerning their *Wealth* and *Strength*; It is also material to examin, how many of them do get more than they spend, and how many less.' The English population, though smaller, was better distributed: commoners were wealthier and artisans and seamen more numerous. France had too many of the wrong kind of people: 250,000 churchmen, outside the labour force but living off it, reduced the effective population to under 13 million.[59] Though deficient in absolute terms, England was 'naturally near as considerable for Wealth and Strength' as France.

Further, 'the Impediments of *Englands* greatness' were 'but contingent and removable', matters of mistaken policy or failures to capitalize on situation.[60] Several were familiar from the *Treatise of Taxes*: 'the different Understanding of several Material Points' touching the powers of king and Parliament; the fact 'That Taxes ... are not Levied upon the *expence*, but upon the whole *Estate*' and thus 'chiefly upon Land'; the crazy-quilt of parishes and precincts, 'which do hinder the Operations of Authority ... as a Wheel irregularly made, and excentrically hung'; more tentatively, in a Hobbesian vein, the problem 'that the power of making War, and raising Mony be not in the same Hand.'[61] Petty's response to these problems was also familiar. Chapter II argued for taxes that redistributed wealth from spendthrifts to improvers; chapters VI–X argued that England's people, trade, and coin could sustain tax reform, maintain the civil administration and a 90,000-strong military, generate £2 million per annum by employing 'spare hands', and 'drive the Trade of the whole *Commercial World*.'[62] The framework of situation, trade, and policy simply juxtaposed politics and nature more directly than the *Treatise* had done: 'None of the Impediments are Natural', Petty proclaimed, and 'As these Impediments are contingent, so they are also removeable'.[63]

Two impediments, however, stood out. The first concerned England's expanding empire, whose '*Territories* ... are too far asunder, and divided by the Sea into many several *Islands* and Countries; and ... into so many Kingdoms, and several Governments.'[64] The sea was an impediment not easily removed, but it was the attendant divisions of state and population for which Petty saw no 'naturally substantial reasons from the Situation, Trade, and Condition of the People'.[65] A host of political, legal, and administrative

---

[59] Petty, *Political Arithmetick*, 75–78.
[60] Petty, *Political Arithmetick*, 87.
[61] Petty, *Political Arithmetick*, 91–94.
[62] Petty, *Political Arithmetick*, 35–51, 96–116.
[63] Petty, *Political Arithmetick*, 94–95.
[64] Petty, *Political Arithmetick*, 87.
[65] Petty, *Political Arithmetick*, 88.

divisions within and between Charles's kingdoms and colonies—artefacts of policy including the Navigation and Cattle Acts—obviated the potential advantages of imperial geography by manufacturing internecine rivalries. Petty's sketchy solution was a form of imperial union: the creation of 'Two such Grand Councils, as may equally represent the whole Empire, one to be chosen by the King, the other by the People'.[66] This would not solve every problem (colonies might still drain people from the metropole), but it would at least reduce a multiplicity of governments to a single state.[67] Natural policies might then more easily reduce the population to '*Unity, industry,* and *obedience,* in order to the Common Safety, and each Man's particular Happiness.'[68] The rational administration of the empire and the optimal disposition of its population faced a second impediment, however. This was Ireland.

The political anatomy of Ireland

Chapter IV of *Political Arithmetick* had given ten pages to 'a jocular, and perhaps ridiculous digression', namely,

> that if all the *moveables* and People of *Ireland,* and of the Highlands of *Scotland,* were transported into the rest of *Great Brittain*...then the King and his Subjects, would thereby become more *Rich* and *Strong,* both *offensively* and *defensively,* than now they are...I have heard Wise Men (in such their Melancholies) wish, that (the People of *Ireland* being saved) *Island* were sunk under Water: Now it troubles me, that the Distemper of my own mind in this point, carries me to dream, that the benefit of those wishes, may practically be obtained, without sinking that vast Mountainous Island under Water.[69]

Petty presented this as a 'Dream, or Resvery', but reminded readers that Thomas More and Descartes had commented on the difficulty of distinguishing dreams from reality.[70] It was indeed hard to tell the difference. Condensing the population by 'transplanting about Eighteen Hundred thousand People, from the poor and miserable Trade of Husbandry to more beneficial Handicrafts' in lowland cities and towns would, Petty

---

[66] Petty, *Political Arithmetick,* 88–91.   [67] Petty, *Political Arithmetick,* 91.
[68] Petty, *Political Arithmetick,* 117.   [69] Petty, *Political Arithmetick,* 65–66.
[70] Descartes discusses this in the first of his *Meditations;* see Descartes (trans. John Cottingham, Robert Stoothoff and Dugald Murdoch), *The Philosophical Works of Descartes,* 2 vols (Cambridge: Cambridge University Press, 1984), 2:13. I have not located any comparable passage in More.

now suggested, increase the ratio of hands to lands and the proportion of the population employed in profitable sectors of the economy. Increased rents, consumption ('every Man desiring to put on better apparel when he appears in Company') and revenues, greater specialization, and decreased expenses for church and state would follow.[71] These were the very processes Petty had seen behind Dutch success; the only apparently fantastic element was the massive transplantation of people required to get them started in Britain.

Just twenty pages later, transplantation reappeared in Petty's catalogue of impediments to England's greatness:

> The third impediment [of England's greatness] is, That *Ireland* being a Conquered Country, and containing not the tenth part as many *Irish* natives, as there are *English* in both Kingdoms, That natural and firm Union is not made, between the two Peoples, by Transplantations, and proportionable mixture, so as there may be but a tenth part, of the *Irish* in *Ireland*, and the same proportion in *England*; whereby the necessity of maintaining an Army in *Ireland*, at the expence of a quarter of all the Rents of that Kingdom may be taken away.[72]

Transplantation here was no dream, but a step towards the real, natural, and necessary goal of union. Union itself was not simply a matter of institutional conglomeration but depended on the 'proportionable mixture' of populations. Finally, while transplantation, mixture, and union addressed fiscal-military challenges—freeing up revenues by removing the need for a standing army in Ireland—they worked differently from conventional policy. The Dutch promoted wealth and strength through legislative or institutional means (allowing liberty of conscience, promoting trade, setting up banks); the success of these policies was reflected in the size and disposition of the population. Transplantation manipulated demography directly. Understanding how Petty could see so invasive a policy as a natural solution to the unnatural impediment of disunion requires seeing political arithmetic as a product of both Petty's natural philosophy and his understanding of Ireland's problems. *The Political Anatomy of Ireland* brought these together.

Although its appearance may have been prompted by different concerns—there was encouragement from official quarters for a 'state of Ireland' to be made available—*Political Anatomy* can be read as an extended application to Ireland of the approach adumbrated in the *Treatise*

[71] Petty, *Political Arithmetick*, 66–74.   [72] Petty, *Political Arithmetick*, 92.

of Taxes and elaborated in *Political Arithmetick*.[73] Petty's rhetoric shifted from mathematics to medicine, but Baconian natural philosophy was still the key:

> Sir Francis Bacon, in his *Advancement of Learning*, hath made a judicious *Parallel* in many particulars, between the *Body Natural*, and *Body Politick*, and between the Arts of preserving both in Health and Strength: And it is as reasonable, that as *Anatomy* is the best foundation of one, so also of the other; and that to practice upon the Politick, without knowing the *Symmetry, Fabrick*, and *Proportion* of it, is as casual as the practice of Old-women and Empyricks.[74]

As in *Political Arithmetick*, Petty stressed the novelty of his approach and its freedom from faction: 'I ... who profess no Politicks, have, for my curiosity, at large attempted *the first Essay of Political Anatomy*.' He even gave scientific reasons for his choice of Ireland:

> Furthermore, as Students in Medicine, practice their inquiries upon cheap and common *Animals*, and such whose actions they are best acquainted with, and where there is the least confusion and perplexure of Parts; I have chosen *Ireland* as such a *Political Animal*, who is scarce Twenty years old; where *Intrigue* of *State* is not very complicate, and with which I have been conversant from an *Embrion*[.][75]

At the same time, however, he stressed that this science was not so much analytically precise as politically useful:

> 'Tis true, that curious *Dissections* cannot be made without variety of proper Instruments; whereas I have only a common *Knife* and a *Clout* ... However, my rude approaches being enough to find whereabout the Liver and Spleen,

---

[73] *EW*, 1:123.

[74] Petty, *Political Anatomy*, sig. A5r. Tony Aspromourgos sees political anatomy and political arithmetic as opposed models, one algebraic, the other organic; Aspromourgos, 'Political Economy, Political Arithmetic and Political Medicine in the Thought of William Petty', in Peter D. Groenewegen (ed.), *Physicians and Political Economy: Six Studies in the Work of Doctor-Economists* (London: Routledge, 2001), 10–25. He argues (17) that 'algebra eventually won out.' Yet as late as 1687 Petty proposed 'To make Politicall Anatomyes, and keep accompts of his Majesties 3 Kingdomes' ('Advantages humbly offered to the King', BL MS Add. 72866, ff.101–102), and described his 'Treatise of Ireland' as 'An Essay in Political Arithmetick' that included 'The Political Anatomy of that Kingdom' (*EW*, 2:549).

[75] This passage is often read as justifying English colonialism by dehumanizing the Irish, but in his earlier history 'Of making cloth with sheeps wool' Petty had defended the scientific value of 'describing the minutiae of very ordinary and small operations' in identical terms, as comparable to 'the anatomy of a mouse or frog ... as small, and as common, and as cheap as these are.' (Birch, *History*, 1:60.) For Petty's audience, the English colonization of Ireland required no defence; his new science was another matter.

and Lungs lye, tho' not to discern the Lymphatick Vessels, the *Plexus, Choroidus*, the *Volvuli* of vessels within the Testicles ... I have ventur'd to begin a *new* Work, which, when Corrected and Enlarged by better Hands and Helps, I believe will tend to the Peace and Plenty of my Country[.][76]

Ireland's testicles would turn out to be more important than the doctor suggested, but the main point was clear: like political arithmetic, political anatomy was an empirical, approximate, and above all practical discipline.

The text began with matters of number, weight, and measure. The first chapter broadly surveyed Ireland's lands according to area, quality, and ownership before and since the Restoration settlement, which, Petty complained, had given restored 'innocents' ('not 1/20 were really so') more land than they had owned even in 1641.[77] The second turned to 'People, Houses, and Smoaks'. Petty estimated the Irish population at 1,100,000, and divided this several ways. The first and most important division was at once national and confessional: 800,000 Irish 'Papists', as against 300,000 'Non-Papists', of whom 200,000 were English and 100,000 Scots. From an economic angle, Petty estimated that 160,000 families had no fixed hearth, 24,000 one chimney, and 16,000 more than one. He attempted to gauge the proportion of the population available for labour, subtracting 'impotents' (whom he estimated at one five hundredth of the population), children under seven, and soldiers—as well as landowners, ministers, students, and domestic servants—yielding a total of 780,000 'fit for Trade'. Of these, he estimated that 100,000 were employed in tillage, 120,000 in pasturage, and 140,000 in productive trades, leaving roughly 400,000—half, apparently, running alehouses, and the other half useless 'Casherers and Fait-neants'.[78]

Petty's calculations were occasionally shaky, but normative considerations outweighed analytical niceties as his economic anatomy of the population shaded into a programme of social and demographic improvement. The elimination of two-thirds of the alehouses would leave 340,000 free for more useful employment; these might earn £2,380,000 through various projects for 'Local Wealth, or Universal Wealth'. Local projects included building 168,000 stone houses with gardens and orchards 'instead of the lamentable Sties now in use' (that is, by the 160,000 families without fixed hearths), 'Inclosures and Quicksetts', various fortifications and new buildings for Dublin, 'Making several Rivers navigable and mending

[76] Petty, *Political Anatomy*, sig. A5r–v.   [77] Petty, *Political Anatomy*, 1–7.
[78] Petty, *Political Anatomy*, 7–13.

High-Ways', building churches, and setting up 'Workhouses of several sorts, Tan-Yards, Fishing Crofts, Rape-Mills, Allom and Copperas-works, as also Madder, Lead, Salt, &c.' Projects for 'Universal Wealth' promoted Ireland's overseas trade: building up shipping and stocks of wool, hemp, flax, and hides for export.[79] Like Petty's plan to index the number of clerics to Ireland's different religious populations, these projects vividly recalled the *Treatise* if not the Hartlib Circle.[80] In Ireland as in England, the paramount task was to dispose of the population in the most effective way.

Some problems, however, were peculiarly Irish. The fourth chapter, 'Concerning the Late Rebellion', dwelt upon the price of 1641 and its aftermath: 37,000 English killed in the 'massacres' of the first year (a considerable overestimate, but much lower than the then-current figure of half a million) and 112,000 by 1652; 504,000 Irish killed by war, plague, or famine over the same period, and 40,000 transported out of the country as exiles; adjusting for the natural increase of the 1641 population, a total loss of 689,000, 'for whose Blood some body should answer both to God and the King.'[81] Besides this was the material cost—cattle, goods, buildings, and other improvements destroyed, trade cut off, land values decimated, income and revenues lost—£37,255,000 in all, by Petty's reckoning.[82] (This included the loss of Irish labourers, each of whom Petty valued 'as Slaves and Negroes are usually rated, viz. at about £15 one with another.' Englishmen, he thought, were worth £70 apiece.)[83] Legacies of the rebellion and turmoil over the land settlement lingered, hindering recovery and improvement. Still other problems—chronic currency shortages and troublesome trade restrictions associated with absentee landlords, tax farmers, and the Navigation and Cattle Acts—derived from Ireland's long-term slide towards colonial status, a tendency the postwar settlements merely confirmed.[84]

Though new legislation might offer some temporary fixes, Ireland's problems derived ultimately from the interaction of situation, trade, and policy over centuries. Reform would ideally begin with the kind of ex-perimental, quantitative natural history Petty himself had once hoped to provide. He proposed 'long, tedious and reiterated Observations, simple and comparative' of the 'Heat, Coldness, Drowth, Moisture, Weight and Susceptions' of Ireland's air, using the latest instruments, proposing

[79] Petty, *Political Anatomy*, 14–15.   [80] Petty, *Political Anatomy*, 16–17.
[81] Petty, *Political Anatomy*, 17–20.   [82] Petty, *Political Anatomy*, 20–23.
[83] Petty, *Political Anatomy*, 21.   [84] Petty, *Political Anatomy*, 68–75.

'like Expedients' for testing the qualities of the soil.[85] Next he sought to determine the proportional value of land in Ireland's different regions, which wrangling over the settlement had hitherto prevented.[86] A similar question had led him into tricky theoretical territory before; here, he not only repeated the *Treatise*'s call for 'a *Par* and *Equation* between Lands and Labour' to make value expressible in either form, but suggested further pars 'between Art [i.e. skilled work] and Simple Labour', between 'Art and Opinion' and even 'between drudging Labour, and Favour, Acquaintance, Interest, Friends, Eloquence, Reputation, Power, Authority'—'equations' quantifying the sources not simply of economic value but of social power itself.[87] This series of pars (which Petty considered 'of the same kind' as the 'Equation between Land and Labour') would have allowed for a very fine-grained methodization of population indeed.

In practice, however, Petty's assessment of Ireland's situation was confined to rudimentary observations of the sort familiar from *Political Arithmetick*. Like the Dutch, the Irish enjoyed easy access to the sea from most parts of the country, which 'lieth Commodiously for the Trade of the new *American* world; which we see daily to grow and flourish.' Its natural products were well suited to both European and transatlantic trade: 'It lieth well for sending Butter, Cheese, Beef, Fish, to their proper Markets, which are to the Southward, and the Plantations of *America*.'[88] Yet, although Ireland was 'by Nature very fit for Trade,' the Irish were neither equipped nor motivated to produce goods for their 'proper' markets:

> for as hath often been said, the Housing thereof consists of 160,000 nasty Cabbins, in which neither butter nor Cheese, nor Linnen, Yarn nor Worsted, and I think no other, can be made to the best advantage; chiefly by reason of the Soot and Smoaks annoying the same; as also for the Narrowness and Nastiness of the Place; which cannot be kept Clean nor Safe from Beasts and Vermin, nor from Damps and Musty Stenches, of which all the Eggs laid or kept in those Cabbins do partake.

Trade required 'the reformation of these Cabbins' and 'the Institution of ... Corporations' for marketing agricultural commodities.[89] However, the people in the cabins were the real problem. Rather than building upon their situation, they were content to 'live simply, and as it were *ex sponte*

[85] Petty, *Political Anatomy*, 48–58.   [86] Petty, *Political Anatomy*, 58–63.
[87] Petty, *Political Anatomy*, 63–67.   [88] Petty, *Political Anatomy*, 78–79.
[89] Petty, *Political Anatomy*, 79–80.

creatis', generating 'little or no Trade' despite the natural advantages they enjoyed.[90] As Petty summed it up:

> There is at this Day no Monument or real Argument that, when the *Irish* were first invaded, they had any Stone-Housing at all, any Money, any Foreign Trade, nor any Learning but the legend of the Saints, Psalters, Missals, Rituals, *&c. viz.* nor Geometry, Astronomy, Anatomy, Architecture, Enginery, Painting, Carving, nor any kind of Manufacture, nor the least use of Navigation, or the Art Military.[91]

Yet Petty did not blame Irish failures on any inherent incapacity for civilization. Certainly, he affirmed that 'there is much Superstition' among the poor Irish, but he traced this, following Hobbes, to the influence of the grandees and the 'Interest' of the priestly class, who terrorized 'their flocks with dreadful Stories' instead of 'persuading them by Reason, or the Scriptures.'[92] There is little reason to think his opinion of English peasants was any higher. Indulging in some Galenic irony, he promised to 'deduce' Irish 'Manners … from their Original Constitutions of Body, and from the Air; next from their Ordinary Food; next from their Condition of Estate and Liberty, and from the Influence of their Governours and Teachers; and lastly, from their Ancient Customs'. In fact, humoral physiology was as irrelevant to Irish manners as to any other kind. Situation, trade, and policy explained everything:

> Their Lazing seems to me to proceed rather from want of Imployment and Encouragement to Work, than from the natural abundance of Flegm in their Bowels and Blood; for what need they to Work, who can content themselves with *Potato's*, whereof the Labour of one Man can feed forty; and of Milk, whereof one Cow will, in Summer time, give meat and drink enough for three Men, when they can every where gather Cockles, Oysters, Muscles, Crabs, *&c.* with Boats, Nets, Angles, or the Art of Fishing; can build an House in three days?

Ireland's natural fecundity combined with England's unnatural policies to inhibit improvement:

> And why should they desire to fare better, tho with more Labour, when they are taught, that this way of living is more like the Patriarchs of old, and the Saints of later times …? And why should they breed more Cattel, since 'tis Penal to import them into *England*? Why should they raise more Commodities, since there are not Merchants sufficiently Stock'd to take them

---

[90] Petty, *Political Anatomy*, 86.   [91] Petty, *Political Anatomy*, 25.
[92] Petty, *Political Anatomy*, 94–96.

of them, nor provided with other more pleasing Commodities, to give in Exchange for them? And how should Merchants have Stock, since Trade is prohibited and fetter'd by the Statutes of *England*? And why should Men endeavour to get Estates ... where Tricks and Words destroy natural Right and Property?

'They are accused also', he went on, 'of much Treachery, Falseness, and Thievery; none of all which, I conceive, is natural to them'. Treachery was only to be expected, since their priests made them 'believe, that they all shall flourish again' with English defeat; 'As for Thievery, it is affixt to all thin-peopled Countries, such as *Ireland* is'.[93]

These were ultimately matters of quantitative and more especially qualitative demography. Improvement depended upon augmenting the industrious proportion of the population. But this was not just a matter of employing the idle; thanks to the particular interplay of situation and policy over centuries, the Irish altogether lacked the commercial mindset needed to make improvement work. One task of future policy was to instil this quality in the population—to induce the Irish to produce for the market and to create in them the desire for its goods. (Reversing his 1662 endorsement of sumptuary laws, Petty hoped 'to beget a luxury in the 950,000 Plebeians, so as to make them spend, and consequently earn double what they at present do', increasing their own 'splendour, Art and Industry ... to the great enrichment of the Commonwealth.')[94] Most glaring, in the wake of 1641 and in the midst of debates over the French alliance and the Irish land settlement, was the problem of allegiance. Though the rebellion had failed, in practical terms the Irish were still 'govern'd indirectly by Foreign Power'—the Pope—through an 'Internal and Mystical Government' of priests, friars and 'lay patriots', looking for a chance to rebel once more.[95] Turning the Irish into steady producers and enthusiastic consumers depended upon making them into loyal subjects first.

Political Arithmetick had suggested uniting the English and Irish populations by 'transplantation' and 'proportionable mixture'. The fifth chapter of *Political Anatomy*, 'Of the future Settlement of *Ireland*, Prorogation of Rebellions, and its Union with *England*', spelled out exactly what this meant. The Cromwellian reconquest of Ireland had succeeded, but the Restoration settlement, with its restitutions and retrenchments, had failed to secure these gains. 'Wherefore (*Rebus sic stantibus*) what is now to be

---

[93] Petty, *Political Anatomy*, 98–100.   [94] Petty, *Political Anatomy*, 82–83.
[95] Petty, *Political Anatomy*, 36–41.

done is the Question, *viz*. What may be done by natural possibility, if Authority saw it fit?' 'Some furious Spirits have wished, that the *Irish* would rebel again, that they might be put to the Sword. But I declare, that motion to be not only impious and inhumane, but withal frivolous and pernicious even to the who have rashly wish'd for those occasions.'[96] As Gookin had pointed out, Irish labour remained the backbone of English plantation—getting rid of it would solve nothing. Moreover, a series of proportions suggested that 'the *Irish* will not easily rebel again': 'the *British Protestants* and Church have 3/4 of all the Lands; 5/6 of all the Housing in wall'd Towns, and Places of strength[;] 2/3 of the Foreign Trade.' Meanwhile, '6 of 8 of the *Irish* live in a brutish nasty Condition'; 'although there be in *Ireland* 8 *Papists* for 3 others; yet there are far more Soldiers, and Soldierlike-Men' among the Protestants.[97] 'Wherefore,' Petty concluded, 'declining all Military means of settling and securing *Ireland* in peace and plenty, what we offer shall tend to the transmuting one People into the other, and the thorough union of Interests upon natural and lasting Principles'.[98]

Transmutation began with transplantation. Echoing his earlier 'Resvery', Petty remarked that 'If *Henry* the II. had or could have brought over all the people of *Ireland* into *England*, declining the benefit of their Land; he had fortified, beautified and enrich'd *England*, and done real kindness to the *Irish*.' In fact, though 'near four times as hard now to be done as then', the same thing 'might be done, even now, with advantage to all Parties.'

> Whereas there are now 300,000 *British*, and 800,000 *Papists*, whereof 600,000 live in the wretched way above mentioned: If an Exchange was made of but about 200,000 *Irish*, and the like number of *English* brought over in their rooms, then the natural strength of the *British* would be equal to that of the *Irish*; but their Political and Artificial strength three times as great; and so visible, that the *Irish* would never stir upon a National or Religious Account.[99]

However, this was no dream. Petty was quite seriously suggesting a policy of planned, presumably coerced, migration. While this transplantation would disperse 200,000 Irish men, women, and children more or less harmlessly among England's population of nine million, the 200,000 English who replaced them would shift the demographic balance of power in Ireland decisively. From 8:3, the ratio of Papists to Protestants would

---

[96] Petty, *Political Anatomy*, 26. [97] Petty, *Political Anatomy*, 26–27.
[98] Petty, *Politcal Anatomy*, 29. [99] Petty, *Political Anatomy*, 29–30.

now be 6:5—not quite equal, as Petty claimed, but much more nearly so. Since Protestants already dominated Ireland's cities and trade, their 'Political and Artificial' supremacy would be amply confirmed. Rebellion would be unthinkable.

Yet this was hardly the union through proportionable mixture that *Political Arithmetick* promised. That called for a transplantation of a different kind—an exchange not of families but of women:

> There are among the 600,000 ... poor *Irish*, not above 20,000 of unmarried marriageable Women; nor would above two thousand *per Ann.* grow and become such. Wherefore if 1/2 the said Women were in one year, and half the next transported into *England*, and disposed of one to each Parish, and as many *English* brought back and married to the *Irish*, as would improve their Dwelling but to an House and Garden of £3 value, the whole Work of natural Transmutation and Union would in 4 or 5 years be accomplished.[100]

In conjunction with improvements Petty had suggested earlier (for example, the 160,000 stone houses with gardens that Ireland's able-bodied idle would build), the annual exchange of 10,000 women would transmute Irish society from within. English women would marry Irish men, run their households and bear their children; their Irish counterparts, sprinkled across England one to a parish, would take an extended immersion course in good housekeeping. Petty even suggested importing English Catholic priests to replace the troublesome native clergy—effectively granting liberty of conscience while neutralizing Catholicism's national aspect and thus erasing its political significance:

> So as that when the Priests, who govern the Conscience, and the Women, who influence the other powerful Appetites, shall be *English*, both of whom being in the Bosom of the Men, it must be, that no massacring of the *English*, can happen again. Moreover, when the Language of the Children shall be *English*, and the whole Oeconomy of the Family *English, viz.* Diet, Apparel, *&c.* the Transmutation will be very easy and quick.[101]

With transmutation accomplished, institutional fusion 'under one Legislative Power and Parliament' would be simple.[102] Transplantation and mixture would lead to transmutation and union.

Transmutation would solve all the 'Inconveniences of the Not-Union' Petty had lamented elsewhere—the trade restrictions, the treatment of Englishmen in Ireland as aliens, the artificial rivalry between the king's

[100] Petty, *Political Anatomy*, 30.   [101] Petty, *Political Anatomy*, 31.
[102] Petty, *Political Anatomy*, 31.

common subjects. It would not do so alone, of course; it was the core of a whole program of interrelated policies and projects. Perhaps most importantly, it implied, if it did not explicitly require, religious toleration. The point, after all, was to remove the sources of Irish disaffection, not the least of which, in Petty's view, was the political stigma that ecclesiastical uniformity artificially imposed on the Catholic population—a policy that defied human nature, producing few converts but many rebels. More explicit was the fit between Petty's coerced exchange of women and the construction of 160,000 English-style stone houses to house the new couples. These new-model households, linked to towns and ports by improved roads and canals, would produce butter, cheese, linen, and worsted for markets on both sides of the Atlantic, and consume the latest fashions, foods, and manufactures with the money they earned. They would also produce children who, raised by English mothers in English households, would know no difference between Ireland and England but the Irish Sea.

This was more than a pattern of economic development; it was a roadmap to Utopia. Central to it was a policy that can only strike the modern reader as morally repugnant and logistically ludicrous: the coerced 'exchange' of tens of thousands of English and Irish women, followed by the forced marriage of the English women in question to Irish strangers and the consignment of the Irish women to an unspecified fate in England. And yet this was not so implausible in the seventeenth century as we might think. Forced migration was a conspicuous feature of early-modern state-formation and imperial expansion, from the expulsion of Moors and Jews from Spain to the transatlantic slave trade—not to mention the transplantation into Connacht Petty and Gookin had opposed.[103] Nor was the transplantation of women Petty's invention: the Portuguese and Dutch had long since tried exporting single women to their Asian colonies, while *filles du roi* were arriving in New France as Petty wrote. In 1655, in fact, Oliver and Henry Cromwell had discussed sending 'women and maids' to help populate Jamaica—which may well be where Petty, then Henry's secretary, got the idea.[104] Nor, after 1641,

[103] Patrick J. Duffy (ed.), *To and from Ireland: Planned Migration Schemes, c. 1600–2000* (Dublin: Geography Publications, 2004); Emma Christopher, Cassandra Pybus and Marcus Rediker (eds), *Many Middle Passages: Forced Migration and the Making of the Modern World* (Berkeley: University of California Press, 2007); David Eltis, *Coerced and Free Migration: Global Perspectives* (Stanford: Stanford University Press, 2002).

[104] Ramsey, 78–79. See A. J. R. Russell-Wood, *The Portuguese Empire, 1415–1808: A World on the Move* (Baltimore: Johns Hopkins University Press, 1998), 109–111; Jean Gelman Taylor,

would many Englishmen doubt the justice of the project; having defeated a 'national' rebellion, England had at worst 'a Gamester's Right' to do with Ireland what it would.[105] As for the English women involved, Petty compared them to seamen pressed into naval service: 'The King has power to Imprest [sic] men to serve in War', Petty wrote, 'Methinks he may doe the same to prevent war.'[106] Even if we accept that Petty's scheme might appear practicable and legitimate, however, it remains unclear how uprooting and transplanting whole populations could seem *natural*. The key here was Petty's focus on the 'Oeconomy of the Family'. Grasping this allows us to see that transmutation was not a pathological diversion from Petty's economic thinking but the conceptual core of his social science.

The significance of transmutation

Political Arithmetick approached economic writing from without, relying on a conception of natural philosophy distinct from yet fusible with economic discourse as authors like Mun and Child produced it. *Political Anatomy* tackled another genre—English writing on Irish plantation—in a similar way.[107] Though the numbers and ratios by which he expressed them were novel, Petty's complaints about the Irish were commonplace elements of a tradition that began with Giraldus Cambrensis in the twelfth century and flourished from Elizabeth's day.[108] Edmund Spenser's *View of the Present State of Ireland* decried the unsettled habits of the barbaric 'mere' Irish, mocking the mantles they wore—'a fitt house for an outlawe, a meete bedd for a rebel, and [an] apte cloake for a thief'—and attributing their evil customs to Scythian heritage.[109] Fynes Moryson's *Itinerary* expressed disgust at Irish households, and Barnabe Rich's *New Description of Ireland* lingered over the filthy linen and rancid butter ('more

The Social World of Batavia: European and Eurasian in Dutch Asia (Madison: University of Wisconsin Press, 1983), 12–13; George Masselman, *The Cradle of Colonialism* (New Haven: Yale University Press, 1963), 311–312; Yves Landry, *Les Filles du Roi au XVIIe Siècle: Orphelines en France, Pionnières au Canada* (Ottawa: Leméac, 1992).

105 Petty, *Political Anatomy*, 24.
106 Petty, 'Of Counter-Transplanting the Irish & English', BL MS Add. 72879, ff.117–118.
107 McCormick, 'Mixture'.
108 Giraldus Cambrensis (ed. and trans. A. B. Scott and F. X. Martin), *Expugnatio Hibernica: The Conquest of Ireland* (Dublin: Royal Irish Academy, 1978).
109 Spenser, *View*, 63–69.

loathsome then toothsome') they produced.[110] Often this had little to do with the potential export markets Petty stressed; it simply confirmed Irish barbarism. Such attitudes were perhaps even more marked after 1641. Most would have agreed with John Davies's *Discoverie of the Trve Cavses why Ireland was Neuer Entirely Subdued* that 'the maners of the mere Irish are ... little altred since the dayes of King Henry the second'.[111] Worse, the original agents of English civilization had, in Spenser's words, 'degenerated and growen almost mere Irishe' themselves. Made insolent by their power and divided by private interests, the Old English had succumbed to the 'evill ordynance and Institucion of that commonwealth', taking on Irish allies, wives, and finally customs, language and even names—'So much can liberty and ill example doe.'[112]

English views of Ireland were complex, however, and Spenser, Davies and others traced Irish backwardness, at least in part, to social and institutional causes. The Gaelic practice of vesting real property in septs rather than individuals (who might improve their holdings) and passing them on through tanistry rather than by primogeniture (which would allow improvers to benefit their children) discouraged improvement.[113] Tyrannical lords thus squeezed a servile populace, from whom neither honesty nor industry could reasonably be expected, since neither was rewarded. Combining a similar analysis with an anticipation of Petty's trio of situation, trade, and policy, James Perrott wrote that 'the soyle and scituation of the contrie, with the example of the contriemen where any persons have theyr byrth and breedinge, hath a greate stroake to frame mens myndes unto vertue or vice.' But he added that 'likewise education and example are greate motives to make men either rude, rash, well governed, gentle and generous; wherein thoe nature hath ... at the least some sympathy to produce symilitude or anticipate in dissimilitude of manner and conditions, yet suerly education, example, and use bringes forth greate effectes of perfection and imperfection in men'.[114] Ireland's isolated

---

[110] Moryson, 101–114; Barnabe Rich, *A New Description of Ireland: Wherein Is Described the Disposition of the Irish whereunto They Are Inclined* (London: Printed for Thomas Adams, 1610), 25–26.

[111] Davies, *A Discoverie of the Trve Cavses why Ireland was Neuer Entirely Subdued* (Dublin: Printed by Iohn Iaggard, 1612), 3.

[112] Spenser, 62, 82; see Davies, *Discoverie*, 25–30.

[113] Spenser, *View*, 13, 105–107; John Davies, 'The Lawes of Ireland' (1609), Huntington Library MS Ellesmere 7042, ff.1–6; Davies, *Discoverie*, 165–171.

[114] Perrott (ed. Herbert Wood), *The Chronicle of Ireland, 1584–1608* (Dublin: Irish Manuscripts Commission, 1933), 14–15.

'scituation'—an idea later developed by economic writers—explained its
lack of 'commerce with forayn nacions' ('the cheifest meane to begette
civilitie'), which in turn explained the 'meane breeding' of the people.
Taken together, such accounts moved away from viewing the Irish as
inherently barbarous.[115] They suggested that, given a thorough conquest,
the eradication of pernicious native institutions and a systematic program
of reform, Irish civilization was possible. It was tanistry, Perrott wrote,
that made the Irish 'willinge rather to doe eivell then to be idle or well
imployed'. An English property regime 'would make them depend on the
State and not on theyr neere and greate lords'.[116]

These authors favoured various engines of reform and painted divergent
pictures of Ireland's future, but some form of union with England or
the English was a common thread. Spenser argued that 'good staye
of gouernment and stronge Ordynances' could overcome greater Irish
numbers, and hoped

> by an vnion of manners and conformitie of myndes, to bringe them to bee
> one people, and to putt awaye the dislikefull concepte but of the one and
> the other, which wilbe by no meanes better then by this entermingelinge of
> them, that neyther all the Irishe maye dwell together, nor all the Englishe,
> but by translatinge of them, and scattringe them in small numbers, amongst
> the Englishe, not onelye to bring them by dalye conversation vnto better
> lykinge of each other, but also to make both of them lesse able to hurte[.][117]

Settlement in English communities and daily conversation with English
people would literally 'translate' the Irish into English speakers; commerce
with the English in market towns would transmit to them the virtues of
civility.[118] Davies (whose survey of 'impediments' to Irish civility perhaps
prompted Petty's use of the term) looked instead to English law to give
the Irish property rights conducive to improvement and to encourage
conformity to 'the maner of England in al their behauior and outward
formes'. But he expected, much as Spenser did, that given the right English
policy, 'the next generation' of Irish 'will in tongue & heart, and euery way
else, becom English; so as there will bee no difference or distinction, but
the Irish Sea betwixt us.'[119] Spenser had written in the midst and Davies
in the wake of one supposed conquest; we have already heard Vincent
Gookin, writing in the wake of another, predict that 'being mixed with'

---

[115] Perrott, 16.   [116] Perrott, 38–39.   [117] Spenser, 196.
[118] Spenser, 203–205, 212–213.
[119] Davies, *Discoverie*, 270–272; see Hans S. Pawlisch, *Sir John Davies and the Conquest of Ireland: A Study in Legal Imperialism* (Cambridge: Cambridge University Press, 1985).

the English, the defeated Irish 'are likelyer to be swallowed up ... and incorporated into them'.[120]

If Petty's complaints about the Irish resonate throughout English writing on Ireland, then, his proposal for transmuting the Irish into English ties him to a more specific line of thinking that tended, not always consistently, to explain Irish barbarism in structural or contextual rather than essential or racial terms; who therefore tended to see Irish behaviour as rationally comprehensible, though unjustified; who attributed England's failure to civilize Ireland in large part to inadequate plantation policy; and who thought that the right policies—the extension of English law, the encouragement of trade, and, for Spenser and Gookin, mixed settlement of English and Irish—could still unite the Irish with their conquerors. Like Spenser, Petty found the persistence of the Irish language in the face of English conquest 'vnnatural' and unhelpful.[121] He approvingly cited 'Sir *John Davys*', who 'hath expressed much Wit and Learning, in giving the causes why *Ireland* was in no measure reduced to *English* Government ... and withal offers several means whereby what remains to be done, may still be effected.'[122] Above all, Petty—like Davies, Gookin and (implicitly) Spenser—appealed to Irish *interests*:

> As for the Interest of these poorer *Irish*, it is manifestly to be transmuted into *English*, so to reform and qualify their housing, as that *English* Women may be content to be their Wives, to decline their Language, which continues a sensible distinction, being not now necessary ... It is in their Interest to deal with the *English*, for Leases, for Time, and upon clear Conditions, which being perform'd they are absolute Freemen, rather than to stand always liable to the humour and caprice of their Landlords ... [']T]is their Interest to joyn with them, and follow their Example, who have brought Arts, Civility, and Freedom into their Country.[123]

Spenser's translation, Davies's reduction, and Petty's transmutation were varieties of liberation—which, once liberated, the Irish would surely see.

As important as Petty's connection to this tradition, however, was his departure from it. He cared little for converting the Irish because, as he put it in a later manuscript, 'Popery seemes to mee not a Matter of Religion but of politics'; policy, not Protestantism, was the answer.[124] Though he cited Davies approvingly in *Political Anatomy*, he privately

---

[120] Gookin, *Great Case*, 21–22.
[121] Compare Spenser, 87, with Petty, *Political Anatomy*, 106.
[122] Petty, *Political Anatomy*, 25–26.   [123] Petty, *Political Anatomy*, 101–102.
[124] Petty, 'Dialogue on Political Arithmetic' (1675), BL MS Add. 72865, f.104.

thought his predecessor 'bescribbled with Law and Learning. Hee made excellent patches, but set them beside the hole.'[125] For their part, neither Spenser nor Davies (nor, probably, Gookin) would have countenanced the transmutation Petty advocated. For them, 'mixture' meant mixed or perhaps merely adjacent communities of English and Irish families, whose mutual contact would be mediated by English law, English government, and English-style markets. The English would civilize the Irish through institutions, education, and virtuous example, a few at a time and from a safe distance. Petty, by contrast, proposed to marry individual English women to Irish men and insert them directly into Irish households by the thousands. For Spenser and Davies, to say nothing of harder-line authors, this was reckless; without 'good staye of gouernement and strong Ordinance' to preserve English customs from Irish corruption, 'the greater [number] will carrye away the lesse.'[126] Marrying English women to Irish men would puncture these barriers and lead to degeneration even more quickly and surely than the marriage of English men to Irish women had in the past. Reading Petty's manuscript, Lord Chief Justice of Ireland Sir Richard Cox voiced precisely this criticism:

> The expedient of Transmutation is mistaken in the Sex, for if a million of Women were married to as many poor Irish, it is certain they would degenerate into meer Irish & that in a few Years, experience proves my Assertion, besides in reason it must be soe, for women unless elevated by education & a principle of honour are less virtuous than men, that is they are more easy, & sooner allured by temptation or frightned by any thing that is like terrible, they are naturally more slothfull, & love their ease, besides the Irish naturally Lord it over their wives, & are not so uxorious as we English[.]

Cox allowed, however, that transmutation might work 'if a number of young boys were exchangd yearly … for boys bred after the English manner would not marry but with women soe bred, wherefore the Irish women would betake themselves to English service to qualify themselves for such husbands.'[127]

But for Petty it was crucial that women, not men, be exchanged. This was not because he thought English women more virtuous or the Irish more uxorious than Cox did. Indeed, the individual characteristics of the

---

[125] Petty to Southwell, 5 March 1686/7; *PSC*, 260.   [126] Spenser, 196.
[127] Cox's comments are appended to Southwell's copy of *Political Anatomy*, in BL MS Add. 21127, f.54.

women (and for that matter the men) concerned were of no importance. What mattered was the simple fact that they were women, and therefore charged with certain roles that—for Petty and nearly everyone else writing at the time—were virtually natural. It was not as English but as women that they would function as objects for their Irish husbands' natural passions—though the fact that their wives happened to be English would, Petty thought, soften their husbands' attitudes towards England. It was not as English but as women that they were responsible for organizing the household—though improvements in Irish housing would let them perform this function in a suitably English way. Most important of all, it was not as English but as women that they would bear and raise children, teaching them language and customs. Because they were *English* women, the language and customs they imparted would be English; but it was because they were *women* that they could be counted upon to do so. For their part, Irish men would naturally—led first by passion and later by interest—embrace these English women and their dowry of houses, gardens, markets and laws. A later iteration of Petty's proposal, in a 1674 manuscript 'About Exchanging of Women', makes this clear: 'If 7000 English poore Women were yearly brought out of England to Marry the like Number of poorer Irish Men then in 20 Yeares The Mother or Mistress of every of the said familys would bee an English protestant woman, and Consequently The Manners, Language & perhaps the Religion of all the sayd familys would be English.'[128] The 'Oeconomy of the Family', which had sped the degeneration of Old English into Irish, would, once the exchange of women was complete, transmute the Irish into English with the same mechanical necessity.

It was this mechanical necessity that made the transmutation of the Irish into English natural. Here Petty's ideas had less to do with the legacy of English thought about Ireland than with his own background in natural philosophy and specifically in alchemy.[129] As we have seen, Petty had encountered alchemical ideas and practices at several points in his life: during his medical training he spent seven months in a 'chymical laboratory' in Amsterdam, probably in 1645; he engaged in a variety of alchemical projects during his first and most enthusiastic years with the

---

[128] BL MS Add. 72879, f.71.
[129] An early version of this argument appeared in McCormick, 'Alchemy in the Political Arithmetic of Sir William Petty (1623–1687)', *Studies in History and Philosophy of Science* 37:2 (2006), 290–307.

Hartlib Circle, from 1647; in Oxford during 1649 and 1650, he lived above an apothecary's shop and hosted meetings of the 'Philosophical Club' that included alchemical experiments. He was also, of course, a dyer's son, and in 1662 contributed 'A History of Dy[e]ing' to the Royal Society. In other words, he was more familiar than most of his friends or readers with chemical transformations. He was also, like Hobbes, highly critical of inexact language or careless metaphor. Yet, throughout the rest of his life, he continued to speak of 'transmuting' the Irish into English—indeed, he never described his project in any other way. One obvious reason is that transmutation described precisely what Petty intended to do.

The premise of alchemical transmutation was that different substances were mutually convertible: lead could be transmuted into gold, copper into silver. This convertibility was traditionally construed through the Aristotelian theory of the elements. Every substance contained all four elements, which were distinguished by their qualities; earth was cold and dry, water cold and wet, air hot and wet, fire hot and dry. Since each quality could be turned into its opposite (dry becoming wet, cold hot), and thus each element transformed into another, altering the composition of a substance—and thus turning it into another substance altogether—was in theory fairly simple. Onto this framework the eighth-century Muslim alchemist Jabir ibn Hayyan (known to Europeans as Geber) grafted the sulphur-mercury theory of metals, influential in Europe during the later middle ages. Metals were the fruit of a marriage of sulphur and mercury (not the everyday substances, but 'philosophical' variants) in the centre of the earth, believed to ripen as they grew upward towards the surface. Alchemists themselves could capture 'sophic' sulphur and mercury by refining gold and silver; when combined in an instrument called the 'Philosopher's Egg', these gave birth to the Philosopher's Stone—a universal agent of transmutation able to 'heal' inferior metals. The sixteenth-century founder of iatrochemistry, Paracelsus, modified this, proposing the *tria prima* of salt, sulphur, and mercury, and the Dutch iatrochemist van Helmont (in vogue when Petty was a student) modified Paracelsus in turn. Despite these changes, however, the fundamental principle behind transmutation—that one substance could be turned into another if the proportions between its component elements were altered—remained much the same.

Petty had little time for the Philosopher's Stone, for Aristotelian matter theory, or for Paracelsus, but there were alternative paths to transmutation. During the 1660s, his longtime acquaintance and Royal Society colleague

Robert Boyle had developed an account of transmutation well suited to Petty's philosophical temperament and peculiarly adaptable to his political needs. Two of Boyle's works, *The Sceptical Chymist* (1661) and *The Origine of Formes and Qualities* (1666), are especially illuminating.[130] Building on the work of seventeenth-century alchemists, notably the German Daniel Sennert, Boyle confronted both Aristotelians and Paracelsians with a mechanical account of alchemy derived from corpuscularian principles.[131] Instead of four elements or three principles, he supposed a fixed amount of completely uniform matter, differentiated by motion into tiny, impenetrable, and indivisible atoms. These atoms combined into corpuscles, and these corpuscles were the basis of all physical substance. The qualities of different objects were simply the effects of the bulk, figure, and motion of the corpuscles that made them up, and of the relative position and order in which these corpuscles were combined; macro-level sensibilia had micro-level mechanical causes. Further, such sensibilia were all that distinguished one body from another: people called a given body 'lead', for example, because it exhibited a specific set of qualities, lead's 'essential accidents' (grey, heavy, soft, and so on). If the corpuscles composing this lead separated, moved around, or joined with other corpuscles, however, the set of accidents they produced would change. No matter would be destroyed, but the lead would no longer be lead. It would be whatever its new accidents amounted to.[132]

Petty's transmutation worked the same way. Its purpose was to transform the Irish into English—that is, to endow the Irish population with the essential accidents of the English. What made the Irish Irish, in a politically (and economically) meaningful sense, was a set of qualities by no means innate to individuals but produced in the population as a whole, or at least in the 600,000 poor Irish Catholics, by identifiable and alterable causes. Some of these could be addressed on a national scale: toleration, which would help assuage religious disaffection, was one example; the relaxation of trade barriers, which would create incentives for improvement, was another. The root of the problem, however, lay in the 'Oeconomy of the Family'—in Irish households, which, like corpuscles, mechanically produced and reproduced the language and

---

[130] Boyle, *The Sceptical Chymist* (London: Printed by J. Cadwell for J. Crooke, 1661); Boyle, *Origine*.

[131] Newman, *Atoms and Alchemy*; Meinel, 'Early Seventeenth-Century Atomism'.

[132] Boyle, *Origine*, 97–104.

manners that really distinguished Irish from English. By altering the shape of these corpuscles (moving Irish women out and English women in) and their spatial relations (exchanging isolated cabins for stone houses linked by improved roads and canals to markets), Petty proposed to generate, in the population as a whole, new qualities, qualities pre-figured on the micro-level in household relations. Irish industry would reach across the Atlantic, but it would begin in the parlour and kitchen garden; loyalty to the king in England would be avowed at the altar and learned in the crèche. No population would be lost, but the Irish would no longer be Irish. They would be, for all practical purposes, English.

This conflation of chemical and social processes was not careless but crucial. Alchemical language not only captured Petty's ideas more pre-cisely than the traditional political vocabulary of civilization, translation, and reduction could; it also freed him at the outset from the assumptions inherent in that vocabulary. As his inclination to use this idiom suggests, he approached the literature of Irish plantation from without—not as a statesman, to paraphrase the *Treatise of Taxes*, but as a natural philosopher. Like Spenser or Davies, he occasionally spoke of civilizing the Irish or hinted that the transplanted women's children might be raised as Protest-ants; but his appraisal of the problem generally ran along more pragmatic lines. Improvement and security required a loyal and productive Irish population. As long as the Irish population became loyal and productive, little else mattered. The path to peace and plenty emphatically did *not* run through an unnatural policy of uniformity or conversion; the natural way to neutralize the malign *political* influence of Irish Catholic priests, for example, was to substitute English Catholics, who could serve the same spiritual needs without fomenting rebellion. Petty's project ultimately de-pended more on Irish passions and interests—aspects of human nature operative in any population—than on any specifically English civility, religion, or institution. This was what made the transmutative union of Irish and English natural.

Alchemical transmutation had for centuries been attacked as being in some sense artificial: either simply fraudulent, or else demonic; how could mere men produce in a laboratory what it took nature centuries to incubate in the earth? And how could what they produced be considered natural?[133]

---

[133] Newman, *Promethean Ambitions*; Margaret G. Cook, 'Divine Artifice and Natural Mech-anism: Robert Boyle's Mechanical Philosophy of Nature', *Osiris*, 2nd Series, 15 (2001), 133–150.

Boyle answered these questions in two ways. First, corpuscularianism did not distinguish between two substances with the same accidents; if the alchemists' gold looked and behaved like gold from the earth, there was no meaningful difference. Going further, Boyle argued that even if the alchemist's operations were artificial in the sense that they depended on human activity, still

> the Instruments employ'd, are not Tools Artificially fashion'd and shaped, like those of Tradesmen, for this or that particular Work; but, for the most part, Agents of Nature's own providing, and whose chief Powers of Operation they receive from their own Nature or Texture, not the Artificer. And indeed, the Fire is as well a Natural Agent as Seed: And the Chymist that imploves it, does but apply Natural Agents and Patients, who being thus brought together, and acting according to their respective Natures, perform the work themselves; as Apples, Plums, or other fruit, are natural Productions, though the Gardiner bring and fasten together the Sciens and the Stock, and both Water, and do perhaps divers other waies Contribute to its bearing fruit.[134]

Like Boyle's alchemist, Petty's political arithmetician let nature work, channelling its power by creating circumstances in which natural processes would intervene to produce desirable results. Without human effort, ingredients would hardly gather themselves in the laboratory; without state compulsion, English and Irish women would hardly trade places. Yet once the ingredients were combined, nature would assert itself, whether through chemical reactions or in the form of human appetites and affections—of men for women, of mothers for children. Once the right initial conditions had been created, the transmutation of the Irish into English would naturally follow.

A natural science of policy

As outlandish as the transmutation of the Irish into English now seems, it was both the centrepiece of Petty's scheme for Ireland and a paradigmatic example of natural policy. In both respects it was at the heart of political arithmetic. Later regarded—for good reasons and bad—as an early form of social science or political economy, political arithmetic extended Petty's Baconian natural philosophy from inanimate bodies to human

---

[134] Boyle, *Chymist*, 225–226; *Origine*, 87–88.

populations. This entailed many of the prototypically 'modern' emphases Petty is supposed to have brought into the sphere of social thought: inductive rather than deductive reasoning, naturalistic explanations of human behaviour, a focus on quantifiable phenomena and quantitative arguments. But these were just parts of a much larger programme, the purpose of which was not to analyse society but to improve it by direct and in some cases violent means. It was less a social science, in the analytical sense, than a science of social engineering. It was a political science, designed to produce and reproduce industrious, loyal, and efficiently distributed populations in Britain and Ireland alike, for the sake of national wealth and strength. At the same time, it was a natural science, for natural laws and processes defined its scope and provided its instruments. Political arithmetic put nature—the natural world and human nature—at the state's disposal.

Scholars of Petty's work often emphasize the significance of mathematics, and especially his use of quantitative data-gathering and argument, as a precocious anticipation of much later statistical social science or economics. Many correspondingly assume that Petty's *intention* was to produce a statistical form of social analysis. A closer look at his actual proposals suggests otherwise. In the thick of argument it was not precise, absolute numbers but rough, relative proportions that mattered: the ratios of French ships to Dutch, of Protestants to Catholics in Ireland, and so on. These numbers were less important as facts in themselves than as a shorthand for making telling comparisons—props to argument and spurs to action. Perhaps ironically, it was by serving this explicitly discursive function that they extended the potential scope of calculation most dramatically—as Petty's search for equations linking land and labour to art, opinion, interest, reputation, and a host of other conventionally unquantifiable things illustrates. Like so many of his memorable triadic phrases ('situation, trade, and policy', 'symmetry, fabric, and proportion', 'unity, industry, and obedience', and even 'let nature work'), 'number, weight, and measure' is dangerously easy to read as a scientistic slogan. If we consider the kinds of things Petty intended to number, weigh and measure, and his aims in so doing, it has a less familiar ring.

Nothing makes this clearer than his proposal for transmutation, which reduced the politically and economically salient differences between English and Irish to a minimal set of qualities embodied in simple demographic proportions that could, with carefully calibrated effort, be altered. Political arithmetic in fact reduced virtually all of the political and economic

problems to questions of demographic proportion—productive versus un-
productive, peaceful versus disaffected. The task of government was the
manipulation of these ratios. The solution to the problems Petty's ratios described, meanwhile, was alchemical: the transmutation of the Irish
into English, the transmutation of costly idlers into industrious workers,
the transmutation of embittered dissenters into loyal subjects. Political
arithmetic functioned as a Baconian science. It was empirical, even if its
numbers were imprecise. It was collaborative, inasmuch as it not only
served but also—both in gathering data and in acting upon its findings—instrumentalized the state. It was, finally, transformative, designed
to effect by natural means what nature alone would never do. In a later
manuscript Petty admired the ability of a great leader to concentrate the
energy of the vast numbers under him:

> [H]ow wonderfull is it that the spirit of one Generall of an Army should
> Influence, Consimulate & Semetrize the minds, manners & motions of
> 40000. men, or rather that one Monarch should consenture and draw
> together the Mentall & Corporeall facultyes of 10 Millions of men, as
> burning Glasses doe gather and Converge many thousand beams of the Sun
> into one focus or burning point, so as to excite a heat that shall melt Silver,
> where without such burning Glass, the same Raies of the Sunn, would be
> too weake to singe Tinder ... [135]

The political arithmetician, who concentrated the power of population
itself, was part natural philosopher, part general.

Of course, Petty had a considerable professional and personal stake in
Ireland, and it was no accident that his new science began as a bundle
of improvement proposals for Ireland. But implicit in his approach to
the problems of colonial government was a certain indifference to some
of the traditional goals and justifications of plantation, most notably
Protestantization but to a lesser degree civilization itself. To the extent
that political arithmetic turned government into a kind of demographic
alchemy, making Ireland British became less a unique mission of providential significance and more a technical problem of a certain class, privileged

---

[135] Petty, 'Of the Scale of Creatures', Beinecke MS Osborn Shelves fb. 135, document 3,
ff.10v–11r. Rhodri Lewis generously made available his edition of the Beinecke manuscript, a
much more fully realized draft of Petty's 'Scale' than was previously thought to have existed;
Lewis, *William Petty on the Order of Nature: An Unpublished Manuscript Treatise* (Tempe, AZ:
Medieval and Renaissance Texts and Studies, forthcoming in 2009). Partial copies of the
'Scale' are in Osler MS 7614 and BL MS Add. 72898, ff.106r–113v; the latter is printed in *PP*,
2:25–34.

merely by its current political salience. In an era of colonial expansion, confessional division, and economic differentiation, other instances of this class of problem—the management of multiple culturally, socially, or nationally distinct populations within single states, multiple monarchies, or empires—were liable to crop up in other contexts and at other moments. As the next chapters will show, this is just what happened.

CHAPTER 6

Corpuscles, Colonies and Kingdoms

The framework and policies sketched in *Political Arithmetick* and *Political Anatomy* laid the groundwork for a mode of government through social engineering well suited in principle to abstract formulation and general application. In practice, however, this is not how Petty developed his thinking. There would be no 'treatise' of demographic transmutation. There was no audience, and therefore no use, for such a work. Petty's audience was more interested in particular solutions than in general principles; rather than a systematic statement, therefore, there emerged from his pen a dense web of manuscripts dealing with a linked set of problems. Nevertheless, with each new application political arithmetic became more and more a portable method, less and less bound by the political imperatives of the early 1670s. As Petty turned his attention to new topics, his framework and assumptions revealed themselves. The analytical dimension of political arithmetic approximated increasingly to statistical and historical demography, yielding a series of short printed works on English and Irish population, on the relative sizes of London, Paris, and other cities, and on the history of population increase. The practical side, by contrast, remained in manuscript, becoming ever more obviously an art of manipulating demographic proportions for changing political ends.

This chapter will focus on the latter, in part because it is vastly less familiar than Petty's printed analytical work but fundamentally because it is much more important in grasping what Petty was trying to do. *Practice* was central to Petty's conception of natural philosophy and practical problems the impetus for political arithmetic's development; analysis, though eminently safer to publish than policy, was ancillary to it. This is reflected in the pattern of articulation already mentioned: political arithmetic never appeared as a comprehensive, systematic methodology, but took shape through a series of *ad hoc* manuscripts, circulated not to academics but—from beginning to end—to framers of policy. During the early 1670s, the project at the heart of this program was the transmutation of the Irish, the central component of which was the exchange of women. However, from 1673, when Petty re-engaged with the Royal Society as part of a wider effort to reform it, the implications of this programme began to bleed into other areas. Indeed, the fruit of this re-engagement—Petty's idiosyncratic *Discourse ... Concerning the Uses of Duplicate Proportion*—rhetorically inflated political arithmetic into a principle of number, weight, and measure running through nature and society alike. Throughout, analysis served manipulation.

After a brief period of heightened activity, the impetus for reform in the Society petered out. By then, however, Petty had found a new object for his political-arithmetical attentions: England's colonies in North America. This initially took the form of compiling materials for a political anatomy of New England; but by the early 1680s his attention had shifted southward to the new colony of Pennsylvania. Indeed, he even purchased shares in the colony from his new friend, and fellow proponent of toleration, William Penn. Here the problems of political arithmetic differed from Ireland's. Instead of reversing centuries of degeneration via transmutation, the task was to prevent it from starting by facilitating the creation of a stable and growing English population. Yet, again, the solution was a sort of transmutation, this time of Native Americans. While Petty's Atlantic extension of political arithmetic remained little more than a thought experiment, it casts a valuable sidelight on the ethnic dimension of colonial transmutation.

Between 1685 and 1687, political arithmetic took a final, dramatic turn, its last under Petty's hand. Here again, a new problem—not Catholic Ireland but the politics of religion throughout the Three Kingdoms—extended political arithmetic's application; recasting its proximate goals while clarifying its underlying principles. The accession of a Catholic king, James II, reversed the terms of transmutation while vastly extending the field in play: now the task was not the targeted transformation of Irish Catholics into loyal, productive subjects, but rather the *maintenance* of loyalty in the increasingly restive Protestant populations of England, Ireland, and Scotland. Most strikingly, this reversal of terms transformed 'transmutation' itself from a way of Anglicizing Ireland into a program for managing politically troublesome religious demographics across the Three Kingdoms, in part through their 'Catholication'. More profoundly, it transformed political arithmetic from a congeries of colonial and metropolitan projects into an indispensable and implicitly universal instrument of government for a multiple monarchy and a colonial empire. Unfortunately for Petty and James alike, the invasion and revolution of 1688 intervened. When political arithmetic re-emerged, in the 1690s, it had been transformed yet again.

Political arithmetic in manuscript

Important as they were, *Political Arithmetick* and *Political Anatomy*—lengthy manuscripts, divided into independent chapters—were neither the sole nor even the chief vehicles Petty used to transmit his multifarious policy ideas. Petty's more usual manuscript format was a terse bifolio or two, four to eight sides, often fewer. In contrast to the laborious argumentation of the longer works, these *tractiuncli* often included little sustained argument at all. Instead, they frequently comprised series of lists, detailing Petty's proposals, what they would achieve (transmutation, increased revenues, reformed parishes, and so on), how they might be effected (perhaps including a very rough estimate of their cost) and—often the most important part—what might happen if his advice were ignored. This was not a rigid format; any given tract might have fewer, more, or different sets of points or 'heads', with more or less detail to them and in more or less complete sentences. Some papers took wholly different forms. Several sketchy dialogues, for example, survive (though their rough state suggests that they may have been meant to help Petty rehearse his arguments rather than present them to an actual audience). Nevertheless, this format was broadly characteristic of Petty's presentation.[1]

These *tractiuncli* appeared over a sustained period of time, and both the temporal structure of the archive as a whole and the frequency and duration of specific types of proposal demand attention. The vast majority date from the mid-1670s or later, with the largest concentration falling in the mid- and later 1680s. Although the partial survival of the papers raises obvious problems of interpretation, it seems evident that the periodicity of manuscripts within the surviving group at least partly reflects Petty's pattern of production—too much radical, potentially damaging material survives from periods of crisis, and too little of anything from periods of relative calm, for the shape of the archive to be wholly accidental. The paucity of earlier papers, on the other hand, can only be the result of loss or destruction; Petty was an avid proposer of schemes from the 1640s, as we have seen, and there is no reason to think he let up. Nevertheless, it seems likely that the advent of political arithmetic marked a change in both the quantity and quality of Petty's proposals and the beginning of a more aggressive effort at getting his ideas heard.

A few manuscripts show us the key features of Petty's transmutative plan for Ireland gradually taking shape at around the same time as he was

---

[1] Aspromourgos, 'Mind'; Harris, 'Ireland as a Laboratory'.

working on *Political Arithmetick* and *Political Anatomy*. In September 1671 he submitted a series of proposals to the Earl of Arlington, suggesting 'That an exact accompt ought to bee taken of the whole people by there number, age, sex, trade, Office, place of habitation, and by all other there circumstances & qualifications, whereby they improve or impaire the publique wealth'. We have seen something similar in the *Treatise of Taxes*, with its methodization of population, and here, too, Petty's call for a survey led to a discussion of the measures and the principles of value. 'I conceive it expedient, and am ready to offer the proportions which any one person beareth to an other in value; according to his age, trade, office, tythe, Religion or any other qualification, making the Value of [a] full grown Simple Labourer to be the Basis & Radix of all computations.' These computations would not just provide knowledge of 'the Wealth & Power of the whole Kingdome', but also help the King 'to levy with ease certainty & equality, what the reason of his affaires requires' as well as to determine 'The advantages & disadvantages of foraign plantations.'[2] Petty's exploration of value, here as elsewhere, extended well beyond recognizably economic considerations.

Another manuscript, likely from early 1672, listed a range of familiar proposals 'For the People', 'For the King', 'For the Citty of London', and 'For the State'; it also promised, however, 'To Transmute the Irish into English' in nine years.[3] This transmutation would require 'a Particular yearly Accompt of Every Field, Howse & Man of 8 yeares old … as also of the Growth of Cattle Corne & Wooll with the state of Inland Emprovements & forraigne Trade' and included plans 'to reforme the Wretched Howsing' of the Irish.[4] Neither transplantation nor mixture, however, was mentioned. Meanwhile, a second manuscript (also *c*.1672) developed an almost sociological analysis of Ireland's political situation. Entitled 'A Method of Preventing Rebellion, and Intestine warrs in Ireland', it carefully distinguished the different interests absorbed within the Catholic population of Ireland:

1. There are the old Irish, distinguished from others, by the preposition, Mac: & Ô: who bear a great respect and devotion, to the heads of their

---

[2] BL MS 72865, ff.24–28.
[3] BL MS Add. 72865, ff.140–142. Harris dates this tentatively to the 1670s based on the hand. Based on internal evidence, and on its affinities with Petty's proposals of 1671 and differences with *Political Arithmetick*, early 1672 seems likely. Most of the proposals, including that 'to Transmute the Irish into English in 9 yeares', recur in 'A generall Proposall for England & Ireland' (n.d.), BL MS Add. 72865, ff.143–144.
[4] BL MS Add. 72865, f.141.

respective septs, nor are they well pleased, that even the oldest, and most degenerate English ... should have any land amongst them.

2. The next sort are the said Old and degenerate English; who are Irish and Papist, and have little Interest Kindred and Acquaintance in England.

3. Such of both the last mentioned sorts, as have had their breeding in Foreigne parts, as Church-Men, Souldiers, Courtiers, or Merchants, especially such as were abroad with his Majestie during the late troubles; whereunto may be added the Lawyers of the Popish Religion, Clerkes, & the inferior Officers, and Ministers of the Government ...

4. Such of the Irish as can speake no English.

5. Such Irish as were possest of Estates Anno 1641, & are not restor'd unto them.

6. Such are all Church-Men, whom I look upon as discontented for having been outed of their Church-Lands, & Livings[.]

It then turned to the 'varying sorts of English' in Ireland: Old English Catholics, 'Old Protestant' planter families, 'New Protestants' and those who had come over since the Restoration. These categories were not, taken in the abstract, all of one kind; it was only relative to the 'The Severall Quarrells & heartburnings now in Ireland' that they related to each other as rival interests.[5] In other words, Ireland's problems were matters of political demography, clashes of interest between groups whose differences, though often deep-seated, were artificial—artefacts of past plantation policy.

Once Petty began to treat the simple existence of these divisions as the fundamental problem, his thoughts naturally turned to eliminating them—contingent and removable impediments that they were—in a more radical way. *Political Arithmetick* and *Political Anatomy* began to do just this, but manuscripts of 1673 and 1674 continued to articulate a comprehensive programme of transmutation that included the transplantation and intermarriage of certain segments of English and Irish populations, as well as the political and economic union of the English and Irish states. They also kept those in power informed of Petty's thinking. A manuscript written *circa* 1674 listed questions and proposals addressed to a number of members of the Irish Privy Council—including the Earl of Orrery, Sir George Carteret, and Sir Henry Ford, who had helped circulate *Political Arithmetick* in Ireland. While calling for information on population and wealth and arguing for union, Petty here proposed, as

[5] BL MS Add. 72879, ff.36–37.

well as exchanging women 'annually', 'To translate the Bible & Liturgy into Irish', 'To encourage Converts', and 'To obliterate [Irish] Names of Persons & Lands'.[6] Transmutation and mixture would create new families and sever old bonds of kinship; the 'obliteration' of Irish names and the political neutralization of language differences would help remove the last superficial distinctions.

The 'oeconomy of the family' was, however, still the key. Petty's March 1674 paper 'About Exchanging of Women' has already been quoted.[7] Another fragment, echoing Petty's comments to Anglesey, portrayed draconian intervention as political medicine. 'All government is a sort [of] Physick & chirurgery Unpleasant & painfull enough', Petty admitted, 'but when tis administered by licensed & authenticq persons, even death must bee borne with.' Further, 'the qualitys of Exchangd women [were] to bee alike'—they would all be poor—and 'People who have no visible livelihood may bee disposd of [by] the magistrate.'[8] Transmutation enjoyed the same sanction as impressment or the workhouse. Population was, like land, a resource. If waste land overseas justified colonization—an argument John Locke later developed, but traceable to any number of sources, from More's *Utopia* to *Irelands Naturall History*—waste population at home could surely be put to better use 'by licensed & authenticq persons'.[9] The art of government was the improvement and deployment of populations.

By 1675, the complex of policies that made up transmutative political arithmetic could be reeled off by rote. A typical set of heads on union, entitled 'Decrees and Judgments of one Island Executed in the Other', ran: '1. United under One Legislature. 2. Cabbins Reformed. 3. Names of Lands & people Changed. 4. 10,000 young Women per annum exchanged', and so on, up to '7. Schools of English Writing & Arithmetic Instituted.'[10] A set of 'Proposals about the Revenue, Expence, [&] future Estate of Ireland', dated August 1675, listed 'severall things to bee done for the advantage of Ireland out of the revenue of the same'.[11] These included:

4. That the Bible and common Prayer-book, bee translated into Irish, & printed in the Vulgar Character, & that fit persons bee salariated, to preach, Catechise & officiate in Irish, in every part of that kingdome weekly.

[6] BL MS Add. 72879, ff.64–65v.   [7] BL MS Add. 72879, f.71.
[8] 'Of Counter-Transplanting the Irish & English', BL MS Add. 72879, ff.117–118.
[9] More, *Utopia*, 55–56.   [10] BL MS Add. 72879, f.75.
[11] BL MS Add. 72879, ff.84–97, consists of five versions of the same set of proposals: the original, in Petty's hand (ff.84–87 v), three copies by amanuenses (ff.88–89, 'A'; ff.90–91, 'B', used here; ff.92–93, 'C'), and a nineteenth-century transcription (ff.94–97, 'D') based on 'B'.

5. That all the Smoaky-lesse Cabbins [i.e. houses with no fixed hearth] of Ireland, bee made houses worth 4£ each, & fitt for the making of Merchantable Butter, cheese & Linnen yarne in them ...

6. That as many English women bee yearly brought over, as there are Marriages yearly made by the Inhabitants of the said Cabbins, & as many young Irish women sent into England, for Breeding in English manners & huswifery.[12]

At the end of nine years 'a grand account' would assess the 'Emprovements' that had occurred in land and trade—'Howseing ... kilns, forges, Iron-works, fisheryes, mines, Quarryes, & colleryes', livestock and agricultural produce—as well as 'Of the People their names, sex, Ages, Births, Titles, Offices, Trades, Religion &c.'

Again, the criteria of success were not simply economic but matters of social and political demography: how many people, how productive, how loyal. A 1675 'Dialogue on Political Arithmetic' emphasized the political purposes not just of transmutation but also of political arithmetic in general.[13] Two interlocutors, 'A' and 'B' ('Polishing', Petty admitted, 'is not my way'), discussed a manuscript—probably *Political Arithmetick*—that, according to B, 'contaynes the plainest politics I ever yet heard of.'[14]

A: Politics can never bee plaine, you see Geometry which considers the most simple question[s] is extremely difficult. The Science of Motions more, The fabrick of animals yet more, The Minds of Men yet more, But the Genius of Multitude, Which I take to be Politiques, most of all[.] What do you Meane by Politiques[?]

B: Truth, I meane by Politiques not a quarter of all this, but the way how to keep people in Peace and plenty, that is able to resist ... ambitious Conquerors, & the chagrin of discontented persons at home and to [prevent] the land from bearing any Unusefull herb [&] to make the best of all it produces.[15]

If we take 'B' as Petty's spokesman, we can already see political arithmetic emerging as an art of government, geared to ensuring 'peace and plenty' not only by keeping the population productive but also by keeping it loyal against 'ambitious Conquerors' and unified against 'the chagrin of discontented persons'. Yet 'A', too, had a point. Political arithmetic was rooted in Petty's extension of natural philosophy from bodies to minds, and the transmutation of the Irish into English

---

[12] BL MS Add. 72879, f.90.   [13] BL MS Add. 72865, ff.93–107.
[14] BL MS Add, 72865, f.94; Petty to Robert Wood, 10 April 1675, BL MS Add. 72858, f.211.
[15] BL MS Add, 72865, f.94.

depended on this connection. Just as political arithmetic's horizons expanded, the transmutation's corpuscularian underpinnings came again to the fore.

Political arithmetic in nature

The political arithmetician's place was in government. Indeed, Petty's proposals often read like job applications. At the same time, political arithmetic was a practical science, and Petty continued to find attractive the idea of a suitably reformed scientific institution serving as a venue for certain aspects of his programme. Royal Society meetings declined in both frequency and quality after the early years, and already in 1668 suggestions were solicited for a new 'college', though Petty left for Ireland before he could contribute to this discussion.[16] Returning late in the summer of 1673, he found the Society in a worse state than ever. Together with Jonathan Goddard, Nehemiah Grew, Robert Hooke, and Christopher Wren, he now led a much more aggressive push for reform both of meetings and of membership, soliciting and suggesting new experiments, pursuing arrears, and expelling inactive or delinquent members.[17] Differences arose over whether hypothesis-driven experiment or the haphazard compilation of natural histories should take precedence (Petty sympathized with both sides), but in either case a streamlined society of active researchers was the goal. In February of 1674 Petty became, with Wren, co-Vice-President of the Society.[18]

Between 1673 and 1676 Petty re-engaged with the Society and the extensive range of scientific interests he had pursued in its early years. He suggested that it systematically pursue several categories of work at once, proposing 'that there might be a constant apparatus of instruments ready for the making of several kinds of experiments depending on several heads; for instance, for experiments of motion, optical, magnetical, electrical, mercurial, &c.'[19] He diligently attended meetings, hosted Hooke and his telescopes at his house during a lunar eclipse, commented on all manner of work—from Grew's botanical observations to Newton's investigation of light to observations of Icelandic saltwater—and served on a committee appointed to examine John Webster's sceptical *Displaying*

---

[16] Birch, *History*, 2:238–239.
[17] Hunter and Wood; Birch, *History*, 3:102, 110, 119, 123, 136–138, 140–144; BL MS Add. 72898, f.29.
[18] Birch, *History*, 3:123; BL MS Add. 72898, f.32.   [19] Birch, *History*, 3:115.

of Supposed Witchcraft.[20] His own contributions, however, were to a large degree organizational: chasing down arrears, drawing up lists of things to be investigated, classifying the Society's pursuits, pushing for contributions of money or equipment. This may indicate a new sense of the rudimentary administrative control needed to make reform lasting and effective. It also suggests a man more pressed for time—by lawsuits, family responsibilities, estate improvements, and political-arithmetical proposals—than the philosophical bachelor of a decade before.

Yet Petty did make one substantial, and highly idiosyncratic, intellectual contribution. This was *The Discourse ... Concerning the Use of Duplicate Proportion*, originally presented at a meeting in November 1674 and printed the following year. Ostensibly a work of mixed mathematics describing the operation of square relationships in everyday life, the *Discourse* also presented Petty's own hypotheses about the fundamental nature of matter—something he had never before commented on but that was, as we have seen, implicated in the proposals for transmuting the Irish he had been circulating over the previous year and was still producing. More strikingly still, the *Discourse* explicitly linked both mixed mathematics (as proof of natural philosophy's practical utility) and Petty's own version of corpuscularian matter theory to political arithmetic.[21]

Bridging past and present, Petty dedicated the *Discourse* both to Brouncker and to the Duke of Newcastle, who 'did encourage Me 30 years ago' to take up natural philosophy. 'For about that time in *Paris, Mersennus, Gassendy*, Mr. *Hobs*, Monsieur *Des Cartes*, Monsieur *Roberval*, Monsieur *Mydorge*, and other famous men, all frequenting, and caressed by, your Grace and your memorable Brother, Sir *Charles Cavendish*, did countenance and influence my Studies, as well by their Conversation as their Publick Lectures and Writings.'[22] Yet despite this invocation of Parisian physico-mathematics, the *Discourse* owed less to Descartes and the others than to the Baconian vision of natural philosophy Petty had defended against their systems in his letter to Henry More. There is a Hobbesian ring to Petty's promise 'to explain the Intricate Notions, or *Philosophia Prima* of Place, Time, Motion, Elasticity, &c.' and 'to excite the World to the study of a little Mathematicks, by shewing the use of *Duplicate Proportions* in some of the most weighty of Humane affairs'. The notions

---

[20] Birch, *History*, 3:174, 192, 223, 268, 308; Webster, *The Displaying of Supposed Witchcraft* (London: Printed by John Martyn, 1677).

[21] Robert Kargon, 'William Petty's Mechanical Philosophy', *Isis* 56:1 (1965), 63–66; Sharp, 253–355.

[22] Petty, *Discourse*, sig. A8v–A9v.

in question, however, should be such as 'the meanest Member of adult Mankind is capable of understanding' and the mathematics what 'a Child of 12 years old may learn in an hour'—not especially intricate.[23] Utility and accessibility to mean capacities still trumped the theoretical rigour of imaginary principles.

Petty now linked this long-cherished notion of practical science to his new concern with natural policy. Promising 'to store and stock' Newcastle's grandson 'with variety of *Matter, Data* and *Phaenomena*' upon which to hone his mathematical skill, he remarked that 'there is a *Political Arithmetic*, and a *Geometrical Justice* to be yet further cultivated in the World; the Errors and Defects whereof, neither Wit, Rhetoric, nor Interest can more than palliate, never cure', any more 'than vicious Wines can be remedied with Brandy and Honey, or ill Cookery with enormous proportions of Spice and Sugar: *Nam Res nolunt malè administrari.*'[24] Political arithmetic was a branch of applied natural philosophy. As such it was of use to the state and the Royal Society alike. The latter, in particular, had been 'censured ... for spending too much time in matters not directly tending to profit' and 'complained of for producing nothing New.' Avoiding 'all Speculations not tending to Practice' and laying out 'Instances and Applications' of '*Mathematics* to *Matter*', Petty would 'straighten this crooked stick'.[25]

Much as transmutative political arithmetic projected chemical processes onto human populations, mixed mathematics discerned and captured for human use natural ratios obtaining across divergent classes of objects. Most were physical or more demotically 'mechanical': the swing of pendulums, the vibration of strings, the relationships between musical tones; the strength of timber, the power of windmills, 'the Velocities caused by Gunpowder', the height of water raised by pumps, the necessary thickness of sea-walls or land fortifications, 'the *Blast of Bellows*' familiar to Petty from his unsuccessful ironworks.[26] Several had nautical applications; the relative velocities of ships, for instance, were 'the *square Roots* of the *Powers* which either drive or draw them' so that, all things being equal, 'a *quadruple Sail* is requisite to *double* swiftness, and *noncuple* to *treble*'.[27] (Here Petty described experiments he had conducted with Brouncker using a small-scale, simplified 'Apparatus' built for the purpose.)[28] Nor had Petty's older preoccupations with the human senses, alchemy, and even judicial astrology abated. One chapter argued that 'the volume of Space a rarified

[23] Petty, *Discourse*, sig. A4r–A5r.   [24] Petty, *Discourse*, sig. A10v–A12r.

[25] Petty, *Discourse*, 1–3, 5.   [26] Petty, *Discourse*, 41–55, 65–70, 80–82, 88–90, 97–105.

[27] Petty, *Discourse*, 21–22.   [28] Petty, *Discourse*, 34–37.

liquor will fill is the square of the liquor's strength' and thus that 'the space in which [distilled] Spirits rise, are the Roots, whose Squares do show the Spirituosity of those Liquors.'[29] Others applied duplicate proportion to sights, sounds, and smells; in each case, 'the Distances at which they are perceived are the roots of the quantity of Matter out of which they are emitted'—the number of 'musquetts' firing in the heat of battle, the acreage of 'odoriferous herbs' wafting their scent out to sea, the number of candles burning in a distant window.[30] Similar diminutions of power over distance extended beyond the sensory realm: 'this Consideration, I pitch upon, as one of the grounds whereupon I would build a Doctrin concerning the Influence of the Stars, and other Celestial or remote Bodies upon the Globe of the Earth, and its Inhabitants, both Men and Brutes.'[31] The Baconian programme—the improvement of the senses, the superinduction of new natures on substances, even the grasping of astrological influences for human benefit—survived in modified form. Indeed, duplicate proportion united it with Petty's more recent interest in measuring value. Discussing 'the Price of several Commodities', he suggested that the prices of ships' masts, diamonds, pearls, and magnets were all subject to duplicate proportion. The amount of wood in the mast, the weight of the diamond or pearl and the power of the loadstone were each 'but the Roots of their Prices'.[32]

Proportion governed earth and stars, physical and sensible objects, and even commercial exchange. It also governed population. Petty's eleventh 'instance' dealt with 'the Life of Man, and its Duration', and argued that age demography naturally exhibited proportional relationships. 'It is found by Experience,' Petty began, 'that there are more persons living of between 16 and 26 years old, than of any other Age or Decade of years in the whole life of Man (which *David* and *Experience* say to be between 70 and 80 years:)'.[33] On either side of this golden decade, life expectancy varied with a probability expressible by the root of the relevant age:

> I say, that the Roots of every number of Mens Ages under 16 (whose Root is 4) compared with the said number 4, doth shew the proportion of the likelihood of such mens reaching 70 years of Age. As for example; 'Tis 4 times more likely, that one of 16 years should live to 70, then a new-born Babe. 'Tis three times more likely, that one of 9 years old should attain the said age of 70, than the said Infant ... On the other hand, 'tis 5 to 4, that one of 26 years old will die before one of 16; and 6 to 5, that one of 36 will die

[29] Petty, *Discourse*, 93–96.   [30] Petty, *Discourse*, 70–79.   [31] Petty, *Discourse*, 76.
[32] Petty, *Discourse*, 106–110.   [33] Petty, *Discourse*, 82–83.

before one of 26; and 3 to 2, that the same person shall die before him of 16:
And so forward …[34]

These proportions were not merely curious statistical artefacts of a
particular data set; they were, Petty implied, sensible regularities expressing natural features of population. For individuals these laws were
matters of probability, but in the aggregate the pattern was constant.
People as collectivities—setting aside the 'mutable minds' of 'particular
men'—belonged in the same book as observations on pendulums and
distilled spirits because duplicate proportion operated upon each object
with the same necessity. All were objects of the same kind of knowledge,
the same analysis, and the same prediction.

Knowledge was power. Petty had suggested in 1648 that mastery of
judicial astrology might be used to improve public health; here he suggested
that knowledge of demography might do the same thing. He described
how he had determined the average age of a parish, adding the ages of its
inhabitants and dividing the total by their number, yielding a figure (in
this case) of around sixteen:

> which I call (if it be Constant or Uniform) the Age of that Parish, or
> numerous *Index* o[f] Longaevity there. Many of which Indexes for several
> times and places, would make an useful Scale of Salubrity for those places;
> and a better Judg of Ayres than the conjectural Notions we commonly read
> and talk of. And such a Scale the *King* might as easily make for all his
> Dominions, as I did this for this one Parish.[35]

Petty does not seem to have thought policy capable of changing the
patterned age-structure of population. No other instance of duplicate
proportion admitted of such meaningful variation. What he did suggest,
following Graunt, was that the 'salubrity' of a given place—its air, water,
and so on—could affect the average age of the population living there.
Preserving duplicate proportion, this meant that salubrity also affected
the modal or most common age, the pivot around which life expectancy
naturally turned. Since Petty's parish had an average age towards the
low end of the golden decade of sixteen to twenty-six, the implication
seems to have been that this pivot had shifted forward, shortening life
expectancy across the board. The 'index of longevity' thus showed how a
parish's salubrity constrained its demographic possibilities. Salubrity itself
was a component of situation, an element of natural history, and thus a
determinant of natural policy.

---

[34] Petty, *Discourse*, 84–86.   [35] Petty, *Discourse*, 86–88.

While the bulk of the *Discourse* tied political arithmetic, practical science, and mixed mathematics together, the book also featured Petty's own version of the corpuscular mechanism that underpinned chemical and, by analogy, demographic transmutation. In the Preface Petty had defined his terms in corpuscularian fashion—body was 'Matter and Figure considered together', quality 'several Motions considered together'. He proceeded to articulate a theory of matter similar to Boyle's. 'I suppose all the *First Matter* of the World to be *Atoms*; that is, Matter Immutable in Magnitude and Figure. I suppose *Corpuscles* to be as many Atoms joyned together, as make up a *visible* or sensible *Object*, and that all *Juncture* of *Atomes* is made by their *Innate motions*.'[36] Onto this familiar outline, however, he grafted more exotic elements designed to explain these innate motions. Drawing on William Gilbert's 1600 *De Magnete*, Petty posited an essential structural similarity between atoms, magnets, the Earth, and the heavens:

> every Atom is like the Earths Globe or Magnet, wherein are *three Points* considerable, *viz.* two in the surface, called *Poles*, and one within the substance called *Center*, or rather *Byas*, because in Atoms we consider neither *Magnitude* nor *Gravity*. These Atoms also may have each of them such Motions as *Copernicus* attributes to the Earth, or more.[37]

Poles and bias governed the two key motions of these atomic microcosms: first, 'verticity' or 'polarity', the tendency of the magnetic poles of all atoms to form a straight line end to end; second, gravity, a curving motion that drew the biases of neighbouring atoms together to form corpuscles, and drew them too towards the center of the Earth. The conflicting tendencies of these motions—which 'may be of different *Velocities*' and which 'by *Contra-colluctations* ... may balance each other'—were the ultimate causes of all natural phenomena. '[T]he motions of *Corpuscles* are compounded of the abovementioned motions of Atoms; and the motions of bigger and Tangible Bodies (*viz.*, their qualities) are decompounded out of the *Motions*, *Situation*, *Figure*, and *Magnitude* of Corpuscles; and that out of,

---

[36] Petty, *Discourse*, 16–18.

[37] Petty, *Discourse*, 18–19. Petty added in the appendix (126–127) that 'every Atome may move about his own *Axis*, and about other Atoms also, as the *Moon* does about the *Earth*; *Venus* and *Mercury* about the *Sun*; and the *Satellites Jovis* about *Jupiter*, &c.' Compare Gilbert (trans. P. Fleury Mottelay), *De Magnete* (1600; New York: Dover, 1958), 22–23: 'In the heavens, astronomers give to each moving sphere two poles; thus do we find two natural poles of excelling importance even in our terrestrial globe.... In like manner the loadstone has from nature its two poles'. In each case these poles 'are the primary termini of the movements and effects, and the limits and regulators of the several actions and properties' of the bodies concerned.

and by, the premisses all *Phaenomena* in nature must be solved.'[38] Perhaps by way of explaining how they might come to have different velocities, Petty departed from Boyle—aligning himself instead with Gassendi—in allowing '*Atoms* to be of *several Figures* and *Magnitudes*, provided we suppose them *immutable*.'[39]

Most striking of all, in light of the transmutation of the Irish, Petty's atoms differed not only in figure and magnitude but also, more intriguingly, in sex:

> I might suppose (even without a Metaphor) that Atoms are also *Male* and *Female*, and the *Active* and *Susceptive* Principles of all things; and that the above-named Byasses are the Points of Coition: For, that *Male* and *Female* extend further than to *Animals*, is plain enough; the fall of *Acorns* into the ground, being the Coition of Oaks with the Earth. Nor is it absurd to think, that the words in *Genesis*, [*Male and Female created he them*] may begin to take effect, even in the smallest parts of the *first Matter*, For although the words were spoken onely of *Man*; yet we see they certainly refer to other Animals, and to *Vegetables* in manner aforesaid, and consequently not improbably to all other *Principles of Generation*.[40]

It has been suggested that this alchemical reading of Genesis—one of several during the seventeenth century—was designed to defend corpuscularian philosophy from clerical assault.[41] If so, it failed: but there is another possibility, more closely tied to the goals of political arithmetic. This is that in sexing his atoms Petty was taking another cue from Gilbert, who had insisted that what pulled magnets together was not 'attraction' but 'coition': 'for where attraction exists, there, force seems to be brought in and a tyrannical violence rules.'[42] Coition, by contrast, represented a natural union, for atoms as for people.

As we have seen, the essence of Petty's Irish project was literal coition between English women and Irish men—the atoms involved in demographic transmutation. Boyle had not ruled out the transmutation of organic bodies, and his matter theory seems to have been what Petty first had in mind. Why then should Gilbert (whose work Bacon had criticized and Petty had never clearly employed) suddenly appear, unnamed but unmistakable, in the *Discourse*? One reason may simply be that his

---

[38] Petty, *Discourse*, 19–20, 130.   [39] Petty, *Discourse*, 124. See Sorell, 249.

[40] Petty, *Discourse*, 130–132.

[41] Kargon, 65. Compare Arthur Dee (trans. Elias Ashmole) *Fasciculus Chemicus: Or Chymical Collections* (London: Printed by J. Flesher for Richard Mynne, 1650), 212–214.

[42] Gilbert, 97–98.

microcosmic view of magnets appealed to Petty. But another may lie in his reasoned substitution of coition, which was natural, for attraction, which involved 'violence'—that is to say, in Aristotelian language, *unnatural* motion. Much as Boyle emphasized the naturalness of alchemical processes and products—allowing Petty to present his demographic transmutation as natural—Gilbert stressed the natural, unforced, meeting of magnets. But whereas Boyle's streamlined account of corpuscularian transmutation stripped alchemy of its traditional profusion of sexual metaphors, Gilbert's account of magnetism, like Petty's own transmutation scheme, emphasized the sexual aspect of natural union. If this conceptual congeniality is what made Gilbert so suddenly relevant, it suggests that political arithmetic was beginning to influence Petty's synthesis of natural philosophical ideas, instead of the reverse.

Responses to the *Discourse* varied greatly. Newcastle—by now an old man—wrote almost immediately to thank Petty, but had little more to say.[43] Hobbes wrote over a year later, not to Petty himself but to Aubrey, their mutual friend. Both this fact and the letter's contents suggest a certain estrangement, apparently more on Petty's part than on Hobbes's. The older man's assessment of the *Discourse* was nevertheless extremely, perhaps surprisingly, favourable:

> tell him that if I had seene his Booke before it went to the Presse I would not (as he thinks) haue hindred it, but done as the Society did, that is, vrg'd him to print it. For the doctrine is easy to be demonstrated. The last Chap: which is of Elasticity is different from the Principles which I have taken for Naturall Philosophie; but I am of opinion that his Supposition is very true, and will goe a great way.[44]

Opinion among Petty's newer contacts, especially in Ireland, was more mixed. Robert Wood, Petty's friend and the Earl of Essex's secretary, wrote to convey the Lord-Lieutenant's thanks and mentioned that the Solicitor-General of Ireland, Sir John Temple, had also read it. Yet 'I find here that they are more apt to censure then understand it (Even the Sol. Himselfe told me he was angry with you, for saying a Child of 12 yeares old might do in one houre what he found he could not do in many)'. Wood himself had reservations: 'Your Atoms tho very small are yet too big for me to swallow, & indeed I wonder how any Mathematician can, who understand Quantity to be infinitely ... divisible'. Graunt had shown that

---

43 Newcastle to Petty, 27 February 1674/5, BL MS Add. 72850, ff.216–217 v.
44 Hobbes to Aubrey, 24 February/6 March 1675/6, in Hobbes, *Correspondence*, 2:751.

a third of the population was under five years of age, yet Petty claimed that the largest group was between sixteen and twenty-six.[45] (Petty explained that he had meant that the lowest mortality rate fell between these ages.)[46]

That Wood's concerns elicited a series of responses is tribute to Petty's esteem for his friend rather than any inherent respect for criticism.[47] His very inflexibility, however, could lead Petty to rearticulate his aims in revealing ways. He wrote to Aubrey years later that 'As for the opinion of Dr. Woods and others, that the Emanations of Visibles Audibles &c should have been in triplicate (not duplicate) proportion, I say that neither is demonstrably true, but that duplicate doth better agree both with reason and Experience.'[48] Despite appearances, Petty disavowed any pretension either to necessity or to precision:

> what I have done in that discourse was only to keep men from grosse errors and for bringing them into the way of exacter truth. I hope no man takes what I say'd about the motion and burthen of horses and the living and dying of Men for Mathematical demonstration, Yet I say they are better ways of estimating these Matters then I had ever heard from others.[49]

It was enough that duplicate proportion extended the realm of number, weight, and measure; measures themselves were secondary. Likewise, as he had indicated in the *Discourse*, the beauty of his atomic theory was less its verisimilitude than its operational utility: 'all the motions I fancy in my Atoms, may be represented in gross tangible Bodies, an consequently may be made intelligible and examinable.'[50] To be intelligible and examinable was to be an object of scientific knowledge and practical manipulation.

One especially hostile response to the *Discourse* requires special attention. This appeared in a letter from Thomas Barlow, provost of Queen's College, Oxford and later Bishop of Lincoln, a copy of which reached Petty via Anglesey.[51] An Aristotelian and a cleric, Barlow took issue both with Petty's un-scholastic definitions and with the religious implications

[45] Wood to Petty, 30 March 1675, BL MS Add. 72850, ff.218–219 v.

[46] Wood to Petty, 6 April 1675, BL MS Add. 72850, ff.224–225 v.

[47] Wood to Petty, 18 April, 15 May and 28 August 1675, BL MS Add. 72850, ff.226–229 v, 240–241 v.

[48] Petty to Aubrey, 29 May 1678, BL MS Egerton 2231, ff.90–91 v. Wood had suggested triplicate proportion in his letter to Petty of 28 August 1675, BL MS Add. 72850, ff.240–241 v.

[49] BL MS Egerton 2231, f.91r.   [50] Petty, *Discourse*, 133.

[51] The letter was later printed in Barlow, *The Genuine Remains of That Learned Prelate Dr. Thomas Barlow, Lord Bishop of Lincoln* (London: Printed for John Dunton, 1693), 151–156. See Lewis; John Spurr, 'Barlow, Thomas (1608/9–1691)', *Oxford DNB* <http://www.oxforddnb.com/view/article/1439>.

of materialist physics in general: 'though there be several things in it ingeniously said; yet there be too several things highly irrational, and indeed most metaphysical Non-sense, and some things (I fear) impious, if not plainly Atheistical.'[52] Particularly alarming was Petty's atomic rendering of Genesis:

> If such Atomes be the first matter of all things, and by meeting of them all visible bodies be made, and they meet and are join'd by their own innate motion; then 'tis evident Adam was made of such Atomes, and they met in him, (not by God's appointment, and Divine-creating-power), but by their own innate power, and so Epicurus (a Pagan Philosopher) and his Hypothesis, shall have more truth and credit, than the Divine History of the Creation by Moses.[53]

Epicurus had accounted for natural phenomena not by intelligent divine action but by the spontaneous 'swerve' of atoms in the void. Petty's similar attribution of an innate curving motion to atoms contravened Barlow's Aristotelian reading of Mosaic history. More fundamentally, it threatened to make God unnecessary.

Petty replied with characteristic irony: 'though he calls me irrationall, nonsensicall, impious, and Atheisticall, I doe in Christian Charity forgive such his unbrotherly, and unphilosophicall dealings'.[54] He mocked Barlow's Scholastic verbosity and abstruseness. The charge of atheism stung, however, and Petty carefully restated his 'Doctrines' by way of refuting it. First, 'God created Heaven, and Earth, that is, all things, and consequently the first matter of them whether Atoms, or other.' Next, He 'made man of Earth, and afterward breathed into him the Spirit of Life, the Ratio formalis' of which—as Descartes had established—was thinking. And 'What then can be the next principle, but matter for what were thinking without matter to thinke upon'?[55]

> Now if it be not enough for the Churches and Scriptures Vindication to have said (Deus omnia fecit) I shall reinforce the same with another Scripture which is that (God is all in all) the meaning whereof I with submission conceive to be, that God is all Power, all Vertue, all Energy, and all Motion in all things, and in all Beings whatsoever. And consequently that from him proceeded even that innate motion which wee did attribute to Atoms, and from him alone was that Power derived, whereby those Atoms (or most

---

[52] Barlow, 151.   [53] Barlow, 153.
[54] Petty to Anglesey, 3 April 1675, in Bodl. MS Rawlinson A. 185, ff.219–220 v. Another version of Petty's answer is in BL MS 72850, ff.220–223 v.
[55] Bodl. MS Rawlinson A. 185, f.219r–v.

comodious Element) were beautifully, wisely and in infinite variety joyned together in the Fabrick of the Universe, and of all its Severall Parts.[56]

In short, Petty concluded, 'I quietly contemne the having been called (irrationall, Nonsensicall, Impious, and Atheisticall)'.[57]

Barlow's attack left a mark. Many of Petty's later papers—particularly those dealing with the 'multiplication of mankind'—would place new emphasis on confuting 'Scripture Scoffers', linking modern demographic data to scriptural testimony about population.[58] More immediately, Petty launched himself on an explicit apologetic: the 'Scale of Creatures'. Petty began to discuss his 'Scale' with an enthusiastic Southwell late in 1676, but despite occasional bouts of progress never completed it, giving up by early 1679. The purpose of the work was 'to humble that proud Coxcombe man' by showing 'That man hath no reason to put so high a valew uppon himselfe, as if hee were chiefe or next to God' given his actual station on the great chain (or scale) of being.[59] As Petty well knew, the chain was an ancient Platonic theme, but despite occasional references to contemporary works (Southwell seems to have shown Petty a manuscript of Chief Justice Matthew Hale's 1677 *Primitive Origination of Mankind* and excerpted parts of William Bates's 1676 *Considerations of the Existence of God*) his own discussion reflected not only his particular apologetic aims but also, and for present purposes more revealingly, the stubborn persistence of his commitment to Baconian natural philosophy even when least convenient.[60]

Petty posited two scales: 'one whose top is man, and whose bottom is the smallest and simplest animall that man can discern' and another, of which God 'is the top, and man the bottome'. This was humbling in itself, since 'the great multitude of gradations which are upon the small scale' implied 'many more upon the greater scale'—potentially 'millions of beings superior unto man'.[61] He next addressed man's relationship to God,

---

[56] Bodl. MS Rawlinson A. 185, f.220r.   [57] Bodl. MS Rawlinson A. 185, f.220 v.

[58] See for example Petty to Southwell, 20 August 1681, *PSC*, 92.

[59] Beinecke MS Osborn Shelves fb. 135, document 3 (hereafter 'Scale'), f.1r.

[60] Petty summarized points from Hale and Bates in 'Scale', f.1r–v; see Hale, *The Primitive Origination of Mankind, Considered and Examined according to the Light of Nature* (London: Printed by William Godbid for William Shrowsbery, 1677); William Bates, *Considerations of the Existence of God and of the Immortality of the Soul* (London: Printed by J. D. for Brabazon Aylmer, 1676).

[61] Petty, 'Scale', ff.2r, 3r. Discussion of 'holy Angells, Created Intelligences, or subtile Matteriall beings' may have been planned for the second part of the 'Scale' (see f.110 v), only a scrap of which was written. A manuscript note dated tentatively by Harris to the 1680s lists 'Of good & bad Angells', seemingly as a possible essay topic; BL MS Add. 72887, f.35 v.

gauging the 'proportion between the Architect of the whole world and men' by comparing the greatest human creation ('suppose the Piramids') with 'the greatest visible opifitium of God, namely the firmament or Orbe of the fixed stars'. Of course, 'in truth, there be no proportion between them' at all; the juxtaposition of divine and human artefacts paradoxically manifested the incommensurability of man and God.[62] Petty then recast this comparison in describing the two 'Inteligible poles' of religion:

> whereof one is, that as man made and build Houses, shipps, Clocks and other machinaments by a preconceived Idea, models and designes of them, so there is a power namely God, who built and framed the orbe of the fixed starrs, and every thing that is contained within it, according to some preconceived Idea and model also, and who hath (at least) the like power over all things which Man can Imagine as a potter hath over his clay, or as any other Artisan hath over his tools, or Matterialls.[63]

The second 'pole upon which religion turneth' was the notion that man 'was made in the likeness of God'. This did not mean that man was 'godlike' any more than a pot resembled a potter. It simply implied 'that although we see that the Externall & Visible part of man, doth change, perish, desolve and dye, yet there is an other part of him, which is Invisible, Unchangeable and Immortall'—the soul—'between whom and God there is some kind & degree of Affinity, Comunication & Analogy', however distant.[64] Like the analogy between man and God as fellow craftsmen, and indeed like the upper scale itself, these poles of religion at once tied man to God and humbled any pride deriving from the connection.

Turning to the lower 'Scale of Animalls', however, Petty found human abasement harder to maintain. He began by listing a range of reasons for placing man at the top: government, trade and money, travel and exploration, science and observation, complex speech and systems of writing, machines, houses, and ships all set men apart; 'No animall doth consider causes, nor Proportions and Relations, nor hath any signes or footsteps of Religion'—nor, for that matter, did animals dress up in fancy clothing, have sex for pleasure, or make war.[65] The logical next move was to downplay these distinctions by disparaging the human rationality that supposedly underpinned them. Yet the intellectual gaps Petty highlighted mirrored the aims of his own natural philosophy: knowledge of human 'generation & Conception', morbidity and mortality,

---

[62] Petty, 'Scale', f.4r–v.   [63] Petty, 'Scale', f.5r.   [64] Petty, 'Scale', f.5r.
[65] Petty, 'Scale', ff.6 v–7 v.

'Mutations of the Aire' and weather, 'the Riseing and Falling of States and Empires', geography and cosmography, 'the Nature of sence and motion', the manipulation of sensible qualities. (The 'Compounding of all smells & tasts' out of a few basic ingredients 'is not yet known'—but, Petty could not resist adding, 'may bee.')[66] What began as a denigration of mankind ended as an exaltation of science. Man was not incapable of this knowledge and control; he had just not (yet) attained them. The only permanent blind spots of the human intellect were 'The misteries of the Trinity, Incarnation, & the Resurrection', matters above reason, which to explain was to destroy.[67] This would hardly have satisfied Barlow.

Finally, Petty approached the scale from another angle, asking which animal came closest to man on the scale. This was not an exercise in comparative anatomy or natural history but rather a question of 'dignity', which was associated, as in the earlier comparison of God and man, with capability.[68] Elephants, for example, besides a 'wonderfull dexterity' with their trunks not unlike 'the use of a mans hand', displayed longevity, 'memory and Understanding'.[69] As for 'the Ape or rather the Drill', its shape and 'actions ... doe in many points resemble those of a man'.[70] On the other hand, 'Speech is more peculiar unto, & copious in a man then in any other Animall, & Consequently we might in that respect give the 2nd place to Parrotts'—not in place of the elephant (parrots lacked understanding) but perhaps ahead of the apes.[71] Special consideration, finally, was reserved for the bee:

> among all the admirable operations of the Bee, I prefer his pollicy assigneing that faculty for the thing wherein hee comes nearest to man, and pollicy or the Art of Government seems to be the most considerable faculty of a man: for how wonderfull is it that the spirit of one Generall of an Army should Influence, Consimulate & Semetrize the minds, manners & motions of 40000. men, or rather that one Monarch should consenture and draw together the Mentall & Corporeall facultyes of 10 Millions of men, as burning Glasses doe gather and Converge many thousand beams of the Sun into one focus or burning point, so as to excite a heat that shall melt Silver, where without such burning Glass, the same Raies of the Sunn, would be too weake to singe Tinder; I say that if what is reported concerning the policy and Government of bees be true ... their souls seem as like the souls of men as their bodies are unlike.[72]

---

[66] Petty, 'Scale', ff.7 v–8 v.   [67] Petty, 'Scale', f.8 v.   [68] Petty, 'Scale', f.9 v.
[69] Petty, 'Scale', ff.9v–10r.   [70] Petty, 'Scale', f.10r.   [71] Petty, 'Scale', f.10r–v.
[72] Petty, 'Scale', ff.10v–11r.

As Rhodri Lewis argues, Petty's ostensible point was that mankind's seemingly unique characteristics were partly realized in lower species; the distinction between men and animals was one of degree.[73] Again, however, a discourse on human limitations became a celebration of the science that promised to surpass them. Gifted with the art of government, applying policy to nature for his kingdom's benefit, the industrious bee (whose hive graced Petty's new coat of arms) was a tiny political arithmetician.

To be sure, the 'Scale' was not about political arithmetic. To the extent that it maintained a fixed purpose, it was a defence against Barlow's charge of atheism. Yet, as the manuscript grew by fits and starts over the years, its contents drifted with the main current of Petty's thinking. Curiously, this has been ignored even in the one part of the 'Scale' that has attracted scholarly attention, an 'Appendix' considering variations within the human race itself. Having suggested the possibility of separate races of 'Gyants & Pygmies' and the like, Petty hinted at similar differences 'between the Guiny Negroes and the Midle Europeans, and of Negroes between those of Guiny & those who live about the Cape of Good Hope, which last are the most beast like of all the sorts of men with whom our Travellers are well acquainted.'[74] As an apparent anticipation of biological racism, this passage has gained a certain notoriety—in contrast to the 'Scale' as a whole and indeed to the rest of Petty's natural philosophy.[75] But in fact Petty was simply regurgitating the climatic theory of character familiar since the time of Hippocrates and restated in the sixteenth century by Jean Bodin.[76] (He went on to comment on the 'mean' physical and mental stature of 'people who live in the Northernmost parts of the habitable world'.)[77] Geography, not biology, was the key—situation, not race.

This is only what we should expect. Essential biological differences between nations would make nonsense of demographic transmutation. If the 'Scale' does not embody the scientistic racism of later imperialists, however, it nevertheless illuminates Petty's own position. Beyond its neoplatonic trappings—a hierarchical chain of being emanating from God and centred on man—it reveals Petty as neither the atheist Barlow

---

[73] Lewis.   [74] Petty, 'Scale', ff.11v–12r.

[75] Winthrop D. Jordan, *White over Black: American Attitudes Toward the Negro, 1550–1812* (Baltimore: Pelican Books, 1969), 224–225. Jordan treats Petty's emphasis on physiognomic differences as an anticipation of biological racism, but the example of northern Europeans suggests that Petty attributed both physical and mental traits to climate.

[76] Lewis; Julian H. Franklin, *Jean Bodin and the Sixteenth-Century Revolution in the Methodology of Law and History* (New York: Columbia University Press, 1963), 77–78; Olson, 76–77.

[77] Petty, 'Scale', f.12v.

supposed nor the orthodox champion presumably intended, but rather as
committed to a small core of Christian doctrine (Creation, the immortality
of the soul, the salvific role of Jesus) and flexible—favouring toleration but
prepared, like Hobbes, to let the sovereign decide—on other points. This
flexibility, evident in the transmutation scheme, would prove vital under
James II. No less remarkable was Petty's persistent tendency to substitute
praise for blame when discussing human limitations. At times he virtually
suggested that man's place on the scale was in his own hands:

> I doe not only compare man with the Inferiour Creatures of the small Scale,
> but I do also compare the Highest Improvements of Mankind in his masse,
> with the rudest Condition that man was ever in: Thereby Inferring that if
> man hath Improved soe much in the severall past Centuries and ages of the
> World, how far hee might proceed in six Thousand years more, or in any
> other Number of Ages (that is to say) how far hee might advance from the
> bottom (where hee now is) towards the top of the great Scale.[78]

Running against the very logic of the scale, this assertion is strikingly at
odds with the goal of humbling human pride. Here too, it appears that the
'Scale'—which pictured God as an artificer, bees as natural politicians, and
the limits of human reason as temporary impediments—left off damning
'that proud Coxcombe man' to preach the improvement of human science.

Political arithmetic in the Atlantic world

Long before giving up the 'Scale', Petty had begun to cast his thoughts
farther afield—across the Atlantic. The first evidence of his new interest
is a series of notes on New England from February 1675, when the ink
on the *Discourse* was barely dry. How this interest developed is harder
to say. As his stress on population density and his proposals for Ireland
suggested, Petty's attitude towards both territorial expansion and colonial
settlement (beyond the minimum necessary for producing exotic goods
for commercial benefit) was ambivalent, if not hostile: '*Ireland* and the
Plantations in *America* ... are a Burthen to England'.[79] New England was
especially irksome, both because it was literally counterproductive—its
homegrown industry was the despair of mercantilists—and because, from
Petty's perspective, it was the artificial product of unnatural policy, a haven
for exiles created by early Stuart religious persecution.[80]

---

[78] Petty, 'Scale', f.2v.   [79] Petty, *Political Arithmetick*, sig. a2r.
[80] See Maurice Ashley, *Financial and Commercial Policy under the Cromwellian Protectorate*
(London, 1962), 134.

Colonies brought problems. *Political Arithmetick* had identified 'The first impediment of *Englands* greatness' as the fact 'that the Territories thereunto belonging, are too far asunder, and divided by the Sea into many several *Islands* and Countries; and I may say, into so many Kingdoms, and several Governments'.[81] These unnatural divisions multiplied as dominion grew:

> The Government of *New-England* ... doth so differ from that of his Majesties other Dominions, that 'tis hard to say what may be the consequence of it.

> And the Government of the other Plantations, doth also differ very much from any of the rest; although there be not naturally substantial reasons from the Situation, Trade, and Condition of the People, why there should be such differences.

> From all which it comes to pass, that small divided remote Governments, being seldom able to defend themselves, the Burthen of protecting them all, must lye upon the chief Kingdom *England*; and so all the smaller Kingdoms and Dominions, instead of being Additions are really Diminutions[.][82]

Colonies were not simply a source of competition or a drain on population in an absolute sense; by creating divisions they increased the costs of government while diminishing the value of population through geographic dispersal, economic dissociation, political disaffection, and ultimately—as in Ireland—degeneration. Yet correctly managed, colonies could supply the mother country with raw materials and an export market for manufactures, stimulating metropolitan industry and encouraging immigration. *Political Anatomy* attributed Ireland's 'fitness for Trade' in part to the fact that it 'lieth Commodiously for the Trade of the new *American* world; which we see every day to grow and Flourish', while *Political Arithmetick* noted that 'the *American* Plantations employ four Hundred Sail of Ships'—fostering both trade and the training of able seamen, one of the pillars of the commonwealth.[83] Done well, colonization could both multiply the people and improve the population.

The question, once again, was how to remove the unnatural impediments bad policy had created. Here the differences between Ireland and the American colonies were at least as important as the similarities. First, whereas politics, custom, and religion divided Ireland's population, Petty's view seems to have been that all the king's subjects in the

---

[81] Petty, *Political Arithmetick*, 87.   [82] Petty, *Political Arithmetick*, 88.
[83] Petty, *Political Anatomy*, 79; *Political Arithmetick*, sig. a2r–a3v.

Americas were simply English; neither slaves (seen entirely as property) nor Native Americans (apparently seen simply as foreigners) counted.[84] The pressing problem was not, then, to transmute the colonists, but to prevent their degeneration by binding them more closely to England. Accordingly, *Political Arithmetick*'s proposals for the Atlantic colonies were institutional and largely administrative: 'making Two such Grand Councils, as may equally represent the whole Empire, one to be chosen by the King, the other by the People.'[85] What had happened to prior English plantations in Ireland might happen in the other colonies if no action were taken, but it had not happened yet. In the meantime, in fact, dispossessed Irish landowners might themselves be transplanted to America, where they would presumably be less capable of making trouble.[86]

If this was the logic behind Petty's stress on 'grand councils' rather than transmutation in his proposals for the 'English Empire' beyond Ireland, then his assessment of the American scene changed little as years passed. Proposals for administrative and representative institutions (the line between the two is often unclear) proliferated through the 1680s. One such tract, 'Of a Grand House of Peeres', proposed expanding the House of Lords to 520 members, 'Of which 40 to be cald out of Ireland, 30 out of Scotland, and 10 more out of the rest of his majesty's Dominions in Asia, Affrica and America'. This would create a larger pool from which to draw ministers, but the main point seems to have been to unite colonial with metropolitan government both for its own sake and to create a body of loyal servants of the Crown 'greater then that of the House of Commons in England (which is but 513) and greater then the number of any other Assembly within the King's Dominions.'[87] Another paper tentatively dated to 1687 proposing 'a generall Councill for Plantation, Manufacture, Trade, Religion, and Applotment' sketched out a similarly broad elected body, submerging 45 Irish, 30 Scottish, and 11 colonial representatives ('3 for New England, 4 for Virginia, Carolina and Maryland,' and one each

---

[84] Petty makes no mention of Native Americans in any surviving paper before 1675. *Political Arithmetick* (84) included 'The value of the Slaves, brought out of Africa, to serve in our American Plantations' in the total value of English trade, but did not reckon slaves as part of the subject population; from Petty's perspective they were goods, not people.

[85] Petty, *Political Arithmetick*, 88.

[86] In a paper dated to *c*.1675 entitled 'Decrees and Judgments of one Island Executed in the Other' (BL MS Add. 72879, f.75) Petty proposed sending two-thirds of unsatisfied 'divested' Irish landowners to America and the rest to Scotland.

[87] *PP*, 1:8–9.

for Jamaica, the Barbados, 'Asia', and 'Africa') in a sea of 364 English counsellors (including one each for Jersey and Guernsey).[88]

From beginning to end Petty evidently thought that, absent the kind of demographic divisions that tore Ireland, institutional reform could quell incipient colonial insubordination. A 1687 'Table of Chapters' for an unwritten work on empire indicated the shape of Petty's imperial vision. One chapter was to have shown 'That for want of a Union, Even the Protestant and English of Ireland, may as it formerly hath done degenerate, bee estranged, and Rebell'. But given favourable demographic conditions—that is, a predominantly English population—institutional union would serve: 'as Wales is an Example of the good Effects of an Union, so will Ireland bee, to Scotland, New England and the other of his Majesty's out-territorys.'[89] Another paper written the same year noted that 'The King of Englands Empire lyes in 4 parts. Viz His European Islands, His American Islands, His planted lands upon the Continent of America, And his African and East India-Trade.' The task of imperial government was not to expand these territories but to fill them with people who would be more and more the same. 'The Emprov'd Empire' would be a social and political unit bound together by an English sea.[90]

Petty's interest in Native Americans, who might seem to have presented the same problem for this vision as the Irish, developed only gradually. This may be because he did not, at first, see the non-English population as internal to the English dominions in the Americas; transmutative political arithmetic was meant to manipulate *subject* populations. A few pages of 'Notes about New England. Taken 4 February 1674/5' during a conversation between Petty, a Dr Taylor, and two informants identified only as Mr Frost and Mr Bartholomew, are remarkable for their nearly complete lack of reference to the American world outside the English settlements. Petty listed the names of nearly forty Massachusetts towns and the number of families in each and estimated that in all of New England there were 12,080 families, 100,000 'soules', and 16,000 'men fitt for armes'. The document moved on to shipping before listing New England ironworks, 'Principall Merchants' and 'Eminent Ministers', 'Rivers and Harbours on

[88] BL MS Add. 72866, ff.174–175. Petty's allotment of three representatives to New England and only one to Jamaica seems to confirm his exclusion of slaves from the civil population.

[89] BL MS Add. 72885, ff.110–111 and ff.112–113 (two copies).

[90] 'Of the King of England his Naturall & Instrinsic power' (1687), BL MS Add. 72866, ff.148–151. This is one motivation for Petty's preoccupation with *mare clausum*, and probably informed his sense of his role as a judge in the Irish Court of Admiralty.

the Coast', 'Islands', prominent 'Men who have been actually soldiers', 'Present Magistrates', 'Merchants and others of London, Trading & Corresponding with New England', and further 'popular men'. Despite some concern with situation and population, it is impressionistic even by Petty's standards, perhaps reflecting his informants' limitations.[91]

Only with the closing 'Miscellany observations' did some of Petty's more characteristic interests emerge. These included notes about New England's imports from England as well as its home manufactures, the summer and winter wages of labourers and artisans, and further details about the militia, government, and church settlement. Several observations related to crime, such as that 'Adultery is Death by the Law, but scarce ever executed'. There are 'No Beggars in the whole Country', and 'The poorest Houses have ground Roomes & Lofts, & most have Cellars.' Here the contrast with Irish households would have been obvious—Petty's 1673 'Report from the Council of Trade' (a summary of *Political Anatomy* written at Essex's behest) had described 'wretched nasty Cabbins ... worse than those of the Savage *Americans*'.[92] New Englanders, by comparison, maintained recognizably English households. Petty noted that 'The chief Transmigration was between 1631 and 1641', and though he did not comment on its causes he went on to note that 'The Sectaryes at Road Island use extream Lyberty & live quietly enough.' The paper noted in two places without further comment that 'One Mr. Elliot [i.e. John Eliot] translated the Bible into Indian', but the only mention of actual Indians was that the English colonists 'never suffer them to handle Armes.'[93]

A later set of 'Remarques of the people of New England, drawne from Papers sent from Thence' laid out a more limited range of information more systematically, and may reflect a greater degree of selectivity and control on Petty's part than the earlier notes.[94] The paper included estimates

---

[91] *PP*, 2:98–105; BL MS Add. 72867, ff.47–61.

[92] Petty, 'Report to the Council of Trade', 116; manuscript copies are in BL MS Add. 38849, ff.86–93, NA SP 9/2/2, RSL MS Classified Papers XVII, item 18, and TCD MS 888, ff.138–143. Hull dates the 'Report' to 1676 (*EW*, 1:213), but the NA copy is filed under '1673' and dated 'March the 25th, 1673'; both it and the RSL copy refer to 'your Lordship's Act of Council, of January the 20th [16]72 [i.e. 30 January 1673 New Style]' where Hull has 1675; early 1673 seems likely.

[93] *PP*, 2:105–107; John Eliot (trans.), *The Holy Bible containing the Old Testament and the New* (Cambridge, MA: Printed by Samuel Green and Marmaduke Johnson, 1663).

[94] *PP*, 2:107–108. The paper includes militia estimates for Connecticut for 1678. In a letter to Southwell dated 10 September 1678, Petty claimed that his 'collections' on New England 'contain more material truth than I have ever heard from others' (*PP*, 2:95; Petty to Southwell, 10 September 1678, *PSC*, 59). But another paper suggests that Petty thought Rhode Island was an island, and he may have been no better informed about the rest of New England; '6 Points concerning the King's Wealth, Power and Government' (1685), BL MS Add. 72866, ff.17–20.

of the size and distribution of the militia—relatively detailed in the case of 'New England' (Massachusetts Bay and Plymouth), sketchier for Rhode Island and Connecticut (including New Hampshire and Maine). It also contained scattered observations on situation ('Not one Acre of ten or twenty in many places manurable' in New England), improvement ('The Estates [of Connecticut] amount to 110,7881 St[erling]'), and trade ('Commodities imported from England may amount to forty or fifty thousand pounds yearly'). But the paper's focus was demographic, and Petty clearly defined the population that concerned him: 'They account all generally from Sixteen to Sixty ... fitt to bear Arms; except Negroes & Slaves whom they arme not. There are 500 Whites born there yearly & three hundred marriages ... In seven years have been born eight hundred Whites. Four hundred and fifty marriages within the same time.' In Rhode Island, 'Of Whites & Blacks (of the latter there are very few) about two hundred born in a year. About 50 marriages; about four hundred & fifty five Burials in Seaven yeares.'[95]

This lack of interest in Native Americans and the exclusion of 'Negroes & Slaves' from the effective population may surprise, given Petty's absorption in the problems of cultural difference elsewhere. The omission is all the more astonishing since the paper considerably postdates King Philip's War (1675–1676), which made plain the danger Native American neighbours posed to English settlement. It may even be just this that focused Petty's attention on the militia. The most straightforward explanation may be that, on one hand, Petty did not see slaves as a political threat (they were property, whose human characteristics were vaguely assumed but never discussed), and on the other, that he saw Native Americans not as subjects to be manipulated but simply as enemies—analogues not of the 'wild Irish' but of, say, the French. The answer to any problem they posed was diplomatic or military. A rudimentary political anatomy of New England revealed a healthy English population threatened from without, rather than a sickly body politic torn by internal divisions. Transmutation had no role to play.

Between 1679 and 1685, however, Petty began asking questions about Native Americans that closely paralleled those he had asked about the Irish. One likely stimulus was his own limited personal involvement in American colonization, which came about through his acquaintance with William Penn, whom he apparently met while in Ireland in the

1660s.[96] The two shared longstanding interests in both Irish plantation and religious toleration.[97] Petty's interest in American plantation, however, began around 1681, when Elizabeth Petty considered purchasing shares in Penn's American colonial venture, backing out at the last minute.[98] Notes on 'The charge of a share of 5000 acres in Pensilvania', made following conversations with Penn, estimated the cost of clearing land, transporting, housing, and employing labourers, building houses and fencing an estate.[99] But four years later Petty was still weighing 'Whether It bee better to transplant out of England in Ireland or America?' and 'What danger it is to Let people go out of England into Ireland or America, and to which most?'[100] Indeed, he turned down John Aubrey's offer of the chance to buy land in Tobago in 1685 on the grounds that 'the designe is a[s] forraigne and incongruous to my circumstances as any thing can bee, for I am above 60 years old, [and] am under some extraordinary thoughts concerning our affairs in Ireland'.[101] In 1686, however, he went ahead and purchased land in Pennsylvania. A surviving 'Agreement between Penn & Petty about a Colony in Pennsylvania' indicated the terms:

> Penn doth devise to Petty, in Consideration of 5s., a quadrangular peece of Land Lying 12 English Miles upon the river of ____, and 6½ miles broad upwards into the Land, forever; Yeelding & paying for the same one grayne of wheate yearely, together with one hundredth part of all Colts, Calves, Lambs & pigs, as also one hundredth part of all the Wheate, Rye, barly, Rice, Oates & pease, which shall bee gotten & produced out of the said lands forever. To be taken from time to time from & out of the said lands by the said Pen or his assignees, in the same manner as Tythes are now taken & Collected in England.[102]

Nothing came of the purchase in Petty's lifetime besides some un-answered political-anatomical queries and—as we shall see—an illu-minating population scheme.[103] Nearly a century later, however, Petty's

[96] PP, 2:95.

[97] A letter from Penn to Petty dated 30 July 1675 (BL MS Add. 72850, ff.234–235) addressed the latter as 'my old and worthy friend', mentioned speaking with 'the great man' (perhaps the earl of Essex) about Irish affairs, and added 'I entreat thee most earnestly to have In writing what was read to me of England & Ireland...Ireland took as well as England; now is the crisis; therefore pray fail not.' It is possible that Penn was referring to *Political Anatomy*, *Political Arithmetick*, or both, but this is speculation.

[98] PP, 2:96–98.   [99] PP, 2:110–111.   [100] PP, 2:109–110.

[101] Petty to Aubrey, 22 August 1685, BL MS Egerton 2231, f.96; see Aubrey to Petty, 17 August 1685, BL MS Add. 72850, ff.303–304.

[102] PP, 2:121.

[103] See 'Quaeries concerning the nature of the Natives of Pensilvania' (1686), PP, 2:115–119; compare 'Questions concerning Ireland' (1686)—further endorsed '41 Queries concerning

great-great-grandson William, Lord Shelburne, claimed over five thousand acres of countryside and three city lots in Philadelphia on the strength of Petty's presence on the original list of purchasers there.[104]

If his investment suggests the expectation of private gain, Petty remained unsure to the end of his life about the colonies' profitability to the metropole.[105] Profit, however, was not the only consideration, and the political turmoil of James II's reign led him to see 'American Plantations' as a 'desideratum' for England.[106] He worried especially about the resurgence of the Irish Catholic interest under Tyrconnell, which undermined the Protestant settlement of which he was both founder and beneficiary. Some 1685 'Conjectures' predicted both 'That the french & Irish will joyne & invade England & Scotland' and that 'Many will go to America.'[107] That same year Petty wrote that

> It is probable that the French Monarch, doth not onely in generall ayme at the universall Monarchy of the West, but in particular of the Soveraignty of the Seas, so anciently claymed by England; and to bee Master of Trade, unto both which, Ireland by its Scituation since the planting of America, doth eminently conduce.[108]

Untransmuted, Ireland was liable to rebellion or invasion; conquered, it would confer on its masters control of key sea lanes and a platform for invading Britain. Peopling the Atlantic plantations, however, might prevent or at least mitigate these dangers by creating a reservoir of English colonists.[109] A 1686 set of 'Remedies for the King' argued that England's Caribbean colonies could support twice their current population, based on estimates in another paper 'That the King hath Anno 1685, 100 Millions of Statute Acres of Land' around the world and 'That there are unmaried Teeming [i.e. fertile] women, amongst his said subjects, enough to double the said 10 millions of People, in about 25 years'.[110] A third tract called for an Act of

Ireland. Ordinary & Extraordinary, generall & speciall, most of which may serve for any other state'—BL MS Add. 72882, ff.94–97.

[104] *PP*, 2:97–98.

[105] 'For Strengthning the Empire of England', BL MS Add. 72866, ff.104–105.

[106] '40 Desiderata considerata' (1685), BL MS Add. 72866, f.1.

[107] 'Quieting Ireland' (1685), BL MS Add. 72881, f.72.   [108] BL MS Add. 72881, f.88.

[109] 'Twenty Eight Remarkable points in the essay about the Analysis populi' (c.1686), BL MS Add. 72866, ff.53–54.

[110] BL MS Add. 72866 ff.59–60; '6 Points concerning the King's Wealth, Power and Government' (1685), BL MS Add. 72866, ff.17–20.

Parliament 'For regulating ye American Colonys and Encrease of ye people'.[111]

The challenge was to people the colonies without exporting 'teeming women' from England, where they were needed both to counter domestic under-population and to serve as engines of Ireland's transmutation. One solution was to make good the empire's shortage of teeming women from without, for example by marrying English men to Native American women. In light of Petty's proposals for Ireland, and in particular of the 'oeconomy of the family' on which their success relied, however, there was an obvious problem with this. Just as English women installed in Irish households would transmute the Irish (reversing the older but formally identical process by which Irish women had sped the degeneration of the Old English) so Native American women installed in English colonial households—few, scattered, and far from the metropole—would surely induce degeneration in the same way. Had *Political Arithmetick* not stressed the dangers of estrangement between England and the colonies with this in mind? For the peopling of North America to work as Petty wanted, a way had to be found around the mechanism of transmutation that his Irish work relied on.

Throughout the mid-1680s Petty fitfully attempted to apply the lessons of Irish plantation to America. One paper was even endorsed 'The description of a Colony or Towneship to bee made in Ireland or America'; it described a model colony consisting of a walled town surrounded by fields surrounded by further walls, the interlocking economic operations as well as the general maintenance of the whole coordinated and overseen by a colonel.[112] A set of 'General Cautions concerning Pensylvania' included familiar advice regarding census-taking and education (such as to 'Keep an exact accompt of the people' and to 'Discourage the Learning of lattine & greek ... but promote arithmetic & measuring & drawing') but also counseled the reader—perhaps Penn?—to 'Avoyd Stragling plantations', the sort of haphazard private undertakings that had plagued Irish colonization efforts.[113] 'A Proposall concerning American Plantations' proposed a 40,000-acre riverside plantation more or less on the model of the earlier 'Irish colony', while a paper 'Of American Planting' included a map describing the same colony, designed now to

---

[111] 'That there be an Act for taking away all Tests, Oaths, penal Laws and Incapacitys depending upon religion' (c.1686), BL MS Add. 72888, ff.68–69.
[112] BL MS Add. 72867, ff.86–89.   [113] *PP*, 2:114–115.

support 10,000 people at the outset, 'And when there bee 20,000 people To plant as much more on the other side of the River.'[114]

Only in this last paper did Petty suggest the demographic basis for the proposed colonial expansion, and its relationship to the Native Americans outside. First, Native Americans as a group were rigorously excluded from the colonial body politic: 'the Indian may not live within the plantation, but that markets of furres, deere & foule, bee kept neere the Line [i.e. the border of the plantation]'. Second, however, the paper proposed 'That the English may buy Indian girles of under 7 yeares old and use them as wives, even with polygamy regulated by authority.' Both the notion of polygamy and the apparent suggestion of child marriage are alarming, but in fact Petty had speculated about the use of polygamy in Ireland itself. A 1683 paper asked 'whether the Law of God bee not so cleer and absolute for the way of Mariage now practised, That there is no room left for the Soveraigne Magistrate to alter any thing therein',

> Or whether the greatest part thereof bee not the Law of the Land and ancient Custom thereof? And whether the Law of God and Nature, do extend any further then that man and woman shall bee joyned together in Unam Carnem, & bee obliged to make provision for their young Ones t[i]ll they can help themselves? And whether the Law of God doth not leave all other Circumstances to bee setled by the Laws of the Age and Country; for wee see that before the [floud?] and before our Saviour and in severall ages & countrys of the World, the Laws and practis of marriage are very different. Wherefore leaving this matter to Divines, and supposing that the fundamentall Law of God and Nature is, That Men and Women should bee so joyned together, as may produce most Children, and make them most usefull for the Common-Wealth, Wee humbly conceive (at least by way of supposition ... [)] that every ... teeming female, should always and with all decency, bee provided of a Husband[115]

How serious this 'supposition' was is difficult to tell, but it is worth noting that Petty differed from Graunt and others in believing that polygamy increased population growth; the received view was that, like promiscuity, it resulted in barrenness. His American proposal stipulated 'That no youth of between 18 & 58 yeares old, nor woman of between 16 & 41 yeares old, bee unmaryed, without manifest impediment by the magistrate.'[116] Maximal reproduction was a matter of rigorous policy.

[114] *PP*, 2:111–113, 119–120.
[115] 'The naturall & pecul[i]ar Interest of Ireland' (1683), BL MS Add. 72880, ff.128–131. For Petty's thoughts on polygamy (or 'Californian marriage'), see *PP*, 2:49–58.
[116] *PP*, 2:113.

But the key to success was the more shocking notion 'That the English may buy Indian girles of under 7 yeares old and use them as wives'. Petty was *not* advocating child marriage, however. Rather, the girls should be purchased while young, raised in colonial communities, and married as adults. Native American women, as women, might contribute to the English interest; as 'Indian' women, they might destroy it. The solution was to prevent them from becoming Indian women by purchasing them as girls. The formative period of childhood extended, in Petty's and many others' opinions, to around seven years of age.[117] Seven was the age at which children began school or apprenticeships, the age at which they left their mothers, who had given them language and a sense of identity. In Ireland, English women would transmute the population precisely by virtue of their responsibility for children under seven. Thus Indian girls purchased before the age of seven and raised from then on in English households would mature into English women. Degeneration would be circumvented, the economy of the family preserved, marriage promoted, and population—*English* population—maximized.

Petty's Indian marriage proposal, unlike his Irish transmutation scheme, never developed beyond the sketchiest of drafts. He may have shared them with Southwell, but there is no reason to think he seriously attempted to promote the idea among those with real power to act; it remained a vague speculation built on analogical foundations and very limited knowledge of the conditions in the colonies for which it was intended. It is precisely those analogical foundations, however, which let us see the elaboration of political arithmetic from a specific set of policies grounded in Irish and English politics to a more obviously generalizable set of assumptions and practices enabling government through demographic manipulation. American problems were different from Irish ones, and Petty's solutions differed accordingly: but the natural processes in operation were the same. The economy of the family worked the same way, degeneration was still a threat, acculturation still a possibility. In Pennsylvania as in Ireland, people were matter to be moulded to the state's convenience. Ethnicity was a matter of timing; race no matter at all.

---

[117] BL MS Add. 72880, f.127. The northern European late-marriage pattern entailed independence from an early age, but may also have blurred the gendered division of labour Petty assumed; see Mary S. Hartman, *The Household and the Making of History: A Subversive View of the Western Past* (Cambridge: Cambridge University Press, 2004).

Political arithmetic and the politics of religion

Just as Petty was extending political arithmetic across the Atlantic, a new need for it arose at home. In one sense, the accession to the throne in 1685 of James II—an openly practising Catholic with a Catholic queen and soon a Catholic heir—appeared to realize the Protestant nightmare Petty, as a landowner, had partially shared: the triumph of a resurgent Catholic interest in Ireland under Tyrconnell, the abrogation and perhaps ultimately the destruction of the Protestant settlement, the reversal of conquest. In another sense, however, it did not so much exacerbate the situation political arithmetic had been designed for as turn it on its head. In pushing transmutation Petty had linked the protection of Protestant Ireland with the survival of the monarchy. Now the threat to Protestant Ireland derived from royal policy itself. At the same time, the threat to monarchy was not Catholic rebellion in Ireland but Protestant rebellion across the Three Kingdoms. Torn between these two problems, no longer jointly soluble, Petty ultimately opted for the second. As it expanded to embrace the politics of religion on both sides of the Irish Sea during 1686 and 1687, political arithmetic became a way of turning anyone into anything the king needed—English or Irish, Protestant or Catholic.

Understanding how such a reversal was possible requires an examination of Petty's attitude to religion and its relationship to the body politic. As we have seen, he favoured toleration for both pragmatic and principled reasons: conscience could not be forced, and trying was counterproductive. There is little unambiguous evidence about Petty's own beliefs, but his friends remarked on a humorous skepticism in sectarian matters. As Aubrey wrote, 'He can be an excellent comedian (if he has a mind to it) and will preach *extempore* incomparably, either the Presbyterian way, Independent, Capucin frier, or Jesuite.'[118] Petty himself remarked to Southwell on the worthlessness of denominational labels:

> When any Boddy would have you to bee a Roman Catholiq, a Papist, a Protestant, a Church of England man, a Presbiterian, Annabaptist, Quaker, fanatick &c, or even Whig or Tory, Let them quit all those giberish denominations and uncertaine phrases, but make you a list of *Credenda* and *Agenda* necessary for your Eternall happinese, and give you their reasons for the same.[119]

That is by no means to say that he did not believe—we have seen how Barlow's accusation stung. Petty's will maintained that

---

[118] Aubrey, 243.   [119] Petty to Southwell, 1 April 1686, *PSC*, 186–187.

As for Religion I dye in the profession of that faith & the practice of such worship as I find established by the Law of my country not being able to believe what I please my self, nor to worship God better then by doing as I would be done unto & observing the laws of my country & expressing my love & honour to almighty God by such signes & tokens as are understood to be such by the people with whome I converse God knowing my heart even without any at all.[120]

There seems little reason to look for a secret creed concealed beneath this. A few essential inward convictions and a dispassionate attitude towards outward forms—coupled with a recognition that *some* form of worship, which the sovereign could decide, was essential for society to function—seem to sum Petty's position up.

Petty favoured toleration, but he was not invariably tolerant. Indeed, he responded with particular frostiness to John Graunt's conversion to Catholicism: 'As for difference in Religion you have done amise [sic] in sundry particulars'. He ended on a slightly more forgiving note: 'wee leave these things to God & be mindfull of what is the summe of all riligeon'.[121] Despite this, however, he informed a mutual friend that 'I converce lesse then formerly with Mr. Gra[u]nt, he having declared himselfe a Papist, & of a religion which I take to be both false and inconvenient.'[122] Since Petty had elsewhere pronounced the truths of religion above the reach of reason, the key word was 'inconvenient'. Persecuting consciences in the name of 'giberish denominations' was reprehensible, but so was risking life, limb, and property for their sake. For Petty as for Hobbes, the sovereign had the ultimate say. Graunt's mistake was not spiritual but political.

This view implied that the social utility of religion was detachable from its denominational content, and like many Petty strove to define the essentials of doctrine so that artificial divisions caused by inessentials (*adiaphora*) could be dispensed with. As religious tensions rose—from the debate over toleration of dissent in the early 1670s, through the Popish Plot, to James's accession—this pursuit grew in vigour. Many of the very numerous papers on religion in Petty's archive emphasize the social and political function of both public worship and some form of private belief.[123] Religion played an essential role in building faith between rulers

---

[120] BL MS Sloane 2903, f.18.

[121] Petty to Graunt, 18 January 1672/3, in BL MS Add. 72858, f.82.

[122] Petty to Holland, 23 August 1673, in BL MS Add. 72858, f.111.

[123] Three boxes of Petty's BL manuscripts (several hundred folios) are catalogued as 'religious', and dozens of papers in other boxes might easily be so described. By contrast, the fifteen papers

and ruled, ensuring public peace, and promoting obedient and faithful service:

> Man is a Religious Animall, and onely men hope that their Earthly Soveraines will deale very justly, when such soveraines believe there is a most Just God above them … Men, either for the Love of God or the feare of Hell, will forbeare doing such mischief to their Neighbour as the Law canot reach … Men beare paines & wrongs more patiently, when they hope that God will balance all in the next life … Soldiers will be most valiant & faithfull when They believe Death to bee the doore of happines.[124]

Religion should not be superficial. Petty denigrated 'What is vulgarly meant by Worshipping, honoring, & glorifying God'—that is, 'Enriching, obeying, & fighting for those who pretend to be his priests', 'Praying … for such benefits as Man canot give us', and (a linguistic and moralistic critique) 'By patheticall Metaphoricall expressions & allusions to set forth in a general way his power, wisedom, mercy &c, when wee either deny or ignore them in particulars.' The 'Disadvantages to the world by the same' included 'The vast expence of sacrifices & preists', 'The great bloodsheds by wars', and various 'Miscariages by superstitions'—among them the 'needlesse restraints put upon [matrimonial] conjugations', which hindered the multiplication of mankind.

If Petty had no interest in furthering 'vulgar' religion, however, he believed that 'God would be much honored' by the investigation of nature and that political arithmetic might both benefit and benefit from ecclesiastical reforms.[125] He began a slew of works on 'the multiplication of mankind' by way of helping 'a good Man … Writing against Atheism … answering Cavills against the Resurrection', and considered his estimates of the size and rate of growth of human population 'a brave argument against Scripture Scoffers and Prae-Adamites.'[126] Such men were every bit as harmful as the peddlers of superstition. Petty's clearest arguments for toleration are often also his strongest affirmations of religion's role as a supplement to

---

on 'religion' printed in Lansdowne's selection amount to thirty pages of text (*PP*, 1:113–145), all drawn from one box (BL MS Add. 72887). Meanwhile, Lansdowne printed nearly every extant paper relating to American plantation (*PP*, 2:93–121), taking up roughly the same amount of space. The resulting impression, that Petty devoted roughly equal time to both topics, is profoundly misleading.

124 'Religion' (c.1680s), *PP*, 1:116–117.   125 *PP*, 1:117–118.
126 Petty to Southwell, 20 August 1681, *PSC*, 92.

the law and a pillar of the state. 'The Effects of a Good Religion' (c.1685) sums it up:

No man ought to disturb another in that Religion

1. Which makes & keepes him good morally.
2. Which keepes him from secret sins not cognizable by the Magistrate & contrivances of the same.
3. Which gives him courage in adversity.
4. Which keepes him from dreading death & the infirmities & paines of Old age.
5. Which makes him conformable to the Lawes of the Land & Customes of the Country.
6. Which breakes violent passions & appetites.[127]

Just as political arithmetic methodized secular government, so Petty proposed reforming the church that oversaw the body politic at prayer:

The Church is the People congregated & Incorporated upon the accompt of seeking eternall happines after Naturall death & extraordinary advantages before. The Guides of ye People on the way to these ends are called Ministers, Priests or Divines. The Places of their flocks dwelling are called Parishes, which are to consist of as many familys or people as One Priest can officiate for, that is of so many adult persons as can hear him preach.[128]

This theologically streamlined, administratively rationalized national church would play a vital role in monitoring and maintaining the improved population political arithmetic promised to create.

It might also play a vital role in the advancement of learning. Arguing that knowledge of God came from nature as well as scripture, Petty recommended that ministers study mathematics, natural philosophy, natural history, antiquities, languages, and the skills of textual criticism. The primary point of this was to prepare skilled moral instructors:

the Work of divines is not to distr[ac]t their fl[o]ck wth their owne Philosophicall opinions & conceits, but to teach them thoroughly ye establishd lawes & customs of Religion, and to show them how God doth punish & reward ye observence & breaches of them, and to … punish their [Motions?] & temptations to Sin & to apply generall & particular Rem[e]dyes unto Each of them.[129]

---

[127] *PP*, I:118.   [128] BL MS Add. 72887, f.28.   [129] BL MS Add. 72887, f.29.

Yet shoring up parish morals required a thorough knowledge of the parish itself, and this meant gathering a considerable body of data over a length of time:

> the Priest ought not onely to know in generall the Number & Names of every Soule under his care but also their ages, sex, condicon, Trade, sect [and] pr[iva]te opinion, their art[,] their births, sicknesses, marr[ia]ges, deaths, their Estates, their thriving & decaying ... their dealings & bargain[in]gs, the differenc[e] between Seesonable & unseesonable Weather, fru[i]tfull & barren lands, yeares of plenty & dearth, hea[l]th & Mortality, barranesse & fecundity, War & peace, the Settlement & [Commotion?] of Mens Mind, Obedience & Sedition &c. To the end, That when Sin abounds hee may bee really able to tell the people how why & wherein the Same is, Who the Judgment & anger of god hath been shewne, [in the?] Number of those who dyed in the yeares of Sin more then in yeares of godlines lesse number borne, more have been sick, corne & fruite more scarse, Mor[e] tempestuous weather, more Murrayne among the Cattle, how & what Spe[cie?]s of grayne & fruite has fayld, And not talk at Random when hee himselfe is angry wth his parishi[o]ners.[130]

Charged with directing his parishioners' moral life, the priest must interpret God's will as expressed not only in scripture but also providentially through the ongoing history—demographic, economic, political—of parish and country. The priest, like the political arithmetician, determined policy by gathering data and interpreting situation. Returning yet again to his Baconian roots, Petty turned the parish into a sort of Nosocomium and the priest into its director.

This role, for good or ill, was not in principle limited to 'the Anglicane Church'.[131] It characterized any church worthy of the name, even, perhaps, the Church of Rome. *Political Anatomy* had suggested replacing Irish Catholic priests with English Catholic ones, as part of his project of reconciling English and Irish interests. Petty also proposed, in 1675, that the Church of Ireland pay for translating the Bible into the Irish language and 'character' and 'salariate fitt persons to preach & catechise Weekely in all parts, Or to all people in Ireland, in an intelligible language'—probably less to promote Protestantism than to instill some religion in those who lacked any (he described the Irish situation as a 'Scandall of Religion &

---

[130] BL MS Add. 72887, f.30.
[131] 'A Dutifull and moderate answer, to the Papers concerning Religion, the Catholiq Church, the Churches of Rome & England &c, left by the late King Charles the 2d' (1686), BL MS Add. 72887, ff.78–91, f.88.

Civility').[132] In his 'Proposals about the Revenue, Expence, future Estate of Ireland', Petty suggested 'That the Number of [Catholic] Priests conived at, bee no more than are necessary, & that such priests do procure the abroga[tion] of 12 holly dayes in the year, Unnecessary Churchmen, & hollydayes, being a great damage to an underpeopl[e]d country.'[133] He did not, however, propose eliminating the priesthood, and it seems to have been the deleterious economic effects of large numbers of holy days that most offended him. In 'An Appendix concerning Papists & Protestants' (c.1685), he suggested that papal authority was a threat not only to English government but, more immediately, to health and property.[134] He made the same point in a manuscript of thirty folios entitled 'The naturall & pecul[i]ar & present Interest of Ireland',[135] dated 1683:

> [T]o allow the Pope a Power of forbiding of meats, is to give him power over the Lives and Healths of all the People; and to allow him to forbid Labour as many dayes as hee pleases, is to impower him to empoverish the People to what Degree hee pleases; and to allow him the Supreame Power in Matrimoniall Cawses, is to enable him to dispose of the Inheritance of Lands, and the Succession to Kingdomes.[136]

From this perspective the question was one of social utility and political authority, not religious belief. Papal control of diet, calendar, and marriage—factors in the health and productivity as well as the loyalty of the Irish population—was unacceptable.

Yet there were more fundamental political as well as epistemological problems with Catholicism—with the apportionment of spiritual and temporal power, that is, and with the demands of Catholic belief. Petty discussed these in 'The naturall & pecul[i]ar & present Interest of Ireland', mentioned above. 'Papists,' he wrote, 'differ from other Religionarys in two principall Points, which … affect their Temporall Interest, That is to say in the Popes supremacy, and Transubstantiation.' Papal supremacy caused obvious problems for Catholics both as potential office-holders and as subjects:

> [F]or with what reason can men bee admitted to Elect or bee elected to the Legislative Power, who profess that the Supreme or Legislative Power in Ireland, (as to matters of Chief concernment) is in the Pope, a forraigne Prince? Or why should the Subjects of the Pope, bee allowed any Jurisdiction over the King of Irelands Subjects? And may not great severitys bee used to

---

[132] 'A Proposal for Ireland' (1675), BL MS Add. 72879, ff.98–103, ff.99–100.
[133] BL MS Add. 72879, f.90.   [134] BL MS Add, 72888 ff.18–20, f.20.
[135] BL MS Add, 72880, ff.121–151.   [136] BL MS Add. 72880, f.147.

hold the hands of the Papists of Ireland, when It is but suspected they will lett in and assist Papists from abroad to prejudice their own Country?

'As for Transubstantiation,' Petty went on,

It makes men become as Senslesse; brings them to deny the Judgement of their Senses, to admit of impossibilitys and contradictions, as that a Priest cannot onely change Bread into Flesh, but Bread (which is a Body) into the Incorporiall Substance of a Mans Soule, and into the transcendentall Substance of God himself[.][137]

This was both philosophically and socially crippling: 'I say it is unsafe to deal or converse with such men, who cannot trust their owne senses.'[138] Men who could 'admit of impossibilities and contradictions' could hardly function as witnesses or jurors, much less as judges. Again, however, the content of faith was peripheral to its social and political implications.

Determined to make toleration safe nonetheless, Petty persistently sought ways around these problems. 'It is the Interest of Peacable Papists to quit this Supremacy and Transubstantiation', he acknowledged. 'But perhaps it is the Interest of governing Protestants, to lett them continue in the same,' if only 'That they may never want a fair pretence to punish and empoverish them.'[139] In any event Catholics were no worse than Protestant 'Fanaticks ... who are governed by their owne private Spirit' and 'Who dislike Episcopall Government'. He was 'inclind to believe that If the said Popish and Fanatick Dissenters would give security not to disturb the Publiq Peace; Nor actively violate the Lawes of the Land, That a convenient Liberty might bee allowed to both the said Dissenters, excepting the said two grand Points' of supremacy and transubstantiation.[140] These were indeed grand points, but Petty's various proposals for loyalty oaths, church comprehension, and toleration of Catholics as well as Dissenters suggest that they did not seem insurmountable to him. A 1685 'Essay concerning the Tolleration of heterodox p[er]sons' asked 'Whether The Soveraigne of a Country may or ought to give License to all or any of his Subjects to speake professe & practise What they please (differing from ye Lawes) about the Worship of God & beliefe in Divine matters'. The answer was 'No', but Petty did suggest that the articles of every faith should be codified in law. Dissenters might then take oaths affirming their belief in a given set of articles as well as their allegiance to the laws and the government. Once registered they could pay a tax and be tolerated, subject

---

137 BL MS Add. 72880, f.146.   138 BL MS Add. 72880, f.147.
139 BL MS Add. 72880, f.147.   140 BL MS Add. 72880, f.148.

only to a weekly 'State sermon'.[141] There were limits to liberty: 'As for Sceptisismes concerning the Person and Family of the King, and Forme of Government, I take them to bee not Matters of Religion, but such as must bee regulated by the Laws of the Land.'[142] Yet if the dissenting population were methodized and regulated, these limits could be extended.

From toleration to 'Catholication'

Distinct as politics and religion may have been in Petty's mind, they were practically inseparable in the political culture of the three Stuart kingdoms. The disintegration of the Cabal ministry that was taking place as Petty completed *Political Arithmetick* and *Political Anatomy* was bound up with the failure of Charles II's pro-French strategy (enshrined in the Treaty of Dover, one of whose secret articles stipulated that Charles would declare himself a Catholic at the earliest convenience), which had implicated the King in an unsuccessful and unpopular war with the Dutch and a disastrous Declaration of Indulgence. As Petty's two large manuscripts circulated in London and Dublin through early and mid-1673, the Test Act purged the English administration of both Dissenters (including Benjamin Worsley, who left his position on the Council for Trade and Plantations, to be replaced by John Locke) and Catholics (including the Duke of York). The defining event of Charles II's reign, however, came in 1678, with the revelation of the Popish Plot—a purported scheme to assassinate Charles and put his brother on the throne—and with the Exclusion Crisis over the succession that ensued.

Petty's opinion of the Plot and of the anti-Catholic hysteria that surrounded it left few traces. A letter to Southwell written from Dublin in February of 1679 glibly reported: 'Here is some news—not so much of Plotts as of Counter-plotts, and of papists prodding protestants into Plotts'.[143] Over a month later Petty alluded to some trouble the Plot had apparently caused Southwell (his patron Ormond's moderate handling of the crisis in Ireland had drawn fire from English Whigs and some Irish Protestants).[144] He noted that 'the parliaments zeale to defend Ireland against the Pope and King of France is very gratefull to many'.[145]

---

[141] BL MS Add. 72889, ff.7–8.   [142] BL MS Add. 72880, f.148.
[143] Petty to Southwell, [February, 1679], *PSC*, 67.
[144] Several letters from Ormond to Southwell allude to this: see, e.g., Ormond to Southwell, 1 March 1678/9, BL MS Add. 21484, ff.44–45.
[145] Petty to Southwell, 8 April 1679, *PSC*, 73.

Some of his papers drew renewed attention to the military significance of demographic, economic, and geographical data.[146] He believed in the Plot—indeed, he even thought he might have spotted one of the men named as a suspect in the murder of Sir Edmund Bury Godfrey, the judge who had first heard Titus Oates's fabricated evidence—but his reaction was hardly overheated.[147] He was as worried about the Protestant reaction as the threat of a Catholic coup.

His reaction to Whig attempts to exclude the Duke of York from the line of succession was correspondingly cold. Though direct evidence is limited, Wood's letters to Petty leave little doubt. Writing in March 1681—a pivotal moment, just before the Oxford Parliament (whose prorogation marked the beginning of the Tory reaction), Wood disparaged Whig radicalism:

> The Court should go towards Windsor in the way to Oxford the 10th instant … but there is some whisper of a Prorogation, Elections running mostly in the old Channels [i.e. in favour of the Whigs]. There is an 8° lately come forth calld Plato redivivus writ dialogue wise, as tis said by H. Nevill, upon the Oceana Principle of Dominion founded on Property, much read by the discontented Partie. He concludes not for a Democracie (I suppose because he thinks the matter not (yet) capable of such a Forme) But that a Parl[iament] be chosen annually … That Elections be regulated. That the Parl[iament] choose 4 Committees to manage and governe these 4 things viz 1st Forreign Alliances, Peace & warr. 2. The Militia at Home. 3. The Tresury & Revenue. 4. The Principall Officers of State as Judges &c … That this is the only way to preserve the Monarchy & King: I much doubt his Majestie will not be of that opinion.[148]

In September he recommended to Petty perhaps the best-known piece of Tory literature to come out of the crisis, 'a marvelous smooth Poem called Absalom & Achitophell', as 'exceeding ingenious', even sending a 'Key' to the allegorical personae in Dryden's poem: 'Abs[alom] Munmouth', 'Achit[ophel] Shaftsb[ury]', and so on.[149] Petty's pursuit of toleration put him at odds with both 'High Church' Tories and Whig critics of popery and arbitrary government. But his politics were first and foremost monarchist, and therefore anti-Whig (a 1682 paper even defined 'a Whig' as

---

[146] 'The Uses of the Booke mention'd by W.P.' (1679), *PP*, 1:172–175.

[147] Ormond to Southwell, 13 March 1679, Bodl. MS Carte 118, ff.184–185.

[148] Wood to Petty, 1 March 1680/1, in BL MS Add. 72850, f.271–272; Henry Neville, *Plato Redivivus, or, A Dialogue concerning Government* (London: Printed for S. I., 1681).

[149] Wood to Petty, 22 September 1681, in BL MS Add. 72850, 292–293; John Dryden, *Absalom and Achitophel* (London: Printed for J. T., 1681).

'one who hates the King's person and family and the forme of monarchicall Government and even the present established Government').[150] In these respects, they were close to those of James II himself.

James's reign saw Petty produce more papers than ever before; even allowing for accidents of survival, the contrast with the years immediately previous is striking. This new production reflected a new tension between two of Petty's, and political arithmetic's, central aims: the preservation of the Irish settlement and the promotion of state power and national wealth through natural policy. These goals had evolved together. Transmutation was both the solution to Irish disaffection and the extreme form of the demographic manipulation Petty elsewhere proposed to promote industry in England and population growth in the American colonies. Yet in the peculiar circumstances of James's reign they began to diverge, as the king courted Irish Catholic support—appointing Richard Talbot, Earl of Tyrconnell and the leader of the anti-settlement lobby, Lord Deputy of Ireland—and endured the growing opprobrium of Protestants in all Three Kingdoms for (among other things) his pursuit of toleration. Caught between defending a settlement his king seemed bent on undoing and defending the king himself, Petty chose the king. The result was a final twist in political arithmetic designed to save a failing monarchy, based on a view of the body politic that foreign invasion and internal war would soon make irrelevant.

Petty's first concern when James came to the throne, other than his own advancement, was how a new religious policy would affect political stability. In a paper probably written late in 1685 and suggestively entitled 'The Dangers & Evills of disloyalty demonstrated', Petty sketchily assessed possible projects for the new reign, including religious innovations ('Scotland Mild towards popery & Ireland more able for it'), and tried to map the dangers facing king and subjects alike.

> There have been 15 formes of government (all Vanished) between 1 Novemb. 1640 & the same day 1685. Q. What a Man worth £10,000 would give, to have the present government demolishd, & One of the other 14 set up in its Roome? ... The King hath 10 Non-papist subjects for One papist. Q. what is the hazard of setting up popery, without liberty to others, or taking away Abby Lands &c? ... Since Conscience cannot bee forced, what is the danger of [?] worshipping of God, in a way set up by the Law of the Land or Vox populi & like what has been practisd over all Europe for about 1300 yeares.

[150] 'A Colloqui between A: B: C: concerning a New Instrument of Government' (1682), *PP*, 1:103. 'The New Instrument of Government' itself is in BL MS Add. 72880, ff.60–71.

Rather then following every Man his owne Judgement upon the Sence of the Scriptures? … How have the people fared, where the Soveraigne hath been of One Religion & the bulk of the people of another or of many others[?][151]

Another paper described these '15 formes of government between 1 November 1640 & the same day 1685', the first being the government of Charles I, the fourteenth the short-lived 'Attempt to make Monmouth Monark' after Charles II's death, and the last 'King James the 2 Crowned, with 2 houses of parliament Very conformable, an additionall Revenue, London quelled[,] an army of 18000 Men, a great Navy, Argile & Monmouth vanquished the 3 last mentioned projects Nulled & punished and the way of the 11th forme [i.e. government according to the Test Act of 1673] Established.'[152] Stability across the Three Kingdoms depended not only on James's firm grasp of the reins but also on his judiciousness in forming and executing policy. As Petty's constant reference to the relative proportions of different confessional groups suggested, political arithmetic—'a new instrument of government'—was meant to assure both.

Meanwhile, the Irish settlement came under fresh attack. In 1685 the pseudonymous *Twelve Quaeries relating to the Interest of Ireland*—building on an earlier critique, Nicholas French's 1668 *Narrative of the Settlement and Sale of Ireland*—argued that the Irish had been driven to rebellion by religious persecution, and had remained consistently loyal to the King against Parliament; the Cromwellian and Restoration settlements victimized loyal Catholics and rewarded rebellious Protestants.[153] Petty's 'Answer to certain Queries made by the Irish about July 1685 signed G.F.D.' flatly rejected the insinuation 'that the Plantiffs [against the settlement] are Cavaliers, vizt such as fought in Ireland for the King upon the same questions and Quarrell as the Cavaliers did in England' and the corollary 'that the Defendents are the Creatures of Oliver Cromwell and murderers of K. Charles the first, who fought in Ireland, onely to make Cromwell chiefe in both Kingdomes.'[154] On the contrary:

> the Suite is between the Persons who suffered in the Irish Insurrection, with their kindred, friends & Neighbors … and those who begun the Murders, Massacres, robbing, plundering and exiling the aforementioned sufferers[,] who changed the Government from Monarchy into a Supreme Councill and

---

[151] BL MS Add. 72881, f.77.   [152] BL MS Add. 72866, ff.3–4, f.3.
[153] G.F.D., *Twelve Quaeries relating to the Interest of Ireland* ([s.n.], 1685); Nicholas French, *A Narrative of the Settlement and Sale of Ireland* (Louvain: [s.n.], 1668). French was titular Bishop of Ferns.
[154] BL MS Add. 72883, ff.51–60, f.52.

generall assembly, who endeavoured to alienate the Empire of Ireland from
the Crowne of England, to severall forraine Potentates, Or to the Romish
Clergy on the other part. Which latter sort may bee Stiled Oneilians
[i.e. followers of O'Neill], Renucinians [i.e. followers of Rinuccini, papal
nuncio to the Catholic confederacy], & Clerocratians, not Cavaliers and
Innocents; Whereas the former party are to bee stiled English Patriots,
who endeavoured to avenge the murders and desolations abovementioned,
to preserve the Government and Religion established, and did by the best
ways they could ... deliver all up to the King (as they really did) and takeing
what hee should please to allow them for their Service and Sufferings in the
premisses. So as wee humbly affirme the War generally speaking to have
been between Irish Rebells & English Patriots.[155]

English and Irish struggles in the 1640s had been fundamentally different,
though some of the protagonists had been the same. The Civil War
was an internal political conflict, whereas the Irish Rebellion, as *Political
Arithmetick* put it, was 'national' and 'religious', justly punished regardless
of events elsewhere. The Irish Protestant interest was the foundation of
English authority in Ireland, and the settlement was the foundation of this
interest. A more detailed 'Answer of the substance of a Treatis Intituled
The Sale & Settlement of Ireland' made much the same case.[156] As long
as Ireland and England, religion and politics could be held apart in this
way, neither Petty's nor anyone else's royalism or tolerationism need call
the settlement into question.

   In practice, however, these distinctions quickly collapsed. Through 1685
and into 1686 Petty generated numerous papers explaining the rationale
for toleration to Dissenters and mainstream Protestants, but as James's
Catholicizing program became clearer they steadily abandoned him. For
his part, James fell back for support on a smaller and smaller coterie of
Catholic advisers, the Earl of Tyrconnell foremost among them. Petty
did his best to court this new audience—while he used the memory of
1641 to attack the author of the *Quaeries*, he met what he took to be
Tyrconnell's plans with counterproposals purporting to serve Catholic
interests without undoing the settlement or precluding union. But here,
too, events told against him. In mid-July 1686 Petty noted the presence
of hundreds of Jesuits in England and Ireland and the issue of 160
commissions for Catholic officers in the Irish Army, which Tyrconnell was

---

[155] BL MS Add. 72883, ff.52–53.
[156] BL MS Add. 72883, ff.75–94; See 'Another more true and calm Narrative of the
Settlement & Sale of Ireland', *PP*, 1:49–55; 'Some Articles (not of faith) but of Sense, concerning
the Rebellion in Ireland' (c.1685–1686), BL MS Add. 72884, ff.71–74.

purging of Protestants; to allay Protestant fears he desperately suggested an exchange not of women but of English and Irish troops—turning each population into collateral for its army's good behaviour towards the other.[157] Recognizing that the land settlement might be doomed whatever he did or said, Petty clung to the task of preserving English power in Ireland and Stuart authority in Britain.

One sign of his new thinking was a series of papers setting Catholicism in a new light, no longer as 'false and inconvenient' but rather as an inescapable reality and, moreover, a reality with potential benefits. He began to distinguish between more and less dangerous brands of Catholicism, writing in one paper (rather ungraciously, given his education) 'That the Jesuites are but as Mountebanks in ye Catholiq Religion.'[158] Many more papers emphasized the basic elements of Christianity and tried to reduce Catholic and Protestant doctrinal differences to accidents of ritual rather than essentials of faith. Petty even weighed the political advantages 'of a Living infallible Judge in Spirituall matters', something he managed to connect to his own thinking on the inaccessibility of such matters to reason.[159] A paper entitled 'Moderate Thoughts concerning Popery' noted that the idea 'That temporall paines are due for sin, Which are satisfied by Indulgence, penance or purgatory is a better doctrine to keep men from Sin, than that Christ takes all away without any paines.'[160] Yet however valuable they are as evidence of Petty's thinking, these arguments were politically worthless. No amount of arguing would unify the contending parties.

If unity was not to be had, however, stability might yet be secured. Petty retained considerable status as an expert on Ireland—which the publication in 1685 of his Irish atlas, based on the Down Survey, reinforced—and in May 1686 he was able to meet with Tyrconnell himself, both to discuss his ideas and to submit several papers 'in order to an accomodation.'[161] The first of these sketched 'The State of Ireland for 500 Yeares', by way of showing the historically contingent emergence—and hence the potential removal—of Irish political divisions.[162] The second surveyed Ireland's profitable land and the 'Partys & Classis' that owned it in

[157] 'Catholiq News', 19 July 1686, BL MS Add. 72888, f.64; 'Some materiall Points in the State of Ireland the 16th July 1686', BL MS Add. 72882, ff.43–46. On exchanging troops between all three kingdoms, see also BL MS Add. 72888, ff.65–66.
[158] BL MS Add. 72888, ff.48–49.   [159] BL MS Add. 72888 ff.54–63.
[160] BL MS Add. 72888, ff.46–47.
[161] Petty, Hiberniae Delineatio; Petty, Geographicall Description; BL MS Add. 72885, ff.3–6.
[162] BL MS Add. 72885, ff.7–8.

1641 and in 1686.[163] By themselves these were unremarkable, but the next two marked a real departure: Petty proposed raising £300,000 for the relief of distressed Irish Catholics—victims, that is, of the land settlement—and even included 'Lists of Nocents … Nominees & others who may bee thought fitt to have a share in the said Grand Summe'.[164] There followed 'A List of Matters to be Prepared' classifying different kinds of landowners, and further papers, not identifiable in the present archive, fleshed out a significant revision of the settlement—including a retrenchment of Protestant claims by thirds, as in the 1660s.[165] New taxes would either pay off dispossessed Catholics or buy the Protestants out on their behalf.[166]

This was a startling reversal. Up to this point, Petty had stoutly refused to consider the exactions of the settlement anything but the just deserts of rebellion. But by mid-1686 the rights and wrongs of the settlement were moot; abandoning it was more and more obviously the price of preserving the Three Kingdoms. Petty set forth his fears in 'A Dialogue of Ireland':

A. What News of Ireland?

B. They say It shall bee governd by the Kings Lieut[enant] and 12 Irish Catholiques, according to the Articles made in 1648, as to forces, Revenue, Religion, repealing old and making new Lawes &c., pardoning all done amisse Anno 1641.

A. By that Method, all that was done & intended Anno 1641, will bee justifyed and allowed.

B. And Ireland will bee thereby made an Asylum and Security for all his Majestys Catholiq friends in the world, in Case his Majesty in his life time should faile to protect them, or in Case his successor should bee hard upon them.

A. Why then all Protestants ought to bee disarmd there, and a full Army of Irish Catholiq's putt into pay. The Church Livings transferred to Catholiques; The Judges, Sherrifs & Justices of Peace & officers of the Revenue to bee all Catholiques, and most of the English stript of their

---

[163] This seems to be BL MS Add. 72885, ff.9–12.   [164] BL MS. Add. 72885, ff.3–4, 13–14.

[165] BL MS Add. 72885, ff.15–16. See also 'Vade mecum May 1686', BL MS Add. 72885, f.1.

[166] See for instance 'Considerations Leading to pitch upon a Sum of Mony for remedy of Evills & Wrongs arising from & consequent to the Act of Settlement and Explanation' (BL MS Add. 72882, ff.25–30); 'An Undertaking how to pay 600,000 pounds in Remedy of Wrongs to provide for the Catholiq Clergy forthwith, and for the Catholiq & Protestant Clergy after the present Protestant Incumbents' (BL MS Add. 72882, ff.31–32); 'A Proposal how the English may Buy Out the Interest of the Irish Papists in Ireland and Advance the Roman Catholique Interest in England' (PP, 1:64).

Lands and scarse any tolleration given to the exercise of any Religion, but Catholiques.[167]

Making Ireland a Catholic 'asylum' would destroy the demographic mixture on which the peace, strength, and coherence of James's dominions ultimately depended. Among Petty's '17 arguments against the Lord Tirconells design' were that it would 'Drive away the English', provoke 'fear of the French', remove any 'meenes of Union', and introduce the 'Danger of Democracy' by incurring another rebellion—this time of Protestants.[168] These were not remote possibilities. As Petty warned in 'A Memento to the Lord Tirconell', reckless policies in Ireland risked not only 'The Extirpation or Slavery of the Irish Nation language & Religion & that Irrecons[il]ably' but also the fall of James II. 'The Princesse of Orange, & Princesse Anne & Prince of Orange are not willing That Ireland should bee retrencht from England, Nor that the Pope should have [a] share in the English Empire. Whoever attempts these things may bring a War upon the King from Holland'.[169] Petty did not live to see it, but this is just what happened.

His last-ditch attempt to prevent it transformed political arithmetic from a way of 'transmuting the Irish into English' into an instrument for what Petty called the 'Catholication of the 3 Kingdomes'.[170] Reversing the polarity of his original transplantation schemes, Catholication would shore up James's authority in England by increasing the relative demographic preponderance of his coreligionists there. At the same time, it would also reduce the risk of rebellion in Ireland by correspondingly reducing Catholic dominance there. Exactly how great the demographic shift would be varied from paper to paper, much as Petty's estimates of the time and numbers transmutation required had done. He reckoned that 'Catholiques to Nonpapists in Engl[an]d are as 1 to 280' and 'In great Brittane ... as One to 300' (while 'In Ireland the Catholiques are as 6 to One'); different tracts proposed increasing the Catholic population of Britain to an eighteenth, a twelfth, or even an eighth of the total.[171] If political arithmetic had begun as a way of making Ireland British, it was now a way of tailoring both the qualities of the population and the proportions between its component

---

[167] BL MS Add. 72882, ff.41–42 v.   [168] BL MS Add. 72882, f.67.
[169] BL MS Add. 72885, f.2.
[170] 'Of Catholication of the 3 Kingdomes of Engl[an]d Scotland & Ireland' (1686), BL MS Add. 72888, ff.37–38 v.
[171] BL MS Add. 72888, f.37r-v; '7 Distinct Proposals concerning Ireland and Religion' (1686), BL MS Add. 72882, ff.51–52.

parts to the needs of the monarchy, needs that changed from kingdom to kingdom and from reign to reign.

The shift from transmutation to Catholication is also crucial to understanding one of Petty's last, and most notorious, Irish schemes. This was his proposal to remove most of Ireland's population into England, leaving Ireland as a massive, thinly staffed cattle-farm. First mooted in manuscripts of 1686, the 'cattle farm' scheme was the centrepiece of Petty's last major manuscript, the 1687 'Treatise of Ireland'.[172] From one perspective, this can be seen as the ultimate expression of mercantilist imperialism, disposing of a whole population and reducing an entire country to institutional and economic dependence with a few strokes of the pen.[173] Yet Petty's earlier proposals show that he could deal similarly with his own countrymen (and especially women) when circumstances warranted; further, the scheme would undo the Cattle Acts—the most important mercantilist legislation then affecting Ireland. Neither an ethnic cleansing programme nor a plantation scheme, the 'ranchification' of Ireland was in fact a corollary of the 'Catholication' of Britain. Emphasizing its effect on political divisions in both England and Ireland, and thus the security of both from rebellion and invasion, the very papers that propose the scheme make this clear.[174]

By far the clearest and most detailed is the 'Treatise'. Roughly the same length as *Political Anatomy* or *Political Arithmetick*, it focused exclusively on securing the 'perpetual Settlement of Ireland' and the 'Natural Improvement and Union of England and Ireland, by Transplanting a Million of People (without Distinction of Parties) out of Ireland into England: Leaving in Ireland only enough Hands to manage as many Cattle as that Countrey will feed.'[175] Petty devoted nine chapters and a lengthy appendix (including a dialogue and a series of tables) to establishing the project's feasibility—using 'Number Weight and Measure'

---

[172] The final version of the 'Treatise' is in BL MS Add. 21128, ff.52–142; drafts and related materials are in BL MS Add 72886, ff.1–215. The 'Treatise' is printed in *EW*, 2:545–621.

[173] David Armitage, 'The Political Economy of Britain and Ireland after the Glorious Revolution', in Ohlmeyer, *Political Thought*, 228–230; Hugh Goodacre, 'William Petty and the Early Colonial Roots of Development Economics', in Kwane Sundaram Jomo (ed.), *The Pioneers of Development Economics* (London: Zed Books, 2005), 10–30.

[174] See for example 'A Probleme', *PP*, 1:64–67; 'Questions and assertions ariseing from & depending upon the Maine question of Transporting a Million of people out of Ireland into England' (*c*.1686), BL MS Add. 72882, ff.59–62 v; 'The State & Settlement of Ireland considered the 16th day of July 1686', BL MS Add. 72882 ff.43–46 v; 'Advantages in particular to Ireland by the Transplantation and other practises within mentioned And in generall to the King, all his Kingdoms and subjects' (c.1686), BL MS Add. 72882 ff.65–66 v.

[175] *EW*, 2:551.

to make 'puzling and perplexd Matters ... demonstrable'—and explaining its goals.[176] The first chapter outlined what these were: to multiply England's Catholic population thirty-six times (making it one eighth of the total), to increase trade and revenues by means of this influx, and 'To cut up the Roots of those Evils in Ireland, which the Differences of Births, Extractions, Manners, Languages, Customs, and Religions, have continually wasted the Blood and Treasure of both Nations for above 500 Years'.[177]

The third chapter fleshed these purposes out in a remarkable way. Discussing the exact numbers involved, Petty argued that the transplantation he proposed would reduce Protestant dominance in England from 283:1 to 8:1; at the same time, because the transplantation out of Ireland would be undertaken 'without distinction of parties'—that is, Protestants as well as Catholics would be removed—the ratio there would remain 8:1 in favour of Catholics. The point, in other words, was not to reduce the Catholic proportion of the Irish population, or even simply to increase English population at Ireland's expense, but to make England's confessional demography the mirror image of Ireland's. As in the earlier exchange of troops, so here the minority group in each country would function as collateral for the safety of its opposite number—English Catholics standing surety for Irish Protestants, and vice versa. Petty cited 'the Conquerors of ancient Times and even now in the Oriental Countreys,' who 'execute their Conquest, by Carrying away Captives into their own Countreys, and not by Maintaining great Armies, in the Conquer'd Countreys'. In James II's multiple monarchy, however, the hostage-taking would be mutual: 'it will be the Profit, Pleasure, and Security of both Nations and Religions to Agree herein.'[178]

Compared to the careful calibration of passions and manipulation of household economies transmutation required, this removal of whole populations simply to establish abstract ratios may seem ham-handed, perhaps a mere thought-experiment never fully worked out. Yet the uncharacteristic length and organization of the 'Treatise' are evidence of Petty sincerity, and in any case he had already circulated many of the ideas it contained at the highest levels. Nor did he abandon the long-term goal of transmutation—indeed he insisted 'That this Proposal was intended for an Union of the Two Nations, which is a real blessing to both, according to that of *Faciam eos in Gentem Unam*.'[179] Here he quoted from Ezekiel 37:22: 'And I will make them one nation upon the land

---

[176] *EW*, 2:554.   [177] *EW*, 2:557–558.   [178] *EW*, 2:561.   [179] *EW*, 2:577.

in the mountains of Israel; and one king shall be king to them all: and they shall be no more two nations, neither shall they be divided into two kingdoms any more at all.' As his successive projects for transmuting the Irish, populating the American colonies and Catholicating the three kingdoms showed, different circumstances called for different measures to bring about loyalty, industry, and unity. But to the end of his life these goals, political arithmetic's central place in achieving them, and the philosophical outlook that enabled it to do so, remained the same.

The problems posed by Atlantic colonization and especially the shifting politics of religion under James II provoked a surge in Petty's manuscript production; the solutions he proposed effected a gradual transformation of practical political arithmetic from a specific project for Ireland to a general art of government through social engineering. This art deployed a repertoire of strategies—institutional and legislative reform, transplantation and proportionable mixture, marital and national union—derived from past imperial experience and from contemporary natural philosophy. Capturing naturalized social, biological, and chemical processes alike, political arithmetic conferred on the state the power to manage both the quality and quantity of the population, instilling industry and loyalty, maximizing effective numbers while managing—and, with nature's assistance, removing—troublesome divisions. Created for a sovereign whose confessional identity fluctuated and whose subjects were divided by nation, language, and religion, it was an instrument for governing a multiple monarchy and a colonial empire. Petty meant it, and marketed it, as such.

CHAPTER 7

Political Arithmetic in Circulation

Though Petty was, in his own lifetime, political arithmetic's sole practitioner, he did not practice it alone. Not only did the various strands
woven into his work tie it to different intellectual communities—natural
philosophers, economic writers, Irish policymakers, and improvers; its
very purpose was deeply political. It was a program designed to solve real
problems through new policies, and Petty promoted it as such among a
necessarily select but unquestionably important audience. Without people
to act on his recommendations (and only the very powerful *could* act on
them), political arithmetic was just a disorderly pile of papers. Only if the
state embraced his ideas could it become the transformative program of
natural policy he intended, and only by access to the right people would
these ideas be heard. Political arithmetic needed a network.

We have traced the changing shape of political arithmetic from the early
1670s to the end of Petty's life. We turn now to the people it addressed: not
the faceless reading public that would buy Petty's posthumously printed
books, but a carefully cultivated network of friends, contacts, and potential
patrons—men who could be trusted to handle his often alarming notions
with discretion and to pass his papers onward and upward to the privy
councillors, lords lieutenant, and even monarchs whose backing he sought.
This network changed over time. Relationships warmed and cooled,
political tides ebbed and flowed. At any given moment, not every link
in the chain is visible from the papers and correspondence that survive.
It has seemed better, therefore, to offer a synchronic reconstruction of
Petty's pattern of 'scribal publication' here, rather than to fragment the
evidence further, distributing it year by year through earlier chapters.
Although partial, such a reconstruction affords the best view we can
hope for of political arithmetic's early 'social' history: the paths of its
dissemination, the circles in which it moved, the way it was supposed to
effect real change—and the reasons why it ultimately failed. It also provides
perhaps the deepest insight we can have into Petty's understanding of his
purposes.

Petty on Petty

> I do not reckon all my right and reasoning to be worth a straw, till I can get
> some powerfull person to consider it. I compose curious peeces in Music and
> play them accurately; but all this while my hearers are as deaf as haddocks,
> nor will their eares (I feare) ever be opened with just applications, till Wee
> run a Spit into them made of some convenient Metall.[1]

Petty had a very high opinion of his own abilities, an opinion widely but
not universally shared. As the years passed, he also developed a strong
and perhaps understandable sense of frustration with the limited attention
and still more limited resources given to him by potential patrons. He
generally attributed his failure either to the unorthodoxy and originality
of his own work, or to the corruption and stupidity of the circles in
which he tried to promote it. Though self-indulgent, both views probably
had something to them. Petty's opinions on religion, in particular, were
undeniably bold at a time when such boldness was a dangerous thing.
To the extent that political arithmetic was bound up with opinions on
toleration, comprehension, and doctrinal matters, then, Petty's concerns
('shew not these things but where you are sure of Candor and Safety',
he wrote to Southwell in 1677) seem justified.[2] This is one reason why so
much of Petty's political-arithmetical production is in the form of brief,
sometimes cryptically sketchy, manuscripts. Politically sensitive material,
whether satirical poems, pamphlets or state papers, often remained out
of print.[3] Nor, in matters to be decided by a few select, high-ranking
people, as in the case of so many of Petty's and others' projects, would
printing have made economic sense. These conditions, combined with
Petty's tendency to see in virtually all his projects implications for the
wealth and security of the state, go far towards explaining his mode of
literary production.

Petty's opinion of his court audience, however, was never very high, and
the mixed reception his work received (remember the Double-Bottom)
confirmed him in it. He was always solicitous, but quickly defensive.
Writing to the Earl of Anglesey about *Political Arithmetick* late in 1672,
Petty noted that 'I never was successfull in any Thing of this Nature', but
stressed that 'I am not wary of pursuing honest Intentions' and hoping

[1] Petty to Southwell, 2 August 1681, *PSC*, 91.
[2] Petty to Southwell, 4 August 1677, *PSC*, 31.
[3] Love, *Culture*; Harris, 'Ireland as a Laboratory', 84–85.

that 'perhaps some may have an Ear to heare' them.[4] A week later he wrote anxiously to John Graunt that 'I never heard you say any thinge of the Politicall Arithme[ti]ck, nor whether the world knows or accepts it &c.'[5] Later, though, entrusting his translation of the one hundred and fourth Psalm to Southwell for publication, Petty declined to print *Political Arithmetick* and remarked with characteristic self-pity, 'You know I have no Luck with my politicks. Slight Court tricks have advanced many men, but the solid study of other men's peace and plenty ruines mee.'[6] Earlier in the same year he had written to John Aubrey in a similar vein:

> As for the Reprinting the booke of Taxes [i.e. the 1662 *Treatise of Taxes and Contributions*] I will not meddle with it, I never had thanks for any publick good I ever did nor doe I own any such booke, As for that of Duplicate proportion [*A Treatise ... Concerning the Use of Duplicate Proportion*, 1674], I take Mr. Lodewicks paynes to put that discourse into the real character to be an honour to Bishop Wilkins and myself, but doubt of its acceptance in the world.[7]

Petty was disdainful but nevertheless keenly aware of his competitors for patronage, and was usually ready to admit that he lacked the necessary social skills for success at court. In this, too, there was some truth.

Such pessimism never detracted from Petty's confidence in his work, however, and it is worth noting that all of the above pronouncements, some of the darkest he made, date from the 1670s, while he was first working on political arithmetic but well before the burst of pamphlets he produced in the last days of Charles II and under James II. Even then, amid a flurry of criticism of his 1674 *Discourse*, he was bold enough to write:

> As for Mens Cencuring mee, for not understanding mee, Tis a Signe of Enmity or Envy, for If I were a popular and belovd person, People would applause [sic] my writings the more, for their little understanding them. So the Report of the Council of Trade, so much Exploded & thought criminall by some, is now in every great mans Archives.[8]

Petty's disdain for 'slight court tricks' was lasting, but his anxiety about the court fluctuated. He had some basis for confidence, having gone from serving Henry Cromwell to enjoying audiences with Charles II and

[4] Petty to Anglesey, 17 December 1672, BL MS Add. 72858, f.73.
[5] Petty to Graunt, 24 December 1672, BL MS Add. 72858, f.78.
[6] Petty to Southwell, 5 October 1678, *PSC*, 61.
[7] Petty to Aubrey, 29 May 1678, BL MS Egerton 2231, f.90.
[8] Petty to Wood, 10 April 1675, BL MS Add. 72858, f.211.

James II, both of whom expressed interest in his ideas and projects. His Irish career, in particular, had given him a reputation for expertise and numerous connections. Each new political tide, in London or in Dublin, brought new hope.

Beyond the vagaries of Restoration politics, Petty's personal characteristics affected the reception of his work among higher-ups. His overbearing and under-informed performance as a judge of the Irish Admiralty Court from 1676, coupled with his abrupt departure from the post, can hardly have impressed his superiors. It is also worth remembering that his actual dealings with officials in Ireland and England were dominated most of the time not by political arithmetic but by the web of litigation in which his Irish estates involved him, sometimes in direct conflict with men whose patronage he sought. Petty's correspondence, and much correspondence between other parties regarding Petty, is littered with references to what was by all accounts a complicated, tedious, and interminable business.

This was further complicated by the degree to which Petty's legal problems and his political projects were connected, for both revolved around the question of the Irish settlement; even at a distance of centuries it is not always easy to tell one set of interests from the other, distinct though they sometimes were. In this sense, Petty was a victim of his own success. It may have been hard for anyone with his knowledge of or interest in settling Ireland to escape the same trap, but Petty never really tried. In fact, he explicitly connected what we would be tempted to identify as professional with private interests. Sometimes this was with obvious humour, as when he writes to Southwell that, along with his philosophical work on the 'Scale of Creatures', 'I might write a Treatis and call it *The Scale of Devills*, studying whereabout to place the Farmers' of the Irish revenue, his frequent legal antagonists.[9] At other times, however, there is a strong suggestion that Petty's philosophical and financial interests mingled too freely for his own good: 'The world do feare and therefore hate that Things should bee tried by Number, Weight and Measure. I cannot bring the Farmers to any accompt.'[10] It is not surprising that someone with Petty's intellectual abilities should tend to develop theoretical justifications for his private as much as for his public interests. But this propensity to be right in all things at whatever cost did not endear him to many of the more practical people whose favour he sought.

---

[9] Petty to Southwell, 10 November 1677, *PSC*, 38.
[10] Petty to Southwell, 4 October 1681, *PSC*, 97.

Despite this, Petty consistently portrayed himself as an essentially disinterested, if misunderstood and abused, servant of the public good. In late letters to Southwell Petty describes 'my 53 chests of Papers containing the Epitomy of my services and sufferings', and proudly asserts that he was 'never the Toole or Turne-Shovell of any Person or Party.'[11] The pose of the noble martyr was one Petty often found congenial, even in rare moments of apparent modesty ('Surely I am either not Good enough or not Bad enough to live in this World!').[12] He sent some of his poems to Southwell with the disclaimer that they 'are cramd with a sort of dry matter, and describe the truth of things, but they all want the Flame and very spirit of Poetry.' But he went on, warming to a theme that had begun self-critically: 'So also do my other proceedings want the Poetry of Craft, the Lying Flattery, dissimulation, base complacency &c, and therefore are unsuccessfull.'[13] Such professions reflect not only Petty's propensity for self-pity, but also, more importantly, his sense of being both burdened with and uniquely equipped for a mission that was, politically speaking, a hard sell: the settlement of Ireland by means of a transmutative union of English and Irish. 'All I can say is that I meane well to the whole, and not ill to any person in particular. If it bee so taken, I am contented to be a martyr for my Country. Bee it how it will, I have the Vanity to think That no body else can handle this Important Matter in this way.'[14]

Colleagues

A brief turn in the Admiralty Court aside, Petty never held a regular office in government after the Restoration. No great project replaced the Survey, and no great patron stepped into the gap Henry Cromwell left. The Royal Society, as we have seen, was happy to receive Petty's histories and to hear reports of his progress, but was never a source of much material support. It was, in any case, no venue for politically ambitious projects, and although it furnished Petty with some useful social connections, as an institution it remained peripheral to the development, circulation, and reception of political arithmetic. Nevertheless, Petty had a number of important friends, below the level of patrons but possible channels for contact with them. These included Sir Robert Southwell, Samuel Pepys, Sir Peter Pett,

[11] Petty to Southwell, 17 July 1686, *PSC*, 220.
[12] Petty to Southwell, 28 April 1677, *PSC*, 28.
[13] Petty to Southwell, 29 September 1677, *PSC*, 36–37.
[14] Petty to Southwell, 3 May 1679, *PSC*, 77.

Robert Wood, John Aubrey, John Evelyn, and, more distantly, others like
William Penn and Thomas Sheridan, various Fellows of the Royal Society
and former colleagues from Oxford, Gresham College, and Ireland. To
speak of these men as Petty's 'colleagues' is slightly misleading, in that they
did not work together and were not in any exact sense equals. But they did
share certain interests, and they were more nearly equal with each other
than any of them were with the kinds of men Petty sought as patrons.
These were the men to whom Petty sent his manuscripts, among whom
copies of them were exchanged and who in many cases responded with
comments and suggestions before passing them on to their own patrons
for perusal. They form what there is of Petty's coterie, and connect at the
margins with higher, more influential circles.

The most important of these was Sir Robert Southwell, who was Petty's
cousin by marriage after 1667, his most regular correspondent from the
mid-1670s on, and 'at once his most intimate friend and his literary
censor.'[15] Southwell was a clerk of the Privy Council, envoy to Lisbon,
Brussels, and Brandenburg and later, under William III, Secretary of
State. More importantly for Petty, he was a protégé of the Duke of
Ormond, with whom he frequently interceded on Petty's behalf in legal
and political matters alike. But Southwell was much more to Petty than
a door to greater things. From the historian's point of view, he deserves
the credit for the survival of so much of Petty's unprinted (and, but for
Petty's correspondence with him, undated) work; he collected Petty's ideas
and papers assiduously, passing them along but always keeping copies
for himself. He reminded Petty more than once of 'that Ebony Cabinet
wherein I keep, as in an Archive, all the effects of your Pen', and urged
him to spend more time on his writing and less in litigation.[16]

Southwell was also an important interlocutor for Petty, less on economic
than on political, philosophical, and religious questions. The two had a
common interest in Ireland; Southwell's grandfather and great-uncle had
been 'undertakers' in the Munster plantation under James I, and he
exchanged numerous letters with Petty over the course of the 1670s and
1680s alluding nervously to threats to the settlement. Petty sometimes
likened this to a ship,[17] proposing in April 1687 'That if wee had a dry
dock, These few timbers [troublesome parts of the settlement] might bee

[15] *PSC*, xii. See Toby Barnard, 'Southwell, Sir Robert (1635–1702)', in *Oxford DNB*
<http://www.oxforddnb.com/view/article/26066>.

[16] Southwell to Petty, 15 September 1677, *PSC*, 34.

[17] See for instance Petty to Southwell, 22 May 1686, *PSC*, 200–201.

mended without prejudice even to the mold of the present Hull.'[18] Ireland was a mutual interest and a natural topic of comment between two cousins who owned Irish estates, and both seemed to share more or less the same view of things, which they only occasionally articulated—as, for instance, when commenting on the appearance of anti-settlement pamphlets. Rarely do these exchanges throw very much light on political arithmetic, though the evident flow of papers from Petty to Southwell at least highlights the latter's place in its circulation. It was in a letter to Southwell that Petty first used the phrase, and it is to Southwell that Petty's very last thoughts on the subject seem to have been communicated.

More substantial are Petty's and Southwell's discussions of religion and population, which often accompanied or followed on political-arithmetical papers by Petty touching one or both subjects. As in Petty's correspondence with Robert Wood following the 1674 *Discourse*, questions raised by regular readers like Southwell often led Petty to work on new problems, to clarify some of his claims, and to assess the nature of his commitment to them, though rarely to reconsider positions he had taken up in earnest. Petty and Southwell traded thoughts on Matthew Hale's and Edmund Halley's pronouncements on the origins of mankind and the history of population since the Flood, and Southwell was occasionally able to supply Petty with unfamiliar but useful material.[19] This sort of collaboration is most evident during Petty's work on the 'Scale of Creatures', in the later 1670s:

> As for the *Scale of Creatures*, I thank you for the paragraph you have sent me out of Dr. [William] Bates. You know I am no good book man, and therefore do not know what authors have written of this subject ... I desire you to enquire further what hath been written already; But whatever it bee, you shall shortly see mine, which will be an originall, although you should find the like hath been done a thousand times already.[20]

Few passages so neatly sum up their literary relationship, but it seems to have continued and even deepened over the remaining years of Petty's life—and despite, or perhaps because of, the occasional disagreement. In 1685 a long exchange about the desirability or otherwise of an increase in population brought out several long letters from Petty on 'full peopling' that emphasized not only its economic benefits but also its place in the

---

[18] Petty to Southwell, 7 April 1687, *PSC*, 267.
[19] Southwell to Petty, 2 January 1676/7, and Petty to Southwell [December 1677], *PSC*, 12, 44–48.
[20] Petty to Southwell, 3 April 1677, *PSC*, 23.

progress of the history of the world.[21] A running commentary, often very amusing, on the education of the young Pettys and Southwells fed into a critique by Petty of a paper by Pascal that Southwell sent him, which in turn led Petty to make some of his clearest statements on education.[22] Southwell's interest in Petty's thoughts on religion led the latter to come up with a brief catechism and plan of Bible study—Southwell used it to teach his children, Petty as the basis for a comprehensive scheme of national worship.[23] It is difficult to overstate the importance of Southwell's friendship and correspondence on the development of Petty's thought in the 1670s and 1680s—he was by turns Petty's research assistant, editor, literary agent, publisher and audience, and, all the while, his closest friend.

Southwell's position was unique, but a number of other friends and acquaintances served as important readers and contacts for Petty and for early political arithmetic. John Graunt, as we have seen, helped Petty gain his position at Gresham College in the 1650s.[24] By the early 1670s, however, Gresham College had 'almost sunk'[25] and Graunt, too, had fallen on hard times, suffering apparently irrecoverable losses in the Great Fire in 1666.[26] Petty was constitutionally indisposed to sympathy, and we have seen that Graunt's conversion to Catholicism aggravated him. When Robert Wood asked after Graunt, Petty replied coldly: 'Captain Graunt is now an open and zealous champion for popery. Wherefore I have not so much Intimacy with him as formerly.'[27] As suggested earlier, his objection seems to have been more on pragmatic than principled grounds, Catholicism being 'both false and inconvenient.'[28] Petty sanctimoniously scolded Graunt: 'As for

[21] *PSC*, 143–147, 150–155, 160–168, 171, 173–176.

[22] *PSC*, 148–149, 152, 157–159, 169–170, 173, 180–182, 187–198.

[23] See for example *PSC*, 172–174. Petty wrote the catechism in Latin and English; the English portion is printed in *PP*, 1:128–130. The original, 'The Christian Religion of little Children' (1685), is in BL MS Add. 72887, f.13. For Petty's scheme of Bible reading see Petty to Southwell, 29 August 1685 (*PSC*, 142):

> I think there needs be no formal Essay about what I hinted for reading the Scriptures, for (1st) We hold all equally canonized. (2) Tis Manifest that St. Luke and the Acts are the best History of Christ and the Apostles. (3) The Epistles of Peter, James, John and Jude, are stile[d] Catholiq or Generall Epistles, directed to the whole world, and not to Particular Churches upon speciall occasions. (4) They do manifestly contain the whole Christian Doctrine. I only add that the 2 Bookes of the Chronicles is the like Epitome of the History of the Jewish nation and Church.

[24] *EW*, 1:xxxiv–xxxviii.

[25] Petty to Henry Ford, 13 October 1674, BL MS Add. 72858, f.173.   [26] *EW*, 1:xxxvii.

[27] Petty to Robert Wood, 2 August 1673, BL MS Add. 72858, f.107.

[28] Petty to Holland, 23 August 1673, BL MS Add. 72858, f.111.

difference in Religion you have done amise in sundry particulars, which I need not mention, because yourself may easally conjecture my meanings.'[29]

Yet when Graunt died in 1674, it was reported that 'Sir William Petty was conspicuous for his grief.'[30] He had been an immensely important figure in Petty's early career, and although Petty was unsentimental, he was not devoid of feeling.[31] Graunt had certainly also played some part in the early circulation of *Political Arithmetick*, probably as a London distributor for Petty, who was then in Dublin—in much the same way that John Petty had acted in Dublin for Petty, then in London, twelve years earlier.[32] A letter from Petty to Graunt sent December 1672 asked anxiously about *Political Arithmetick's* reception.[33] There is also a letter from Graunt to Petty, undated but probably from the early or mid-1660s, in which Graunt reported conversations he had had about Petty with Sir Robert Moray and the Earl of Anglesey, so that he may have played a role in circulating Petty's name and ideas among people of some influence.[34] However, Graunt himself did not live long enough to do very much more for Petty. His most important contribution to the project was the intellectual stimulus his *Observations* provided.

Robert Wood's connection to Petty went back to their mutual affiliation with the Hartlib Circle, but considerably outlasted it. The two men were nearly the same age, had a number of interests in common, and followed relatively similar paths early in their careers. Wood came to Ireland in 1656 as a retainer of Henry Cromwell, then Petty's patron and protector as well, but soon left to become a fellow at the short-lived Durham College. Like Petty he attended meetings of Harrington's Rota Club, and like Petty he was a Fellow of the Royal Society—though not until 1681. Wood returned to Ireland after the Restoration, initially as Chancellor of the diocese of Meath, later as a revenue commissioner, and finally as Accountant-General of Ireland, the post he held at his death in 1685.[35]

---

[29] Petty to Graunt, 18 January 1672/3, BL MS Add. 72858, f.82.

[30] Thompson Cooper, 'Graunt, John (1620–1674), Statistician', *Oxford DNB* archive <http://www.oxforddnb.com/view/olddnb/11306>.

[31] Southwell, stung by a distastefully cheerful letter of condolence on the death of his wife, remarked, 'Cousin, you doe wipe off Teares at a very strange rate'; Southwell to Petty, 29 May 1686, *PSC*, 201.

[32] John Petty to Petty in BL MS Add. 72858 ff.15, 18, 28, 29, 41, 43, 47.

[33] Petty to Graunt, 24 December 1672, BL MS Add. 72858, f.78.

[34] Graunt to Petty (undated), BL MS Add. 72858, ff.126–127. Arthur Annesley is referred to as the Earl of Anglesey, which puts the letter in 1661 or later; Graunt's position in the Royal Society argues for a date before 1666.

[35] Carlyle, 'Wood, Robert', *Oxford DNB*.

Wood thus shared Petty's interest in Irish government and politics, and by the 1670s he was in a position Petty might have envied.

Wood's surviving correspondence with Petty—especially two dozen or so letters from 1672–75 and 1680–82—provides the most important evidence of Petty's methods of literary production and circulation. Among other things, it included a relatively protracted exchange regarding Petty's 1674 *Discourse*, which Lindsay Sharp has examined, along with the *Discourse* itself, in considerable depth.[36] Outside of Petty's correspondence with Southwell this is one of the only instances in which Petty was forced—or felt the need—to defend himself at length in intellectual terms, and Wood's criticism of some of his friend's philosophical claims was deeper and more persistent than anything in Southwell's letters; where Southwell was an admiring and enthusiastic friend, Wood was a critical though constructive commentator. The content of this particular exchange is not pertinent to political arithmetic per se, but the fact that it occurred is indicative of Wood's place in Petty's circle.

The first evidence of Wood's function as a contact, on the other hand, is provided by several letters from early 1672, around the time Petty was completing a draft of *Political Arithmetick*. These letters initially concern Petty's so-called 'Treatise of Navall Philosophy', which was in reality, like so many of Petty's productions, not a book but a scheme, in this case a sort of prospectus or set of heads for a treatise on naval matters of all sorts, from shipbuilding to what Petty referred to as 'Naval Oeconomy'.[37] Wood wrote on 6 January 1672, thanking Petty for the 'Treatise' as well as for '[an]other Treatise', which is not named. It might possibly be Petty's 1662 *Treatise of Taxes*, though why Wood should need a copy from Petty ten years after its publication is admittedly difficult to see; at any rate it does not appear to have been *Political Arithmetick*.[38] Three weeks later Wood wrote to say he had not yet shown Petty's papers to 'my Lord', apparently meaning the Earl of Essex, then Lord Lieutenant of Ireland, but expected to do so presently.[39]

There is then a letter, puzzlingly dated 5 December 1671 (but Petty was in Ireland in 1671; a date of 1673–75, while Petty was in London,

---

[36] Sharp, 253–335. About twenty letters from Wood to Petty are in BL MS Add. 72850; copies of a few from Petty to Wood are in BL MS Add. 72858.

[37] Southwell's copy of 'A Treatise of Navall Philosophy' is now in BL MS Add. 72854, ff.99–105.

[38] Wood to Petty, 6 January 1671/2, BL MS Add. 72850, ff.172–174.

[39] Wood to Petty, 27 January 1671/2, BL MS Add. 72850, ff.174–175.

would make more sense given the content), that shows Petty's circulation strategy paying off. Though the date is confusing, it seems that the work in question was probably the 'Treatise of Navall Philosophy'. In any case, the letter gives so vivid and amusing a picture of how Petty's connections worked that it is worth quoting at length:

> I come just now from the Castle where I had opportunity of presenting your Duty to my Lord Lieutenant alone in his Closet, who asking how you did, I began to tell him what you were doing viz what you had written, what kind of Arguments you had used, & how you had designed to have concerned his Lordship in shewing the Treatise you had made to the King &c ... That no body had yet seen it, but that I had permission to shew the Heads thereof (which was all I had) to his Lordship if he pleased to see them: He Answered, most gladly, & so I pulld out a copie I had taken of them, supposing he would desire to keepe it, which he read over with much greediness, crying out severall times Excellent things! rare! &c. and then fell to commend you, & asked what you would have him to do, whether to write to the King about it, or to send those Heads, or expect the Booke it selfe, (which he hoped you would let him see) or to send you a letter to give the King with the Booke? any thing he would do to promote that which he though tended so much to the public good. I replyed, I knew nothing more of it then what I had imparted to your Lordship from your letter, nor whether things were yet ripe for publication. He then desired me to remember him unto you, & asked shall we see him in Ireland againe? & when?[40]

Petty ultimately received a judgeship in the Admiralty Court, which ended badly. Nevertheless, the episode shows that manuscripts circulated among Petty's connections could bring him the attention and possibly the patronage of higher-ups. Rather than publication as we think of it, this was Petty's goal.

On this point a brief digression is appropriate, to raise the more general question of the relationship between Petty's literary form and his intentions. It is telling that all the Lord Lieutenant can have seen of Petty's 'Treatise of Navall Philosophy' was a prospectus; this is all that ever existed of the 'Treatise'. Wood had also shown someone referred to as 'honest J.B.' Petty's 'naval scheme, which he tooke thankfully ... But (added he) when shall we see the Treatise of which you gave us the Heads?'[41] This sounds like a fair enough question, but it was in fact rarely asked and hardly

---

[40] Wood to Petty, 5 December 1671[?], BL MS Add. 72850, ff.192–193v.
[41] Wood to Petty, 10 February 1671/2, BL MS Add. 72850, ff.176–177.

ever answered. Frances Harris, Petty's most recent and most thorough archivist, has remarked on this phenomenon perceptively:

> once [Petty] had put down the broad outlines of an idea in manuscript they had the same weight in his mind (and in those of his admirers) as a completed and published work. He claimed for example that a Dutch book on naval matters which was 'infinitely cry'd up at Court' (probably Nicolaas Witsen's *Book of Building Ships* of 1671) did not contain a fraction of what was in his own 'Treatise of Naval Philosophy', although the latter ... existed only in a few pages of synopsis passed around in manuscript amongst his friends, who hoped that one day he might be persuaded to expand it.[42]

This was merely one instance of a larger pattern. Petty produced vast numbers of heads, few of which bear much resemblance to the small number of recognizable books he wrote. His *tractiuncli* vary between skeletal lists and concise summaries, hardly ever longer than five or six pages, and more often half that. It would be slightly perverse to see them as no more than heads—unlike the naval 'Treatise', which did at least purport to be the plan of a larger work, they are often essentially self-contained, and complete as they stand, however terse. But among their primary functions was one that they shared with sets of heads like the 'Treatise', namely, impressing upon the relevant authorities a sense of Petty's ability, both conceptual and, potentially, administrative. This purpose was evidently just as well served by a brief set of heads that could be read in a few minutes as it would have been by hundreds of pages of high-flown theory or tiresome detail. Petty was not engaged in an academic exercise; he wanted a job. The way forward was through 'every great mans Archives', not through the libraries of all and sundry. Petty did not want to be known as the author of a great book on naval administration (or economic policy, or political demography), but to be a great administrator. It may well be that such heads were all he thought he needed.

Even where a more complete work did exist, Petty's contacts seem to have found it expedient to cut it up into digestible chunks for their elite audience. Here, too, a letter from Wood gives the best evidence. While *Political Arithmetick* passed whole, *The Political Anatomy of Ireland*, had to be broken up and served to Essex *à la carte*:

> Sir. H. Ford at his going for England left me with your Pol. Arithm. But under this promise or Injunction That I should give my Lord [Essex] a Copie, which accordingly I did fairely written not very long after, my Lord

---

[42] Harris 'Ireland as a Laboratory', 87.

since told me he had read it over & with much satisfaction, commended
your ingenuity & c. I then took occasion to tell his Lordship, You had since
writ a Discourse particularly about Ireland [i.e. *The Political Anatomy*], That
I had the first draught thereof by me, That I would if his Lordship pleased
bring him the Heads of the Chapters, That if his Excellency pleasd to select
any or have them all writ out for his reading he might, being then written
in a fast hand not so legible. He desired I would do so & when I brought
him the Heads, he chose out which he would have first, & when I carried
them, he told which next &c so by degrees I wrot him out 7 or 8 chapters,
not according to the order in the Anatomy but as he fancied. Thus he has
already had those about the Rebellion, Future Settlement, Mony, Trade,
Valuation of Lands &c. I thought it was better to let his Lordship have
them as he might digest them as well as I write them, then stay to have all
together; & I believe he had had the whole before this but for my sickness;
for what he had he seemed still to be desiring more. And thus your Politicall
Anatomy was dissected.[43]

Like Wood's earlier letter, this gives a rare view of the way Petty's
manuscript publications were circulated and read. It also allows us to see
the sort of labour involved in producing manuscripts for circulation. Like
Southwell, Wood played a dual role as contact and as interlocutor, and
both roles involved editorial and scribal work. Wood's editorial input is
suggested by an earlier letter on *Political Anatomy*, wherein he offered
Petty some advice on organization: 'If you cause the P. Anatomy to be
transcribed againe, I thinke the Paragraff about the Chancellor would be
well inserted in the Chapter of Government just before the Ecclesiasticall
part, & would together with that of the mysticall Government richly
embellish that chapter.'[44] It appears, though it is hard to be certain, that
Petty followed Wood's advice.[45]

In terms of circulation, both the numbers and the quality of copies
seemed to be a constant concern.

I have a[t] length got the Copy of your Report [i.e. the 1673 'Report from
the Council of Trade'] from Sir Harry [Ford] … but cannot prevaile for the
Polit. Arithm., only he tells me my Lord [Essex] has it & likes it, I tell him
however you would not willingly be thus utterly bereaved of your children:
which I see at present moves not: nevertheless courage! I can at worst bid

[43] Wood to Petty, 28 April 1674, BL MS Add. 72850, ff.202–204.
[44] Wood to Petty, 16 August 1673, BL MS Add. 72850, ff.198–199.
[45] Chapter VI of the printed version of *Political Anatomy*, 'Of the Government of Ireland',
mentions the Lord Chancellor (both with reference to the Court of Chancery and as responsible
for the appointment of Justices of the Peace), the ecclesiastical government, and the 'Internal
and Mystical [that is, Catholic] Government of Ireland' in that order; *EW*, 163–164.

faire for the supply of that loss, if it should prove so, out of a copy I scribbled in hast.[46]

The gratifying news of Essex's attention was apparently tempered with anxiety about the fate of the manuscript itself, and as the letter of 28 April indicates, Wood recovered the one good copy, lent by Ford to Essex, only by promising to replace it with a new one—eight months after Petty himself had asked Ford to deliver it up to Wood.[47] Petty seems to have sent out one or two manuscripts at a time, trusting to each reader to transcribe what he wanted to keep or give away, and to keep the thing moving. Coterie circulation avoided the political pitfalls and financial risk of print, but was only as efficient and controlled as the coterie itself.

That it was worth the cost suggests that Petty had a very specific audience in mind that did not require print but did require dedicated friends like Wood. Although Wood's letters from 1680–82 do not provide the detail of his earlier letters, it seems that he continued to be an important agent for Petty.[48] Robert Hooke noted in his diary on 13 October 1678: 'I gave Dr. Wood Sir W. Petty's paper ['The Improvement of Ireland'], he lent me Sir W. Petty's *Political Arithmetick*.'[49] And although letters from Southwell and Wood provide most of the evidence for Petty's manuscript publication, their letters consistently indicate that they were part of a larger circle. Wood's letters in particular mention Sir Henry Ford, who appears to have been the first one to bring *Political Arithmetick* to the attention of Essex, then Lord Lieutenant of Ireland. Like Petty, Ford was a Fellow of the Royal Society, though expelled in 1682 for letting his subscription fall into arrears. Like Wood, but more briefly, Ford was part of the Irish administration: Secretary of State under Lord Robartes during the latter's brief Lord-Lieutenancy in 1669–70, he returned in the same capacity for a time under Essex.[50] It was during this time that Ford seems to have functioned as a contact for Petty and an agent for the circulation of *Political Arithmetick*; after 'his going for England' in 1674 references to him ceased.

Another contact worthy of mention is Sir Peter Pett, who, like Petty, had been at Oxford in the late 1640s and was an original Fellow of the

---

[46] Wood to Petty, 25 August 1673, BL MS Add. 72850, ff.200–201.

[47] Petty to Ford, 23 August 1673, BL MS Add. 72858, f.111.

[48] Petty returned the favour, distributing copies of Wood's 'Almonac'; see Wood to Petty, 14 September 1680, BL MS Add. 72850, f.284.

[49] Hooke (ed. Henry W. Robinson and Walter Adams), *The Diary of Robert Hooke, MA, MD, FRS, 1672–1680* (London: Wykeham Publications, 1968), 380.

[50] Stuart Handley, 'Ford, Sir Henry (*bap.* 1617, *d.* 1684)', *Oxford DNB* <http://www.oxforddnb.com/view/article/9859>.

Royal Society (like Ford, expelled for falling into arrears in 1675). Pett had sat in the Irish Parliament in the 1660s, later became Advocate-General of Ireland, and was knighted by the Duke of Ormond. He was a natural contact for Petty, and the two were also good friends. Their extant letters are few but chatty, Pett addressing Petty with good-natured ribbing as 'Noble Sir William' and ending one letter 'And so (as old Primate Bramhall was wont to end his letters) God blesse us.'[51] It seems likely that many letters have not survived. The two exchanged poetry (their own and others'), sometimes of a distinctly lowbrow sort, as well as various projects.[52] In late 1682, for instance, Pett wrote that Hugh Chamberlaine had sent him and was shortly to send Petty a proposal for setting up a bank in London, and invited Petty to join them to discuss the matter over a drink.[53] In 1685 a letter from Pett describes their exchange of books:

> I here send you by Marke Pardo An Index (that I promised to Lend you) elucubrated by a Great Disciple of yours, & worshipper of the 2d part of your Politicall Arithmetic, calld your other Essay [i.e. *Another Essay in Political Arithmetick concerning the Growth of the City of London*, 1682] ... I entreat you to send me by Mark Pardo your Copy of Sir Jonas Moore's Survey of the River of Thames & it shall be Carefully & speedily restored you.[54]

How and to what extent Pett functioned as a channel for Petty's proposals to those higher up is not clear from the surviving letters, though Mark Goldie has made a case for such a relationship, at least under James II.[55] What is most significant is that Pett—like Southwell and Wood, and in contrast to Ford and Graunt—could and probably did continue to play a role in circulating Petty's manuscripts in the 1680s, when the bulk of them were produced.

Not all of Petty's contacts were old or good friends. In August 1686, Petty wrote to Southwell that 'I am just now going to Winsor ... to get an Essay read to the King, that London hath more people and Howses

---

51 Pett to Petty, 28 July [1674?], BL MS Add. 72850, ff.196–197.

52 The Petty Papers include three Latin poems on political arithmetic, at least one of which is by Pett: 'Sir Peter Pett's Pindarick on the Politicall Arithmetic' (n.d.), BL MS Add. 72899, ff.60–61. On Petty's 'Leonine' poems, see Harold Love, 'Sir William Petty, the London Coffee Houses, and the Restoration "Leonine"', *The Seventeenth Century* 22:2 (2007), 381–394.

53 Pett to Petty, 10 [December] 1682, BL MS Add. 72850, ff.298–299.

54 Pett to Petty, 11 July 1685, BL MS Add. 72850, f.302.

55 Mark Goldie, 'Sir Peter Pett, Sceptical Toryism and the Science of Toleration in the 1680s', in W. J. Sheils (ed.), *Persecution and Toleration: Papers read at the twenty-second summer meeting and twenty-third winter meeting of the Ecclesiastical History Society, Studies in Church History* 21 (1984), 247–273.

than Paris and Rouen put together'.[56] The essay—part of an ongoing dispute between Petty and the French natural philosopher Adrien Auzout over the relative populations of London and Paris—was the basis of Petty's posthumously printed *Five Essays in Political Arithmetick*.[57] The reader was William Blathwayt, clerk of the Privy Council, secretary at war and surveyor and auditor-general of royal revenues in the American plantations.[58] Blathwayt had been in contact with Petty for some time at this point—Petty sent him a copy of a paper addressing the debate over recoinage, which Blathwayt transcribed—and his capacity for forwarding Petty's proposals is obvious.[59] The two were in some ways similar, the younger man having, like Petty, 'raised himself by his industry from very moderate circumstances', as Evelyn put it.[60] There is little evidence that they were ever close, but Blathwayt was an ideally placed contact for Petty's purposes, and evidently functioned as such.

Probably the last name worthy of much attention in the context of the circulation of political arithmetic among Petty's colleagues is that of Samuel Pepys, who needs little introduction. As we have heard, Pepys was a firm believer in the Double-Bottom even before he knew Petty. The two became friends, and over time Pepys sought out Petty's opinions on a range of topics, from religion to population. His professional interest in 'Navy Oeconomy & Rules' made him an avid reader of Petty's 'Treatise of Navall Philosophy', and he thanked Wood for lending him a copy.[61] His notes on religion, meanwhile, include memoranda to himself such as 'Consult Sir William Petty about the Number of Men in the World &c', 'Remember Sir William Petty's Note of the suddaine Extra[ordinary] Growth of the sect of Quakers even to a Mericle', and 'Sir William Petty's saying seems to employ a great deale, that much the greatest part of all humane understanding is lost by our discoursing and writeing of Matters Nonsensically that is in Words subject to more Sences then one to the

---

[56] Petty to Southwell, 14 August 1686, *PSC*, 231; see also Petty to Southwell, 18 January 1686/7, *PSC*, 252.

[57] Petty, *Five Essays in Political Arithmetick* (London: Printed for Henry Mortlock, 1687).

[58] Barbara C. Murison, 'Blathwayt, William (*bap.* 1650, *d.* 1717)', Oxford *DNB* <http://www. oxforddnb.com/view/article/2626>; Gertrude Ann Jacobsen, *William Blathwayt: A Late Seventeenth Century English Administrator* (New Haven: Yale University Press, 1932).

[59] See Petty to Southwell, 16 and 27 September 1682, *PSC*, 104–106; the manuscript was posthumously published as *Sir William Petty's Quantulumcunque Concerning Money, 1682* (London: [s.n.], 1695).

[60] Evelyn, 2:266.

[61] Bodl. MS Rawlinson A.171, f.89; Pepys to Wood, 16 June 1682, Bodl. MS Rawlinson A.194, f.279. The doomed Pepys wrote of Petty's 'Treatise': 'I am under so impatient a desire of possessing the rest.'

rendring disputations Infinite upon every proposition that can be made in any Science whether divinity, Law &c.'[62] Here, Pepys was getting Hobbes in the Petty version. Pepys's archive even includes 'A Dialogue between A & B', an important paper by Petty on religious toleration, which he endorsed as 'Sir William Petty's Paper written at my desire & given mee by himselfe a little before his Death.'[63] He also had a copy of one of Petty's letters to Southwell on population, of the letter defending the 1674 *Discourse*, and of the 1673 'Report from the Council of Trade'.[64] Direct evidence of a more critical role is harder to come by; but a letter from Petty written in September 1687 is suggestive:

> I am just now sent from Bath where the King will be on Tuesday for the papers in your hands. I blush to presse you for your perusal of them, & to make your Remarques with that friendly Severity you promised. As for the Truth in Matter of fact I am content to venture them at the peril of my Veracity & Reputation. But whether the King will be pleasd to have these Matters to be discussed & published, is beyond my reach. Those only can advise mee who converse much with him: I am sure I meene well, but that may not bee enough[.][65]

At this point Petty had three months to live, but was producing papers at an incredible rate. The political situation created by James II's religious reforms and the resistance these encountered gave Petty's work a new urgency, but also seemed to create new opportunities for him. Pepys's involvement as a reader and adviser at this critical point, when Petty was at the height of his intellectual powers and appeared to be approaching new heights of influence over the king, argues for his inclusion in Petty's coterie.

There are other figures whose activity in circulating Petty's ideas is more shadowy, due not to their unimportance but rather to a lack of sources. During James II's reign, for instance, Thomas Sheridan connected Petty to the Earl of Tyrconnell, whose secretary he was—though the extent and nature of the material he passed along is not clear.[66] Petty mentioned to Southwell only that 'I have given many notes to Thom Sheridan, at my Lord Tirconell's Importunity, who pretends to write the History of

---

[62] 'Notes from Discourses Touching Religion', Bodl. MS Rawlinson A.171 ff.218–221.

[63] Bodl. MS Rawlinson A.171 ff.274–275; another copy is in BL MS Add. 72889 ff.11–12.

[64] Petty to Southwell, 20 August 1681, Bodl. MS Rawlinson A.178, f.71 (*PSC*, 91–93); Petty to Anglesey, 3 April 1675, Bodl. MS Rawlinson A.185, ff.219–220 (a shortened version of BL MS Add. 72850, ff.220–223).

[65] Petty to Pepys, 4 September 1687, Bodl. MS Rawlinson A.189, ff.17–18.

[66] Petty to Southwell, 5 March 1686/7, *PSC*, 259. See John Miller, 'Thomas Sheridan (1646–1712) and his "Narrative"', *Irish Historical Studies* 20:78 (1976), 105–128.

Ireland', but other papers clearly made it over; Petty lamented that 'To what a good passe had I brought matters to with that great man, till Dick Nagle [a critic of the land settlement] came over!'[67] Others read Petty's papers but played more peripheral roles in their transmission. John Aubrey thought of Petty as 'my singular friend', and read his work with enthusiasm. He corresponded with Petty as well as with Robert Wood and even Thomas Hobbes on Petty's 1674 *Discourse*, but this was a matter of philosophical interest rather than potential patronage, and unlike Wood he did not attempt to enter the debate.[68] He later tried to interest Petty in taking a share in the purchase of the island of Tobago; this occasioned some meditations from Petty on population increase, and nothing more.[69] More revealingly, when it did come to the production and distribution of Petty's work, Aubrey seems to have thought in terms of print publication rather than manuscript circulation. Petty put off Aubrey's inquiry about reprinting the *Treatise of Taxes*, and answered a similar query regarding *Political Arithmetick* by writing that 'I am not forward to Print my Political Arithmaticke, but doe wish that what goeth abroad were compared with the Coppy in Sir R. Southwell's hand, which I corrected March 1679/80.'[70] Aubrey does not appear to have been a vital part of the circuit along which Petty's political-arithmetical manuscripts moved.

Patrons

However much can be said for Petty's coterie circulation of manuscripts, and however many fascinating exchanges of opinions his correspondence includes, any account of the early production and distribution of political arithmetic has to take into account one basic fact: it failed. That is, Petty's proposals and petitions did not lead to his appointment to any significant office, and although political arithmetic did eventually achieve success as a way of talking about certain problems of government, it never became the instrument of government that Petty wanted it to be. English and Irish government in the 1670s and 1680s was too plagued by short-term problems to be susceptible to programmatic reform, and turnover of personnel and

---

[67] Petty to Southwell, 5 March 1686/7, *PSC*, 259.
[68] Petty to Aubrey, 29 May 1678, BL MS Egerton 2231, ff.90–91; Hobbes to Aubrey, 24 February/6 March 1675/6, Hobbes, *Correspondence*, 2:751–753.
[69] Aubrey to Petty, 17 August 1685, BL MS Add. 72850, ff.303–304; Petty to Aubrey, 22 August 1685, BL MS Egerton 2231, ff.95–98.
[70] Petty to Aubrey, 12 July 1681, BL MS Egerton 2231, ff.92–94.

policies alike was too high to give much scope for potential reformers to act effectively. The history of Petty's search for patronage throws as much light on political circumstances as it does on political arithmetic, and his failure to find it reflects on both. The situation was too unstable; the program was too comprehensive; Petty himself, both personally and politically, was too troublesome.

Petty naturally tended to pursue successive Lords-Lieutenant of Ireland. Ireland had given Petty his wealth and his first taste of administration, and its problems inspired much of his subsequent work; alterations in his proposals correspondingly signalled changes in the politics of the settlement or in the attitude of his would-be patrons to it. When he began developing political arithmetic, in the early 1670s, Irish politics were in a state of flux. Arthur Annesley, since 1661 Earl of Anglesey, with whom Petty seems to have been on good terms, had been turned out of his Irish offices in 1667 as the result of a politically motivated investigation of Ireland's finances directed at the then Lord-Lieutenant, the duke of Ormond, who lost his place two years later.[71] After Lords Robartes and Berkeley took brief turns at the job, the earl of Essex was appointed Lord-Lieutenant in 1672, just as drafts of *Political Arithmetick* and *The Political Anatomy of Ireland* seem to have begun circulating via Wood and Ford. Essex initially showed considerable interest in Petty's work, getting him to produce as a state paper a 'Report' which summarized one of his treatises, and eventually giving him a minor appointment as an admiralty judge, in 1676. Yet one suspects that the latter came only after considerable importunity on Petty's part; already in 1673 Essex found Petty's ambitious, even grasping nature wearying: 'I am confident that in all his majesties three kingdoms, there lives not a more grating man than Sr Wm Petty; I dare say the practices of Empson and Dudley [Henry VII's infamous councillors] would be found nothing in comparison'.[72]

The story of the judgeship is itself revealing. In fact the position was less important than Petty imagined (and tried to make it). 'The Admiralty of Ireland is a very raw thing,' he wrote to Southwell in 1677, 'and must bee brought to Maturity by many and mature thoughts', presumably his own.[73] Yet forced to admit his own lack of experience, he bewailed the absence of authoritative guidance: 'Wee here are the Blind, leading the Blind.'[74] Even

---

[71] McGuire.

[72] Essex to the Lord Chancellor, 4 May 1673, in BL MS Stowe 213, f.189v. Thanks to Jason McHugh for drawing this letter to my attention.

[73] Petty to Southwell, 18 November 1677, *PSC*, 40.

[74] Petty to Southwell, 10 November 1677, *PSC*, 38.

as he churned out papers on the possibility of enforcing a 'Mare Clausum' in the seas surrounding Britain (he sometimes took the expression literally, envisioning a physical barrier of manned buoys guarding fixed boundary lines) his comments on the job itself degenerated into complaints about the cost of the postage it entailed. Before long he came to feel that, far from being a path to greater influence, it kept him from more important things.[75] He gave up the post in 1683, but had farmed out his duties well before then. The overall picture is of an officious busybody sloughing off his robes when he tired of them—hardly the picture of a reformer, but of a piece with Petty's personality.[76]

While he courted Essex, Petty maintained contact with Anglesey. The two may have known each other from the last days of the Protectorate, when both sat in Parliament; in any case both were major participants in the Irish settlement after the Restoration, and by that point they certainly knew one another.[77] Anglesey had been appointed in 1661 to the first of several commissions charged with enforcing the Act of Settlement. Ten years later, when yet another commission was formed to investigate the settlement, Anglesey was once again on it—and this time, rather alarmingly, began to change sides. In 1673 he was made Lord Privy Seal, apparently back in favour at court. A friendly figure with influence over the fate of the Irish land settlement, Anglesey was both a natural target and apparently a receptive reader of Petty's proposals. One of the earliest occurrences of the phrase political arithmetic, 'whereupon I thinke depends The Politicall Medicine of that Country', is in a letter to him.[78]

Just as Anglesey was linked with political arithmetic at its inception, so he may have been connected with the explosion of pamphlets fifteen years later.[79] A dispute with Ormond in 1681–82, arising from the circulation of the memoirs of the Earl of Castlehaven, cost Anglesey his position as Lord Privy Seal. This dispute, which centred on Ormond's role during the Irish Rebellion and Confederacy, touched off a series of histories important for their different justifications of and challenges to the settlement.[80] Despite

    [75] Petty to Southwell, 19 March 1677/8, *PSC*, 48–52.

    [76] Kevin Costello, 'Sir William Petty and the Court of Admiralty in Restoration Ireland', in Paul Brand, Kevin Costello and W. N. Osborough (eds), *Adventures in the Law: Proceedings of the Sixteenth British Legal History Conference* (Dublin: Four Courts Press, 2005), 106–138.

    [77] Richard L. Greaves, 'Capel, Arthur, first earl of Essex (*bap.* 1632, *d*. 1683)', *Oxford DNB* <http://www.oxforddnb.com/view/article/4584>.

    [78] Petty to Anglesey, 17 December 1672, BL MS Add. 72858, f.73.   [79] Goldie.

    [80] On this dispute see Michael Perceval-Maxwell, 'The Anglesey-Ormond-Castlehaven Dispute, 1680–1682: Taking Sides about Ireland in England', in Carey and Lotz-Heumann, 213–230.

this second fall from grace under Charles II, Anglesey recovered (while Ormond lost ground) with the accession of James, and in 1686 he was rumoured to be a possible replacement for Ormond as Lord-Lieutenant. He died before this could happen, but not too soon to provoke new hopes of influence among writers like Petty and Sir Peter Pett, who had adopted political arithmetic as 'a therapy for national religious dissention' in England as well as for political and economic settlement in Ireland.[81] At the very least, this is a valuable indication of who (besides his colleagues and, perhaps, James II) Petty's numerous writings on religion were meant to impress. It also links the first generation of political arithmetic with the project of religious toleration, indulgence, or comprehension in the interests of political stability.

From the Restoration almost until the end of Petty's lifetime, however, the pre-eminent figure in Anglo-Irish politics was James Butler, first duke of Ormond, scion of one of the greatest Old English families in Ireland, loyal defender of Charles I's cause there, and one of Charles II's most senior advisers during and after the Restoration.[82] Ormond was Lord-Lieutenant of Ireland twice. His first tenure, from 1661 to 1669, ended when he was brought down by the machinations of enemies in Ireland such as the Earl of Orrery, and by his association with the recently deposed Clarendon.[83] Ormond stood for the moderate enforcement of religious uniformity; although of Old English Catholic descent, he had been raised in the Church of England as a ward of the Crown. In Ireland, he sought an at least relatively equitable enforcement of the Acts of Settlement and Explanation, which punished only those Catholics guilty of rebellion and rewarded, if possible, only those Protestants not too blatantly guilty of it themselves. For both reasons hard-line New Protestants, led by Orrery, distrusted him. Ormond returned to office in 1677, but when, in 1685, James II briefly managed to unite Protestant dissent with the Catholic lobby in the supposed pursuit of religious toleration, his time was up.

Petty began courting Ormond at the Restoration. In a letter of 1 March 1660/1, he sent Ormond 'certain proposals for the improvement of Ireland',

---

[81] Goldie. However, the Ormond-Anglesey dispute put Southwell squarely in the Ormond camp (see Bodl. MS Carte 98) without harming his relations with Petty. After Anglesey's death Petty wrote to Southwell that 'My Lord of Anglesey's friends tell mee that his Lordship desired I should perfect his History of Ireland if he were snacht away', but that he himself would rather 'Let the Dead bury the Dead'; Petty to Southwell, 5 March 1686/7, *PSC*, 260.

[82] Toby Barnard, 'Butler, James, first duke of Ormond (1610–1688)', *Oxford DNB* <http://www.oxforddnb.com/view/article/4191>.

[83] McGuire.

'an obscure draft of what I mentioned to your Lordship under the name of a Registry.' Then fresh from the Down Survey, Petty presented himself as disinterested but well-informed and above all confident that he was the man to solve Ireland's problems:

> I do not appear a projector to shark for my necessities nor because the newness of my thoughts hath intoxicated me, but because I have so often slept with them ... as that I can hope to say some things soberly enough concerning my proposition. I should have presented this thing to your Lordship in gratitude ... but I do it now because I know few hands besides your own from which Ireland will endure to receive any new thing ... And as for debating the feasibility and usefulness of the thing, let it be done most publicly ... for having 'scaped pretty well in several new proposals already, I have the courage to venture being laughed at once more.[84]

Nothing came of this proposal at the time, but given the confused state of Ireland and the settlement during the early 1660s that is not surprising. By the 1670s things had changed both for Ireland and for Petty. In the intervening years he had enjoyed modest favour under Essex, and with his marriage to Elizabeth Fenton his circle of acquaintance widened considerably. He now counted Robert Southwell, Elizabeth's cousin, among his closest friends. The biggest difference, however, was political arithmetic. In his 1661 letter to Ormond, Petty had offered a proposal for a registry that might have come from any number of Hartlibian or other projectors. By 1677 he was thinking in much more comprehensive terms—not Irish projects but a programme for Ireland. This difference is captured in an undated (probably late 1670s) letter from Southwell to Ormond about Petty: 'I verily believe if hee be seconded by Authority in the method propos'd by him hee will be a great Instrument to make that Rocky Lawless places, that lyes now beyond Authority, to become English.'[85] Ormond was initially receptive, and after Southwell forwarded him a sycophantic poem Petty had written celebrating his reappointment as Lord-Lieutenant, he gave Petty an encouraging audience. Southwell wrote to his patron on 9 October 1677 thanking him for this kindness, again stressing that Petty's 'talent is very considerable, and he has several

---

[84] Petty to Ormond, 1 March 1660/1, *HMC Ormonde*, 3:11.

[85] Southwell to Ormond (undated), BL MS Add. 72901, f.70. The letter asks for Ormond's help both with Petty's programme and with his lawsuits: 'if this Anxiety of his mind were over, he would be at leisure ... to think of many useful things for the Publick.' Southwell refers to Petty as 'a Kinsman', which puts it at 1667 or after. If by Ormond's 'Authority' Southwell means that of the Lord-Lieutenancy, the letter must be from 1677 or later.

admirers of it'.[86] For his part, Ormond was 'glad Sir William Pet[t]y is satisfied with my reception of him' and hoped that 'I may have opportunity to advantage myself by his excellent partes & conversation.'[87]

As time went on, however, Petty's parts increasingly irritated the Lord-Lieutenant. The Popish Plot and its aftermath caused Ormond a lot of trouble but gave Petty new inspiration—Petty's schemes grew grander just as Ormond's fuse shortened. Beyond that, the two simply had very different personalities. Ormond often lacked the patience and perhaps the intellectual curiosity to hear Petty out, while Petty was intellectually domineering and often unwilling to simplify or compromise his schemes enough to make them practicable in the short term. The comprehensive, programmatic nature of political arithmetic itself was, in Ormond's mind, its greatest problem. 'I do not wonder that a man of so fruitful an invention as Sir William Petty lets it loose now,' he wrote. 'It is most certain he has very many useful notions but they must for the most part be separated and singled out for practice and he bears not retrenchments either of land or of notions with much patience.'[88] Petty did, however, impress Ormond as 'our best computer' in matters of population, and even when misquoting Petty's estimates the Lord-Lieutenant cited his name.[89] In this respect, Ormond's reception of Petty marked the beginning of a pattern that second-generation political arithmeticians like Gregory King and Charles Davenant, and many later historians, would reproduce. In the relatively narrow realm of population estimates, Petty became an authority very early on.

However, although Ormond used Petty as an authority on population, and continued to show interest in his ideas, he became increasingly critical both of Petty's accuracy (at least on matters other than population) and of the practicality of his program. Some of Ormond's criticism betrayed a personal impatience with pedantry bordering at times on anti-intellectualism: but much of it was doubtless fair—he was, after all, trying to govern a difficult place at a difficult time. When he wrote, apropos of the debate over coinage, that 'Sir Wm. Petty and Col. Lawrence have showed

[86] Southwell to Ormond, 9 October 1677, *HMC Ormonde*, 4:377.

[87] Ormond to Southwell, 20 October 1677, BL MS Add. 21484, f.11.

[88] Ormond to Southwell, 23 April 1679, *HMC Fourteenth Report*, 2:286.

[89] Ormond to Southwell, 8 November 1679, *HMC Fourteenth Report*, 2:294. Here Ormond claims that Petty put the ratio of Irish Catholics to Protestants at 15:1, whereas Petty had said it was 8:3. Southwell wrote back to correct him; Southwell to Ormond, 18 November 1679, *HMC Ormonde*, 4:558. If nothing else, this illustrates both the general ignorance of population statistics and Ormond's faith in Petty as a statistician.

their skill in tumbling the argument of coins up and down, but with little edification to the hearers',[90] it is not hard to sympathize. Ormond was not operating, and had neither the time nor the inclination to operate, on Petty's level. He was not alone in this. Regarding Petty's project for licensing ale and liquor (a project encouraged by Ormond and the Earl of Rochester), the Earl of Arran struck a similar note: 'I confess I do not comprehend it well enough to give my opinion on the project, and am the less edified by his bringing Doctor Wood to me to explain and demonstrate the thing.'[91] Yet even Arran wound up convinced that Petty's ideas were good.[92] The problem was apparently more with Petty's presentation of them than with their substance.

There was also the considerable problem of Petty's endless absorption in lawsuits to do with his estates. This was a time-consuming distraction that Southwell, and, at certain moments, Petty himself, despaired of. It was also a major political liability that he would not let go. In 1677, careless comments about the Lord Chancellor (already stung, as we have heard, by his inability to grasp duplicate proportion, which Petty presented as child's play) made in the course of one lawsuit even landed Petty briefly in prison.[93] But, even with much greater sensitivity, patience, and intellectual modesty than he possessed, Petty would probably still have been handicapped by his legal battles and other estate-related conflicts, many of which pitted him against the same people whose attention and favour he hoped to secure, notably Ormond.[94] Even given the comparatively lax standards of the seventeenth century, the idea of giving Petty an office raised doubts about conflicts of interest that his difficult personality did little to assuage. Enclosing papers from Petty in a letter to his son, the highly esteemed Earl of Ossory, Ormond offered some revealing comments on their author:

> I send you herewith some notions of Sir William Petty's upon the subject [of Tangier, naval questions, etc.], but I omit his computations of charge because they are too much mistaken, and that we can have them more certainly elsewhere. I have no objection to Sir Wm. Petty's being a Privy Councellor, but that he will make so many objections and propose so many notions that much of our time will be lost in them; besides, till a dispute

[90] Ormond to the Earl of Arran, 17 April 1683, *HMC Ormonde*, 7:14.
[91] Arran to Ormond, 28 November 1683, *HMC Ormonde*, 7:162.
[92] See Arran to Ormond, 19 December 1683, *HMC Ormonde*, 7:170.
[93] Petty to Southwell, 10 February 1676/7, *PSC*, 14–18.
[94] See for example Orrery to Ormond, 23 July 1667, Bodl. MS Carte 48, ff.116–117, in which Petty is accused of cutting down trees on Ormond's land.

between him and the Farmers is over it will be highly inconvenient to have him there.[95]

Petty's most fervent supporters would have found this difficult to deny.

Three years later, with James II on the throne and Ormond on his way out of office, Petty was chasing down more promising figures—James, whom he had known for some time, and even the Earl of Tyrconnell, whose long campaign against the Irish settlement seemed now close to fruition. This final change of direction brought out a further feature of Petty that may have held him up: his apparent untrustworthiness and even disloyalty. Of course, anyone who had survived the changes wrought by the Protectorate and then the Restoration could seem either mercenary or merely sensible, depending on one's point of view. But there seems to have been a particular streak in Petty—it surfaced in his relationships with the Hartlib Circle and with John Graunt—that was more than simple political self-preservation. Ormond was no political naïf, yet Petty's behaviour still struck him: 'Sir William Pet[t]y is not so very confident of the assureance given him but that hee thinks it prudence to secure himself by applications to men in power & if hee can not save all will try to save one.'[96] It may seem romantic to pin the failure of a programme of colonial governance on the vagaries of personal relationships. Yet two considerations should be borne in mind. The first is the extent to which Restoration politics generally—and Irish politics in particular—was a matter of personal relationships, at the highest levels at least. The second, more particular to this case, is the peculiar way in which the programme of political arithmetic was bound up with the person, if not the personality, of Sir William Petty. He was its progenitor and, before the late 1680s at the earliest, its sole practitioner. Until other writers took it up, its fate depended on Petty's ability to get himself heard by a very select group of individuals. Given all this, the importance of Petty's personal history may be seen in its proper perspective.

The last two names to add to the roster of patrons are those of Charles II and James II. As we saw in an earlier chapter, Petty enjoyed occasional audiences with Charles from the Restoration on; he brought him papers to read, or read them himself. This might seem promising, but the heterogeneous character of the proposals Charles heard—everything from the

[95] Ormond to Ossory, 16 June 1680, *Ormonde*, 5:336.
[96] Ormond to Southwell, 27 October 1686, BL MS Add. 21484, f.64. In fact Petty had been suspected of machinations against Ormond nearly twenty years earlier; see correspondence between Ormond and his son Ossory from 1667 and 1668 in Bodl. MS Carte 48, ff.221–222 and 237–238; 220, ff.431–432.

improvement of Ireland to, most famously, the Double-Bottom—sounds a cautionary note. It is probably not the case, as many historians have suggested, that Petty was never anything other than a source of amusement for Charles, the fate of his ship notwithstanding.[97] It is, however, certain that Charles was a changeable man, and an occasional audience with him, while encouraging, meant nothing in policy terms, particularly for a man of Petty's relatively low standing. Petty's own frustrations suggest that he knew this only too well. The way to get things done was to go to the doers themselves—the Essexes and Ormonds. Charles offered prestige, but inaction. James was a different matter. He expressed sincere interest in naval schemes, Petty's included, and later and more interestingly in religious toleration and projects for securing liberty of conscience. At the same time, his Catholic sympathies represented a serious threat to the Irish settlement, confirmed by his support for the Earl of Tyrconnell's Catholicizing policies in Ireland. As we have seen from the Pepys correspondence above, Petty secured at least one audience with James II at this crucial time. He also met and submitted proposals to Tyrconnell himself, once cautioning him to 'have a care to lay good foundations for the next settlement, which perhaps will bee called by your name.'[98] The threat of Catholicization in Ireland and the opportunity for liberty of conscience throughout the Three Kingdoms ultimately led Petty to reorient his programme considerably, to make it both relevant to the changed situation and palatable to James. But here too, he failed—he died in December 1687. At that point, political arithmetic ceased to be a programme and became, instead, a language.

---

[97] See Petty to Sir Robert Moray, 29 November 1662, RSL Letterbook P.1., ff.28–29, wherein Petty mentions 'his Majesties kindness towards me (who was outwardly obnoxious enough, &c.)'. Even the ridicule surrounding the double-bottom may have been exaggerated somewhat: Peter Pett, for one, wrote to Wood that Charles 'doth often speak with ... the ... Commissioners of the Navy about Sir Wm Petty's Sluce Ship & doth not in the least ridicule it or play with it in his way of descant, but looks on it as an important invention, & so doth all the Navy board here.' Pett to Wood, 27 November 1684, BL MS Add. 72894, f.46.
[98] Petty to Tyrconnell, 19 May 1687, BL MS Add. 72850, ff.163–164.

CHAPTER 8

Death and Afterlife

Petty's end

Over the last few chapters our focus has shifted away from other aspects of Petty's life and work towards political arithmetic. In some ways this is fitting: Petty's last years were, in terms of manuscript production, his busiest, and under James II in particular his pursuit of a lasting settlement based on the political-arithmetical tools he had forged over two decades became frenetic. Yet he was always more than a political arithmetician—it was precisely his multifaceted nature that allowed him to create political arithmetic in the first place. Through the 1680s he remained as interested and involved in natural-philosophical and other scientific matters as ever, becoming in 1683 the first President of the Dublin Philosophical Society, which he and William Molyneux designed as a younger sister to the Royal Society. A larger fish in a smaller pond than he had been in 1660, Petty pursued in Dublin the same sorts of experiments and some of the same reforms he and his friends had attempted in London. He cautioned against admitting members of whatever status whose commitment to science was lacking, and his 'Advertisements' of the Dublin group and the lists of experiments and equipment he drew up for it attracted interest from the Royal Society.[1] In 1684 he returned to another Restoration project, launching his final double-bottomed ship, and he experimented all the while with lead, dyes, soils, waters, meteorology, magnets, lenses, and—a response to Kerry's rocky roads—land carriages.[2] In one 1683 Royal Society meeting, his name came up in discussions of chemical salts, artillery, and the usefulness or otherwise of walking through a bean field while holding a salmon.[3] The Baconian imperatives of his early days remained a constant spur to the end.

While continuing in some of his familiar paths, however, Petty devoted a larger share of his time to his family. Against a background of lawsuits,

---

[1] See *PP*, 2:88–92; Birch, *History*, 4:353, 374, 378, 397.

[2] See *PP*, 2:71–76, 150–151; Birch, *History*, 4:175, 183, 192, 273–275, 294–295, 297.

[3] Birch, *History*, 4:194.

estate projects, and political worries, correspondence with Southwell
attests to his care in educating his children and the pride he took in their
accomplishments, tracing Charles's and Henry's (and to a lesser extent
Anne's) progress from fairy tales and play-acting to serious study, detailing
their reading lists and suggesting both courses of study and mathematical
puzzles for Southwell's own son Edward and his sisters. Characteristically,
however, this affection was far from blind. An early admirer of Newton's
Principia, Petty told Southwell that 'I would give £500 to have been the
author of it, and £200 that Charles [his eldest] understood it.'[4] Nor did it
extend to his natural daughter, Frances, the product of a fleeting encounter
in 1664 and his only child to reach adulthood in his lifetime. With her
allowance nearing its end and her 'sallary in the Play-House' where she
acted insufficient, she wrote first to Petty and then to Elizabeth in late
1684, asking for money.[5] Petty's reply suggests the cold authority he could
assume:

> I have perus'd the Letter you sent My Wife, Concerning your Retirement.
> There was in it enough of Witt Shift & Evasion, but not much of that
> Sincerity fairness & Complyance that I expected ... I take noe Pleasure to
> make a Long Cataloge of my Provocations. I will pitch at present but upon
> one, which is that when your Mother swore that you were my Child, she
> allso swore that I was then Maried to her to which I say, that I know the
> falsity of the one, but doe not know the truth of the other ...
>
> Wherefore my Resolutions Concerning you are as followeth.
>
> Viz: 1st. that you part from your Mother allowing her so much of your
> Pension, as you think absolutely Necessary.
>
> 2. that you be never seen in the Parke nor Play-Houses, Nor visitt any
>   Woman of an ill Reputation.
>
> 3. that by reason of your Mothers afore-mention'd oath, which renders the
>   Main point so doubtfull you quit my Name, & take that which stands
>   in the Church Booke of St Clements Parishe wher you were Cristned in
>   Jan: 1664/5; or what else you pleas ...
>
> 4. I foresee many mischiefs that may arise from the ill use you have made of
>   my Late Indulgences, wherefore I would not have you visitt my Family,
>   nor wonder that I should not visitt you if I were at London.
>
> 5. I expect according to your promise how you have dispos'd of the £100
>   I gaue you, not that I intend to retrenche any parte thereof, or of your

[4] Petty to Southwell, 23 July 1687, *PSC*, 279.
[5] Frances Petty to Petty, 9 December [1684] and [December 1684–February 1685], BL MS
Add, 72850, ff.110–113.

present allowance, which may assure you, that these precepts doe not proceed from Malice, Nor from a hasty beliefe of all that may be said against you, but out of a Rationall Care of you, & of my nearer Relations to whom I must be iust.[6]

(Frances knew her man, however; though a weak writer, she made sure to include calculations of income and expenses that supported her claims. This Pettian strategy evidently worked on her father, whose expenses for 21 August–21 October 1685 included £30 for her half-yearly allowance.)[7] Petty doted, by contrast, on his younger daughter Anne—'That shall be a countesse, if her pappa can'.[8] Charles and Henry died without issue; it was she who secured the family legacy.

Petty's own death came on 16 December 1687, the unexpected result of an infection in his leg. It caught him at the height of his polemical powers; laid up three days earlier, he had Elizabeth initial a letter inveighing against the Irish revenue farmers, and a new tract on religion was found in his pocket after his death.[9] However, its effect on political arithmetic was hardly less sudden or permanent than its effect on the man himself. Ending his circulation of manuscripts, it left his printed works to stand alone. The effects of this were soon compounded by the Revolution of 1688, which swept away both the political circumstances and many of the people that the manuscript proposals had addressed. Without a Catholic king there was no need to 'Catholicate' Britain; nor, in the wake of Orange victories at the Boyne and Aughrim, was there any perceived need to conciliate Catholic Ireland. Even had it not disappeared physically, the practical political arithmetic Petty had so carefully tailored to the government of populations in the Stuart multiple monarchy lost its political meaning with James II's deposition, William III's conquests, and the definitive settlement in 1701 of a Protestant succession. What remained was the analytical political arithmetic of Petty's few, short printed works, and it was from these that a second generation of political arithmeticians fashioned their discipline. Paradoxically, the 'age of political arithmetic' that historians have identified between the arrival of William and Mary and the death of Queen Anne saw no simple elaboration of Petty's pioneering work but rather a radical reinterpretation of it, inscribed in the blank space the *tractiuncli* left behind.

---

[6] Petty to Frances Petty, 24 February 1684/5, BL MS Add. 72850, ff.159–160.
[7] BL MS Add, 72857, ff.140–141.
[8] 'Sir Wm. Petty to His Daughter Anne' (1679), *PP*, 2:255.
[9] Petty to Southwell, 13 December 1687, *PSC*, 331; '12 Articles of a Good Catholiq & Good Patriots Creed', BL MS Add. 72866, ff.178–179v.

Political arithmetic in print

During the same years that his manuscripts extended political arithmetic's political applications across the Atlantic and then the Irish Sea, Petty published a string of short works, some just a few pages in length, of comparative and historical demographic analysis: *Another Essay in Political Arithmetick, Concerning the Growth of the City of London* (1683), *Observations upon the Dublin-Bills of Mortality, MDCLXXXI* (1683), *An Essay Concerning the Multiplication of Mankind* (1686), *Further Observations upon the Dublin-Bills* (1686), *Two Essays in Political Arithmetick, Concerning the People, Housing, Hospitals, &c. of London and Paris* (1687), *Observations upon the Cities of London and Rome* (1687), and *Five Essays in Political Arithmetick* (1687).[10] Peripheral to his practical work, these were vital to political arithmetic's articulation after his death. Even before then, they spread his reputation and did much to define political arithmetic for the learned and wider reading public, as distinct from the officialdom Petty's manuscript tracts targeted. (The *Two Essays* and the *Five Essays* were immediately translated into French; Petty's claims about the relative sizes of Paris and London sparked an inconclusive cross-Channel battle with Adrien Auzout of the Académie des Sciences.)[11] Most important, they continued what Graunt had begun, establishing population as an object of knowledge, susceptible to measurement and subject to graspable regularities—natural laws.

Even here, it is dangerous to presume familiarity with Petty's analytical intent simply because he presented numerical data in tabular format. His failure to identify the geometrical progress of population seems astonishing, for example, particularly in a man who ranked himself with Archimedes and Descartes as a mathematician.[12] But Petty's thoughts on the 'multiplication of mankind' were in part an attempt 'To justifie the *Scriptures*' statistically, by linking specific 'doubling' periods (numbers of

---

10 Petty, *Another Essay in Political Arithmetick, Concerning the Growth of the City of London* (London: Printed by H. H. for Mark Pardoe, 1683); *Observations upon the Dublin-Bills; An Essay Concerning the Multiplication of* Mankind (London: Printed for Mark Pardoe, 1686); *Further Observations upon the Dublin-Bills* (London: Printed for Mark Pardoe, 1686); *Two Essays in Political Arithmetick, Concerning the People, Housing, Hospitals, &c. of London and Paris* (Printed for J. Lloyd, 1687); *Observations upon the Cities of London and Rome* (London: Printed for Henry Mortlocke, 1687); *Five Essays*.

11 Petty, *Deux Essays d'Arithmetique Politique, Touchant les Villes de Londres et Paris* (Londres: Chés B. G., 1686); *Cinq Essays sur L'Arithmetique Politique* (Londres: Imprimie pour Henry Mortlock, 1687); Petty, *Five Essays*, 2–12; Petty to Southwell, 25 December 1686 and 9 July 1687, *PSC*, 248–249 and 276–277; RSL MS Classified XVII, item 24; *EW*, 2:522–523.

12 Petty to Edward Southwell, 3 November 1687, *PSC*, 321–322. See Reungoat, 213.

years within which population naturally doubled itself) with specific eras
of biblical history: ten years for the first century after the Flood, two
hundred and ninety years in Moses' time, four hundred in King David's,
and seven hundred and fifty at the birth of Christ.[13] The aim was less
to determine how population worked than to find a way for it to work
with scriptural chronology—something less surprising in the author of the
'Scale of Creatures' than in the pioneer economist of later historiography.[14]
Petty equated the progress of population with the march of sacred history.
The 'full peopling' of the Earth, taking perhaps two further millennia,
would 'give one Head for every two Acres of Land in the *Habitable* part of
the *Earth*'—'And then, according to the *Prediction* of the *Scriptures*, there
must be *Wars* and great *Slaughter*, &c.'[15] This may sound like a Malthusian
'positive check' in scriptural clothing, but Petty's comments to Southwell
give it a very different colour:

> I say that as in great Cittys and Cohabitations of men art and sciences are
> better cultivated than in Deserts; so I say That if there were as many men on
> Earth as It could bear, the works and wonders of God's Wisdome would be
> the sooner discovered and God the sooner honored really and heartily... I
> should ad to my last head that, it being probable That the world shall not
> be destroyed, nor the Day of Judgement come till the whole Earth bee
> peopled ... Then we must wish the speedy peopling of the Earth.

Full peopling would lead not to Malthusian crises but to Baconian reformation, fulfilling the apocalyptic promise of Daniel 7:12: 'many shall run to
and fro, and knowledge shall be increased.' Multiplication was luciferous
in the nearer term, too: 'To come nearer the point (Good Cozen) our Lands
in Ireland may 12 years hence bee double in value to what they are now'.[16]

Both the flatly statistical and the more providential aspects of Petty's
printed work influenced political arithmetic's reception and articulation
in the years after his death—the age of physico-theology as well as of
fire and life insurance. Its most obvious use was simply as a source of
data on the size, growth, and age-structure of various populations, both
for risk-assessment and in continuing disputes over the relative sizes
of different urban populations.[17] William Nicolson's *English Historical*

[13] Petty, *Another Essay*, 18–19.   [14] Petty to Southwell, 20 August 1681, *PSC*, 92–93.
[15] Petty, *Another Essay*, 16–17.   [16] Petty to Southwell, 19 September 1685, *PSC*, 153–155.
[17] Though see John Ward, *Clavis Usurae; Or, A Key to Interest, both Simple and Compound*
(London: Printed by J. M. for W. Taylor, 1710), 105–107, which drew on Petty's discussion
on population in his 1674 *Discourse*. The Friendly Society used Petty's estimates in calculating
insurance rates; *Land Security, for Establishing a Perpetual Insurance upon Lives, Of Men, Women,
and Children, &c.* (London: [s. n.], 1715), 30.

Library (1696) used Petty ('one of the most eminent Mathematicians and Virtuoso's of this Age') as his authority for London's pre-eminence, and both English and French geographical and historical writers continued to cite—and criticize—his comparisons of London, Paris and Rome.[18] His data were used to criticize doubtful sources; Maximilien Misson, doubting Marco Polo's claims for Chinese cities, remarked that 'Likely [Petty] had no great faith for [Polo], for else he would not have said … that London is the largest, and most populous City in the World.'[19] They were also deployed, as Petty intended, 'To justifie the *Scriptures* and all other good *Histories* concerning the *Number* of the People in Ancient Time.'[20] William Nicholls's 1696 *Conference with a Theist* used Petty's account of doubling to argue against the infinity of the world, and later that year William Whiston's *New Theory of the Earth* followed suit, quibbling over the details.[21] Two decades later, George Cheyne did the same:

> Sir *William Petty*, from Observations on Births and Burials has discover'd, that in 360 Years the Mass of Mankind is doubled in these Countries. Had they thus increas'd from all *Eternity* in other Countries, all the *Planets* within our *System* had not been able to have contain'd them by this time; yea, if in many *millions* of Years they had but increas'd by an Unity continually, their Number had been infinite by this time. But it's plain, both the Number of Mankind, and that of other *Animals* and *Vegetables*, must have perpetually increas'd, if the World has been from all *Eternity* as it is at present. And since their Number is but finite at present, it's evident, this World has not been forever as it now is. And indeed the present Number of Animals does answer very well to the common *Aera* of the Creation.[22]

Petty could not have put it better himself.

---

[18] William Nicolson, *The English Historical Library*, 2 vols (London: Printed for Abel Swall, 1696), 1:47–48. Nicolson also described Petty (1:48) as 'the Chief Director and Author' of Graunt's *Observations*. See John Beaumont, *The Present State of the Universe* (London: Printed by Randall Taylor, 1694), 41–43; [?] de Souligné, *A Comparison between Old Rome In its Glory, As to the Extent and Populousness, and London, as it is at Present* (London: Printed by John Nutt, 1706), 25.

[19] Maximilien Misson, *A New Voyage to Italy*, 4 vols (4th ed., London: Printed for R. Bonwicke, Ja. Tonson, W, Freeman, Tim. Goodwin, J. Walthoe [*et al.*], 1714), 1:24. The reference to Petty does not occur in the first edition (1695).

[20] Petty, *Another Essay*, 19.

[21] William Nicholls, *A Conference with a Theist* (London: Printed by T. W. for Francis Saunders and Tho. Bennet, 1696), 66–76; William Whiston, *A New Theory of the Earth, from Its Original to the Consummation of All Things* (London: Printed by R. Roberts for Benj. Tooke, 1696), 383–388.

[22] George Cheyne, *Philosophical Principles of Religion: Natural and Revealed* (London: Printed for George Strahan, 1715), 174.

Petty's printed political arithmetic was thus widely read as a source of numbers that functioned as evidence for various kinds of claims, whether economic or theological; in the *tractiuncli*, by contrast, numbers were used not so much to describe states of affairs accurately as to indicate objects to be moved, mixed, and separated. It was the former dimension that Petty's successors during the 1690s—the first writers to self-consciously create their own political arithmetic—developed, applying an ever more analytical and mathematical political arithmetic across an ever greater range of contexts but leaving overt policy prescriptions to others. In his 1691 *Proposal for Improvement of Husbandry and Trade*, John Houghton suggested systematically gathering data on weights, measures, and commodity prices, trade policies of other nations, as well as compiling histories of trade and—'for the *Political Arithmeticians* that desire to know the *Increase* and *Decrease* of Places'—tracking population change in the localities.[23] In one sense a throwback to the Office of Address, Houghton's project identified political arithmetic with generalized demographic data gathering.

John Arbuthnot's *Of the Laws of Chance* (1692)—mostly a translation of Christiaan Huygens's 1654 *De ratiociniis in ludo aleae*—went further. Talk of chance, Arbuthnot argued, revealed 'nothing but want of Art', ignorance of the physical causes that governed all events. Probability, 'the Laws of Chance', pulled back the curtain, permitting rational calculation.[24]

> There are very few things which we know, which are not capable of being reduc'd to a Mathematical Reasoning, and when they cannot, it's a sign our knowledg of them is very small and confus'd; and where a mathematical reasoning can be had, it's as great folly, to make use of any other, as to grope for a thing in the dark when you have a Candle standing by you.[25]

The progress of knowledge was the expansion of mathematics—including its expansion into the political realm: 'all the Politicks in the World are nothing else but a kind of Analysis of the Quantity of Probability in casual Events, and a good Politician signifies no more, but one who is dexterous at such Calculations'.[26] Petty could hardly have disagreed. Yet Arbuthnot's extension of number, weight, and measure was more facile and in a sense shallower than Petty's:

> There is…a Calculation of the Quantity of Probability founded on Experience, to be made use of in Wagers about any thing; for example, it is

[23] John Houghton, *A Proposal for Improvement of Husbandry and Trade* (London: [s.n.], 1691), 1.
[24] John Arbuthnot, *Of the Laws of Chance* (London: Printed by Benj. Motte, 1692), sig. A6v.
[25] Arbuthnot, sig. A8r–v.   [26] Arbuthnot, sig. A9r.

odds, if a Woman is with *Child*, but it shall be a *Boy*; and if you would know the just odds, you must consider the Proportion in the Bills that the Males bear to the Females: The Yearly Bills of Mortality are observ'd to bear such Proportion to the live People as 1 to 30, or 26; therefore it is an even Wager, that one out of thirteen, dyes within a Year ... because, at this rate, if 1 out of 26 dyes, you are no loser.[27]

This sounded like Petty, but Arbuthnot went on to apply the same reasoning to very different sorts of demographic category. Not only was it 'but 1 to 18 if you meet a *Parson* in the Street, that he proves to be a *Non-Juror*, because there is but 1 of 26 that are such'; but 'It is [also] hardly 1 to 10, that a *Woman* of Twenty Years old has her *Maidenhead*'.[28] Demographic proportion had come unmoored, available for any situation that struck the fancy. Political arithmetic now gained its purchase not through some unique aptness for specific kinds of problem—the transmutation of the Irish, the management of colonial population, the government of a multiple monarchy—but rather through its applicability, given sufficient quantitative information, to anything. Indeed, neither philosophical discussions nor ultimate goals had any place in the political arithmetician's office: however dexterous the calculator, 'the Principles which are made use of in the Solution of such Problems,' as distinct from the problem-solving itself, 'can't be studied in a Closet, but acquir'd by the Observation of Mankind.'[29] For Petty, political arithmetic arose in the course of a political project; the numbers, constructed to serve their purpose, came afterwards. For Arbuthnot, the numbers were given; their use was decided elsewhere.

Gregory King, Charles Davenant, and an art of reasoning

As Petty came to be remembered as a purveyor of statistics, so political arithmetic came to signify a practice of computation—most often, the analysis of quantitative accounts of national demography. Both tendencies are clearly visible in the 'LCC Burns Journal', one of two surviving notebooks of perhaps more than fifty kept by Gregory King between 1695 and 1700 (the 'Journal' is marked no. 51).[30] King, the first major practitioner

---

[27] Arbuthnot, sig. A9v–A10r.   [28] Arbuthnot, sig. A10r–v.
[29] Arbuthnot, sig. A9r.
[30] A facsimile reproduction of 'The LCC Burns Journal'—along with King's *Natural and Political Observations on the State of England* (written in 1696 but first printed in London in 1802) and Graunt's *Observations*—is printed in Peter Laslett (ed.), *The Earliest Classics: John Graunt and Gregory King* (Farnborough: Gregg International Publishers, 1973).

of political arithmetic after Petty, was not entirely unlike his predecessor: 'a skilful herald, a good accomptant, surveyor, and mathematician, a curious penman, and well-versed in political arithmetick.'[31] Like Petty, too, his most interesting work was never printed but remained in manuscript form, sometimes in brief proposals that can be identified as state papers. Paradoxically, however, it was Petty's printed work that influenced King's manuscripts, and King's reception even of this was in certain respects highly critical. In both the form his work took and the conception of political arithmetic behind it, King illustrates the transition between Petty, on the one hand, and King's friend Charles Davenant—whose printed work explicitly recast both political arithmetic and Petty's place in its history—on the other.

King's notebook reveals a working knowledge not only of Petty's printed work on population but also of at least some of his earlier scientific work. A section entitled 'General Propositions touching the Number of People' noted that 'Sr Will. Petty in his Treatis of Duple Proportion, printed anno 1674 gives several Instances of the operation of Duple Proportion & among the rest p. 82 His 11th Instance is, in the life of man and its duration.'[32] He went on to summarize Petty's chapter and make notes on his method of argument. He seems to have known very little, by contrast, about Petty's manuscript work. His notes on *Political Arithmetick* do record that it was 'writ about 1676 but published ... 1690', though in fact a manuscript had been in circulation some years earlier.[33] However, he showed no awareness of Petty's *tractiuncli*, and although his own major work on the subject, the *Natural and Political Observations and Conclusions upon the State and Condition of England* remained in manuscript (written in 1696, it was printed only in 1802), it was evidently meant for the press.[34] Despite his own recourse to manuscript, King envisioned political arithmetic as primarily a print genre, a way of capturing the state with numbers and making those numbers public.

[31] Monument to Gregory King in the Church of St. Benet, Paul's Wharf, London, quoted in Negley B. Harte, 'The Economics of Clothing in the Late Seventeenth Century', *Textile History*, 22:2 (1991), 277. See Julian Hoppit, 'King, Gregory (1648–1712)', in *Oxford DNB* <http://www.oxforddnb.com/view/article/15563>; Peter Laslett, 'Introduction', in Laslett (ed.), *The Earliest Classics*, 1–10; Laslett, 'Natural and Political Observations on the Population of Late Seventeenth-Century England', in Kevin Schurer and Tom Arkell (eds), *Surveying the People: The Interpretation and Use of Document Sources for the Study of Population in the Later Seventeenth Century* (Oxford: Leopard's Head Press, 1992), 6–30. On King's relationship to Petty and Davenant, see Hoppit, 'Political Arithmetic in Eighteenth-Century England', *Economic History Review* 49:3 (1996), 516–540; Slack, 'Government'; Slack, 'Measuring the National Wealth in Seventeenth-Century England', *Economic History Review* 57:4 (2004), 607–635.

[32] King, 'Burns Journal', 21.   [33] King, 'Burns Journal', 181.   [34] Harte, 277.

Petty was the genre's pioneer, and his printed works were its models. Despite appearances, the title of King's *Natural and Political Observations* probably referred not to Graunt but to Petty, then widely presumed to have written the 1662 *Observations*. The book itself attempted an updated fusion of *Political Anatomy* and *Political Arithmetick*: the first section dealt with 'The Number of People in England and Wales, calculated from the Assessments on Marriages, Births, and Burials', the second with 'The Proportion of England, in Acres, and People, to France, and Holland, to Europe, and to the World in general', and later sections with the age, sex, and social structure of the population as well as with estimates of annual income and consumption—making constant reference, as Petty had, to France and Holland.[35] Yet King did not follow Petty blindly. He was very careful to distance himself, in particular, from what he saw as a tradition of patriotic exaggeration in 'all former calculations of this kind', Petty's emphatically included.[36] As he put it in his notebook, 'Sr William Petty was lookt upon as the best Computer of his time, But in all his Computations of the Numbers of People in England and London, It is Evident he designd to Represent both the one and the other much greater then they truly were'.[37]

That is not to say that King's work was in fact more disinterested or objective than Petty's; on the contrary, Paul Slack has convincingly shown that Petty's successors bent their estimates to suit their political preferences much as Petty did, using the same statistical tools, though enjoying more plentiful data.[38] What is significant is that, unlike Petty, King expressly affirmed that his own numbers were both neutral and 'come very near the truth'; inaccuracies, he implied, resulted from the limitations of his data or errors in calculation rather than external bias.[39] In *Political Arithmetick*, Petty had claimed only that his figures were 'not so false as to destroy the argument they are brought for'. King denied having any arguments to make:

> If, to be well apprized of the true state, and condition of a nation, especially in the two main articles, of its people, and wealth, be a piece of political knowledge, of all others, and at all times, the most useful and necessary; then, surely at a time when a long and very expensive war against a potent Monarch, (who, alone, has stood the shock of an alliance and confederacy of

---

[35] King, *Observations*, 33–38.   [36] King, *Observations*, 31.
[37] King, 'Burns Journal', 49. King later repeated (63) that Petty's estimate of London's size evinced 'a Design to magnify London beyond its true Value.'
[38] Slack, 'Measuring'.   [39] King, *Observations*, 31.

the greatest part of Christendom), seems to be at its crisis; such a knowledge
of our own nation must be of the highest concern[.][40]

This knowledge was in some sense political in its content, but King's point
was that it was not, to use our word, *politicized*. Even when King's numbers
implied a political position—for instance, that given 'The State of the
Nation' and its revenues, 'the war [against France] cannot well be sustained'—the reader was given to understand that the numbers compelled
King's conclusions, and not the other way around.[41] The door remained,
theoretically, open to other views. Revenues might increase, new sources
of credit might materialize, the fortunes of war might change. Political
arithmetic crunched the numbers, projected likely forecasts and presented
possible options, but by itself it decided nothing. Indeed, its very usefulness
in policymaking was now predicated on its independent presentation of
neutral data. Using inflated numbers to rationalize prior commitments,
Petty had erred. 'And tho Writing to the Publick might make it Excusable
so to do,' King conceded, there was a danger that 'those Publick accounts of
His should be too much Rely'd on by those who sit at the Helm, to whom a
true Account of the Kingdom is more necessary then to others'.[42] The irony
of this is that Petty's most important political-arithmetical proposals had
not been written 'to the public' but precisely for 'those who sit at the helm'.

King's disinterested, decontextualized political arithmetic was also neutral as to subject matter. Far from solving a unique order of political
problem, it now embraced almost any mathematical calculation made in
any political, economic, or social context; universal applicability might
even certify its value neutrality. King's papers offer admirable testimony
to possibilities thus created. A bundle of his 'Exercises in polit[ica]l
Arithmetic' preserved in the National Archive includes 'An accompt of
the Receipt of the Publick R[e]venue at the Exch[eque]r from 28 Sept.
1701 to 26 Dec. following', a proposal for a 'Tax upon Windows', 'An
Extract of the Number of Houses and People from the Assessment
upon Marriages Births and Burials Anno Domini 1695', a manuscript
booklet containing 'The Names of the People in Harfield near Uxbridge in
Co[unty] Midd[lese]x. with their ages. Taken the latter End of Oct 1699',
a 'Scheme of the Charge of Settling 2000 Palatines in Martin Meer', and
various scribblings on population and notes on Petty and Graunt.[43] It also
includes 'Computations of Horses and Men Running' (a topic treated in

---

[40] King, *Observations*, 31.   [41] King, *Observations*, 61–63.
[42] King, 'Burns Journal', 49.
[43] NA MS T64/302, ff.3–5, 11–12v (the latter two manuscripts are unfoliated).

Petty's 1674 *Discourse*) and, touchingly, a 'Computation of the No. of Great and Small Flowers to be wrought in Mrs Kings fine Callico Gown Begun by Mrs Mince … Tuisd[ay]-noon 17 Apr 1711.'[44] King's political arithmetic could calculate the number of people who populated the kingdom or the number of flowers that populated a gown. What mattered was that it was equally accurate in either case, that its computations gave a 'true account'.

King's work reflected and reinforced the main trends in political arithmetic's reception and rearticulation after 1688: the emphasis on analysis rather than intervention, on accuracy rather than utility, on a public audience rather than a private coterie. It was left to King's friend Charles Davenant to give these changes formal expression in what was effectively the first attempt at defining political arithmetic as a practice.[45] Unlike Petty or King, Davenant was neither a natural philosopher nor a scholar but a pamphleteer and a bureaucrat, serving first as an Excise Commissioner under Charles II and James II and then as Secretary to the Commissioners for the Union with Scotland and Inspector-General of Imports and Exports under Anne.[46] Familiar with Petty and Graunt, in part via King, Davenant set out to define political arithmetic's method and purpose in an essay 'Of the Use of Political Arithmetick, in all Considerations about the Revenues and Trade', the first of his *Discourses on the Publick Revenues, and On the Trade of England* (1698).[47] Together with his historical sketch of its development, the definition he framed was immensely influential for both practitioners and later scholars (to the point that Davenant's views are sometimes attributed to Petty).[48] Yet even as Davenant enshrined Petty's founding role in political arithmetic as a 'computing faculty', he deepened King's criticism of Petty's practice. In the political arithmetic of the Williamite era, Petty's ambitions had no place.

'By Political Arithmetic,' Davenant wrote, 'we mean the Art of Reasoning, by Figures, upon things relating to Government.'[49] In line with

---

[44] NA MS T64/302, unfoliated and ff.9–10.

[45] See McCormick, 'Transmutation, Inclusion, and Exclusion: Political Arithmetic from Charles II to William III', *Journal of Historical Sociology* 20:3 (2007), 259–278, elements of which appear below.

[46] The most thorough study of Davenant is still D. A. G. Waddell, 'The Career and Writings of Charles Davenant (1656–1714)' (D.Phil., University of Oxford, 1954); see also Waddell, 'Charles Davenant (1656–1714): A Biographical Sketch', *Economic History Review*, 2nd series, 2:2 (1958), 279–288; Finkelstein, *Harmony*, 219–246.

[47] Davenant, *Discourses on the Publick Revenues, and on the Trade of England* (London: Printed for James Knapton, 1698), 1–35.

[48] Deane (23) attributes Davenant's definition to 'Petty and his followers'.

[49] Davenant, *Discourses*, 2.

King, he described an abstract set of computational practices applicable to all kinds of objects. So general an art could hardly have been invented by a single individual, but he gave Petty ('who as yet has been followed by very few') particular credit for both its methodological formulation and its use in economic matters: 'The Art it self is undoubtedly very ancient; but the Application of it, to the particular objects of Revenue and Trade, is what *Sir William Petty* first began ... he first gave it that Name, and brought it into Rules and Method'.[50] Petty's own use of this method left much to be desired, but this was chiefly for technical reasons:

> The Foundation of this Art is to be laid in some competent Knowledge of the Numbers of the People: And in all his [i.e. Petty's] Inquiries, he took for Guides the Customs, Excise and Hearth-Mony, and the Accompts of those Revenues were not fully stated, and their Produce was not known, at least to him, when his Books were written.[51]

Such limitations were obviously beyond Petty's control, and Davenant had no doubt that Petty's 'excellent Wit would have carry'd it very far, if he had liv'd to this Time; for his skilful Hand did all along want right Materials to work upon, with which he might have been furnish'd, by the variety of new Taxes that have been levied in this Kingdom.'[52] It was simply unfortunate that 'the very Grounds upon which he built his Calculations, being probably wrong, he must ... be mistaken in his Superstructure'.[53]

At this point, however, Davenant abruptly shifted from a technical appraisal of Petty's results to an essentially moral criticism of his practice. '[T]hrough the whole Course of [Petty's] Writings,' Davenant now claimed, 'it may be plainly seen, by any observing Man, that he was to advance a Proposition, not quite right in itself, but very grateful to those that govern'd.'[54] The whole argument of *Political Arithmetick* (Davenant supplied page references in the margins of his work) had been designed to flatter the lazy vanity of Charles II:

> The Growth of the *French* King, and chiefly of his Naval Power, was a very unpleasant Object, for the Parliament, and the People of *England* to contemplate; and no doubt it did disquiet the Mind of King *Charles* II. But this Prince, delighting to be sooth'd in his Ease and Pleasures, and to have no anxious Thoughts, was very glad to see one of Sir *William Petty's* Repute for Calculations of this Nature, affirm, That France exceeded England very little in Territory; That we came near 'em as to the Numbers of Men; and

---

[50] Davenant, *Discourses*, 2.   [51] Davenant, *Discourses*, 2–3.
[52] Davenant, *Discourses*, 2.   [53] Davenant, *Discourses*, 4.
[54] Davenant, *Discourses*, 5.

that our Numbers were as effectual in point of Strength ... That France was
under a Natural and Perpetual Impediment of being Powerful at Sea ...

and so on.[55] 'Every good Englishman does undoubtedly wish all this had
been true', Davenant allowed, but the fact remained that Petty 'rather made
his Court, than spoke his Mind'.[56] Embroiled in a costly war with France,
the nation paid the price for such flattery. 'The King was well pleas'd to be
lull'd asleep by a flattering Council ... it excus'd his Breach of the Triple
Alliance [with the United Provinces and Sweden, against France] and all
the other Measures which have since prov'd so pernicious to the Interest
of *England*.'[57] By betraying his method, Davenant suggested, Petty had
betrayed his country.

As history, this picture was deeply flawed. The Petty we have seen
certainly courted favour when opportunity offered, but neither his extraordinarily bold policy proposals (most of which Davenant never saw)
nor his stubbornness in the face of criticism from whatever quarter suggest
the spineless courtier Davenant portrayed. But Davenant was not really
interested in giving an account of political arithmetic's original substance
and purposes, which he conveniently if perhaps half-consciously assumed
to reflect the whims of the debased and now defunct Restoration court.
What he offered instead was both a morality tale about political arithmetic's right use and a defence of its potential utility. By allowing political
goals to drive his analysis, Petty had corrupted his numbers, harming his
nation. By rigorously separating statistical facts from political values, Davenant—following King's lead—would rescue Petty's admirable method
from his deplorable politics. This illuminates, if it does not entirely explain, the ambivalence of Davenant's account. Petty had both pioneered
and perverted a method he was incompetent, for both technical and moral
reasons, to practise.

Self-serving though it undoubtedly was, Davenant's cant nevertheless
reflected a real change in the meaning of political arithmetic: once
explicitly an art of government, it was now, its practitioners stressed,
an art of reasoning. This rhetorical shift hardly purified the data that a
new generation of political arithmeticians presented, though biases were
perhaps more carefully concealed. But it was essential to the radically
different political and institutional contexts in which they operated. Petty
put his most important ideas down in manuscripts he then circulated
among a small number of powerful crown appointees, in whose hands

---

[55] Davenant, *Discourses*, 5.   [56] Davenant, *Discourses*, 6.
[57] Davenant, *Discourses*, 6.

alone the fate of his programme ultimately rested. Davenant, writing in the wake of the Glorious Revolution, worked to reinvent political arithmetic as a putatively apolitical tool of quantitative analysis suitable for an expanding fiscal-military bureaucracy (of which he was himself an agent) and available, via the printing press, for use in parliamentary and public debate. His 1695 *Essay upon Ways and Means of Supplying the War* had blamed the erroneous 'Opinion ... That the War [with France] could not last' on 'the vanity, natural to our Nation, of over-rating our own Strength, and undervaluing that of our Enemies.'[58] Only political arithmetic, he now wrote, could deflate such 'Extravagant hopes'.[59] It was indeed an essential instrument of government: 'The Abilities of any Minister have always consisted Chiefly in this Computing Faculty; nor can the Affairs of War or Peace, be well manag'd without reasoning by Figures, upon Things.'[60] However, it could function this way only once its original political purposes were forgotten.

From people to numbers

Davenant's political arithmetic was not a programme but a practice. Concretely, it purported to tie certain types of numbers to certain aspects of politics and society. In this respect it served to codify many of the guiding assumptions of contemporary economic thinking: the central importance of population, the natural ratio of population to land, the relation of both to trade, and the relation of all to national strength.[61] These relationships had been identified by many earlier writers—not just Petty, but men like Child, Coke, Mun, Temple, Worsley, and others as well—so that the novelty of Petty's work was seen to be his use of numbers. In terms of its policy implications, indeed, the actual content of much of the so-called political arithmetic of the 1690s has much more in common with the trade pamphlets of Mun and Child than with the political arithmetic of Petty's manuscript tracts. But the conception of political arithmetic itself had changed, even as Petty was enshrined as its inventor. It now embodied the rhetoric of disinterestedness, maximal probability, and precision—of objective, factual analysis—that increasingly characterized both the economic writing as well as the scientific work of the late seventeenth and early eighteenth century.

---

[58] Davenant, *An Essay upon Ways and Means of Supplying the War* (London: Printed for Jacob Tonson, 1695), 1.

[59] Davenant, *Essay*, 2.   [60] Davenant, *Discourses*, 6–7.

[61] See for example Davenant, *Discourses*, 10–11.

It was also a bureaucratic conception. The new political arithmetic was a set of computational operations detached from any specific material or goals, not an expertise based on any particular experience or an art designed to produce any particular effect; the second-generation political arithmetician was a professional who applied these operations neutrally to a given body of quantitative data, rather than an expert, much less a Baconian natural philosopher. Indeed, Petty's particular experiences and commitments had become liabilities, in that they tied him, and his method, to a particular set of interests. Davenant's political arithmetic, by contrast, derived its epistemological credit not from any aspect of his identity but precisely from the fact that, *qua* political arithmetician, he had none. Its functions were routine and impersonal. As politics was increasingly seen as a matter of numbers, in political arithmetic it was increasingly the numbers that mattered. As policy-making centred less and less on the shadowy comings and goings of a handful of courtiers and more and more on Parliamentary party politics, political arithmetic evolved into a language that could be learned and used by anyone, in or out of power, to advance or to critique any policy—and to do so in print, for all to see.[62]

John Brewer's account of the rise of the bureaucratic fiscal-military state after 1688, beginning with William III's commitment of English resources to a large-scale continental war, indicates the imperatives that shaped and raised to prominence this new, putatively apolitical political arithmetic.[63] Current scholarship identifies the period between William's accession and the death of Anne (Gregory King died in 1712 and Davenant in 1714) as political arithmetic's 'golden age'.[64] There are good reasons for this. Though he printed nothing, for example, Gregory King may have contributed to the 1695 Marriage Duty Act, which taxed bachelors for not contributing to the increase of population.[65] Davenant was a living example of political arithmetic in government, spending over a decade in one part of England's fiscal bureaucracy and entering another with the return of

[62] Peter Buck, 'Seventeenth-Century Political Arithmetic'; Buck, 'People Who Counted: Political Arithmetic in the Eighteenth Century', *Isis* 73:1 (1982), 28–45. The lapse in 1695 of the Licensing Act undoubtedly helped to make political arithmetic a public language.

[63] John Brewer, *The Sinews of Power: War, Money, and the English State, 1688–1783* (Cambridge, MA: Harvard University Press, 1990).

[64] Hoppit.

[65] His papers in the National Archives include 'A Probable Calculation of the Annual Income To be raised by a Tax on Marriages, Burials, and Legacies', endorsed on the back as 'Fryth's Project of the Duty on Marriages Births and Burials' (NA MS T64/320 ff.2–3v). See Colin Brooks, 'Projecting, Political Arithmetic and the Act of 1695', *English Historical Review* 97:382 (1982), 31–53; Slack, *Reformation*, 103; Slack, 'Government'.

the Tories to power under Queen Anne. Set against a backdrop of war, the revenue projections and tax incentives King and Davenant proffered have seemed to some scholars altogether more serious than Petty's often speculative, and mostly untried, social engineering schemes. Geoffrey Holmes states this view neatly: 'as late as 1688 [political arithmetic's] distinguished practitioners had been few. However, over the next six or seven years what had started as a largely academic study received the stamp of deadly earnestness from the War of the League of Augsburg.'[66]

In fact, political arithmetic had been neither less 'earnest' nor more 'academic' in the 1670s or 1680s than in the 1690s. It had simply been a different sort of enterprise. Petty's political arithmetic, evolving as a branch of natural philosophy, made policy a Baconian science. Not unlike Davenant's, it was empirical, depending not only on raw numerical data about trade and population but also on observations of how these naturally functioned. Again somewhat like Davenant's—though in a very different institutional setting—it was collaborative, in the sense that gathering these materials and applying the policies that resulted was the work of the state as a whole; much as in the Down Survey, Petty would sit at the top, directing things, while hundreds milled and sifted beneath him. But most importantly, and unlike Davenant's, its ambitions were emphatically trans-formative. Just as Bacon's natural philosopher superinduced new natures on the substances he worked with, Petty's political arithmetician—or the state, with his help—superinduced new qualities (Englishness, industry, loyalty to the Crown) on human populations. Both worked, crucially, by turning natural processes to human uses, whether the processes in question were physical, chemical, or biological.

One of the central contentions of this book has been that Petty wrote political arithmetic as a natural philosopher, and in particular as a self-conscious follower of Bacon, though shaped by a variety of other influences—his Jesuit education, his training in chemical medicine, his encounters with Hobbes and Harrington, his time with the Hartlib Circle, and his work in and experience of Cromwellian and Restoration Ireland. Like many of his better known colleagues, Petty continually emphasized that what mattered to the new philosophy he pursued—in contrast with both scholastic disputatiousness and Cartesian abstraction—were not words but things. Seen from this perspective, his political arithmetic carried the New Philosophy into government not so much by introducing an empirical or quantitative sensibility as by reorienting political practice

---

[66] Holmes, 'Gregory King', in Holmes, *Politics*, 285.

from the pronouncement of laws to the manipulation of populations. This implies that the real political analogue of the Scientific Revolution was not an eighteenth-century revolution in statistical reasoning consolidated by a nineteenth-century 'avalanche of numbers', but rather a late seventeenth-century revolution in social engineering whose connection to numerical precision, as Petty's own words and works attest, was often tenuous.[67]

The writers who took up political arithmetic in the 1690s were not natural philosophers but bureaucrats. In their eyes, Petty had invented an 'Art of Reasoning, by Figures'—a method of using the language of numbers, not a way of transforming things. In this respect the shift from self-conscious social engineering to self-effacing social analysis was a step back not only from Petty's questionable political commitments but also from the notion of applied natural philosophy that guided his endeavours and underlay the invention of political arithmetic itself. Yet these new men inherited more than they acknowledged or perhaps realized. Petty's extension of science from bodies to minds, begun with the Down Survey and completed with political arithmetic, turned human populations into natural objects, the state into a scientific agent, and government into a sort of collaborative scientific project. Whatever their analytical pretensions, the political arithmeticians, bureaucrats, and colonial administrators of the next generation—who witnessed and in some cases drove in the establishment of Protestant ascendancy in Ireland, the extension of colonization in North America, and the explosion of the transatlantic slave trade—treated populations as objects without having to think about it, much less to construe their work in natural-philosophical terms. Petty had done this thinking for them.

[67] Ian Hacking, *The Taming of Chance* (Cambridge: Cambridge University Press, 1990), 118. See also Hacking, *The Emergence of Probability*; Lorraine Daston, *Classical Probability in the Enlightenment* (Princeton: Princeton University Press, 1988).

Conclusion: William Petty's Political Science

Since Davenant wrote, William Petty has been cast in many roles: disciple of Thomas Hobbes, servant of Oliver Cromwell, precursor of Adam Smith—a wide-ranging 'genius' at home among the heroes of the Scientific Revolution. Yet he has rarely been treated as a natural philosopher in his own right. As the early chapters of this book have shown, however, mechanical philosophy, experimental method, corpuscularian matter theory, and, above all, a Baconian understanding of the purposes of 'real learning' structured Petty's work throughout his career, and played an essential role in shaping his political arithmetic. It might be perverse—and it would certainly be futile—to try to put Petty on the same historiographical plane as Bacon, Boyle, or Newton. However, the point is that understanding what political arithmetic meant demands, in part, that we grasp its evolution as a component of what Petty and many of his contemporaries thought natural philosophy should be. At once as natural as meteorology, and, like alchemy, an art, it both followed and improved nature, channelling natural forces to superinduce desirable qualities on its given subject matter. As this suggests, what made political arithmetic a science in the seventeenth century bears only a faint resemblance to what has made it 'scientific' for so many historians since.

If political arithmetic's combination of art and nature was characteristic of other early modern sciences, what set it apart were the forms—policy on one side, population on the other—that art and nature took within its frame. In this sense, it was less remarkable for its attention to economic questions or its focus on data-gathering than for its Baconian reinterpretation of politics, or what Petty called 'the Genius of Multitude'.[1] This 'biopolitics' *avant la lettre* made the quantitative and qualitative manipulation of populations the purpose of policy; Petty envisioned the state as a scientific agency, organ and beneficiary of this demographic alchemy.[2]

---

[1] BL MS Add. 72865, f.94.

[2] See Patrick Carroll, *Science, Culture, and Modern State Formation* (Berkeley: University of California Press, 2006), especially 52–80. I regret that I became aware of this work too late to engage with it in more detail.

'Number, weight, and measure' correspondingly mattered less for the analytical precision they permitted than for the control—the extension of 'human empire', in Bacon's language—they conferred. On the practical level, this distinction may look like hair-splitting: numbers matter, surely, because of the decisions they guide. As Davenant's denunciation of Petty illustrates, however, such hair-splitting is crucial when it comes to justifying political decisions or validating knowledge claims. What makes statistics usable, for us as for Davenant, is that they conceal their purposes. Knowledge should not be politicized. Social science should not look like social engineering.

Petty, however, wore his purposes on his sleeve. He meant political arithmetic as an 'instrument of government' after the fashion of his own Down Survey—a collaborative project explicitly geared towards political and social transformation. As we have repeatedly seen, and as he readily acknowledged, political priorities determined both the extent and the kind of quantitative knowledge he sought. But this is merely to say that Petty brought to political arithmetic the same Baconian conviction he embraced in his other work, namely, that the goal of any real science was to 'produce great & Noble pieces of art, tending to the happines of Mankind'.[3] In this light, it should no longer be surprising that his 'political medicine'—designed 'to transmute the Irish into English', to preserve English demographic integrity in America, and to assuage sectarian strife in Britain and Ireland—required only such rough numbers as would not destroy the arguments they were brought for. Petty's cavalier attitude to the statistics that subsequently made him famous reflected not some lack of resources or of political will, as Davenant supposed, but a conscious and principled ordering of priorities. To use Petty's own metaphor, finding the mathematical formula to describe the path of a tennis ball would not make anyone a better player. Or, to return to medicine: diagnosis was important, but treatment was the point.

This order of priorities was embedded in Petty's conception of natural philosophy and of himself as a natural philosopher. The priorities themselves, however—the ambitions of political arithmetic explored throughout the later chapters of the book—reflected both his intellectual background and the political context in which he wrote. Face to face with the disastrous consequences of confessional diversity in Cromwellian Ireland, Petty came to identify the fragmentation of the commonwealth into distinct subpopulations as both the natural consequence of post-lapsarian

---

[3] Petty to Hartlib [early 1649], HP, 7/123/1a.

human factiousness and—in so far as the confessional, national, or social principles dividing these subpopulations impinged on their civil allegiance—the proper object of political intervention. Combining his scientific commitments with a range of pre-existing imperial tactics and economic idioms, and gradually extending his view to the problems of colonial settlement overseas and the politics of religion throughout the Stuart multiple monarchy, Petty created a Baconian science of natural policy that put the power to shape and reshape populations, using natural processes and artificial aids, in the hands of the state.

The creation of political arithmetic and its subsequent transformation into an early social science was neither a simple nor a necessary process. Somehow, a combination of mixed mathematical, mechanical, and alchemical ideas and Baconian aspirations reacted against the vicissitudes of Irish and English politics and religion to generate a new kind of social engineering predicated on a new kind of quantitative analysis; and somehow, out of this social engineering, came something that modern economists, statisticians, and demographers identify as their own. This was no simple application of numbers to social questions, although in retrospect that did occur. It was, rather, the eventual and unintended product of a series of attempts to deal with a series of political and intellectual challenges—specific moves made in specific contexts. The very form of Petty's archive—dominated as it is by the fragmentary remnants of his fitful office-seeking—is a monument to this contingency.

Looking backwards, it is easy to talk about Petty's economics or his demography and to dismiss or ignore his alchemy or even his politics: but this is not only to oversimplify, it is to miss the point. Petty's successors enunciated more carefully than he did the idea of a value-neutral science of society. However, they pursued their own brand of social engineering no less ruthlessly, and much more effectively. The forced movement, mixture, and separation of populations did not stop in 1687. On the contrary, it had scarcely begun. From the slavery and transplantation of Petty's day to the eugenics, ethnic cleansing, and nation-building more familiar to our own, the connection between analyzing populations and manipulating them has been often hidden but never cut. If Petty—whose reputation in print stands in sharp contrast to his forgotten manuscripts—tells us anything, it is that the history of social science, which is to say the history of our own pre-eminent worldview, has always been about both.

Epilogue: From Petty to Marx

Following the twists and turns of political arithmetic through the eighteenth century would be another book, and would no doubt tell a story very different from the one told here—although a story built upon this one. As Julian Hoppit has written of eighteenth-century practice:

> Political arithmetic was not ... confined to estimates of national income and population, for it might also explore public finances, economic performance, poor relief, military matters, religious affiliation, social order, and so on. The dimensions of public policy set the agenda and, therefore, the potential subject matter of political arithmetic was unfixed and could change from one period to another ... Political arithmetic was both thematically and methodologically a broad church.[1]

However multifaceted, it remained fundamentally a method of calculation; from Davenant's seminal definition to Adam Smith's cursory and somewhat dishonest dismissal of it eighty years later in *The Wealth of Nations*, the foundational work of its successor science, political economy. 'I have no great faith in political arithmetick,' Smith declared, having just quoted some economic statistics, 'and I mean not to warrant the exactness ... of these computations.'[2] Minus exact computations, he implied, political arithmetic had nothing to offer the new science of political economy; indeed, he never mentioned Petty's name. Yet just eighty years after Smith wrote, Petty would re-emerge as the 'founder' of political economy itself.[3] Stressing the historical contingency of both the economic arrangements and the analytical categories Smith and his followers naturalized, Karl Marx began his story with Petty.

The history of political economy

Much like modern historians of economics, Marx was interested in Petty chiefly to the extent that his theoretical contribution to the discipline remained significant. What distinguished Marx's treatment was the criterion of significance he employed. Rather than measuring Petty's

---

[1] Hoppit, 517.   [2] Smith, *Wealth of Nations*, 2:121.   [3] Marx, *Theories*, 1.

pronouncements against current theory, Marx was interested in how Petty's thinking, in historical context, reflected the contingency of theories whose universal claims Marx rejected. The proper critique of political economy, in other words, was not dogmatic but historicist, rooted in a detailed examination of the origins of political economy. As Marx wrote in early 1852, 'I should in general remark to the democratic gentlemen that they would do better first to acquaint themselves with bourgeois literature before they presume to yap out their contradictions of it ... Before they try to criticise the criticism of political economy they should try to acquaint themselves with the first foundations of political economy.'[4] Petty had laid these first foundations of 'classical political economy' now embraced by 'all the economists who, since the time of W. Petty, have investigated the real internal framework of bourgeois relations of production, as opposed to the vulgar economists who only flounder around within the apparent framework of those relations.'[5] What especially distinguished Petty was his grasp of commodities and his reach towards a theory of value. The early pages of *Political Arithmetick* had distinguished 'very prettily and very naïvely' between ordinary consumable commodities ('wealth, but *hic et nunc*') and gold and silver—money—as 'eternal commodities' and hence a medium for the accumulation of wealth over time.[6] More important than this distinction (which Marx also found in Xenophon), however, was Petty's inkling that just as specific types of labour produced the use-values embodied in short-lived commodities, so labour in general lay behind value in general.[7] Petty was thus among 'the first economists ... to have seen through the nature of value.'[8] Specifically, 'Value as such has no other "material" but labour itself. This determination of value, first indicated by Petty, clearly worked out by Ricardo, is merely the most abstract form of bourgeois wealth.'[9]

The insight of classical political economy, however, was also its blindness: 'it has never once asked the question why this content has assumed that particular form, that is to say, why labour is expressed in value', and the

[4] Marx to Georg Weydemeyer, 5 March 1852, in Marx and Friedrich Engels (trans. Dona Torr), *Correspondence, 1846–1895: A Selection with Commentary and Notes* (London: Lawrence and Wishart, 1934) [hereafter *Marx–Engels Correspondence*], 56.

[5] Marx (trans. Ben Fowkes), *Capital: A Critique of Political Economy*, vol.1 ([1867]; London: Penguin 1990), 174–175 n.34.

[6] Marx (trans. Martin Nicolaus), *Grundrisse*, ([1939]; London: Penguin, 1993), 170, 646. Marx quotes *Political Arithmetick* at length in *Grundrisse*, 231–232.

[7] Marx, *Grundrisse*, 170.   [8] Marx, *Capital*, vol.1, 142 n.18.

[9] Marx to Engels, 2 April 1858, in *Marx–Engels Correspondence*, 106.

nature of the transformation between them.[10] Marx's desire to understand
this blindness no doubt underscored Petty's importance to the classical
tradition of political economy. 'Political economy, which first emerged
as an independent science during the period of manufacture, is only able
to view the social division of labour in terms of the division found in
manufacture'; but Petty had written before the rise of large-scale manufacturing, and before political economy existed as a discipline.[11] Petty's
historical position thus gave his views considerable significance for Marx's
investigation of how a contingent regime of labour, associated with a mode
of production not yet dominant in Petty's day, came gradually to seem
natural among his successors. In the third volume of *Capital*, Marx con-
trasted the Physiocrats of the eighteenth century with the 'mercantilists',
who focused on commercial or circulating rather than productive capital,
and 'Who in their crude realism form the true vulgar economists of their
day and whose practical self-interest pressed the beginnings of scientific
analysis by Petty and his school right into the background.'[12] For Marx,
the effacement of Petty's science—though not, to be sure, of his natural
philosophy—underpinned the development of his economics.

When Petty wrote, his words were not orthodoxy. In his analysis
of ground-rent, indeed, Petty was 'closer to the feudal period' than to
Ricardo: in the seventeenth century, 'the agricultural population are still
the overwhelming majority of the nation' and 'the landowner still appears
as the person who appropriates in the first instance the excess labour
of the immediate producers'; 'ground-rent is the normal form of surplus
value' and 'Landed property thus still appears as the chief condition of
production.'[13] The economic context in which Petty, his contemporaries,
and his immediate successors wrote explained why 'instead of deriving
the valorization of capital from the exploitation of labour-power, they
explain the productivity of labour-power by declaring that labour-power
itself is this mystical thing, interest-bearing capital.'[14] Petty's analysis was
important not because he avoided these shortcomings but precisely because
he embodied them in their most comprehensible form: 'The older writers,
like Petty … bring out the capitalist character of the division of labour
as applied to manufacture more clearly than Adam Smith does.'[15] Petty
threw the specificity of bourgeois political economy into relief.

---

[10] Marx, *Capital*, vol.1, 174.   [11] Marx, *Capital*, vol.1, 486.
[12] Marx (trans. David Fernbach), *Capital: A Critique of Political Economy*, vol.3, ([1870];
London, 1991), 920.
[13] Marx, *Capital*, vol.3, 919.   [14] Marx, *Capital*, vol.3, 596.
[15] Marx, *Capital*, vol.1, 486 n.53.

In reading Petty, however, Marx combined a mastery of the available sources with a blindness of his own. Given the range of material he cites, his impressive research habits and the facilities at his disposal (the British Library in London, and Chetham's Library in Manchester), it is very likely that he had read the full range of Petty's not particularly voluminous printed work. It is unlikely, however, that he had read anything more; and as the foregoing chapters have shown, Petty's printed works were neither comprehensive nor straightforwardly representative of his thinking or goals. Further, Marx read with a very specific question in mind: what had Petty to say about labour, value, commodities, money—the basic concepts with which any analysis of economic relations must begin? He located and elucidated Petty's comments on these topics with great efficiency, theoretical brilliance and an uncommon degree of historical sensitivity. Once he had supplied himself with a historicized interpretation of Petty's economic ideas, however, he moved on. Paradoxically, Marx's interest in Petty's historical context established a tradition of reading Petty by the light of current economics. It is a great irony that the peculiar nature of Marx's interest in Petty's economics obscured their strangely similar interests in transforming Ireland.

The perils of union

Petty spent much of his life arguing for the union of English and Irish; bringing this union about was what political arithmetic was invented to do. Marx, meanwhile, sought a rather different and much more famous union of his own: 'Working men of all countries, unite!' This juxtaposition may look like a bit of word-play, but if we examine what Marx and Engels had to say about Ireland, there is something more to it than that. Petty tried to reconcile opposed political interests by uniting the demographic groups that embodied them and the composite polity they inhabited. Marx, two centuries later, sought to unify an economic class driven by political differences by splitting the polity they shared in two. Petty saw a future Anglo-Irish political union as the institutional backdrop to the transmutative union of English and Irish interests into one; Marx saw in the actual Union of 1801 the institutionalization of inequality between two persistently distinct nations. The union Petty sought to create, Marx sought, for strikingly similar reasons (in formal terms, at least), to destroy.

The English colonization of Ireland interested Marx and Engels both as a matter of practical politics and as an example of colonial practice. Of special importance was the relationship between the fact of Irish subjugation and the perception of English liberty. Following a tour of Ireland in 1856, Engels wrote to Marx that 'Ireland may be regarded as the first English colony and as one which because of its proximity is still governed exactly in the old way, and here one can already observe that the so-called liberty of English citizens is based on the oppression of the colonies.'[16]

He described a country 'completely ruined by the English wars of conquest from 1100 to 1850 (for in reality both the wars and the state of siege lasted as long as that),' and how through 'consistent oppression' the Irish themselves 'have been artificially converted into an utterly demoralised nation and now fulfil the notorious function of supplying England, America, Australia, etc., with prostitutes, casual labourers, pimps, thieves, swindlers, beggars and other rabble.'[17] Exploring the history of this oppression took Engels through some of the same sources Petty himself had drawn on as an agent of it:

> Last week I waded through the tracts by old Sir John Davies (Attorney-General for Ireland under James). I do not know if you have read them, they are the main source; at any rate you have seen them quoted a hundred times ... From these tracts it is clear that communal property in land *still existed* in full force in Ireland in the year 1600, and this was brought forward by M. Davies in the pleas regarding the confiscation of the alienated lands in Ulster, as a proof that the land did not belong to the individual owners (peasants) and therefore either belonged to the lord, who had forfeited it, or from the beginning to the Crown. I have never read anything finer than this plea.[18]

Noting that Davies 'gives an exact description of the income, etc., of the chief of the clan', Engels offered to send Marx the details.[19] Marx responded warmly: 'I have read a lot of *Davies* in extracts. The book itself I had only glanced through superficially ... So you would do me a service if you would copy out the passages relating to *common property*.'[20]

Constructing their own anatomy of Ireland, the two drew on some of the same materials Petty had used in his. Their aims, of course, were different; but their positive conclusions about the relationship of Irish and English political and social divisions—and about what could be done to alter these relationships—overlapped in remarkable ways.

---

[16] Engels to Marx, 23 May 1856, in *Marx–Engels Correspondence*, 93.
[17] *Marx–Engels Correspondence*, 94.
[18] Engels to Marx, 29 November 1869, in *Marx–Engels Correspondence*, 275.
[19] *Marx–Engels Correspondence*, 275–276.
[20] Marx to Engels, 10 December 1869, in *Marx–Engels Correspondence*, 281.

Irish history shows one how disastrous it is for a nation when it has subjugated another nation. All the abominations of the English have their origin in the Irish Pale. I have still to work through the Cromwellian period, but this much seems certain to me, that things would have taken another turn in England but for the necessity of military rule in Ireland and the creation of a new aristocracy there.[21]

Historically, the exploitation of Ireland had prolonged the life of a backward English regime, and it continued to do so in the present. 'Ireland is the bulwark of the English *landed aristocracy*,' Marx wrote in 1870. 'The exploitation of this country is not only one of the main sources of their material wealth, it is their greatest *moral* strength.' The English ruling classes 'represent the *domination of England over Ireland*. Ireland is therefore the great means by which the English aristocracy maintains *its domination in England* itself.'[22] English revolution required Irish liberation:

> it is in the direct and absolute interest of the English working class to get rid of their present connection with Ireland ... For a long time I believed that it would be possible to overthrow the Irish regime by English working class ascendancy ... Deeper study has now convinced me of the opposite. The English working class will *never accomplish anything* before it has got rid of Ireland. The lever must be applied in Ireland. That is why the Irish question is so important for the social movement in general.[23]

Though Marx and Petty would have been on opposite sides of the question, the idea that the stability of the English ruling class depended on English political control of Ireland was common to both. For Petty, bent on shoring up England's rulers, the answer was a union that would consolidate English authority. For Marx, bent on the workers' revolution, the answer was to liberate the Irish from their English masters. 'If ... the English army and police were withdrawn to-morrow you would at once have an agrarian revolution in Ireland'; 'the overthrow of the English aristocracy in Ireland ... has as a necessary consequence its overthrow in England. And this would fulfil the prerequisite for the proletarian revolution in England.'[24]

Achieving this meant getting English workers to identify their interests with those of the Irish—a goal conceptually very close to Petty's own,

[21] Engels to Marx, 24 October 1869, in *Marx–Engels Correspondence*, 264.
[22] Marx to Siegfried Meyer and A. Vogt, 9 April 1870, in *Marx–Engels Correspondence*, 288.
[23] Marx to Engels, 10 December 1869, in *Marx–Engels Correspondence*, 280–281.
[24] Marx to Meyer and Vogt, *Marx–Engels Correspondence*, 288.

despite the very different ends in view.[25] Still more striking than this conceptual convergence of both writers on the notion of a union of interests is the unmistakable echo of Petty in Marx's analysis of the obstacles to union:

> [E]very industrial and commercial centre in England now possesses a working-class population *divided* into two *hostile* camps, English proletarians and Irish proletarians. The ordinary English worker hates the Irish worker as a competitor who lowers his standard of life. In relation to the Irish worker he feels himself a member of the *ruling* nation and so turns himself into a tool of the aristocrats and capitalists *against Ireland*, thus strengthening their domination *over himself*. He cherishes religious, social and national prejudices against the Irish worker. His attitude towards him is much the same as the 'poor whites' to the 'niggers' in the former slave states of the U.S.A. The Irishman pays him back with interest in his own coin. He regards the English worker as both sharing in the guilt for the English domination in Ireland and at the same time serving as its stupid tool.[26]

Marx faced, in formal terms, the same problem as Petty: artificial divisions articulated in terms of nation, religion or culture, 'artificially kept alive and intensified by the press, the pulpit, the comic papers, in short by all the means at the disposal of the ruling classes', obscured a natural identity of interests.[27] But whereas for Petty political union had been an institutional prop for demographic and cultural fusion, for Marx the real effect of the Union in conditions of labour mobility was to maintain ethnic chauvinism even in the teeth of material interest. Petty's answer to national sentiment was an ambitious programme of demographic transmutation legitimated by the sovereign power of Leviathan. Marx's answer was an appeal to reason justified in terms of a new international order. Both failed. It is tempting to wonder what Marx would have said if he had read Petty's manuscript proposals, and if he had appreciated Petty's own distinction between 'artificial' obstacles and 'natural' possibilities as the cultivated product of an engagement with Baconian natural philosophy rather than a preliminary gesture towards Smithian naturalism. Petty, at any rate, would certainly have agreed with the last of Marx's 'Theses on Feuerbach', which echoed his own letter to Henry More: 'The philosophers have only *interpreted* the world in various ways; the point is to *change* it.'

[25] See for instance Marx to Kugelmann, 29 November 1869, in *Marx–Engels Correspondence*, 278–279.
[26] Marx to Meyer and Vogt, *Marx–Engels Correspondence*, 289.
[27] *Marx–Engels Correspondence*, 289–290.

Bibliography

MANUSCRIPTS

Trinity College Library, Dublin
MSS 544, 888, 1180

British Library, London
Additional MSS 4292, 21127, 21128, 21484, 38849, 72850, 72852, 72854, 72857, 72858,
    72865–72867, 72878–72889, 72891, 72894, 72897–72899, 72901
Egerton MS 2231
Harveian MS 3360
Sloane MS 2903
Stowe MS 213

National Archives, London
MS T64/302, 320
SP 9/2

Royal Society Library, London
MS 366
Classified Papers XVII (Miscellaneous Papers)
Letterbook P. 1

Osler Library, McGill University, Montreal
MS 7614

Beinecke Library, Yale University, New Haven
Osborn Shelves fb. 135, document 3

Bodleian Library, University of Oxford, Oxford
Carte MSS 40, 53, 98, 118
Rawlinson MSS A. 171, 178, 185, 189, 194

Huntington Library, Pasadena
Ellesmere MS 7042

Sheffield University Library, Sheffield
*The Hartlib Papers: A Complete Text and Image Database of the Papers of Samuel
    Hartlib (c. 1600–1662)* (2nd ed. on CD-ROM, HROnline for the Humanities
    Research Institute: University of Sheffield, 2002)

PRINTED PRIMARY SOURCES

Aglionby, William. *The Present State of the United Provinces of the Low-Countries.* London: Printed for John Starkey, 1669.

Arbuthnot, John. *Of the Laws of Chance.* London: Printed by Benj. Motte, 1692.

Aubrey, John (ed. Richard Barber). *Brief Lives.* Woodbridge: Boydell Press, 1982.

Bacon, Francis. *The Essayes or Covnsels, Civill and Morall, of Francis Lo. Verulam.* London: Printed by Iohn Haviland for Hanna Barret, 1625.

—— *Sylva Sylvarum: or A Naturall Historie.* London: Printed by Iohn Haviland and Augustine Mathewes for William Lee, 1628.

—— (ed. Brian Vickers). *Francis Bacon.* Oxford: Oxford University Press, 1996.

—— (ed. and trans. Lisa Jardine and Michael Silverthorne). *The New Organon.* Cambridge: Cambridge University Press, 2000.

Barlow, Thomas. *The Genuine Remains of That Learned Prelate Dr. Thomas Barlow, Lord Bishop of Lincoln.* London: Printed for John Dunton, 1693.

Bates, William. *Considerations of the Existence of God and of the Immortality of the Soul.* London: Printed by J. D. for Brabazon Aylmer, 1676.

Beaumont, John. *The Present State of the Universe.* London: Printed by Randall Taylor, 1694.

Birch, Thomas (ed.). *A Collection of the State Papers of John Thurloe, Esq.* 7 vols. London: The Executor of the late Mt. Fletcher Gyles, Thomas Woodward and Charles Davis, 1742.

—— *The History of the Royal Society of London for Improving of Natural Knowledge, from Its First Rise.* 4 vols. London: A. Millar, 1756–1757.

Boate, Gerard. *Irelands Naturall History.* London: Printed for John Wright, 1652.

Boyle, Robert. *The Sceptical Chymist.* London: Printed by J. Cadwell for J. Crooke, 1661.

—— *The Origine of Formes and Qualities.* Oxford: Printed by H. Hall for Ric: Davis, 1666.

—— (ed. Michael Hunter, Antonio Clericuzio and Lawrence Principe). *The Correspondence of Robert Boyle.* 6 vols. London: Pickering & Chatto, 2001.

Brathwaite, Richard. *The Chimney Scuffle.* London: [s.n.], 1662.

Burdet, W. *A Wonder of Wonders.* London: J. Clowes, 1651.

Carpenter, Andrew (ed.). *Verse in English from Tudor and Stuart Ireland.* Cork: Cork University Press, 2003.

Cheyne, George. *Philosophical Principles of Religion: Natural and Revealed.* London: Printed for George Strahan, 1715.

Child, Josiah. *Brief Observations Concerning Trade, and Interest of Money.* London: Printed for Elizabeth Calvert and Henry Mortlock, 1668.

Chymical, Medicinal, and Chyrurgical Addresses made to Samuel Hartlib, Esquire. London: Printed by G. Dawson for Giles Calvert, 1655.

Coke, Roger. *A Discourse of Trade.* London: Printed for H. Brome and R. Horne, 1670.

——*A Treatise Wherein Is Demonstrated, That the Church and State of England, Are in Equal Danger with the Trade of It.* London: Printed by J. C. for Henry Brome and Roger Horn, 1671.

——*Reasons of the Increase of the Dutch Trade.* London: Printed by J. C. for Henry Brome and Roger Horn, 1671.

Culpeper, Nicholas. *Culpeper's Directory for Midwives: Or, A Guide for Women. The Second Part.* London: Printed by Peter Cole, 1662.

Davenant, Charles. *An Essay upon Ways and Means of Supplying the War.* London: Printed for Jacob Tonson, 1695.

——*Discourses on the Publick Revenues, and on the Trade of England.* London: Printed for James Knapton, 1698.

Davies, John. *A Discoverie of the Trve Cavses why Ireland was Neuer Entirely Subdued.* Dublin: Printed by Iohn Iaggard, 1612.

A Declaration from Oxford, of Anne Green. London: Printed by J. Clowes, 1651.

Dee, Arthur (trans. Elias Ashmole). *Fasciculus Chemicus: Or Chymical Collections.* London: Printed by J. Flesher for Richard Mynne, 1650.

Descartes, René (trans. John Cottingham, Robert Stoothoff and Dugald Murdoch). *The Philosophical Works of Descartes.* 2 vols. Cambridge: Cambridge University Press, 1984.

Dryden, John. *Absalom and Achitophel.* London: Printed for J. T., 1681.

Du Chesne, Joseph (trans. Thomas Tymme). *The Practise of Chymicall, and Hermeticall Physicke, for the Preseruation of Health.* London: Printed by Thomas Creede, 1605.

Dury, John. *The Reformed Librarie-Keeper.* London: Printed by William Du-Gard, 1650.

Dymock, Cressy. *An Invention of Engines of Motion, Lately Brought to Perfection.* London: Printed by I. C. for Richard Woodnoth, 1651.

Eliot, John (trans.). *The Holy Bible containing the Old Testament and the New.* Cambridge, MA: Printed by Samuel Green and Marmaduke Johnson, 1663).

Evelyn, John (ed. William Bray). *Diary and Correspondence of John Evelyn, F. R. S.* 4 vols. London: Henry G. Bohn, 1862.

Farrell, Allen P., S. J. (trans.). *The Jesuit Ratio Studiorum of 1599.* Washington: Conference of Major Superiors of Jesuits, 1970.

Fludd, Robert. *Mosaicall Philosophy: Grounded upon the Essentiall Truth, or Eternal Sapience.* London: Printed for Humphrey Moseley, 1659.

Fortrey, Samuel. *England's Interest and Improvement.* Cambridge: Printed by John Field, 1663.

French, Nicholas. *A Narrative of the Settlement and Sale of Ireland.* Louvain: [s.n.], 1668.

Friendly Society. *Land Security, for Establishing a Perpetual Insurance upon Lives, Of Men, Women, and Children, &c.* London: [s.n.], 1715.

G.F.D. *Twelve Quaeries relating to the Interest of Ireland.* [s.n.], 1685.

Gentleman, Tobias. *The Best Way to make England the Richest and Wealthiest Kingdom in Europe*. London: [s.n.], 1660.

Gilbert, William (trans. P. Fleury Mottelay). *De Magnete*. 1600; New York: Dover, 1958.

Giraldus Cambrensis (ed. and trans. A. B. Scott and F. X. Martin). *Expugnatio Hibernica: The Conquest of Ireland*. Dublin: Royal Irish Academy, 1978.

Glauber, Johann Rudolph (trans. John French). *A Description of New Philosophical Furnaces*. London: Printed by Richard Coats for Tho: Williams, 1651.

Gookin, Vincent. *The Great Case of Transplantation in Ireland Discussed*. London: Printed for I.C., 1655.

—— *The Author and Case of Transplanting the Irish into Connaught Vindicated*. London: Printed by A. M. for Simon Miller, 1655.

Graunt, John. *Natural and Political Observations, Mentioned in a following Index, and made upon the Bills of Mortality*. London: Printed by Thomas Roycroft for James Martyn, James Allestry, and Thomas Dicas, 1662; 5th ed., London: Printed by John Martyn, 1676.

Hale, Matthew. *The Primitive Origination of Mankind, Considered and Examined according to the Light of Nature*. London: Printed by William Godbid for William Shrowsbery, 1677.

Harrington, James. *Aphorisms Political*. London: printed by J. C. for Henry Fletcher, 1659.

—— *A Discourse upon This Saying: The Spirit of the Nation is not yet to be trusted with Liberty*. London: Printed by J. C. for Henry Fletcher, 1659.

—— (ed. J. G. A. Pocock). *The Commonwealth of Oceana* and *A System of Politics*. Cambridge: Cambridge University Press, 1992.

Helmont, Jean Baptiste van (trans. J. C.). *Van Helmont's Works: Containing his most Excellent Philosophy, Chirurgery, Physick, Anatomy*. London: Printed for Lodowick Lloyd, 1664.

Heydon, Christopher. *A Defence of Iudiciall Astrologie*. Cambridge: Printed by Iohn Legat, 1603.

Historical Manuscripts Commission. *Fourteenth Report*, Appendix, Part VII: *The Manuscripts of the marquis of Ormonde, preserved at the Castle, Kilkenny*. 2 vols. London: Historical Manuscripts Commission, 1895.

—— *Calendar of the Manuscripts of the Marquis of Ormonde, K.P. Preserved at Kilkenny Castle*, New Series. Vols 3–7. London: Historical Manuscripts Commission, 1905–1912.

Hobbes, Thomas. (ed. Richard Tuck). *Leviathan*. Cambridge: Cambridge University Press, 1991.

—— (ed. Noel Malcolm). *Thomas Hobbes: The Correspondence*. 2 vols. Oxford: Oxford University Press, 1994.

Hooke, Robert. *Micrographia*. London: Printed by Jo. Martyn and Ja. Allestry, 1665.

——(ed. Henry W. Robinson and Walter Adams). *The Diary of Robert Hooke, MA, MD, FRS, 1672–1680*. London: Wykeham Publications, 1968.

Houghton, John. *A Proposal for Improvement of Husbandry and Trade*. London: [s.n.], 1691.

J.H. *The Censure of the Rota Upon Mr Miltons Book, Entituled, the Ready and Easie Way to Establish a Free Common-Wealth*. London: Paul Giddy, Printer to the Rota, 1660.

Keymor, John. *A Cleare and Evident Way for Enriching the Nations of England and Ireland, and for Setting Very Great Numbers of Poore on Work*. London: Printed by T. M. & A. C., 1650.

——*John Keymors Observation Made Upon the Dutch Fishing, About the Year 1601*. London: Printed for Sir Edward Ford, 1664.

King, Gregory. 'The LCC Burns Journal'. In Peter Laslett (ed.), *The Earliest Classics: John Graunt and Gregory King*. Farnborough: Gregg International Publishers, 1973.

——*Natural and Political Observations on the State of England* [London, 1802]. In Peter Laslett (ed.), *The Earliest Classics: John Graunt and Gregory King*. Farnborough: Gregg International Publishers, 1973.

Kinner, Cyprian (trans. William Petty). *A Continuation of Mr. John-Amos-Comenius School-Endeavours*. London: Printed for R. L., 1648.

Laslett, Peter (ed.). *The Earliest Classics: John Graunt and Gregory King*. Farnborough: Gregg International Publishers, 1973.

Lawrence, Richard. *The Interest of England in the Irish Transplantation, Stated*. Dublin: Printed by William Bladen, 1655.

Leybourn, William. *The Compleat Surveyor*. London: Printed by R. and W. Leybourn for E. Brewster and G. Sawbridge, 1653.

Lodwick, Francis. *A Common Writing*. London: Printed for the author, 1647.

Lifford, James Hewitt (ed.). *A Collection of Tracts and Treatises Illustrative of the Natural History, Antiquities, and the Political and Social State of Ireland, at Various Periods prior to the Present Century*. 2 vols. Dublin: Alexander Thom & Sons, 1860–1861.

Mahaffy, Robert Pentland Mahaffy (ed.). *Calendar of State Papers relating to Ireland, Preserved in the Public Record Office. 1663–1665*. London: Stationery Office, 1907.

Marx, Karl (trans. Emile Burns). *Theories of Surplus Value, Part I*. [1861]; Moscow: Progress Publishers, 1967.

——(trans. Ben Fowkes). *Capital: A Critique of Political Economy*. Vol. 1. [1867]; London: Penguin, 1990.

——(trans. David Fernbach). *Capital: A Critique of Political Economy*. Vol. 3. [1870]; London, 1991.

——(trans. Martin Nicolaus). *Grundrisse*. [1939]; London: Penguin, 1993.

Marx, Karl, and Friedrich Engels (trans. Dona Torr). *Correspondence, 1846–1895: A Selection with Commentary and Notes*. London: Lawrence and Wishart, 1934.

Milton, John. *The Readie and Easie Way to Establish a Free Commonwealth.* London: Printed by T. N. for the Author, 1660.

Misson, Maximilien. *A New Voyage to Italy.* 4 vols. 4th edn, London: Printed for R. Bonwicke, Ja. Tonson, W. Freeman, Tim. Goodwin, J. Walthoe [*et al.*], 1714.

Montanus, Arnaldus (trans. John Ogilby). *Atlas Japannensis.* London: printed by Thomas Johnson for the author, 1670.

——(trans. John Ogilby). *Atlas Chinensis.* London: printed by Thomas Johnson for the author, 1671.

More, Thomas (ed. George M. Logan and Robert M. Adams). *Utopia.* [1516]; Cambridge: Cambridge University Press, 1989.

Moryson, Fynes (ed. Graham Kew). *The Irish Sections of Fynes Moryson's Unpublished Itinerary.* Dublin: Irish Manuscripts Commission, 1998.

Mun, Thomas. *A Discovrse of Trade, from England Vnto the East-Indies.* London: Printed by Nicholas Okes for John Pyper, 1621.

——*England's Treasure by Forraign Trade.* London: Printed by J. G. for Thomas Clark, 1664.

Neville, Henry. *Plato Redivivus, or, A Dialogue concerning Government.* London: Printed for S. I., 1681.

Nicholls, William. *A Conference with a Theist.* London: Printed by T. W. for Francis Saunders and Tho. Bennet, 1696.

Nicolson, William. *The English Historical Library.* 2 vols. London: Printed for Abel Swall, 1696.

Ogilby, John. *America: Being the Latest and Most Accurate Description of the New World.* London: Printed by Thomas Johnson for the author, 1670.

Pell, John (ed. Noel Malcolm and Jacqueline Stedall). *John Pell (1611–1685) and His Correspondence with Charles Cavendish: The Mental World of an Early Modern Mathematician.* Oxford: Oxford University Press, 2005.

Pender, Seamus (ed.). *A Census of Ireland, circa 1659.* Dublin: Irish Manuscripts Commission, 2002.

Pepys, Samuel (ed. J. R. Tanner). *Private Correspondence and Miscellaneous Papers of Samuel Pepys, 1679–1703.* 2 vols. London: G. Bell & Sons, 1926.

——(ed. Robert Latham and William Matthews). *The Diary of Samuel Pepys.* 11 vols. London: G. Bell and Sons, 1970–1983.

Perrott, John (ed. Herbert Wood). *The Chronicle of Ireland, 1584–1608.* Dublin: Irish Manuscripts Commission, 1933.

Petty, William. *The Advice of W. P. to Mr. Samuel Hartlib For The Advancement of some particular Parts of Learning.* London: [s.n.], 1647 [1648].

——*Double Writing.* London: [s.n.], 1647 [1648].

——*A Declaration Concerning the newly invented Art of Double Writing.* London: Printed by R. L. for R. W., 1648.

——*A Brief of the Proceedings between Sr. Hierom Sankey and Dr. William Petty.* London: [s.n.], 1659.

—— *Reflections on some Persons and Things in Ireland.* London: John Martin, James Allestreye, and Thomas Dicas, 1660.

—— *A Treatise of Taxes and Contributions.* London: Printed for N. Brooke, 1662.

—— *Some of the Observations made by W. P. Upon the Trade of Irish Cattel.* London: [s.n.], 1673.

—— *The Discourse Made before the Royal Society the 26. of November 1674. Concerning the Use of Duplicate Proportion in Sundry Important Particulars.* London: Printed for John Martyn, 1674.

—— *Observations upon the Dublin-Bills of Mortality, MDCLXXXI, and the State of that City.* London: Printed for Mark Pardoe, 1683.

——*Another Essay in Political Arithmetick, Concerning the Growth of the City of London.* London: Printed by H. H. for Mark Pardoe, 1683.

—— *A Geographicall Description of the Kingdom of Ireland.* London: Published by Francis Lamb, 1685.

——*Hiberniae Delineatio.* London: [s.n.], 1685.

——*An Essay Concerning the Multiplication of Mankind.* London: Printed for Mark Pardoe, 1686.

——*Further Observations upon the Dublin-Bills.* London: Printed for Mark Pardoe, 1686.

——*Deux Essays d' Arithmetique Politique, Touchant les Villes de Londres et Paris.* Londres: Chés B.G., 1686.

—— *Two Essays in Political Arithmetick, Concerning the People, Housing, Hospitals, &c. of London and Paris.* London: Printed for J. Lloyd, 1687.

—— *Observations upon the Cities of London and Rome.* London: Printed for Henry Mortlocke, 1687.

——*Five Essays in Political Arithmetick.* London: Printed for Henry Mortlock, 1687.

—— *Cinq Essays sur L' Arithmetique Politique.* Londres: Imprimie pour Henry Mortlock, 1687.

——*Political Arithmetick.* London: Printed for Robert Clavel and Henry Mortlock, 1690.

—— *The Political Anatomy of Ireland.* London: Printed for D. Brown and W. Rogers, 1691.

—— *Sir William Petty's Quantulumcunque Concerning Money, 1682.* London: [s.n.], 1695.

—— *Tracts; Chiefly Relating to Ireland.* Dublin: Printed by Boulter Grierson, 1769.

—— (ed. Thomas Aiskew Larcom). *The History of the Survey of Ireland, Commonly Called the 'Down Survey'.* Dublin: Irish Archaeological Society, 1851.

—— (ed. Charles Henry Hull). *The Economic Writings of Sir William Petty.* 2 vols. Cambridge: Cambridge University Press, 1899.

—— (ed. Marquis of Lansdowne [H. W. E. Petty-Fitzmaurice]). *The Petty Papers: Some Unpublished Writings of Sir William Petty.* 2 vols. London: Constable & Co., 1927.

Petty, William (ed. Marquis of Lansdowne [H. W. E. Petty-Fitzmaurice]). *The Petty-Southwell Correspondence*. London: Constable & Co., 1928.

——(ed. Rhodri Lewis). *William Petty on the Order of Nature: An Unpublished Manuscript Treatise*. Tempe, AZ: Medieval and Renaissance Texts and Studies, forthcoming 2009.

Philipps, Fabian. *The Reforming Registry*. London: Printed by Tho. Newcomb for the author, 1662.

Plattes, Gabriel. *A Discovery of Infinite Treasvre, Hidden Since the Worlds Beginning*. London: Printed by Iohn Legat, 1639.

——*A Discovery of Subterraneall Treasure*. London: Printed by I. Okes for Iasper Emery, 1639.

——*A Description of the Famous Kingdome of Macaria*. London: Printed for Francis Constable, 1641.

Renaudot, Théophraste (trans. G. Havers). *A General Collection of Discourses of the Virtuosi of France, upon Questions of all Sorts of Philosophy, and Other Natural Knowledg*. London: Printed for Thomas Dring and John Starkey, 1664.

——(trans. G. Havers and J. Davies). *Another Collection of Philosophical Conferences of the French Virtuosi, upon Questions of All Sorts*. London: Printed for Thomas Dring and John Starkey, 1665.

Rich, Barnabe. *A New Description of Ireland: Wherein Is Described the Disposition of the Irish whereunto They Are Inclined*. London: Printed for Thomas Adams, 1610.

Smith, Adam. *An Inquiry into the Nature and Causes of the Wealth of Nations*. 2 vols. London: Printed for W. Strahan and T. Cadell, 1776.

Smith, John. *The Trade & Fishing of Great-Britain Displayed*. London: Printed by William Godbid, 1661.

Souligné, de. *A Comparison between Old Rome In its Glory, As to the Extent and Populousness, and London, as it is at Present*. London: Printed by John Nutt, 1706.

Spenser, Edmund (ed. W. L. Renwick). *A View of the Present State of Ireland*. London: Eric Partridge Ltd. at the Scholartis Press, 1934.

Sprat, Thomas. *Observations on Monsieur De Sorbier's Voyage into England*. London: Printed for John Martyn and James Allestry, 1665.

—— *The History of the Royal-Society of London, for the Improving of Natural Knowledge*. London: Printed by T. R. for J. Martyn, 1667.

Stubbe, Henry. *The Rota: Or, News from the Common-Wealths-Mens Club*. London: [s.n.], 1660.

Temple, John. *The Irish Rebellion: Or, an History of the Attempts of the Irish Papists to Extirpate the Protestants in the Kingdom of Ireland*. London: Printed by R. White for Samuel Gellibrand, 1646; rpr., London: R. Wilks, 1812.

Temple, William. *Observations upon the United Provinces of the Netherlands*. London: Printed by A. Maxwell for Sa. Gellibrand, 1673.

Tentzel, Andreas (trans. Ferdinando Parkhurst). *Medicina Diastatica or Sympatheticall Mumie*. London: Printed by T. Newcomb for T. Heath, 1653.

Walton, Izaak. *The Lives of Dr. John Donne, Sir Henry Wotton, Mr. Richard Hooker, Mr. George Herbert.* 4th edn, London: Printed by Tho. Roycroft for Richard Marriot, 1675.

Ward, John. *Clavis Usurae; Or, A Key to Interest, both Simple and Compound.* London: Printed by J. M. for W. Taylor, 1710.

Watkins, Richard. *Newes from the Dead.* Oxford: Printed by Leonard Lichfield for Thomas Robinson, 1651.

Webster, John. *The Displaying of Supposed Witchcraft.* London: Printed by John Martyn, 1677.

Wheeler, William. *A List of some of the Chief Workes which Mr. William Wheeler offereth to undertake.* Amsterdam: Printed by George Trigg, 1653.

Whiston, William. *A New Theory of the Earth, from Its Original to the Consummation of All Things.* London: Printed by R. Roberts for Benj. Tooke, 1696.

Worsley, Benjamin. *The Advocate.* London: Printed by William Du-Gard, 1651.

UNPUBLISHED THESES

Heitman, Kristin. 'Hobbes, Wallis and Seventeenth-Century Mathematical Method'. Ph.D., The Johns Hopkins University, 2000.

Sharp, Lindsay G. 'Sir William Petty and Some Aspects of Seventeenth-Century Natural Philosophy'. D.Phil., University of Oxford, 1976.

Waddell, D. A. G. 'The Career and Writings of Charles Davenant (1656–1714)'. D.Phil., University of Oxford, 1954.

PUBLISHED SECONDARY WORKS

Amati, Frank, and Tony Aspromourgos. 'Petty *contra* Hobbes: A Previously Untranslated Manuscript'. *Journal of the History of Ideas* 46:1 (1985), 127–132.

Andrews, J. H. *Shapes of Ireland: Maps and their makers 1564–1839.* Dublin: Geography Publications, 1997.

Appleby, Joyce. *Economic Thought and Ideology in Seventeenth-Century England.* Princeton: Princeton University Press, 1978.

Armitage, David. 'The Political Economy of Britain and Ireland after the Glorious Revolution'. In Jane Ohlmeyer (ed.), *Political Thought in Seventeenth-Century Ireland: Kingdom or Colony*, (Cambridge: Cambridge University Press, 2000), 221–243.

Aspromourgos, Tony. 'Political Economy and the Social Division of Labour: The Economics of Sir William Petty'. *Scottish Journal of Political Economy* 33:1 (1986), 28–45.

—— 'The Life of William Petty in relation to His Economics: A Tercentenary Interpretation'. *History of Political Economy* 20:3 (1988), 337–356.

Aspromourgos, Tony. 'New Light on the Economics of William Petty (1623–1687): Some Findings from Previously Undisclosed Manuscripts'. *Contributions to Political Economy* 19 (2000), 53–70.

—— 'The Mind of the Oeconomist: An Overview of the "Petty Papers" Archive'. *History of Economic Ideas* 9:1 (2001), 39–102.

—— 'Political Economy, Political Arithmetic and Political Medicine in the Thought of William Petty'. In Peter D. Groenewegen (ed.), *Physicians and Political Economy: Six Studies in the Work of Doctor-Economists*. London: Routledge, 2001, 10–25.

—— 'The Invention of the Concept of Social Surplus: Petty in the Hartlib Circle'. *European Journal of the History of Economic Thought* 12:1 (2005), 1–24.

Barber, Sarah. 'Settlement, Transplantation and Expulsion: a Comparative Study of the Placement of Peoples'. In Ciaran Brady and Jane Ohlmeyer (eds), *British Interventions in Early Modern Ireland*. Cambridge: Cambridge Universty Press, 2005, 280–298.

Barnard, Toby C. 'Miles Symner and the New Learning in Seventeenth-Century Ireland'. *Journal of the Royal Society of Antiquaries of Ireland* 102:2 (1972), 129–142.

—— 'The Hartlib Circle and the Origins of the Dublin Philosophical Society'. *Irish Historical Studies* 19:73 (1974), 56–71.

—— 'Sir William Petty, His Irish Estates and Irish Population'. *Irish Economic and Social History* 6 (1979), 64–69.

—— 'Sir William Petty, Irish Landowner'. In Hugh Lloyd-Jones, Valerie Pearl, and Blair Worden (eds), *History and Imaginaton: Essays in Honour of H. R. Trevor-Roper* (London: Duckworth, 1981), 201–217.

—— 'Sir William Petty as Kerry Ironmaster'. *Proceedings of the Royal Irish Academy* 82C:1 (1982), 1–32.

—— 'The Hartlib Circle and the cult and culture of improvement in Ireland'. In Mark Greengrass, Michael Leslie, and Tim Raylor (eds), *Samuel Hartlib and the Universal Reformation: Studies in Intellectual Communication*. Cambridge: Cambridge University Press, 1994, 281–297.

—— 'The Protestant Interest, 1641–1660'. In Jane Ohlmeyer (ed.), *Ireland from Independence to Occupation, 1641–1660*. Cambridge: Cambridge University Press, 1995, 218–240.

—— *Cromwellian Ireland: English Government and Reform in Ireland, 1649–1660*. [1975]; 2nd edn, Oxford: Oxford University Press, 2000.

Bevan, Wilson Lloyd. 'Sir William Petty: A Study in Economic Literature'. *Publications of the American Economic Association* 9:4 (1894), 13–102.

Biagioli, Mario. *Galileo, Courtier: The Practice of Science in the Culture of Absolutism*. Chicago: University of Chicago Press, 1993.

Bonar, James. *Theories of Population from Raleigh to Arthur Young*. London: George Allen and Unwin, 1931.

Boran, Elizabethanne. ' "Propagating Religion and Endeavouring the Reformation of the Whole World": Irish Bishops and the Hartlib Circle in the

Mid-Seventeenth Century'. In Vincent P. Carey and Ute Lotz-Heumann (eds), *Taking Sides? Colonial and Confessional Mentalities in Early Modern Ireland: Essays in Honour of Karl Bottigheimer*. Dublin: Four Courts Press, 2003, 165–184.

Bos, Erik Jan. 'Regius, Henricus'. In Daniel Garber and Michael Ayers (eds), *The Cambridge History of Seventeenth-Century Philosophy*, 2 vols. Cambridge: Cambridge University Press, 1998, 2:1459.

Bottigheimer, Karl S. *English Money and Irish Land: The 'Adventurers' in the Cromwellian Settlement of Ireland*. Oxford: Oxford University Press, 1971.

—— 'The Restoration Land Settlement in Ireland: A Structural View'. *Irish Historical Studies* 18:69 (1972), 1–21.

Boyce, D. George, Robert Eccleston, and Vincent Geoghegan (eds). *Political Discourse in Seventeenth- and Eighteenth-Century Ireland*. Basingstoke: Palgrave, 2001.

Brady, Ciaran, and Jane Ohlmeyer (eds). *British Interventions in Early Modern Ireland*. Cambridge: Cambridge Universty Press, 2005.

Brand, Paul, Kevin Costello, and W. N. Osborough (eds). *Adventures in the Law: Proceedings of the Sixteenth British Legal History Conference*. Dublin: Four Courts Press, 2005.

Brewer, John. *The Sinews of Power: War, Money, and the English State, 1688–1783*. Cambridge, MA: Harvard University Press, 1990.

Brooks, Colin. 'Projecting, Political Arithmetic and the Act of 1695'. *English Historical Review* 97:382 (1982), 31–53.

Brown, Stuart. 'Renaissance Philosophy Outside Italy'. In G. H. R. Parkinson (ed.), *The Renaissance and Seventeenth-Century Rationalism*. London: Routledge, 1993, 70–103.

Buck, Peter. 'Seventeenth-Century Political Arithmetic: Civil Strife and Vital Statistics'. *Isis* 68:1 (1977), 67–84.

—— 'People Who Counted: Political Arithmetic in the Eighteenth Century'. *Isis* 73:1 (1982), 28–45.

Cañizares-Esguerra, Jorge. *Nature, Empire, and Nation: Explorations of the History of Science in the Iberian World*. Stanford: Stanford University Press, 2006.

Canny, Nicholas. *Making Ireland British, 1580–1650*. Oxford: Oxford University Press, 2001.

Carey, Vincent P. and Ute Lotz-Heumann (eds). *Taking Sides? Colonial and Confessional Mentalities in Early Modern Ireland: Essays in Honour of Karl Bottigheimer*. Dublin: Four Courts Press, 2003.

Carroll, Patrick. *Science, Culture, and Modern State Formation*. Berkeley: University of California Press, 2006.

Chandaman, C. D. *The English Public Revenue, 1660–1688*. Oxford: Oxford University Press, 1975.

Christopher, Emma, Cassandra Pybus, and Marcus Rediker (eds). *Many Middle Passages: Forced Migration and the Making of the Modern World*. Berkeley: University of California Press, 2007.

Clark, George N. *Science and Social Welfare in the Age of Newton*. 2nd edn, Oxford: Oxford University Press, 1970.

Clarke, Aidan. *The Old English in Ireland, 1625–42*. Dublin: MacGibbon and Kee, 1966.

—— *Prelude to Restoration in Ireland: The End of the Commonwealth, 1659–1660*. Cambridge: Cambridge University Press, 1999.

Clericuzio, Antonio. 'New Light on Bejamin Worsley's Natural Philosophy'. In Mark Greengrass, Michael Leslie, and Tim Raylor (eds), *Samuel Hartlib and the Universal Reformation: Studies in Intellectual Communication*. Cambridge: Cambridge University Press, 1994, 236–246.

Clucas, Stephen. 'In Search of "The True Logick": Methodological Eclecticism among the "Baconian Reformers"'. In Mark Greengrass, Michael Leslie, and Tim Raylor (eds), *Samuel Hartlib and the Universal Reformation: Studies in Intellectual Communication*. Cambridge: Cambridge University Press, 1994, 51–74.

Coleman, D. C. (ed.). *Revisions in Mercantilism*. London: Methuen, 1969.

Cook, Harold J. *Matters of Exchange: Commerce, Medicine and Science in the Dutch Golden Age*. New Haven: Yale University Press, 2007.

Cook, Margaret G. 'Divine Artifice and Natural Mechanism: Robert Boyle's Mechanical Philosophy of Nature'. *Osiris*, 2nd series, 15 (2001), 133–150.

Corcoran, Irma. *Thomas Holme, 1624–1695: Surveyor General of Pennsylvania*. Philadelphia: American Philosophical Society, 1992.

Costello, Kevin. 'Sir William Petty and the Court of Admiralty in Restoration Ireland'. In Paul Brand, Kevin Costello and W. N. Osborough (eds), *Adventures in the Law: Proceedings of the Sixteenth British Legal History Conference*. Dublin: Four Courts Press, 2005, 106–138.

Cottingham, John. 'Descartes: metaphysics and the philosophy of mind'. In G. H. R. Parkinson (ed.), *The Renaissance and Seventeenth-Century Rationalism*. London: Routledge, 1993, 201–234.

Coughlan, Patricia. 'Natural history and historical nature: the project for a natural history of Ireland'. In Mark Greengrass, Michael Leslie, and Tim Raylor (eds), *Samuel Hartlib and the Universal Reformation: Studies in Intellectual Communication*. Cambridge: Cambridge University Press, 1994, 298–317.

—— 'Counter-currents in colonial discourse: the political thought of Vincent and Daniel Gookin'. In Jane H. Ohlmeyer (ed.), *Political Thought in Seventeenth-Century Ireland: Kingdom or Colony*. Cambridge: Cambridge University Press, 2000, 56–82.

Creighton, Anne. '"Grace and Favour": The Cabal Ministry and Irish Catholic Politics, 1667–1673'. In Coleman A. Dennehy (ed.), *Restoration Ireland: Always Settling and Never Settled*. Aldershot: Ashgate, 2008, 141–160.

Dale, P. G. *Sir W. P. of Romsey*. Romsey: Lower Test Valley Archaeological Study Group, 1987.

Daston, Lorraine. *Classical Probability in the Enlightenment.* Princeton: Princeton University Press, 1988.

Deane, Phyllis. *The State and the Economic System: An Introduction to the History of Political Economy.* Oxford: Oxford University Press, 1989.

Dear, Peter. 'Totius in Verba: Rhetoric and Authority in the Early Royal Society'. *Isis* 76:2 (1985), 145–161.

—— *Discipline and Experience: The Mathematical Way in the Scientific Revolution.* Chicago: Chicago University Press, 1995.

Debus, Allen G. *The Chemical Philosophy: Paracelsian Science and Medicine in the Sixteenth and Seventeenth Centuries.* 2 vols. New York: Neil Watson Academic Publications, 1977.

Dennehy, Coleman A. (ed.). *Restoration Ireland: Always Settling and Never Settled.* Aldershot: Ashgate, 2008.

—— 'The Irish Parliament, 1661–1666'. In Dennehy (ed.), *Restoration Ireland: Always Settling and Never Settled.* Aldershot: Ashgate, 2008, 53–68.

Des Chene, Dennis. *Physiologia: Natural Philosophy in Late Aristotelian and Cartesian Thought.* Ithaca: Cornell University Press, 1996.

Desrosières, Alain (trans. Camille Naish). *The Politics of Large Numbers: A History of Statistical Reasoning.* Cambridge, MA: Harvard University Press, 1998.

Dickson, Donald R. 'Johann Valentin Andreae's Utopian Brotherhoods'. *Renaissance Quarterly* 49:4 (1996), 760–802.

Duffy, Patrick J. (ed.). *To and from Ireland: Planned Migration Schemes, c. 1600–2000.* Dublin: Geography Publications, 2004.

Edie, Carolyn A. 'The Irish Cattle Bills: A Study in Restoration Politics'. *Transactions of the American Philosophical Society*, New Series, 60:2 (1970), 1–66.

Eltis, David. *Coerced and Free Migration: Global Perspectives.* Stanford: Stanford University Press, 2002.

Feingold, Mordechai. *The Mathematician's Apprenticeship: Science, Universities and Society in England, 1560–1640.* Cambridge: Cambridge University Press, 1984.

—— 'Jesuits: Savants'. In Mordechai Feingold (ed.), *Jesuit Science and the Republic of Letters.* Cambridge, MA: MIT Press, 2003, 1–45.

—— (ed.). *Jesuit Science and the Republic of Letters.* Cambridge, MA: MIT Press, 2003.

Finkelstein, Andrea W. *Harmony and the Balance: An Intellectual History of Seventeenth-Century English Economic Thought.* Ann Arbor: University of Michigan Press, 2000.

Finch, Jeremiah S. *Sir Thomas Browne: A Doctor's Life of Science and Faith.* New York: Collier, 1961.

Fitzmaurice, Edmond. *The Life of Sir William Petty, 1623–1687.* London: John Murray, 1895.

Ford, Alan. ' "Firm Catholics" or "Loyal Subjects"? Religious and Political Allegiance in Early Seventeenth-Century Ireland'. In D. George Boyce, Robert

Eccleston, and Vincent Geoghegan (eds), *Political Discourse in Seventeenth- and Eighteenth-Century Ireland*. Basingstoke: Palgrave, 2001, 1–31.

Frank, Robert G., Jr. *Harvey and the Oxford Physiologists: A Study of Scientific Ideas*. Berkeley: University of California Press, 1980.

Franklin, Julian H. *Jean Bodin and the Sixteenth-Century Revolution in the Methodology of Law and History*. New York: Columbia University Press, 1963.

Freedman, Joseph S. 'Aristotle and the Content of Philosophy Instruction at Central European Schools and Universities during the Reformation Era (1500–1650)'. *Proceedings of the American Philosophical Society* 137:2 (1993), 213–253.

Furniss, Edgar S. *The Position of the Laborer in a System of Nationalism: A Study in the Labor Theories of the Later English Mercantilists*. [1921]; New York: Augustus M. Kelley, 1965.

Garber, Daniel, and Michael Ayers (eds). *The Cambridge History of Seventeenth-Century Philosophy*. 2 vols. Cambridge: Cambridge University Press, 1998.

Gaukroger, Stephen. 'Descartes: Methodology'. In G. H. R. Parkinson (ed.), *The Renaissance and Seventeenth-Century Rationalism*. London: Routledge, 1993, 167–200.

—— *Descartes: An Intellectual Biography*. Oxford: Oxford University Press, 1995.

—— *Francis Bacon and the Transformation of Early-Modern Philosophy*. Cambridge: Cambridge University Press, 2001.

Gillespie, Raymond. *The Transformation of the Irish Economy, 1550–1700*. Dundalk: Studies in Irish Economic and Social History 6, 1991; rpr., 1998.

Glass, D. V. 'John Graunt and His Natural and Political Observations'. *Proceedings of the Royal Society of London* 19:1 (1964), 63–100.

Goblet, Y. M. *La Transformation de la Géographie Politique de l' Irlande dans les Cartes et Essais Anthropogéographiques de Sir William Petty*. 2 vols. Nancy, Paris and Strasbourg: Imprimerie Berger-Levrault, 1930.

Goldie, Mark. 'Sir Peter Pett, Sceptical Toryism and the Science of Toleration in the 1680s'. In W. J. Sheils (ed.), *Persecution and Toleration: Papers Read at the Twenty-Second Summer Meeting and Twenty-Third Winter Meeting of the Ecclesiastical History Society, Studies in Church History* 21 (1984), 247–273.

Goodacre, Hugh. 'William Petty and the Early Colonial Roots of Development Economics'. In Kwane Sundaram Jomo (ed.), *The Pioneers of Development Economics*. London: Zed Books, 2005, 10–30.

Grafton, Anthony. *Bring Out Your Dead: The Past as Revelation*. Cambridge, MA: Harvard University Press, 2001.

Greengrass, Mark, Michael Leslie, and Tim Raylor (eds). *Samuel Hartlib and the Universal Reformation: Studies in Intellectual Communication*. Cambridge: Cambridge University Press, 1994.

Greenwood, M. 'Graunt and Petty'. *Journal of the Royal Statistical Society* 91:1 (1928), 79–85.

Groenewegen, Peter D. 'Authorship of the *Natural and Political Observations upon the Bills of Mortality*'. *Journal of the History of Ideas* 28:4 (1967), 601–602.

——(ed.). *Physicians and Political Economy: Six Studies in the Work of Doctor-Economists*. London: Routledge, 2001.

Hacking, Ian. *The Taming of Chance*. Cambridge: Cambridge University Press, 1990.

——*The Emergence of Probability: A Philosophical Study of Early Ideas About Probability, Induction and Statistical Inference*. 2nd edn, Cambridge: Cambridge University Press, 2006.

Hall, A. Rupert. *Henry More: Magic, Religion and Experiment*. Oxford: Blackwell, 1990.

Hall, A. Rupert, and Marie Boas Hall. 'The Intellectual Origins of the Royal Society—London and Oxford'. *Notes and Records of the Royal Society of London* 23:2 (1968), 157–168.

Harris, Frances. 'Ireland as a Laboratory: The Archive of Sir William Petty'. In Michael Hunter (ed.), *Archives of the Scientific Revolution: The Formation and Exchange of Ideas in Seventeenth-Century Europe*. Woodbridge: Boydell Press, 1998, 73–90.

Harris, Tim. *Restoration: Charles II and His Kingdoms, 1660–1685*. London: Penguin, 2006.

——'Restoration Ireland—Themes and Problems'. In Coleman A. Dennehy (ed.), *Restoration Ireland: Always Settling and Never Settled*. Aldershot: Ashgate, 2008, 1–17.

Harris, Tim, Paul Seaward, and Mark Goldie (eds). *The Politics of Religion in Restoration England*. Oxford: Oxford University Press, 1990.

Harrison, Peter. *The Bible, Protestantism, and the Rise of Natural Science*. Cambridge: Cambridge University Press, 1998.

Harte, Negley B. 'The Economics of Clothing in the Late Seventeenth Century'. *Textile History*, 22:2 (1991), 277–296.

Hartman, Mary S. *The Household and the Making of History: A Subversive View of the Western Past*. Cambridge: Cambridge University Press, 2004.

Heckscher, Eli F. (trans. Mendel Shapiro). *Mercantilism*. 2 vols. London: George Allen & Unwin, 1934.

Higgs, Edward. *The Information State in England: The Central Collection of Information on Citizens since 1500*. Basingstoke: Palgrave Macmillan, 2004.

Holmes, Geoffrey. *Politics, Religion and Society in England, 1679–1742*. London: Hambledon Press, 1986.

——'Gregory King and the Social Structure of Pre-Industrial England'. In Geoffrey Holmes, *Politics, Religion and Society in England, 1679–1742*. London: The Hambledon Press, 1986, 281–308.

Hoppit, Julian. 'Political Arithmetic in Eighteenth-Century England'. *Economic History Review* 49:3 (1996), 516–540.

Houghton, Walter E., Jr. 'The History of Trades: Its Relation to Seventeenth-Century Thought: As Seen in Bacon, Petty, Evelyn, and Boyle'. *Journal of the History of Ideas* 2:1 (1941), 33–60.

—— 'The English Virtuoso in the Seventeenth Century: Part I'. *Journal of the History of Ideas* 3:1 (1942), 51–73.

—— 'The English Virtuoso in the Seventeenth Century: Part II'. *Journal of the History of Ideas* 3:2 (1942), 190–219.

Hull, Charles Henry. 'Graunt or Petty?'. *Political Science Quarterly* 11:1 (1896), 105–132.

—— 'Petty's Place in the History of Economic Theory'. *Quarterly Journal of Economics* 14:3 (1900), 307–340.

Hunter, Michael. *Science and Society in Restoration England.* Cambridge: Cambridge University Press, 1981.

—— *The Royal Society and Its Fellows, 1660–1700: The Morphology of an Early Scientific Institution.* 2nd edn, London: British Society for the History of Science, 1994.

—— (ed.). *Archives of the Scientific Revolution: The Formation and Exchange of Ideas in Seventeenth-Century Europe.* Woodbridge: Boydell Press, 1998.

Hunter, Michael, and Paul B. Wood. 'Towards Solomon's House: Rival Strategies for Reforming the Early Royal Society'. *History of Science* 24:1 (1986), 49–108.

Jacob, Margaret C. 'Factoring Mary Poovey's *A History of the Modern Fact*'. *History and Theory* 40 (2001), 280–289.

Jacobsen, Gertrude Ann. *William Blathwayt: A Late Seventeenth Century English Administrator.* New Haven: Yale University Press, 1932.

Johnson, E. A. J. *Predecessors of Adam Smith: The Growth of British Economic Thought.* New York: Prentice Hall, 1937.

Jomo, Kwane Sundaram (ed.). *The Pioneers of Development Economics.* London: Zed Books, 2005.

Jordan, Thomas E. *A Copper Farthing: Sir William Petty and his Times, 1623–1687.* Sunderland: University of Sunderland Press, 2007.

Jordan, Winthrop D. *White over Black: American Attitudes Toward the Negro, 1550–1812.* Baltimore: Pelican Books, 1969.

Kargon, Robert. 'William Petty's Mechanical Philosophy'. *Isis* 56:1 (1965), 63–66.

Kraye, Jill. 'The Philosophy of the Italian Renaissance'. In G. H. R. Parkinson (ed.), *The Renaissance and Seventeenth-Century Rationalism.* London: Routledge, 1993, 16–69.

Landry, Yves. *Les Filles du Roi au XVIIe Siècle: Orphelines en France, Pionnières au Canada.* Ottawa: Leméac, 1992.

Laslett, Peter. 'Introduction'. In Peter Laslett (ed.), *The Earliest Classics: John Graunt and Gregory King.* Farnborough: Gregg International Publishers, 1973, 1–10.

—— 'Natural and Political Observations on the Population of Late Seventeenth-Century England'. In Kevin Schurer and Tom Arkell (eds), *Surveying the People:*

The Interpretation and Use of Document Sources for the Study of Population in the Later Seventeenth Century. Oxford: Leopard's Head Press, 1992, 6–30.

Leng, Thomas. *Benjamin Worsley (1618–1677): Trade, Interest, and the Spirit in Revolutionary England*. Woodbridge: Boydell and Brewer, 2008.

Letwin, William. *The Origins of Scientific Economics*. London: Methuen, 1963.

Lewis, Rhodri. Introduction. In Rhodri Lewis (ed.), *William Petty on the Order of Nature: An Unpublished Manuscript Treatise*. Tempe, AZ: Medieval and Renaissance Texts and Studies, forthcoming in 2009.

Lindemann, Mary. *Medicine and Society in Early Modern Europe*. Cambridge: Cambridge University Press, 1999.

Lloyd-Jones, Hugh, Valerie Pearl, and Blair Worden (eds). *History and Imaginaton: Essays in Honour of H.R. Trevor-Roper*. London: Duckworth, 1981.

Losonsky, Michael. 'Language and Logic'. In Donald Rutherford (ed.), *The Cambridge Companion to Early Modern Philosophy*. Cambridge: Cambridge University Press, 2006, 170–197.

Love, Harold. *The Culture and Commerce of Texts: Scribal Publication in Seventeenth-Century England*. Amherst: University of Massachusetts Press, 1998.

—— 'Sir William Petty, the London Coffee Houses, and the Restoration "Leonine"'. *The Seventeenth Century* 22:2 (2007), 381–394.

Macinnes, Allan I. *The British Revolution, 1629–1660*. Basingstoke: Palgrave Macmillan, 2005.

Magnusson, Lars. *Mercantilism: The Shaping of an Economic Language*. New York: Routledge, 1994.

Malcolm, Noel. *Aspects of Hobbes*. Oxford: Oxford University Press, 2002.

Mancosu, Paolo. *Philosophy of Mathematics and Mathematical Practice in the Seventeenth Century*. Oxford: Oxford University Press, 1996.

Masselman, George. *The Cradle of Colonialism*. New Haven: Yale University Press, 1963.

McCormick, Ted. 'Alchemy in the Political Arithmetic of Sir William Petty (1623–1687)'. *Studies in History and Philosophy of Science* 37:2 (2006), 290–307.

—— 'Transmutation, Inclusion, and Exclusion: Political Arithmetic from Charles II to William III'. *Journal of Historical Sociology* 20:3 (2007), 259–278.

—— '"A Proportionable Mixture": Sir William Petty, Political Arithmetic, and the Transmutation of the Irish'. In Coleman Dennehy (ed.), *Restoration Ireland: Always Settling and Never Settled*. Aldershot: Ashgate, 2008, 123–139.

McCracken, Charles. 'Knowledge of the Existence of Body'. In Daniel Garber and Michael Ayers (eds), *The Cambridge History of Seventeenth-Century Philosophy*, 2 vols. Cambridge: Cambridge University Press, 1998, 1:624–648.

McGuire, J. I. 'Why Was Ormond Dismissed in 1669?'. *Irish Historical Studies* 18:71 (1973), 295–312.

McKenny, Kevin. 'The Seventeenth-Century Land Settlement in Ireland: Towards a Statistical Interpretation'. In Jane Ohlmeyer (ed.), *Ireland from*

Independence to Occupation, 1641–1660. Cambridge: Cambridge University Press, 1995, 181–200.

Meinel, Christoph. 'Early Seventeenth-Century Atomism: Theory, Epistemology, and the Insufficency of Experiment'. *Isis* 79:1 (1988), 68–103.

Mercer, Christia. 'Heereboord, Adriaan'. In Daniel Garber and Michael Ayers (eds), *The Cambridge History of Seventeenth-Century Philosophy*, 2 vols. Cambridge: Cambridge University Press, 1998, 2:1433.

——'de Raey, Johannes'. In Daniel Garber and Michael Ayers (eds), *The Cambridge History of Seventeenth-Century Philosophy*, 2 vols. Cambridge: Cambridge University Press, 1998, 2:1458.

Miller, John. *Popery and Politics in England, 1660–1688.* Cambridge: Cambridge University Press, 1973.

——'Thomas Sheridan (1646–1712) and his "Narrative"'. *Irish Historical Studies* 20:78 (1976), 105–128.

—— *Charles II.* London: Weidenfeld and Nicolson, 1991.

Molland, George. 'Science and mathematics from the Renaissance to Descartes'. In G. H. R. Parkinson (ed.), *The Renaissance and Seventeenth-Century Rationalism* (London: Routledge, 1993), 104–139.

Momigliano, Arnaldo. 'Ancient History and the Antiquarian'. *Journal of the Warburg and Courtauld Institutes* 13:3/4 (1950), 285–315.

Mora, Jose Ferrater. 'Suarez and Modern Philosophy'. *Journal of the History of Ideas* 14:4 (1953), 528–547.

Moran, Bruce T. *Distilling Knowledge: Alchemy, Chemistry, and the Scientific Revolution.* Cambridge, MA: Harvard University Press, 2005.

Newman, William R. *Promethean Ambitions: Alchemy and the Quest to Perfect Nature.* Chicago: Chicago University Press, 2004.

—— *Atoms and Alchemy: Chymistry and the Experimental Origins of the Scientific Revolution.* Chicago: University of Chicago Press, 2006.

Newman, William R., and Anthony Grafton (eds). *Secrets of Nature: Astrology and Alchemy in Early Modern Europe.* Cambridge, MA: MIT Press, 2001.

——'Introduction: The Problematic Status of Astrology and Alchemy in Premodern Europe'. In William R. Newman and Anthony Grafton (eds), *Secrets of Nature: Astrology and Alchemy in Early Modern Europe.* Cambridge, MA: MIT Press, 2001, 1–37.

Newman, William R., and Lawrence M. Principe. 'Alchemy vs. Chemistry: The Etymological Origins of a Historiographic Mistake'. *Early Science and Medicine* 3:1 (1998), 32–65.

—— *Alchemy Tried in the Fire: Starkey, Boyle, and the Fate of Helmontian Chemistry.* Chicago: University of Chicago Press, 2002.

Ochs, Kathleen. 'The Royal Society of London's History of Trades Programme: An Early Episode in Applied Science'. *Notes and Records of the Royal Society of London* 39:2 (1985), 129–158.

Ohlmeyer, Jane (ed.). *Ireland from Independence to Occupation, 1641–1660*. Cambridge: Cambridge University Press, 1995.

—— (ed.). *Political Thought in Seventeenth-Century Ireland: Kingdom or Colony*. Cambridge: Cambridge University Press, 2000.

Olson, Richard. *The Emergence of the Social Sciences, 1642–1792*. New York: Twayne Publishers, 1993.

Ó Siochrú, Micheál. *Confederate Ireland, 1642–1649: A Constitutional and Political Analysis*. Dublin: Four Courts Press, 1999.

Oxford Dictionary of National Biography. Oxford: Oxford University Press, 2004; online ed., 2007. <http://www.oxforddnb.com>.

Parkinson, G. H. R. (ed.). *The Renaissance and Seventeenth-Century Rationalism*. London: Routledge, 1993.

Pawlisch, Hans S. *Sir John Davies and the Conquest of Ireland: A Study in Legal Imperialism*. Cambridge: Cambridge University Press, 1985.

Pearson, Karl, and E. S. Pearson. *The History of Statistics in the 17th and 18th Centuries*. High Wycombe: Charles Griffin and Company, 1978.

Perceval-Maxwell, Michael. 'The Anglesey-Ormond-Castlehaven Dispute, 1680–1682: Taking Sides about Ireland in England'. In Vincent P. Carey and Ute Lotz-Heumann (eds.), *Taking Sides? Colonial and Confessional Mentalities in Early Modern Ireland: Essays in Honour of Karl S. Bottigheimer*. Dublin: Four Courts Press, 2003, 213–230.

—— 'The Irish Land Settlement and its Historians'. In Coleman A. Dennehy (ed.), *Restoration Ireland: Always Settling and Never Settled*. Aldershot: Ashgate, 2008, 19–34.

Pincus, Steven C. A. *Protestantism and Patriotism: Ideologies and the Making of English Foreign Policy, 1650–1668*. Cambridge: Cambridge University Press, 1996.

Pocock, J. G. A. *The Discovery of Islands: Essays in British History*. Cambridge: Cambridge University Press, 2005.

Poovey, Mary. *A History of the Modern Fact: Problems of Knowledge in the Sciences of Wealth and Society*. Chicago: University of Chicago Press, 1998.

Principe, Lawrence M. *The Aspiring Adept: Robert Boyle and His Alchemical Quest*. Princeton: Princeton University Press, 1998.

Principe, Lawrence M., and William R. Newman. 'Some Problems with the Historiography of Alchemy'. In William R. Newman and Anthony Grafton (eds), *Secrets of Nature: Astrology and Alchemy in Early Modern Europe*. Cambridge, MA: MIT Press, 2001, 385–431.

Ramsey, Robert W. *Henry Cromwell*. London: Longmans, Green and Co., 1933.

Rattansi, P. M. 'The Intellectual Origins of the Royal Society'. *Notes and Records of the Royal Society of London* 23:2 (1968), 129–143.

Reif, Patricia. 'The Textbook Tradition in Natural Philosophy, 1600–1650'. *Journal of the History of Ideas* 30:1 (1969), 17–32.

Reungoat, Sabine. *William Petty: Observateur Des Îles Britanniques*. Paris: Institut National d'Études Démographiques, 2004.

Rodis-Lewis, Geneviève (trans. Jane Marie Todd). *Descartes: His Life and Work.* Ithaca: Cornell University Press, 1998.

Roncaglia, Alessandro. *Petty: The Origins of Political Economy.* Armonk: M.E. Sharpe, 1985.

Rozbicki, Michal J. 'Between East-Central Europe and Britain: Reformation and Science as Vehicles of Intellectual Communications in the Mid-Seventeenth Century'. *East European Quarterly* 30 (1996), 401–419.

Russell-Wood, A. J. R. *The Portuguese Empire, 1415–1808: A World on the Move.* Baltimore: Johns Hopkins University Press, 1998.

Rutherford, Donald (ed.). *The Cambridge Companion to Early Modern Philosophy.* Cambridge: Cambridge University Press, 2006.

Sarasohn, Lisa T. 'Nicolas-Claude Fabri de Peiresc and the Patronage of the New Science in the Seventeenth Century'. *Isis* 84:1 (1993), 70–90.

—— 'Thomas Hobbes and the Duke of Newcastle: A Study in the Mutuality of Patronage before the Establishment of the Royal Society'. *Isis* 90:4 (1999), 715–737.

Seed, Patricia. *Ceremonies of Possession in Europe's Conquest of the New World, 1492–1640.* Cambridge: Cambridge University Press, 1995.

Shapin, Steven, and Simon Schaffer, *Leviathan and the Air-Pump: Hobbes, Boyle, and the Experimental Life.* Princeton: Princeton University Press, 1985.

Shapiro, Barbara J. *A Culture of Fact: England 1550–1720.* Ithaca: Cornell University Press, 2000.

Simms, J. G. 'The Civil Survey, 1654–6'. *Irish Historical Studies* 9:35 (1955), 253–263.

Skinner, Quentin. 'Hobbes's Disciples in France and England'. *Comparative Studies in Society and History* 8:2 (1966), 153–167.

—— *Visions of Politics.* 3 vols. Cambridge: Cambridge University Press, 2002.

Slack, Paul. *From Reformation to Improvement: Public Welfare in Early Modern England.* Oxford: Oxford University Press, 1999.

—— 'Government and Information in Seventeenth-Century England'. *Past and Present* 184 (2004), 33–68.

—— 'Measuring the National Wealth in Seventeenth-Century England'. *Economic History Review* 57:4 (2004), 607–635.

Sloane, A.W. *English Medicine in the Seventeenth Century.* Durham: Durham Academic Press, 1996.

Smolarski, Dennis C. 'Teaching Mathematics in the Seventeenth and Twenty-First Centuries'. *Mathematics Magazine* 75:4 (2002), 256–262.

Smyth, William J. 'Society and Settlement in Seventeenth Century Ireland: The Evidence of the "1659 Census"'. In William J. Smyth and Kevin Whelan (eds), *Common Ground: Essays on the Historical Geography of Ireland, Presented to T. Jones Hughes, M.A., M.R.I.A.* Cork: Cork University Press, 1988, 55–83.

—— 'Wrestling with Petty's Ghost: The Origins, Nature and Relevance of the So-Called "1659 Census"'. In Seamus Pender (ed.), *A Census of Ireland,*

circa 1659: With Essential Materials from the Poll Money Ordinances, 1660–1661
(Dublin: Irish Manuscripts Commission, 2002), iii–lxii.

——*Map-making, Landscapes and Memory: A Geography of Colonial and Early Modern Ireland*, c. *1530–1750*. Cork: Cork University Press, 2006.

Smyth, William J., and Kevin Whelan (ed.). *Common Ground: Essays on the Historical Geography of Ireland, Presented to T. Jones Hughes, M.A., M.R.I.A.* Cork: Cork University Press, 1988.

Sorell, Tom. 'Seventeenth-Century Materialism: Gassendi and Hobbes'. In G. H. R. Parkinson (ed.), *The Renaissance and Seventeenth-Century Rationalism* (London: Routledge, 1993), 235–272.

Stimson, Dorothy. 'Amateurs of Science in 17th Century England'. *Isis* 31:1 (1939), 32–47.

——'Hartlib, Haak and Oldenburg: Intelligencers'. *Isis* 31:2 (1940), 309–326.

Strangeland, Charles Emil. *Pre-Malthusian Doctrines of Population: A Study in the History of Economic Theory*. [1904]; New York: Augustus M. Kelley, 1966.

Strauss, Erich. *Sir William Petty: Portrait of a Genius*. Glencoe, IL: The Free Press, 1954.

Struik, D. J. Review of J. E. Hofman, *Frans van Schooten der Jüngere*. *The American Mathematical Monthly* 70:9 (1963), 1030–1031.

Sutherland, Ian. 'John Graunt: A Tercentenary Tribute'. *Journal of the Royal Statistical Society*, Series A, 126:4 (1963), 537–556.

Taylor, Jean Gelman. *The Social World of Batavia: European and Eurasian in Dutch Asia*. Madison: University of Wisconsin Press, 1983.

Tolmacheva, Marina. 'The Medieval Arabic Geographers and the Beginnings of Modern Orientalism'. *International Journal of Middle East Studies* 27:2 (1995), 150–151.

Trevor-Roper, Hugh. *The Crisis of the Seventeenth-Century: Religion, the Reformation, and Social Change*. New York: Harper & Row, 1967.

——'Three Foreigners: The Philosophers of the Puritan Revolution'. In Hugh Trevor-Roper, *The Crisis of the Seventeenth-Century: Religion, the Reformation, and Social Change*. New York: Harper & Row, 1967, 219–271.

——*Renaissance Essays*. Chicago: University of Chicago Press, 1985.

——'The Paracelsian Moment'. In Hugh Trevor-Roper, *Renaissance Essays*. Chicago: University of Chicago Press, 1985, 149–199.

Tuck, Richard. 'The Institutional Setting'. In Daniel Garber and Michael Ayers (eds), *The Cambridge History of Seventeenth-Century Philosophy*, 2 vols. Cambridge: Cambridge University Press, 1998, 1:9–32.

Turnbull, G. H. *Hartlib, Dury and Comenius: Gleanings from Hartlib's Papers*. London: Hodder & Stoughton, 1947.

Ullmer, James H. 'The Macroeconomic Thought of Sir William Petty'. *Journal of the History of Economic Thought* 26:3 (2004), 401–413.

Verbeek, Theo. *Descartes and the Dutch: Early Reactions to Cartesian Philosophy, 1637–1650*. Carbondale, IL: Southern Illinois University Press, 1992.

Waddell, D. A. G. 'Charles Davenant (1656–1714): A Biographical Sketch'. *Economic History Review*, 2nd series, 2:2 (1958), 279–288.

Wear, Andrew. *Knowledge and Practice in English Medicine, 1550–1680*. Cambridge: Cambridge University Press, 2000.

Weber, Max (trans. Talcott Parsons). *The Protestant Ethic and the Spirit of Capitalism*. [1930]; London: Routledge, 2001.

Webster, Charles. 'The Authorship and Significance of *Macaria*'. *Past and Present* 56 (1972), 34–48.

—— 'New Light on the Invisible College: The Social Relations of English Science in the Mid-Seventeenth Century'. *Transactions of the Royal Historical Society*, 5th series, 24 (1974), 19–42.

—— *The Great Instauration: Science, Medicine and Reform 1626–1660*. London: Duckworth, 1975.

—— 'Benjamin Worsley: Engineering for Universal Reform from the Invisible College to the Navigation Act'. In Mark Greengrass, Michael Leslie, and Tim Raylor (eds), *Samuel Hartlib and the Universal Reformation: Studies in Intellectual Communication*. Cambridge: Cambridge University Press, 1994, 213–235.

Weeks, Andrew. *Paracelsus: Speculative Theory and the Crisis of the Early Reformation*. Albany: SUNY Press, 1997.

Wennerlind, Carl. 'Credit-Money as the Philosopher's Stone: Alchemy and the Coinage Problem in Seventeenth-Century England'. *History of Political Economy* 36 (2004), 235–262.

Wheeler, James Scott. *Cromwell in Ireland*. Dublin: Gill and Macmillan, 1999.

Wise, John E. 'Jesuit School Beginnings'. *History of Education Quarterly* 1:1 (1961), 29–30.

Wood, Ellen Meiksins. *The Origin of Capitalism: A Longer View*. London: Verso, 2000.

Index

User's Note: The order of entries is word-by-word. References to footnotes are indicated by the letter 'n', followed by the note number, and to epigraphs by the letter 'e'. References to illustrations are printed in italics, viz: *167* (Figure 4).

Lightning Source UK Ltd.
Milton Keynes UK
UKOW06n0809181116
287968UK00016B/417/P